The Politics of Economic Adjustment

The Politics of Economic Adjustment

INTERNATIONAL CONSTRAINTS, DISTRIBUTIVE CONFLICTS, AND THE STATE

Edited by Stephan Haggard and Robert R. Kaufman

WITH CONTRIBUTIONS BY

Peter Evans, Stephan Haggard and Robert R. Kaufman,
Miles Kahler, Joan M. Nelson, Barbara Stallings,
and John Waterbury

PRINCETON UNIVERSITY PRESS

PRINCETON, NEW JERSEY

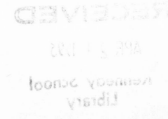

AMC 4736-4/2

Copyright © 1992 by Princeton University Press
Published by Princeton University Press, 41 William Street,
Princeton, New Jersey 08540
In the United Kingdom: Princeton University Press, Oxford

Library of Congress Cataloging-in-Publication Data

The Politics of economic adjustment : international constraints,
distributive conflicts, and the state / edited by Stephan Haggard
and Robert R. Kaufman ; with contributions by Peter Evans . . . [et al.].
p. cm.
Includes bibliographical references and index.
1. Structural adjustment (Economic policy). 2. Economic stabilization.
I. Haggard, Stephan. II. Kaufman, Robert R. III. Evans, Peter B., 1944–   .
HD87.P65 1992 338.9–dc20 91–38423 CIP

ISBN 0-691-04300-0 (alk. paper) — ISBN 0-691-00394-7 (pbk.: alk. paper)

This book has been composed in Linotron Times Roman

Princeton University Press books are printed on acid-free paper
and meet the guidelines for permanence and durability of the
Committee on Production Guidelines for Book Longevity of the
Council on Library Resources

Printed in the United States of America
10 9 8 7 6 5 4 3 2 1
10 9 8 7 6 5 4 3 2 1
(Pbk.)

Contents

Figures and Tables

Contributors

PETER EVANS is professor of sociology at the University of California, Berkeley. He is coeditor of *Bringing the State Back In* (1985) and continues to do comparative research on the role of the state in industrial development.

STEPHAN HAGGARD is professor at the Graduate School of International Relations and Pacific Studies, University of California, San Diego. He is the author of *Pathways from the Periphery* (1990) and coeditor with Tun-jen Cheng of *Political Change in Taiwan* (1992). He is currently working with Robert Kaufman on a project on the political economy of democratic transitions.

MILES KAHLER is professor at the Graduate School of International Relations and Pacific Studies, University of California, San Diego, and chairs the Committee on Foreign Policy Studies of the Social Science Research Council. He is the author of *Decolonization in Britain and France: The Domestic Consequences of International Relations* (1984); and editor of *The Politics of International Debt* (1988).

ROBERT R. KAUFMAN is professor of political science at Rutgers University. He is the author of *The Politics of Debt in Argentina, Brazil, and Mexico: Economic Stabilization in the 1980s* (1988), and coeditor with Barbara Stallings of *Debt and Democracy in Latin America* (1989).

JOAN M. NELSON is senior associate at the Overseas Development Council. She is author of *Access to Power: Politics and the Urban Poor in Developing Nations* (1979); coauthor with Samuel Huntington of *No Easy Choice: Political Participation in Developing Countries* (1976); and the editor of the two previous volumes stemming from this research project, *Fragile Coalitions: The Politics of Economic Adjustment* (1990) and *Economic Crisis and Policy Choice: The Politics of Adjustment in the Third World* (1990).

BARBARA STALLINGS is professor of political science and former director of the Latin American Studies Program at the University of Wisconsin, Madison. She is the author of *Class Conflict and Economic Development in Chile 1958–1973* (1978); *Banker to the Third World: U.S. Portfolio Investment in Latin America, 1900–1986* (1987); and coeditor with Robert Kaufman of *Debt and Democracy in Latin America* (1989).

JOHN WATERBURY is William Stewart Tod Professor of Politics and International Affairs, Princeton University. He is the author of *The Egypt of Nasser and Sadat: The Political Economy of Two Regimes* (1983) and coauthor with Alan Richards of *A Political Economy of the Middle East: State, Class, and Economic Development* (1990).

Preface

THIS VOLUME is the product of a research project that is virtually as old as the debt crisis itself. By 1984, each author was already engaged in research on the political dimensions of economic policy. Joan Nelson, in particular, had written some of the first articles on the politics of stabilization and structural adjustment. Miles Kahler, Robert Kaufman, Stephan Haggard, and Joan Nelson met at a series of workshops organized by Kahler at the Lehrman Institute in the fall of 1984 that led to his book, *The Politics of International Debt* (Ithaca, Cornell University Press, 1986). In late May 1985, a number of the participants in the project met again at a conference on the political economy of stabilization sponsored by the Yale Center for International and Area Studies and the Institute for Social and Policy Studies; Colin Bradford played a central role in bringing that meeting together.

At this meeting, we agreed to develop a larger comparative project on the topic. At an early workshop, we received useful guidance from Christine Bogdanowicz-Bindert, Hollis Chenery, Gerry Helleiner, Daniel Schydlowsky, and John Williamson. Joan Nelson developed a proposal that was generously funded by the Ford and Rockefeller foundations; without her leadership, the project would not have come to fruition. We owe special thanks to Tom Bayard, then at the Ford Foundation, and Catherine Gwin of the Rockefeller Foundation for their support, advice, and, above all, forebearance. Ford and Rockefeller funding provided us the luxury of a number of lively and intense authors' meetings from which we all gained immensely. Administrative support for the project was provided initially by the Lehrman Institute, and since mid-1987 by the Overseas Development Council (ODC). We would like to thank John Sewell and Richard Feinberg of the ODC for their interest in and support of this project, as well as Valeriana Kallab for her editorial help and Ingeborg Bock for the management of project finances.

The project unfolded in three overlapping phases. At each step, we received assistance and criticism that contributed substantially to this volume; it is thus a pleasure to acknowledge these debts.

When we began, the monographic literature on the topic was thin. We therefore decided to develop a set of comparative case studies that would provide the basis for broader comparisons. They were published in a volume edited by Joan Nelson entitled *Economic Crisis and Policy Choice: The Politics of Adjustment in the Third World* (Princeton: Princeton University Press, 1990). In addition to an introduction and conclusion by Nelson and an overview of the intellectual debate on adjustment by Kahler, the volume contained studies of Argentina, Brazil, and Mexico by Kaufman; Chile, Peru, and Colombia by Barbara Stallings; Costa Rica, the Dominican Republic, and Jamaica by Nelson; Ghana, Zambia, and Nigeria by Thomas Callaghy; and the Philippines by Haggard. This volume also profited substantially from meetings with foreign scholars. Carlos Roces hosted a large meeting at El Colegio de México that brought together forty-five participants from ten countries. The political science department of the University of Nairobi sponsored a workshop to review the African materials from the first volume; our thanks to Michael Chege for his efforts on behalf of that meeting. The first volume also profited from detailed comments by Thomas Biersteker, Gerry Helleiner, Tony Killick, Azizali Mohammed, Robert Russell, and John Sheahan.

The second phase of the project drew on the case studies to speak to a policy audience. In particular, we were interested in addressing the interaction of economic liberalization and democratization. In addition to an introduction by Nelson, the volume contained chapters on the political management of reform by John Waterbury; two chapters on economic adjustment and democratization, one by Haggard and Kaufman, the second by Laurence Whitehead; a chapter on the politics of pro-poor adjustment by Nelson; an analysis of the role of the state by Callaghy; and an overview of the role of the international financial institutions by Kahler. This volume was edited by Joan Nelson as *Fragile Coalitions: The Politics of Economic Adjustment* (New Brunswick: Transaction Books, 1989), and appeared in the Overseas Development Council's Policy Perspective Series. The authors benefited from workshops held at the ODC that discussed earlier drafts of both published manuscripts, as well as the chapters in this volume. For their attendance and comments at these ODC meetings, we would like to thank Robert Bates, Henry Bienen, Mark Chona, Vittorio Corbo, Richard Cooper, Max Corden, Gary Cowan, Benjamin Crosby, Vinod Dubey, Richard Erb, Richard Feinberg, James Fox, Alan Gelb, David Gordon, Merilee Grindle, Ann Henderson, Carol Lancaster, David Lehman, John Lewis, Robert Liebenthal, Azizali Mohammed, Kent Osband, Jacques Polak, Gus Ranis, Sylvia Saborio, John Toye, and John Williamson.

The current volume has thus had a long gestation period. In addition to the ODC meetings, drafts were presented at the International Studies Association meeting in London and a workshop at the University of Sussex in the spring of 1989. We are particularly indebted to John Toye for his assistance in setting up the Sussex workshop and in sharing the results of his work with Jane Harrigan and Paul Mosely with us. Our thanks to the participants at the Sussex workshop for addressing the idiosyncratic concerns of North American social scientists with constructive criticism: Teddy Brett, Rolf Cappel, Chris Colclough, Enrico Colombatto, Stephen Ellis, Mike Faber, Emanuel Gyimak-Boadi, Jane Harrigan, Tony Killick, Colin Kirkpatrick, James Manor, Jean-François Medard, Stephen Riley, Mark Robinson, Erik Svendsen, Brian Thomson, and Robert Wade. A second conference was held in the fall of 1989 at Harvard's Center for International Affairs, at which we received useful, if often withering, comments from Robert Bates, Jeffry Frieden, Merilee Grindle, Sylvia Maxfield, Michael Shafer, and Eliza Willis.

In this third stage of the project, we were very pleased to be able to co-opt two authors who had been working on similar themes for some time: John Waterbury and Peter Evans.

The editors of this volume have accumulated a number of additional debts. Our initial collaboration is contained in our contribution to a project on developing country debt sponsored by the National Bureau of Economic Research. Jeffrey Sachs directed that project and goaded us to contribute to it. Stephan Haggard benefited from support and time made available to him by the Center for International Affairs and the U.S.-Japan Program; he would like to thank Samuel Huntington and Susan Pharr, the directors of these two institutions, for their support. Ongoing collaborative efforts with Susan Collins, Richard Cooper, and David Lindauer strengthened Haggard's understanding of the economics of adjustment. Haggard also presented the introduction twice at Harvard: to the Working Group on the Politics of International Debt and Finance organized by Leslie Armijo, and to a faculty seminar on comparative politics organized by Jorge Domínguez that included Houchang Chehabi, Frances Hagopian, Sam Huntington, Ashutosh Varshney, and Jennifer Widner.

In 1990, Haggard was on leave from Harvard at the Macroeconomics and Growth Division of the World Bank on a Council on Foreign Relations International Affairs Fellowship. He had the opportunity to present parts of this book in several seminars at the Bank. He would like to thank Tony Dunn at the Council and Johannes Linn at the World Bank for helping him realize that fellowship. A number of individuals at the World Bank made the stay a rich learning experience. These include particularly Vittorio Corbo, director of the Macroeconomics and Growth Division, who was kind enough to invite a political scientist into his division, and Steven B. Webb, with whom Haggard is co-directing a project on economic adjustment in new democracies for the World Bank. Karim Sharif taught Haggard some econometrics, and Max Corden shared his wisdom over a number of stimulating lunches. Nancy Gillespie, Brian Levy, and Barbara Nunberg also helped make his stay both pleasant and stimulating.

None of the findings, interpretations, and conclusions of this volume can be attributed to the World Bank, the board of directors, its management, or any of its member countries.

Kaufman received helpful comments from participants in seminars held at Harvard, Princeton, Brown, and Rutgers at which he presented earlier versions of chapters 1, 7, and 8. He is also grateful for the general encouragement of colleagues and graduate students in the Rutgers political economy program, including Ken Finegold, Mike Shafer, Eric Davis, and for the very able research assistance provided by Bill Clark.

We both owe particular gratitude to the "founding members" of this project: Thomas Callaghy, Joan Nelson, Miles Kahler, and Barbara Stallings. Over the past seven years, these people have been collaborators in the broadest sense, contributing not only their essays, but also participating as partners in the design and execution of the project as a whole.

Finally, we would like to thank Nancy Gilson and Laura Schoen, who put up with our seemingly endless phone calls to one another over the last two years.

Stephan Haggard, Cambridge, Massachusetts
Robert R. Kaufman, New Brunswick, New Jersey
May 1991

The Politics of Economic Adjustment

Institutions and Economic Adjustment

Stephan Haggard and Robert R. Kaufman

FOR DEVELOPING country debtors, the 1980s was a decade of increasingly insistent calls for economic policy reform: to reduce budget deficits and tighten monetary policy; to liberalize trade and exchange rate regimes; and most generally, to expand the role of market forces and the private sector. Reforms of this sort have been urged on developing countries before, but the collapse of the international lending boom of the 1970s and the economic crisis that ensued forced fundamental reassessments of policy across the developing world. Unlike the 1930s, when external shocks generated heterodox policy experiments,[1] international pressures in the 1980s pushed toward a scaling back of the state's developmental and redistributive commitments. Rather than breaking with orthodoxy, developing countries were urged to embrace it.

Although international pressures on the developing countries have been substantial, responses to the crisis have not been uniform. These differences raise critical questions for comparative political analysis. Why did some governments avoid difficulty in the first place while others still struggle unsuccessfully with problems of stabilization and structural adjustment? Why did some countries hew to orthodox policies while others experimented with alternatives or failed to arrive at coherent policy responses of any sort?

The essays in this volume address these differences, exploring how international and domestic politics affect policy choice. The shifting perceptions of decision makers and personal differences in political style and skill naturally introduce a degree of indeterminacy into any effort to explain policy choice, and good or bad tactics sometimes emerge as the most

In addition to the extensive comments from members of this project, we would like to thank the members of the faculty seminar on the politics of development at Harvard's Center for International Affairs organized by Jorge Domínguez, and including Houchang Chehabi, Frances Hagopian, Samuel Huntington, Ashutosh Varshney, and Jennifer Widner. We would also like to thank the members of the Working Group on the Politics of International Debt and Finance, Center for International Affairs, Harvard University, organized by Leslie Armijo.

[1] See Peter Gourevitch, *Politics in Hard Times: Comparative Responses to International Economic Crisis* (Ithaca, N.Y.: Cornell University Press, 1986).

compelling explanation of success and failure. But it is also clear that decision makers operate in a matrix of international, social, and institutional incentives and constraints that sets limits on the range of policy alternatives. The pages that follow provide a comparative examination of these incentives and constraints, seeking a clearer understanding of the conditions under which policymakers will adopt and sustain economic policy reforms.

OBJECTIVES, SCOPE, OUTLINE

The present volume contains the results of the second phase of a collaborative research project. In the first phase, we pursued an inductive, comparative case study approach to provide a preliminary survey of the political forces shaping adjustment decisions to derive some first-order generalizations and to generate hypotheses for further exploration.[2] In this volume, we build on this empirical foundation, as well as on the growing theoretical literature on the politics of economic policy. Our objective is to forge more explicit connections to the central theoretical debates in comparative and international political economy, and to provide broader cross-national comparisons. We also seek to exploit the rich monographic literature on the politics of adjustment that appeared in the late 1980s.[3] The essays thus draw on the "core cases" discussed in the

[2] Those studies were published as *Economic Crisis and Policy Choice: The Politics of Adjustment in the Third World* (Princeton: Princeton University Press, 1990), Joan Nelson, ed. The case studies included in that volume were: Argentina, Brazil, and Mexico (Robert Kaufman); Chile, Peru, and Colombia (Barbara Stallings); Costa Rica, the Dominican Republic, and Jamaica (Joan Nelson); Ghana, Zambia, and Nigeria (Thomas Callaghy), and the Philippines (Stephan Haggard).

[3] It is impossible to provide any complete listing of the works in this genre that appeared in the 1980s, but the more noteworthy comparative efforts deserve mention. A comparative project on the political economy of World Bank adjustment lending is contained in Paul Mosley, Jane Harrigan, and John Toye, *Aid and Power: The World Bank and Policy-Based Lending in the 1980s* (London: Routledge, 1991); we are thankful to the leaders of this project for sharing their results with us. John W. Thomas and Merilee S. Grindle summarize their project on the politics of policy reform in *Public Choices and Policy Change: The Political Economy of Reform in Developing Countries* (Baltimore: Johns Hopkins University Press, 1991). The results of a cross-national project on the economics of debt and adjustment undertaken by the National Bureau of Economic Research are summarized in Jeffrey D. Sachs., ed., *Developing Country Debt and the World Economy* (Chicago: University of Chicago Press, 1989) and Jeffrey D. Sachs and Susan M. Collins, eds., *Developing Country Debt and Economic Performance*, vol. 2, *Country Studies: Argentina, Bolivia, Brazil, Mexico* and vol. 3, *Country Studies: Indonesia, Korea, Philippines, Turkey* (Chicago: University of Chicago Press, 1989). Lance Taylor summarizes a seventeen-country research project on stabilization and structural adjustment in *Varieties of Stabilization Experience: Towards Sensible Macroeconomics in the Third World* (Oxford: Clarendon Press, 1988). Among the comparative studies focusing on Latin America are William L. Canak, *Lost*

first volume of the project, but also on the experiences of other countries that have been important in the adjustment debate, either for their apparent success (Korea, Turkey, Bolivia) or failure (Guyana, Zaire, and other low-income African countries).

The economic adjustment choices addressed in this volume can be divided into three clusters of policies: balance of payments management and stabilization; so-called "structural adjustment" measures; and national strategies toward creditors. The first manifestations of the crisis of the 1980s were severe balance of payments problems. In a number of countries, particularly in Latin America, these problems were connected as both cause and effect to unprecedented macroeconomic imbalances and inflationary pressures. Reequilibrating the balance of payments and stabilizing prices entailed adjustment of the real exchange rate and tight fiscal and monetary policies, though more "heterodox" experiments with external controls, incomes policies, and price controls were also attempted.

Short-term balance of payments and price stabilization measures were not sufficient in themselves to rekindle investment and growth. As the decade of the 1980s wore on, attention shifted to broader "structural adjustments" aimed at rationalizing the allocation of resources and strengthening the export sector. In the view of much of the development policy community, economic liberalization has been regarded as the main path toward such goals, and the process of adjustment has been equated with measures such as the reduction of tariffs, the deregulation of financial markets, and the privatization of state-owned enterprises. As Peter Evans argues in his chapter, however, market-oriented reforms are by no means the only conceivable means of adjustment, and in a number of rapidly growing countries the state has played an active and interventionist role in the allocation of resources.

Finally, debtors had to choose the stance they would take vis-à-vis their creditors and the international financial institutions. Debtors had to decide at what point it was no longer rational to service external obligations

---

Promises: Debt, Austerity and Development in Latin America (Boulder, Colo.: Westview Press, 1989); Howard Handelman and Werner Baer, *Paying the Costs of Austerity in Latin America* (Boulder: Westview Press, 1989); John Williamson, ed., *Latin American Adjustment: How Much Has Happened?* (Washington, D.C.: Institute of International Economics, 1990); and Barbara Stallings and Robert Kaufman, eds., *Debt and Democracy in Latin America* (Boulder, Colo.: Westview Press, 1989). On Africa, see Gerald K. Helleiner, ed. *Africa and the International Monetary Fund* (Washington, D.C.: International Monetary Fund, 1986); John Ravenhill, ed., *Africa in Economic Crisis* (New York: Columbia University Press, 1986); Bonnie K. Campbell and John Loxley, *Structural Adjustment in Africa* (New York: St. Martins, 1989); and Thomas M. Callaghy and John Ravenhill, *Hemmed In: Responses to Africa's Economic Decline* (New York: Columbia University Press, forthcoming 1992).

and the extent to which they would comply with the conditions attached to loans from the international financial institutions. As with the other policy decisions, the behavior of developing country debtors varied widely, from compliance, to quiet defection, to outright defiance.

In each of these policy areas, there are three dimensions of choice to be explained. The first is to explain the timing of the *initiation* of policy reform. In a number of countries, the response to crisis was slow. In others, the recurrent announcement of reform packages that subsequently went unimplemented was a similar sign of delay—what Thomas Callaghy has called a "ritual dance" between debtors and creditors.[4] Other countries, by contrast, responded to changed economic conditions with alacrity, or acted preemptively to minimize adjustment costs. Gauging the timing of a policy measure in relation to the problem it is designed to resolve is not always easy. For a number of structural adjustments, it could be argued that reforms are addressing distortions of several decades' duration. Nonetheless, particularly with reference to stabilization and balance of payments adjustment, it is possible to distinguish those governments that acted quickly in the face of warning signs from those that delayed adjustment until facing full-blown crises.

Second, we are interested in explaining the substantive nature of each policy response: its *scope* and its *content*. Scope refers to the breadth of the reforms. We distinguish between those reform efforts that are part of a relatively calculated and internally coherent plan, such as those in Bolivia, Chile, Mexico, Ghana, and Turkey, as opposed to those that unfolded in a more piecemeal and ad hoc way. Content refers to the balance between "orthodox" and "heterodox" measures.

At the beginning of the decade, this distinction was perhaps sharper than it is now; by the early 1990s, there were no longer extensive policy debates about the importance of macroeconomic discipline on the expansion of exports. Throughout the 1980s, however, broad distinctions could usefully be drawn between policy initiatives that relied primarily on market incentives and privates actors, and those that emphasized problems of market failure and a broader role for the government in the promotion of economic growth. Notwithstanding the current convergence between contending policy camps, significant differences do continue to exist over a range of issues, including industrial policy, the pace and extent of deregulation and privatization, price controls, and the scope of public investment.

Finally, we are interested in whether reforms are in fact sustained, or whether they are reversed. By the *consolidation* of reform, we mean not

[4] Thomas Callaghy, "The Political Economy of African Debt: The Case of Zaire," in Ravenhill, *Africa in Economic Crisis*, pp. 307–46.

only that policies have persisted over time, but that they have been instititutionalized within the policy system.

In examining these three dimensions of the reform process, it is not our purpose to assess the validity of contending economic prescriptions. Numerous studies have staked out positions on this question, and the contributors to this volume have somewhat different views. In general, the essays share with "mainstream" economists the assumption that swift action is superior to delay; that developing countries need to pay greater attention to exports, fiscal and monetary discipline, and the price mechanism; and that policies are more likely to succeed if implemented in a consistent fashion. At the same time (perhaps for disciplinary reasons), the contributors stress repeatedly that effective adjustment demands a more activist and capable state than is typically envisioned by neoclassical prescriptions. The point of departure for our analysis, however, is comparative rather than prescriptive. Our primary interest lies in explaining variations in policy choices cross-nationally and over time, differences in the timing of reform initiatives, the degree to which orthodox prescriptions were adopted, and the extent to which reforms were sustained and consolidated.

We cut into these comparisons at three distinct levels of analysis: one international, the second centered on the state, and the third focused on the broader political and institutional setting within which distributional conflicts are waged. The first set of issues centers on the extent to which domestic policy choices are constrained by international market forces and the political leverage of creditor governments, the key multilateral financial institutions—the International Monetary Fund (IMF) and the World Bank—and the commercial banks. The chapters by Barbara Stallings and Miles Kahler address this question. Stallings argues that international economic shocks changed the basic policy agenda during the 1980s, forced some policy changes directly, and generally enhanced the political power of creditors. Looking at the international financial institutions, Kahler is more skeptical about the bargaining power of creditors, and notes the difficulties that arise in attempting to enforce the terms of the "conditionality bargain." The differences in emphasis raise important questions about the mechanisms through which external pressures are transmitted and the role played by domestic political factors in shaping policy responses.

A unifying theme of the essays in the second and third sections of the book is the critical role of political institutions in shaping adjustment decisions. The essays by John Waterbury and Peter Evans focus on the role of the state. The central theoretical debate in this area concerns the importance of state autonomy for the initiation and consolidation of fundamentally new policy directions. On the one hand, because of the free-rider problem facing social groups and the general uncertainty concerning the ultimate beneficiaries of reform, the initiation of policy reform appears more likely when technocratic decision makers enjoy some degree of independence from particularistic interests; this is the case regardless of whether the substantive content of the adjustment program is market-oriented or more activist in orientation. On the other hand, no reform can be sustained in the longer run unless it appeals to, or creates, a new coalition of beneficiaries; this is also true of reforms that have as their objective a reduction of the state's role in the economy. The politics of reform is thus torn between conflicting demands on the state to maintain its autonomy, while also establishing adequate support, or what Evans calls "embeddedness."

Waterbury looks at the state as producer, and considers the paradoxes of government efforts to reduce its role in the economy through privatization. He argues that reform is more likely to be launched by relatively insulated "change teams," but notes that the political use of state-owned enterprises to maintain bases of political support places fundamental limits on the extent of such reforms. Evans tackles the same dilemma by examining the role of the state in a number of earlier cases of "structural adjustment," including the paradigmatic East Asian success stories, Korea and Taiwan. Evans advances a theory of the organizational foundations of the developmental state that focuses on the internal corporate and ideological cohesion of the bureaucracy. Organizationally coherent states are capable of building the linkages with key social actors that are required to support developmental projects, while avoiding the problems of capture and rent seeking highlighted by Waterbury.

The essays by Joan Nelson and Stephan Haggard and Robert R. Kaufman that constitute the third section of the book focus on how distributive conflicts influence adjustment efforts. Again, the key theoretical issue is the weight that should be placed on social and economic interests in explaining the reform process. Both essays argue that distributive conflicts among contending social groups are heavily mediated by state action and the broader institutional milieu. Nelson argues that policy design can itself affect the structure of coalitions and the level of political support and opposition around particular initiatives. By examining the possibilities for integrating "pro-poor" measures into stabilization and structural adjustment programs, Nelson opens the crucial question of leadership and tactics.

In our study of the political sources of macroeconomic stability and instability we give substantial explanatory weight to politicians' independence from the pull of distributive politics in the short run. This, in turn, is shaped by the nature of representative institutions. We suggest how regime type and the party system affect the nature of distributive conflicts, and thus help explain historical patterns of inflation and stabilization.

The remainder of the introduction, and of the book itself, is structured around these three distinct levels of analysis. In the next section of this essay, we outline the debate about the role of international factors in more detail. The last two sections examine respectively "statist" approaches to reform and the effects of the larger political milieu on the adjustment process.

The principal concern of the following studies is with the political determinants of policy choice. In the conclusion to the volume, however, this causal emphasis is reversed, and we turn our attention to the political *consequences* of the adjustment crisis of the 1980s. In particular, we explore the implications of the economic developments of the decade for the establishment and consolidation of political democracy.

THE INTERNATIONAL DIMENSION: SHOCKS, POWER, IDEAS

An essential point of departure for any discussion of policy reform is the adverse external shocks the developing countries experienced in the 1980s. The contributors to this volume all concur that the external environment narrowed the range of policy choice; a central axis of theoretical and empirical debate, however, concerns the extent to which national policy responses can be *explained* by reference to economic shocks or the political power and ideological influence of international creditors and the multilateral institutions.

On the one hand, if we compare economic policy in the 1980s with economic policy in the 1970s, it appears incontrovertible that developing countries were forced to adjust by changes in their external environment and were pressured strongly to adopt more orthodox policy stances. Barbara Stallings argues that this was largely a reflection of economic constraints and the underlying asymmetries in the power relations between creditors and debtors. On the other hand, the variation in national responses to the debt crisis suggests that the relationship between external constraints and policy choice is not as obvious as it may appear. Miles Kahler emphasizes these differences and suggests that creditors often found it difficult to enforce policy conditionality despite apparent power asymmetries. We argue that cross-national variations do provide the justification for a more thorough exploration of the domestic politics of adjustment, but it is important first to explore the theoretical case for and against international explanations of policy in more detail.

The Case for an International Explanation

The strong case for an emphasis on international factors in explaining adjustment policy is found in Stallings' chapter, which reexamines some of the insights of the dependency perspective that was prevalent in the

1960s and 1970s. Stallings argues that there are three distinct ways in which international factors impinge on domestic policy choices. First, developments in international goods and capital markets determine the availability of external resources, which in turn sets important limits on the range of policy options. Second, Stallings points out that policy is influenced by international *linkages*: the transnational social and political networks and coalitions that link domestic and international actors. Finally, debtors were constrained by *leverage*: the financial, political and ideological power exercised by creditors, both directly and through the constitution of the broad rules of the game.

Stallings shows that the range of sustainable policy options, which increased as international trade and lending grew during the 1960s, decreased substantially during the 1980s. Sluggish and erratic growth in the advanced industrial states contributed to the economic difficulties of the less developed countries (LDCs). Trends in developing countries' terms of trade were inauspicious. For countries heavily dependent on commodity exports—with the notable exception of the oil exporters—the first half of the 1980s was especially disastrous. Developments in international financial markets were also adverse. High interest rates increased the cost of servicing external obligations and led to a sharp increase in debt-service ratios. Heavily indebted countries were also forced to adjust to the sharp contraction of international commercial lending that occurred after the Mexican debt crisis of August 1982.[5]

Sharp changes in the terms of trade and the availability of foreign financing affected central decision makers directly through the squeeze on foreign exchange and government revenues. The need for rapid adjustment in the current account forced exchange rate adjustments.[6] External shocks, particularly the withdrawal of foreign lending, also forced demand reduction policies, usually undertaken in conjunction with IMF stabilization programs. These programs included efforts to cut real government expenditure, raise revenues, restrain the growth of wages, and

---

[5] The differential effects of external shocks are most visible in the debt crisis. For Latin America as a whole, net transfers became negative in 1983 and remained large throughout the rest of the decade. For Africa, net transfers to private creditors turned negative in 1983, but the dependence on commercial lending was less and this development was partly offset by continued official flows. For East Asia and the Pacific, net transfers did not turn negative until 1986. Net transfers are obtained by subtracting interest payments on long-term and short-term debt and dividends on foreign direct investments from the aggregate net resource flows, or disbursements minus repayment of principal.

[6] There is a clear link between the retrenchment of foreign lending, depreciation, and the trend toward more flexible exchange rate regimes. See International Monetary Fund, *Developments in International Exchange and Trade Systems* (Washington, D.C.: IMF, 1989), pp. 7–8; Peter J. Quirk et al., *Floating Exchange Rates in Developing Countries: Experience with Auction and Interbank Markets* (Washington, D.C.: IMF Occasional Paper No. 53, 1987).

control money supply growth, usually through, or with the effect of, raising real interest rates.

Several features of the international regime for managing the debt crisis constrained developing country options in the face of external shocks. Creditors were able to coordinate their stance toward the debtors, but cooperation among debtor countries was discouraged, in part through strategic side payments to the most important debtors.[7] As a result, a debtors' cartel failed to materialize. All negotiations over debt rescheduling and adjustment programs were conducted on a case-by-case basis. Moreover, until the late 1980s, it was assumed that all obligations, public and private, would be paid in full, including not only debt owed to commercial banks but bilateral public loans.

The final constraint might be called the *conditionality norm*: the presumption that the costs of adjustment would fall largely on the debtors. The initial difficulties that the debtors had in servicing their obligations forced the banks to reschedule principal and to engage in "concerted" or "involuntary" lending agreements. With very few exceptions, reschedulings of both commercial and public debt were made contingent on the negotiation of high-conditionality, upper-tranche programs with the IMF.[8] According to Stallings, these programs placed that organization in a strategic position to define the adjustment agenda.

The so-called Baker Plan, unveiled at the IMF meetings in Seoul in September 1985, recognized that the problems facing the debtors were of a longer-term nature and promised that international financial institutions would increase their lending in return for which the developing countries would adopt wide-ranging structural adjustment programs. By 1988, however, it was clear that the Baker Plan was inadequate, in part because the plan had no way of inducing new lending from the commercial banks.[9] An increasing number of countries halted repayment and went

[7] See Pamela Metz, "International Bargaining in the 'Lost Decade': A New Look at Some Debt Truisms," Harvard University, January 1990.

[8] Much of the "new money" offered in such agreements was in effect recycled to the banks. In a number of politically important cases, such as Mexico, Turkey, and Poland, creditor governments provided additional assistance and played an active political role in coordinating agreements.

[9] The large money-center banks provisioned themselves against losses, and as their balance sheets improved, concerted lending agreements fell off dramatically. See Jeffrey D. Sachs and Harry Huizinga, "U.S. Commercial Banks and the Developing Country Debt Crisis," *Brookings Papers on Economic Activity* 2 (1989): 555–601. An assessment by the World Bank of the Baker Plan is worth quoting at some length:

"Per capita income in the Baker Plan 17 countries, which were lower in 1985 than in 1982, declined further between 1985 and 1988. Despite large trade surpluses, the Baker 17 countries' total debt continued to rise in relation to exports up to 1986. Their total debt service ratio improved modestly . . . [but] the real depreciation of the currencies of the Baker countries, often necessary to generate the external resource transfer, further increased the

into arrears. In March 1989, U.S. Treasury Secretary Nicholas Brady announced that the United States would support debt reduction.[10] At the end of 1991, the details of the Brady Plan were still evolving, but the concept of conditionality remained central to the new strategy and was even given new force by the fact that an increasing number of countries were undertaking IMF and World Bank programs simultaneously.[11] As Miles Kahler points out, the underlying bargain remained similar over the entire decade: "stringent adjustment for a modest amount of financing."[12]

Reinforcing these specific norms was the decline of the statist ideologies that had prevailed throughout the developing world in the 1970s and the diffusion of more orthodox ideas through various international networks.[13] Stallings emphasizes this factor in her discussion of linkage, Kahler in his analysis of the literature on social learning. There were a number of reasons for the sharp shift in the intellectual climate. The industrial countries appeared much more immune to the threat from the Third World in the 1980s than they had been following the first oil shock and, thus, much less accommodating to developing country demands. The ascendence of conservative governments in Britain, the United States, and Germany also affected the policy discourse and the agenda of the international organizations.

Longer-term intellectual changes were also taking place within the economics profession and the development policy community, including the ascendence of monetarism and a neoclassical revival within the develop-

---

level of external debt relative to domestic output over this period." (World Bank, *World Debt Tables 1989–90*, p. 13.)

[10] On market-oriented debt reduction schemes, see International Monetary Fund, *International Capital Markets: Developments and Prospects*, World Economic and Financial Surveys (Washington, D.C.: IMF, 1989), chap. 3; Stign Claessens, Ishac Diwan, Kenneth A. Froot, and Paul R. Krugman, "Market-Based Debt Reduction: Principles and Prospects," the World Bank, February 1990, mimeo. On Japan's role in pushing for debt service reduction based on an expanded menu approach and additional multilateral and bilateral assistance, see Barbara Stallings, "The Reluctant Giant: Japan and the Latin American Debt Crisis," *Journal of Latin American Studies* 22, no. 1 (February 1990).

[11] In May 1989, both the World Bank and the IMF issued guidelines for the support of debt reduction for middle-income countries. For prudential as well as policy reasons, both organizations insisted on the implementation of acceptable medium-term structural adjustment programs as a condition for Brady Plan money. Similarly, those low-income countries eligible for forgiveness and concessional rescheduling of official bilateral debt under the so-called Toronto terms or for access to the World Bank's debt reduction facility for low-income countries were expected to have IMF- or World Bank-supported adjustment programs in place. Undertaking programs simultaneously with both the IMF and the World Bank entailed either implicit or explicit cross-conditionality.

[12] Miles Kahler, "Orthodoxy and its Alternatives: Explaining Approaches to Stabilization and Adjustment," in Nelson, *Economic Crisis and Policy Choice*, p. 47.

[13] See Kahler, "Orthodoxy and Its Alternatives," and Stephen Krasner, *Structural Conflict: The Third World against Global Liberalism* (Berkeley: University of California Press, 1985).

ment field.[14] These intellectual developments were buttressed by lessons derived, if somewhat selectively, from the contrasting experiences of the export-oriented newly industrializing countries of East Asia and their heavily-indebted and economically-troubled Latin American counterparts. Despite the state's active role in the development of Singapore, Taiwan, and Korea, it was undeniable that these countries had been more aggressive in exploiting their comparative advantage than the Latin American, South Asian or African countries.[15] By contrast, countries such as Brazil and Peru were used to support negative evaluations both of import substitution and of heterodox adjustment strategies, even though ultra-orthodox policies adopted in the late 1970s in Chile, Argentina, and Uruguay experienced equally severe limitations.

No study yet discusses the current diffusion of ideas that parallels Peter Hall's analysis of the spread of Keynsianism,[16] but it is clear that the channels for the dissemination of orthodox policy "lessons" became more developed over the 1980s. The monographic literature consistently reveals that senior economic officials and academic economists were important carriers of neoclassical ideas, forming the core of transnational policy coalitions favoring liberalizing reform.[17] A growing number of these "reformist cadres" served as staff members of the World Bank, IMF, and regional development banks and many had been trained in North American universities. These academics-cum-technocrats had a broader understanding of, if not sympathy for, orthodox policy prescriptions, as well as some comparative knowledge of the adjustment experiences of other countries. These officials were frequently thrust into positions of substantial authority, often acting as interlocutors in negotiations with the international financial institutions.

Stallings argues that these broad economic, political, and ideological changes in the international environment are critical in explaining differences in the pattern of policy choice between the 1970s and the 1980s. She acknowledges that international pressures did not necessarily lead in the same direction in all policy areas. In the area of debt repayment, for example, international constraints became *looser* over the decade. As creditors became somewhat less cohesive in managing negotiations and less willing to make good on promises of renewed access to financial mar-

[14] Kahler, "Orthodoxy and its Alternatives."

[15] For a comparative analysis of the newly industrializing countries of East Asia and Latin America, see Stephan Haggard, *Pathways from the Periphery: The Politics of Growth in the Newly Industrializing Countries* (Ithaca, N.Y.: Cornell University Press, 1990).

[16] Peter Hall, ed., *The Political Power of Economic Ideas* (Princeton: Princeton University Press, 1989).

[17] Perhaps the most explicit development of this argument is Robin Broad, *Unequal Alliance: The World Bank, the International Monetary Fund, and the Philippines* (Berkeley: University of California Press, 1988).

kets, more and more developing countries slipped into arrears on their commercial debts, and even on their obligations to multilateral financial institutions.

Nonetheless, Stallings argues that these variations should not obscure the powerful influence exercised by international constraints over the major adjustment decisions of the 1980s. Adverse developments in the trading system and the drying up of private sources of external finance reduced the resources available to governments to pursue state-led development strategies and increased the leverage both of the multilateral financial institutions and "internationalist" political forces at home.[18] "Since structural change threatens so many entrenched interests," she writes, "most governments will not initiate it without an overwhelming number of factors pushing it forward." By the end of the 1980s a growing number of governments had turned toward conventional stabilization and adjustment programs. A particularly telling point for the internationalist explanation is that the ranks of the orthodox included a number of governments that had been elected or come to power on platforms that explicitly rejected orthodox adjustment measures, including Menem in Argentina, Bórja in Ecuador, Pérez in Venezuela, and Rawlings in Ghana.

Over time, international financial and ideological pressures also had the more profound (though difficult to measure) effect of transforming the nature of the policy debate itself. This intellectual sea change was particularly evident in much of Latin America and sub-Saharan Africa, two regions long resistant to liberal prescriptions. A recent survey by John Williamson claims to find a growing convergence of views among individuals and institutions with a professional interest in Latin America, extending to Latin America itself, around the importance of fiscal discipline, trade liberalization, and the maintenance of realistic exchange rates.[19] Similar changes are visible in the debate within Africa as well.[20]

Limitations on International Explanations

The decade-long trend toward the adoption of more orthodox policy reforms across the developing world would, in itself, seem to constitute strong prima facie evidence for the influence of pressures from the inter-

[18] For an analysis of structural adjustment lending, see the World Bank, Country Economics Department, *Adjustment Lending Policies for Sustainable Growth* (Washington, D.C.: World Bank, 1990).

[19] Contrast Williamson, *Latin American Adjustment* with José María Fanelli, Roberto Frenkel, and Guillermo Rozenwurcel, *Growth and Structural Reform* in *Latin America: Where We Stand* (Buenos Aires: Centro de Estudios de Estado y Sociedad, 1990).

[20] World Bank, *Sub-Saharan Africa: From Crisis to Sustainable Growth* (Washington, D.C.: World Bank, 1989).

national system. Just as many political scientists were turning away from dependency perspectives, the economic, political, and ideological influences emanating from the external environment appeared to be even more binding than they had been in the past. In this regard Stallings' essay provides an important corrective; a reminder of the limits of analyses that rely exclusively on domestic variables.

As Stallings recognizes, however, there are also significant limits, both empirical and analytical, to the range of policy behavior that can be explained without reference to domestic political configurations. One limitation is that the longer-term sources of vulnerability to external pressure often lie with previous policy choices. Changes in commodity prices and the terms of trade can be viewed as largely exogenous; but the public investment booms that contributed to the accumulation of debt in the 1970s, and the overvalued exchange rates that limited export growth and contributed to financial speculation and capital flight, had their origins in domestic spending priorities and development strategies. The debtor countries hardest hit by fiscal crisis and high inflation in the 1980s were generally countries that had experienced repeated inflation-stabilization cycles in the past, often closely connected with domestic political conflicts. Conversely, the relative speed with which the East and Southeast Asian countries adjusted to the shocks of the 1980s reflected both particular coalitional interests and their political capacity to sustain the trade and exchange rate policies that initiated export-led growth in the 1960s and 1970s.

Second, and more importantly, external shocks do not affect policy choice in an unambiguous way. The large Latin American countries responded to the external shocks of the 1930s by turning inward; in the 1980s, external shocks produced efforts to liberalize and strong pressure to abandon import-substituting policies. In attempting to manage balance of payments problems in the 1980s, countries varied in the mix of exchange rate adjustments, demand management, and trade and exchange controls. Countries experiencing comparable shocks varied in the speed with which they adopted stabilization and adjustment programs and the content of those programs.[21] Hard-hit countries such as Korea, Chile, Costa Rica and Ghana responded relatively early in the decade with comprehensive programs of stabilization and structural adjustment, while others, such as Argentina, Peru, and Zambia either experimented with heterodoxy or were unable to sustain adjustment policies of any sort. These variations suggest that domestic economic and political structures are important in understanding national responses to shocks.

Stallings' focus on the long-term convergence of policy approaches in

---

[21] See Joan M. Nelson, "Conclusions," Nelson, *Economic Crisis and Policy Choice.*

developing countries is also more relevant for explaining changes in the policy *agenda* than it is to the actual implementation of policies. Kahler argues that the proper measure of external influence is "the degree to which external actors change the trajectory of national policy from what it would have been in the absence of their intervention." He notes that the "slippage" between announced intentions and actual policy choices is substantial, suggesting the intervening weight of domestic politics. His survey of the record of nineteen governments during the 1980s finds that only nine had implemented coherent stabilization programs, and only five had implemented sustained programs of structural adjustment. In an intensive study of nine countries receiving World Bank structural adjustment loans, Mosely, Harrigan, and Toye find that only two (Turkey and Thailand) actually met more than two-thirds of the conditions attached to structural adjustment and sectoral adjustment loans. Malawi, Ghana, the Philippines, and Jamaica implmented between 55 and 63 percent of the conditions, and Kenya, Guyana, and Ecuador had implementation rates of less than 38 percent.[22] Although this range of variation may have narrowed somewhat over time, it remained substantial at the end of the 1980s.

Kahler's skepticism about the actual leverage of the international financial institutions is not grounded solely on the role of domestic politics; countervailing international factors can also undermine influence. These include the "high" political interests of the creditors, the difficulties in orchestrating cross-conditionality among donors and international financial institutions, and a number of peculiar features associated with the nature of international credit markets that make enforcement difficult.

One reason for diminished leverage is that the potential enforcers—the creditor governments—have multiple and conflicting goals vis-à-vis the debtors. The concern to support a strategically important client can easily override the interest in enforcing conditionality or even ensuring repayment and can result in levels of external financing higher than would have otherwise been provided. This can undermine efforts to coordinate cross-conditionality and produce quite perverse incentives. Where leaders are already committed to a reform program, as in Turkey, additional finance may contribute to program success, though in support of efforts that were likely to have been undertaken anyway. Where nonconditional resources are made available to countries disposed against reform, such as the Philippines under Marcos or Zaire under Mobutu, finance allows governments to postpone, rather than pursue adjustment.

Drawing on a growing literature on dynamic contract theory in economics, Kahler points to a number of other strategic problems that arise

---

[22] Mosely, Harrigan, and Toye, *Aid and Power*, as cited in Kahler, chap. 2, this volume.

out of the attempt to impose external conditions. These include critical informational asymmetries and difficulties in effective monitoring and enforcement. Creditors favor a minimum of finance in return for broad and swift adjustment efforts. Debtor governments, by contrast, seek to maximize available finance while minimizing the political and economic costs of implementing difficult adjustment measures. Debtors have an incentive to exaggerate the difficulty of undertaking reforms, including their political costs, and to seek support or compensation for reforms that might have been undertaken anyway. Depending on the expectations of the political leadership concerning future interaction with creditors, there may also be an incentive to cheat on agreements reached.

Many of the changes in the operations of the international financial institutions (IFIs) over the 1980s can be interpreted as efforts to overcome these strategic dilemmas, including closer monitoring efforts, tranching loan disbursements, insisting on policy actions prior to the disbursement or even negotiation of a loan, moving toward greater specificity and scope in the delineation of conditions, and attempting tighter cross-conditionality. Kahler notes that policy action taken *prior* to securing external support offers a good predictor of the likelihood that programs will be implemented, but this observation only buttresses the point that governments committed to policy reform will probably undertake them in any case and that those opposed will resist. Kahler concludes that only in delicately balanced cases does it appear that the conditionality bargain itself has played an important role in tipping the balance in favor of reform.

Like Stallings, Kahler attaches importance to the diffusion of ideologies through transnational technocratic alliances, a process he calls "social learning," and agrees that this concept helps to account for the tendency toward greater orthodoxy in the late 1980s. Yet he also suggests that it is frequently difficult to tell ex ante how much power technocrats have. Agreements based on technocratic alliances have often broken down because they lack the backing of the president or other segments of the bureaucracy.[23] For such learning to have effect, it must spread to broader segments of the political elite and relevant publics.

We concur with Stallings that there was a substantial narrowing of the feasible policy set over the 1980s as a result of the enhanced role of the IFIs and changing intellectual views of the development problematic. External shocks forced some policy adjustments directly. Nonetheless, political elites still weighed the potential gains of any given adjustment strat-

[23] On these points, see in particular Stephan Haggard, "The Political Economy of the Philippine Debt Crisis," and Thomas Callaghy, "Lost Between State and Market: The Politics of Economic Adjustment in Ghana, Zambia, and Nigeria," in Nelson, *Economic Crisis and Policy Choice.*

egy against its domestic political cost. It is to this decision calculus that we now turn.

THE ROLE OF THE STATE

Collective Action Problems in the Initiation and Consolidation of Reform

The central political dilemma of reform is that though significant benefits may accrue to society as a whole, policy adjustment involves significant startup costs and the reduction of rents to particular groups. How, then, do such innovations come about? The case study literature on the politics of adjustment suggests repeatedly that governmental elites and state institutions are pivotal to the launching of reform efforts.[24] First, government officials play a crucial mediating role between the international and domestic arenas, and thus are directly exposed to pressures that emanate from the world economy, creditor governments, foreign firms and banks, and multilateral financial institutions. Second, because of their unique position in the policy process itself, state actors have substantial power over the policy agenda. Finally, the structure of political institutions, including the state itself, will influence both the capacity of the government to act and the range of societal interests that are represented.

Accordingly, we begin with "state-centered" approaches to policy reform, approaches represented in this volume by the contributions of Peter Evans and John Waterbury. Both authors emphasize that state organizations can be focal points of resistance to reform as well as innovation, yet both also suggest that new adjustment initiatives depend heavily on the capacity of state officials to play an entrepreneurial role.

Since it is common to begin the political analysis of policy reform with reference to its distributional consequences and the power and interests of social groups, a focus on the state demands some theoretical justification. That justification lies in the fact that policy change is plagued by numerous collective action problems. Stable prices can be viewed as a public good, but individuals and firms can gain from policies that undermine stability and might be reluctant to bear the costs of stabilization if others do not do so as well. Similarly, trade liberalization or state enterprise reforms can generate overall efficiency gains, but individual firms or sectors will lobby to retain particularistic benefits.

In institutionalized political systems, where fundamental problems of collective action have been mitigated to some extent and associational life is relatively dense, policy reforms may be explained in terms of shift-

[24] See in particular Grindle and Thomas, *Public Choices and Policy Change*.

ing alignments among interest groups.[25] In many developing countries, however, the classic asymmetry between concentrated losers and diffuse gainers is particularly marked. Powerful business and labor groups in the nontraded goods sector—groups inclined to oppose export-oriented strategies—are likely to be overdeveloped. On the other hand, crucial sectors that might constitute the core of reform coalitions, such as small peasants and landless laborers, informal sector workers, and nontraditional export interests, are less well organized and must overcome significant barriers to collective action in order to be politically effective.

The free-rider problem thus helps explain the difficulty of reform, but precisely for this reason, it makes it difficult to explain the initiation of policy by reference to group interests alone. The types of state leadership discussed by both Waterbury and Evans can be understood as a means of overcoming such collective action problems. Waterbury's study of the state-owned enterprise sector in Egypt, India, Turkey, and Mexico is particularly explicit in this regard. Waterbury argues that the political use of the state-owned enterprise sector crystallizes societal interests within the state itself, and thus poses a particular challenge to comprehensive reform. Nonetheless, to the extent that reform does occur, the impulse will come from technocratic "change teams" within the state that operate outside of routine decision-making channels. Evans suggests that the problems of rent seeking and predation can be mitigated by internally cohesive bureaucracies capable of regulating their links with private sector groups.

Societal forces and economic interests remain essential for understanding the possibilities and limits of reform, but the nature of their influence is frequently misunderstood. As this discussion has suggested, it is useful to distinguish between the politics of initiation and the politics of consolidation, since the two phases of reform demand a somewhat different balance between state autonomy and the representation of interests. Given the problems of collective action outlined, reform initiatives are more likely where and when political institutions insulate politicians and their technocratic allies from particular interest group constraints, at least in the short run.

The consolidation of reform, by contrast, involves stabilizing expectations around a new set of incentives and convincing economic agents that they cannot be reversed at the discretion of individual decision makers.[26]

---

[25] In his analysis of the political responses to the Depression, for example, Peter Gourevitch argues that Keynesian initiatives can be explained on the basis of alliances forged between labor and agricultural groups which were able to bring portions of business together into an implicit pact. Gourevitch, *Politics in Hard Times*, pp. 124–80.

[26] Since government policies are continually being adjusted at the margin, it is difficult to specify exactly what is meant by "sustaining" and "consolidating" a reform. One indicator is simply whether the policy measures are maintained over time by the government in power.

Consolidation is most likely where governments have constructed relatively stable coalitions of political support that encompass major private sector beneficiaries, and have secured at least the acquiescence of the major political forces competing within the political system. Without such tacit or explicit alliances between politicians, technocratic elites, and those gaining from the policy change, reform attempts will necessarily falter.

Despite its merits, the state-centered approach to policy reforms must confront two important puzzles. The first is to understand the preferences of state elites. If elite preferences are not the result of pressures emanating from particular groups or from the logic of political competition, then where do they come from? The second question concerns the organizational characteristics of the state that allow elites to act on their preferences. If statist approaches are to avoid the tautology of defining *capacity* in terms of the ability to realize objectives, they must be able to specify ex ante the state structures that are associated with successful reform. What are the organizational bases of state autonomy? How is state capacity affected by different forms of bureaucratic insulation? What combinations of autonomy and "embeddedness" are associated with the effective initiation and consolidation of reform?

State Preferences for Policy Reform

The new literature on the state has thus far failed to provide a fully satisfactory discussion of the sources of the policy preferences of top executive elites. Several possible sources, however, are suggested in the Waterbury and Evans contributions and in other portions of this study. First, preferences might be driven by a general interest in system maintenance, a view shared by economists who impute to the state some general welfare (or "illfare"!) function. Second, policy preferences might flow from organizational capacity; states may be drawn toward policy solutions for which they are equipped. Third, preferences might be derived from the more general ideological orientation of the political leadership.

The first approach sees policy reform as a response to economic parameters, particularly crises. The catalytic effects of balance of payments and fiscal crises are emphasized by Stallings and play a major role in Waterbury's explanation of elite orientations toward reform of the state-owned enterprise sector. Mexico and Turkey, which experienced severe economic crises, went much further in their efforts to overhaul the parastatal

---

A second, more demanding, criterion is whether a given reform has become an institutionalized feature of government behavior, one that survives changes of government or even of regime.

sector than India and Egypt which, for a variety of reasons, managed to avoid such shocks.

As Margaret Levi has argued most cogently, any analysis of the interests of state elites must begin with material resources, including the extraction of revenue.[27] In economic crises, governments face limits on their capacity to tax and secure foreign exchange, and thus on their ability to spend in support of both economic and political objectives. This argument about "system maintenance" can be extended beyond financial concerns to more general political questions as well. In economic crises, the threats posed by severe economic deterioration and the generalized opposition that accompanies it become an increasingly important component of the survival calculus of governmental elites, and can override the considerations of particular constituencies. Economic crises have led to the adoption of orthodox policy reforms, even by governments that had previously identified with interventionist policies and with groups threatened by market-oriented reforms. Among the more striking examples are Ghana under Rawlings, Bolivia under Paz Estenssoro and Argentina under Menem.

Yet as we have argued in the previous section with reference to international shocks, policy preferences are not easily derived from economic circumstances alone for the simple reason that different governments have widely different threshholds of tolerance for economic distress. In some instances, the systemic concerns of officials may override particularistic and predatory interests, but in others they may give way. As a result, some governments respond to balance of payments and fiscal problems pre-emptively, while others adjust only after reserves have been depleted or inflation has escalated to very high levels. As Waterbury argues, the strongest statement we can make is that some dissatisfaction with the economic status quo is a necessary, but not sufficient, condition for the launching of reform efforts. For a more precise guide to the options selected, it is important to look at other organizational and ideological factors that shape policy preferences.

A second hypothesis is suggested by Peter Evans' analysis of the organizational sources of state capacity. Elite policy preferences may be a function of the level and depth of technical competence in the bureaucracy; preferences may be a function of capabilities. This relationship, however, is by no means obvious. The case studies for this project found, somewhat surprisingly, that a low level of technical competence is not necessarily an impediment to the initial adoption of comprehensive lib-

[27] See Margaret Levi, *Of Rule and Revenue* (Berkeley: University of California Press, 1988).

eralizing reform packages, and may in fact even facilitate them.[28] The Ghanaian and Bolivian governments, for example, were able to use expatriates and to lean heavily on IMF and World Bank staff to design broad-gauged reform packages.

A low level of technocratic competence, however, is likely to be associated with longer periods of policy drift before action is finally taken. In Haiti, Bolivia, Zambia, Zaire, and a number of other low-income African countries, there were few technocratic voices capable of presenting coherent alternatives. If governments with a low level of technocratic and administrative capability do decide to launch reforms, moreover, they are more likely to rely on international agencies for the design of their programs. Both the influence of these agencies and limited administrative capacity may encourage them to select reforms that are comparatively simple to administer, such as trade reform or changing administered prices.

Higher levels of technocratic or administrative capacity have more ambiguous implications for state preferences. On the one hand, the formation of transnational technocratic alliances with strong roots in the national bureaucracy can, as Kahler suggests, work to narrow the range of debate over adjustment questions. But Evans shows in his examination of Korea, Taiwan, Brazil, and India that states with greater technocratic and administrative capacity also have a wider menu of policy options open to them. In East Asia, meritocratic recruitment and informal peer-group networks combined to create highly cohesive military, party, and/or bureaucratic elites, but around a relatively interventionist industrial policy. Such states can combine liberalization with supportive state intervention more effectively and have the capacity to explore more heterodox responses. Even where relatively orthodox measures are adopted, administratively developed governments might tackle more complex reforms or implement them in more complex ways. Thus, for example, the export-led growth strategy pursued by the East Asian newly industrialized countries (NICs) was broadly market-conforming, but also entailed a variety of complex state interventions and institutional supports to business.[29]

The effort to explain policy preferences by reference to economic conditions or bureaucratic capacity yields some insights, but state-centered explanations must often rely in the last instance on the way ideology shapes elite cognitions and values. This again raises the question of the role played by the growing international ascendency of neoliberal economic doctrines during the decade of the 1980s. In some countries, major doctrinal revisions have been reinforced by traumatic historical experiences, such as memories of hyperinflation in Chile, Indonesia, China, and

[28] Nelson, "Conclusions," *Economic Crisis and Policy Choice*, pp. 327–28.
[29] See Haggard, *Pathways from the Periphery*, chaps. 3–5.

Colombia. In most instances, however, it is difficult to pin down precisely processes of learning and socialization that determine the way such ideas are adopted by particular sets of national leaders or incorporated into specific policy contexts. Yet there can be no question that a growing perception of the limits of state intervention has conditioned the way elites interpreted the economic crises of the 1980s and the kinds of policy options necessary to remedy them. Such an interpretation does not necessarily contradict models that view state officials as maximizers, but it does help understand how their preferences over means and ends are conceived. We shall return to this theme at the end of this chapter.

The Implementation of Policy Reform: The Role of State Autonomy and Embeddedness

Given a preference for policy reform, we have suggested that the insulation of central decision makers from distributive claims will enhance the state's capacity to launch new initiatives. Waterbury's discussion of the importance of "change teams" captures important political and institutional characteristics of such innovation. Change teams are relatively autonomous, even free-floating, technocratic actors who are protected from the pressures of interest groups and bureaucratic rivals by strong backing from the chief executive. Though such groups must eventually forge coalitions of social supporters, the centralization and concentration of executive authority outside of normal institutional channels is essential for breaking antireform networks, which in Waterbury's case reside both in the bureaucracy and in the state-owned enterprise sector itself.

Yet the ability to consolidate policy may actually be undermined by the absence of effective channels for communicating with affected political interests. Evans' discussion of "embedded autonomy" in Korea and Taiwan is seminal in this regard, since it highlights institutional features of these states that are of relevance to a broader range of reform efforts. Evans suggests that state autonomy was an important feature of these success stories, but in two somewhat different senses. In the initiation phase, the autonomy required for successful reform rested on discretionary authority of state elites and a rupture with existing bureaucratic routines and channels of societal influence; this sense of the word *autonomy* has been emphasized in particular by Haggard in his study of the East Asian NICs.[30]

Evans argues, however, that the consolidation of reform in these countries rested on a broader organizational autonomy: the capacity of the bureaucracy to retain control over recruitment and the definition of mis-

[30] Ibid., chap. 2.

sion and to regulate the boundaries governing relations with social groups. This form of autonomy refers not to the discretion exercised by individual decision makers, but virtually its opposite: the development of impersonal institutional roles and organizational goals, reinforced by strong informal peer relations within the elite itself. Evans argues that autonomy in this second sense was crucial for establishing the credibility of the export-oriented reforms undertaken in the East Asian NICs in the early 1960s.

Evans argues that this institutional cohesion permitted technocratic agencies to build bases of constituent support among private-sector beneficiaries without the threat of pure capture. The particular form of this embeddedness differed among the East Asian cases; Korea, for example, had more extensive and institutionalized relations with the private sector than the Kuomintang government in Taiwan. Nonetheless, in both countries autonomy and embeddedness were two sides of the same coin. The institutional cohesiveness of the state apparatus enhanced the capacity of elites to set the policy agenda and to construct exchanges with the private sector on terms that were consistent with broad policy objectives. At the same time, embeddedness allowed government agencies to monitor and assess private sector responses and to adjust policy goals in the face of new information.

Embedded Autonomy and the Consolidation of Market-Oriented Reform

To what extent is the concept of "embedded autonomy" relevant for understanding the market-oriented reforms now on the political agenda in many developing countries? Are the aspects of East Asian state organization described by Evans only relevant to the developmentalist policy styles of the 1960s and the 1970s, or do they also have applicability to liberalization efforts?

It is crucial to underscore that economic reforms, including market-oriented ones, vary in their organizational intensity and thus in the nature and extent of the skills required to implement them. Brian Levy notes that dismantling various forms of intervention poses a "negative challenge for bureaucracies—to refrain from actions that had hitherto been part of their organizational function."[31] Where bureaucracies are centered entirely around interventions in the market that are no longer deemed necessary, such as marketing boards or boards of investment that dispense licenses, the bureaucracy may indeed simply be dismantled. Rule-based

---

[31] Brian Levy, "The Design and Sequencing of Trade and Investment Policy Reform," World Bank PRE Working Paper Series 419 (May 1990), p. 25.

forms of intervention that reduce the discretionary power of bureaucracies can also expand state autonomy by reducing the opportunities for rent seeking. The shift from quantitative restrictions to tariffs, the abolition of licensing requirements, and the initiation of auctions for the allocation of foreign exchange are several examples of reforms that can, at least in principle, undercut the formation of rent-seeking alliances between bureaucrats and the private sector.

Yet it is frequently overlooked that many economic reforms—including those aimed at expanding the role of market forces—demand administrative and technical capabilities that are in short supply in developing countries: adequate education among middle- and low-level personnel; specialized training for higher-level and technical staff; and information gathering, processing, and communication capabilities. Moreover, these strategies also require a strengthening of state capacity in the broader sense suggested by Evans. Even purportedly nondiscretionary policies can be undermined if private sector actors are able to circumvent rules by utilizing alternative political channels to secure exceptions. For governments to reduce their role in the economy and expand the play of market forces, the state itself must be strengthened. Miles Kahler has called this the "orthodox paradox."[32]

Examples of the orthodox paradox abound. Privatization, the reform addressed by Waterbury, calls for technical expertise in financial restructuring, rehabilitating companies, and preparing them for divestiture, as well as procedures that guarantee equal access by potential buyers. Entities created to manage privatization must also be politically positioned to resist claims from the state-owned enterprises themselves. Regarding trade policy reform, which is closer to Evans' concerns, drawback and exemption schemes, the provision of overseas market information, and the management of export-processing zones are examples of measures that require new bureaucratic structures or a significant reorganization of existing ones. Similar points can even be made about macroeconomic policy, the subject of our essay on inflation and stabilization. The control of public expenditure and investment, which is central for a stable fiscal policy, requires the establishment of multiyear public investment programs, the capacity to monitor projects once launched, and institutional mechanisms that make expenditures transparent and permit a reconciliation of spending and revenue decisions, such as the combination of spending and control ministries.[33] Improving tax collection is similarly demanding on organizational capabilities. Efficient budgeting and revenue collection

---

[32] Kahler, "Orthodoxy and its Alternatives," p. 55.

[33] See Robert Lacey, "The Management of Public Expenditures: An Evolving Bank Approach," World Bank, Policy, Planning and Research Working Paper No. WPS 46 (January 1989), p. 19.

both demand organizational structures that provide checks on exceptionalism and favoritism.

Comprehensive organizational coherence of the sort that Evans discusses regarding the state apparatus in Japan, Korea, and Taiwan appears rare in the developing world. Nevertheless, both in earlier periods and the present one the development of centralized and relatively insulated bureaucratic agencies have been important features of successful reforms. Colombia's stabilization and trade reforms of the late 1960s were preceded by a constitutional change that transferred both fiscal and exchange-rate authority from Congress to technocratic executive agencies.[34] Mexico's long period of "stabilizing development" (1954–70) rested on a strong Central Bank, backed by the Finance Ministry and close relations with the IMF. Following the model of the currency board, the independence of postcolonial central banks in a number of ex-British colonies, including India, Pakistan, and Malaysia, have been an important factor in the stability of monetary policy.[35]

These cases also seem to support Evans' argument that the formation of links between state officials and strategic producer groups has also been a necessary feature of such reforms. In the Colombian and Mexican cases previously cited, technocratic agencies in the executive were able to mobilize strong support from coffee growers and the private banking sector respectively. Chile in the post-1984 period provides a more recent example of reforms that show signs of consolidation. Following the crisis of the early 1980s, efforts were made to build a network of support among business groups as a component of the recovery strategy engineered by Finance Minister Hernán Büchi. Policies used to accomplish this purpose included the extension of special credits to export-oriented agricultural enterprises, subsidies for the construction industry, and expanding opportunities for stock ownership in privatized state firms for substantial portions of the middle class.[36]

The signs of such alliances elsewhere have been spotty at best; this is true even of those governments considered relatively successful adjustors or which have come to power with private sector backing. Despite the center-right and pro-business orientation of the Özal government in Turkey, for example, private investment has been depressed over most of the 1980s. In the Philippines, the noncrony private sector was an important

[34] David R. Mares, "Domestic Institutions and Shifts in Trade and Development Policy: Colombia 1951–1968," in John S. Odell and Thomas D. Willet, eds., *International Trade Policies: Gains from Exchange Between Economics and Political Science* (Ann Arbor: University of Michigan Press, 1990).

[35] We are indebted to Max Corden for this point.

[36] Barbara Stallings, "Political Economy of Democratic Transition: Chile in the 1980s," in Stallings and Kaufman, *Debt and Democracy in Latin America*, pp. 190–93.

base of Aquino's support, yet levels of investment through the end of the 1980s remained sluggish.

Where private sector beneficiaries of reform are even more scattered or politically weak, as in Ghana and Bolivia, the consolidation of reform is even more precarious. Diffuse public support for adjustment programs has clearly helped to sustain them in both countries, and in Ghana the extraordinary support from international financial institutions has been important. In the absence of concrete bases of private-sector support, however, it is doubtful that such reforms can be institutionalized by small change teams of technocrats and expatriate advisers who are heavily dependent on executive officials.

THE POLITICS OF DISTRIBUTION: SOCIETAL CONFLICTS, PROGRAM DESIGN, AND POLITICAL INSTITUTIONS

The cohesiveness of the state apparatus and the character of its links to the private sector are clearly important for analyzing the process of policy reform. Economic adjustments, however, have wide-ranging distributional consequences that reverberate across a much broader array of social interests and political groups. The essays by Haggard and Kaufman and Nelson focus on the wider arena of distributive politics: the nature of sectoral and class divisions, how they work their way through the political system, and how they are institutionally managed.

As with state-centered approaches, such analysis requires an assessment of how the interests of social groups condition reform efforts; both chapters take such interests as their main point of departure. Yet both essays again raise serious questions about the ability to explain economic policy by reference to distributional outcomes and group interests alone. These limitations on interest group analysis are worth outlining in some detail, since they provide a leitmotif for these essays.

One limit on societal explanations already alluded to concerns the ubiquity of collective action problems. The political power of economic actors depends on their capacity to organize, but organization does not follow from shared economic interests alone. Compared to those who gain from the status quo, the diffuse beneficiaries of reforms may have substantial difficulty organizing, particularly when the gains from the policy reform are ambiguous and uncertain.

An equally important set of limitations on interest group analysis concerns the problem of deriving interests from a group's position in the economy. The ambiguity of groups' policy interests stem from a number of different sources. In the first place, as Nelson shows, individuals and groups occupy a number of positions in the economic structure simultaneously, and may well have a variety of other identifications such as religious or ethnic ones that cut across their economic interests. Incomes are affected through a variety of channels, including labor or other factor income, relative prices, and the provision of public services, transfers and subsidies. Moreover, the actual distributional consequences of policy are highly sensitive to the factor-intensity of output in different sectors, the flexibility of wages and prices, and a number of other complex structural parameters. It may therefore be difficult for groups to calculate the costs and benefits of reform or to weigh the tradeoffs between short-term losses and longer-term gains.

The essays by Nelson and Haggard and Kaufman explore two further limitations on interest group explanations. The first of these, emphasized in Nelson's discussion of the politics of pro-poor measures, is that the packaging and sequencing of policy reform can alter interest groups' calculus. Changes in subsidy programs can be engineered to defuse protest; for example, by targeting politically volatile and important groups for compensation. Similarly, firms that are losers in one area, such as tariff reduction, may be compensated through exchange rate policies or reductions in labor costs. Such packaging of policies in order to reduce resistance and build support is, in a broad sense, a response to political pressures, yet these constraints can themselves be manipulated by political leadership. This opens the door to a more sustained analysis of tactics, strategy, and the political consequences of program design.

The final, and most damaging, limitation on interest group analysis concerns the mechanisms through which interests are translated into policy outputs; this problem is the central focus of our essay on inflation and stabilization. Most coalitional models of politics rest on very simple aggregation rules, or simple decision-making mechanisms such as lobbying, voting, or pure capture of office. The essays in this volume concur that the influence of social groups is a more complex function of the way legal and institutional setting provide or limit opportunities for influence. Political institutions, like markets, structure the incentives to political action and can have a profound effect on the relative standing and power of different groups.

The Distributional Consequences of Adjustment and Reform-mongering

Nelson's essay begins with a sifting of the evidence concerning the distributional consequences for the poor of the adjustment programs initiated in the 1980s. This review identifies two distinct equity problems: one has to do with shielding the very poor and vulnerable groups such as pregnant women and children from destitution, the second with the sharp absolute and relative income losses experienced by somewhat better-off urban groups, including the organized working class and "popular sectors." Each of these equity problems has quite different political dynamics.

Nelson points to a major dilemma in the arguments advocating pro-poor adjustment measures advanced by such influential studies as UNICEF's *Adjustment with a Human Face* (Oxford: Clarendon Press, 1987). It is technically possible to cushion the very poor from the shocks of adjustment through a more careful targeting of subsidies and a redeployment of spending on health and education. But the political incentives to do so are weak unless the benefits can also be extended to the more influential union and white-collar groups. The dilemmas concerning such better-off "popular-sector" groups, however, are precisely the opposite. Such groups have a wider array of political resources for effective protest than do the very poor, and the political incentive to protect them is therefore much stronger. Doing so, however, places serious strains on fiscal resources and works against the integrity of standard adjustment programs.

Nelson notes that there are a number of ways in which governments can reduce the severity of these tradeoffs, however, particularly through the packaging of programs or the manipulation of opposition groups. In some cases, benefits have been permitted to "trickle up" selectively to some middle income groups in order to provide a politically adequate base of support. Program design can be used to create coalitions and preempt opposition. In other instances, popular sector opposition can be finessed or held at bay. Only in a few countries, for example, can unions succeed in scuttling adjustment programs on their own; frequently, unions can be isolated from potential allies through various mixtures of "stonewalling" and strategic concessions.

The array of tactics employed for managing resistance from urban popular sectors is likely to have more limited success in dealing with more powerful groups facing income losses in the face of adjustment programs; compromise is more important when dealing with the privileged. Direct conflict between government and the private sector runs the risk of antagonizing groups that are likely to have more numerous channels of political access. Moreover, such groups can exert pressure on the government through capital flight and investment strikes. Nonetheless, a long-standing literature on reform-mongering has suggested how indirect approaches and tactics may be of use in confronting more powerful sources of resistance as well: the use of ambiguity and obfuscation in presenting programs, the use of less visibly extractive instruments, and the timing of initiatives to exploit moments of high popular support.[37]

[37] The classic statement of the reformist position is Albert O. Hirschman, *Journeys Toward Progress* (New York: Norton, 1973), pp. 251–98. Other primers on reform tactics are

Finally, Nelson's analysis calls into question whether narrow class interests are the only relevant factors in assessing individual or group opposition to adjustment programs. A consistent theme of Nelson's chapter is that political reactions will also be conditioned by broader public opinion concerning the nature of the crisis, the need for government action, and the capacity of the government to organize an effective response. Where crises are broadly recognized and there is confidence in government, political leaders may be able to persuade publics to acquiesce or even actively support quite difficult adjustment measures. One important counterintuitive finding of Nelson's study is that incumbent governments have not necessarily been punished electorally for undertaking difficult measures per se; rather, they have been punished only where such measures *fail*.

The effectiveness of government strategies and the opportunities provided by broad currents of public opinion will always depend to some extent on contingent aspects of the political and economic situation. Nonetheless, as Nelson acknowledges, both distributive conflicts and the possibilities for sustained adjustment will depend heavily on more institutionalized patterns of political representation. Several of these patterns are examined in the chapter by Haggard and Kaufman, including electoral cycles, the nature of the regime, and the structure of the party system.

Electoral Cycles and Changes of Government

The studies from the first phase of this project suggested that the most important political influence on the willingness of state elites to initiate new adjustment policies was connected with changes of government or political regime. Governments facing upcoming electoral challenges, not surprisingly, have generally been reluctant to impose unpopular programs. Incoming governments, by contrast, have capitalized on honeymoon periods and the disorganization or discrediting of the opposition to launch ambitious new reform initiatives.[38]

William Ascher, *Scheming for the Poor: The Politics of Redistribution in Latin America* (Cambridge: Harvard University Press, 1984) and Joan Nelson, "The Politics of Stabilization," in Richard Feinberg and Valeriana Kallab, *Adjustment Crisis in the Third World* (New Brunswick, N.J.: Transaction Books, 1984); and John Waterbury, "The Political Management of Economic Adjustment and Reform," in Joan Nelson, ed., *Fragile Coalitions: The Politics of Economic Adjustment* (New Brunswick, N.J.: Transaction Books, 1989).

[38] For a sample of Latin American countries, Barry Ames finds evidence of expansion prior to elections, but also finds evidence of expansion *following* elections, which he explains in terms of efforts to consolidate new bases of support. See Barry Ames, *Political*

Such policy initiatives cannot simply be understood as the result of the victory of a new political and policy coalition. In many cases, the reform initiatives cut against the interests of followers, suggesting the relative importance of the cycle itself over the constellation of group interests. The most dramatic example of this pattern came in Bolivia under Paz Estenssoro, but similar episodes are visible in Costa Rica under Monge in 1982, in Brazil and Argentina under Collor and Menem respectively, and in Poland under the Solidarity government in 1990.

The evidence of electoral cycles and the effects of changes of government can be seen across a wide range of both democratic and authoritarian political systems, though the effects of electoral cycles and changes in government will also depend on the underlying level of conflict between political groups. New democratic governments in political systems characterized by a high level of party conflict and polarization have had greater difficulty exploiting honeymoons in order to launch reform initiatives, perhaps because of their fragility and the perceived risks of undertaking costly policy actions. In such settings, the second or third posttransition government is more likely to launch initiatives: Brazil under Collor and Argentina under Menem again provide examples. It should be noted, however, that by the time these leaders came to office, there had already been long delays in the formulation of adjustment programs and a significant deepening of the economic crisis. The electoral victories of the opposition forces therefore were not exogenous to economic events; worsening economic circumstances induced a broad cross-section of the population to support efforts by the incoming government to apply shock treatment.

This leads to an important observation on the limits of electoral cycle explanations that is highlighted by Nelson. Despite the fact that incumbent governments are likely to delay reforms prior to elections, it does not appear to be the case that governments that *have* undertaken adjustment programs will necessarily suffer for it electorally. Nelson documents that reform efforts have survived electoral tests where economic conditions prior to the reform were considered disastrous and unsustainable, where governments were decisive, and where there was some evidence that the new order was yielding diffuse benefits, even if they had not reached all sectors of the population.

Elections in authoritarian regimes are, by definition, not wholly competitive; nonetheless, political elites often see them as referenda and use them to legitimate their rule. There is evidence of a political-business cycle in Mexico, for example, despite the monopolization of political power by

---

Survival: Politicians and Public Policy in Latin America (Berkeley: University of California Press, 1987), chap. 2.

the Institutional Revolutionary Party (PRI).[39] As we have suggested elsewhere, the broad political cycles evident in democracies may be reversed
in less institutionalized military regimes. Incoming authoritarian regimes
may play a role in breaking political logjams, but the chances of bold
reform initiatives diminish over time as military governments seek social
bases of support and confront pressures for political liberalization.[40]

The Regime Debate

Differences in regime type are potentially relevant to understanding variations in policy reform; just how relevant has been the subject of one of
the most heated and long-standing debates in the literature on the politics
of stabilization and structural adjustment.[41] Do authoritarian regimes
have greater capacity than political democracies to insulate technocrats,
"manage" opposition, and reorient economic policy?[42]

An analysis of particular cases suggests that such a relationship is plausible. Among the countries this study has examined in depth, the most
comprehensive adjustment initiatives have generally come under the auspices of authoritarian regimes. Chile, Ghana, Turkey, and Mexico all provide prime examples for the 1980s. The capacity of the Korean government and of the Kuomintang on Taiwan to control or repress popular
sector opposition was also an important component of the "developmental state" model outlined by Evans.

At a broader level of comparison, however, these findings do not necessarily hold. Authoritarian regimes do not necessarily guarantee the executive the autonomy required to impose unpopular adjustment programs; nor do the processes of electoral democracy necessarily impede

[39] Edward F. Buffie, with Allen Sangines Krause, "Mexico 1958–1986: From Stabilizing
Development to Debt Crisis," in Sachs, *Developing Country Debt*, p. 144.

[40] Haggard and Kaufman, "The Politics of Stabilization and Structural Adjustment," in
Sachs, *Developing Country Debt*, pp. 244–45.

[41] See Thomas Skidmore, "The Politics of Economic Stabilization in Post War Latin
America," in James Malloy, ed., *Authoritarianism and Corporatism in Latin America* (Pitts-
burgh: University of Pittsburgh Press, 1977); Karen Remmer, "The Politics of Economic
Stabilization: IMF Standby Programs in Latin America, 1954–1984," *Comparative Politics*
19 (October 1986): 1–25; Robert Kaufman, "Democratic and Authoritarian Responses to
the Debt Issue: Argentina, Brazil, and Mexico," and Stephan Haggard, "The Politics of
Adjustment: Lessons from the IMF's Extended Fund Facility," both in Miles Kahler, ed.,
The Politics of International Debt (Ithaca: Cornell University Press, 1986), pp. 187–219
and 157–87; and Scott Siddell, *The IMF and Third World Political Instability* (London:
MacMillan, 1987).

[42] See Guillermo O'Donnell, *Modernization and Bureaucratic Authoritarianism: Studies
in South American Politics* (Berkeley: Institute of International Studies, 1973) and Haggard,
Pathways from the Periphery.

reform.[43] Our study of inflation suggests that a number of democratic regimes, in particular, those based on catchall two-party systems, have quite successful long-term records of macroeconomic management. Moreover, officials in institutionalized democracies often have considerable security against both popular protest and military coups. In Colombia, this security contributed to an extraordinarily rapid response by the Betancur government to the stabilization problems emerging in 1984. In Venezuela, it allowed the newly elected administration of Carlos Andres Pérez to withstand widespread rioting over a very harsh stabilization program in 1989.[44] Although democracies have generally not been able to launch the kinds of sweeping adjustment programs undertaken by some "strong" authoritarian regimes, there are some important exceptions, such as Jayawardene's liberalizing reforms in Sri Lanka in the late 1970s.[45] More incremental but nonetheless significant adjustments were also taken under democratic auspices in the 1980s in Costa Rica, the Philippines, and Jamaica.[46]

Conversely, as Thomas Callaghy has shown for a number of weak African states, formally hierarchical political systems, such as Zambia's one-party state, are frequently penetrated by complex networks of patronage. Such penetration results in highly dualistic decision-making structures that marginalize technocrats and undermine the coherence of policy.[47] Moreover, the very autonomy of authoritarian leaders can facilitate executive interference for political ends. In an excellent study of Brazil's national development bank, Eliza Willis shows how the military governments of the 1970s and 1980s politicized an institution that had been relatively insulated and effective under the preceding civilian regime.[48] In

[43] Haggard and Kaufman, "The Politics of Stabilization and Structural Adjustment," pp. 533–39.

[44] On Colombia, see Barbara Stallings, "Politics and Economic Crisis: A Comparative Study of Chile, Peru, and Colombia," in Nelson, *Economic Crisis and Policy Choice*, pp. 154–61; on Venezuela, see Daniel Levine, "Venezuela: The Nature, Sources, and Future Prospects of Democracy," in Larry Diamond, Juan Linz, and Seymour Martin Lipset, eds., *Democracy in Developing Countries: Latin America* (Boulder: Lynn Rienner, 1989).

[45] See Joan Nelson, "The Political Economy of Stabilization: Commitment, Capacity, and Public Response," *World Development* 12, no. 10 (October 1984): 983–1006.

[46] See Joan Nelson, "The Politics of Adjustment in Small Democracies: Costa Rica, the Dominican Republic, and Jamaica," and Stephan Haggard, "The Political Economy of the Philippine Debt Crisis," both in Nelson, *Economic Crisis and Policy Choice*, pp. 169–215 and 215–57.

[47] See Thomas Callaghy, in Nelson, *Economic Crisis and Policy Choice*. Haggard reached similar conclusions in studies of the Philippines and of the IMF's Extended Fund Facility. See Stephan Haggard, "The Political Economy of the Philippines Debt Crisis," in Nelson, *Economic Crisis and Policy Choice*, and "Lessons from the IMF's Extended Fund Facility."

[48] Eliza Willis, "The State as Banker: The Expansion of the Public Sector in Brazil," Ph.D. diss., University of Texas, 1986.

Mexico, Luis Echeverría extended his personal authority over macroeconomic decision-making and weakened the power of the conservative Ministry of Finance and Central Bank in order to pursue a quasipopulist program. In Korea, Park Chung Hee's personal decision to push a heavy and chemical industry plan resulted in a restructuring of the bureaucracy that undermined the influence of more market-oriented technocrats.

The temptation to use economic policy instruments for political ends increases when authoritarian governments face fundamental challenges to their rule. In the 1980s, such challenges multiplied. A small number of one-party states such as Mexico and Taiwan were able to manage these pressures through a combination of political liberalization and cooptation, and one-party rule has shown surprising resilience in Indonesia. Military regimes, by contrast, had greater difficulty responding to these challenges, in part because of their inability to create institutionalized systems of party or interest group representation linking state and society. As a result, a number of aging authoritarian governments have been characterized by extensive executive interference in policy and a weakening of bureaucratic insulation as military elites sought to bolster their positions during the transition to civilian rule. This pattern contributed to a legacy of political and economic disorganization that impeded adjustment efforts in new democratic governments in a number of Latin American countries, including Argentina, Brazil, Peru, and, under different circumstances, Nicaragua.

Political Alignments and the Structure of the Party System

The ambiguous findings about the relative success of different types of regimes can be clarified by paying greater attention to other aspects of the institutional setting in which distributional conflicts are played out. As we suggest in our essay on inflation and stabilization, it is useful to distinguish countries in which long-term patterns of partisan conflict reinforce class and sectoral cleavages from those in which distributional groups are co-opted into stable multiclass party systems or are penetrated and controlled directly by the state.

These patterns of interest organization and representation cut across the authoritarian-democratic distinction to some extent. In political settings where state or party institutions have suppressed or co-opted distributive groups, there has been little difference in the capacity of state decision makers to initiate and sustain adjustment policies. We have already noted that one-party states such as Mexico and Taiwan have been able to manage a variety of economic pressures through a combination of political reform and cooptation. But multiclass parties have also played a pivotal role in insulating political elites from distributive pressures in democratic countries such as Colombia, Costa Rica, and, in some respects, Venezuela. Potential popular-sector opposition groups were neutralized either because they had been incorporated into parties dominated by governing elites or because they were deprived of electoral influence, or both.

In settings where partisan alignments are more polarized or fragmented, in contrast, political leaders have strong incentives to appeal to the distributive interests of labor and business groups, or to revert to broad populist appeals. In these circumstances, regime type *has* had an impact on adjustment initiatives. In such politically polarized or fragmented settings, incoming authoritarian regimes have in the past been important for breaking social and political stalemates and imposing broad policy initiatives in a number of cases, usually at great cost to the urban working class. The most recent examples are provided by the Turkish military intervention of 1980 and Rawlings coup in Ghana in 1981, but other examples include the Korean military "revolution" of 1961, the Indonesian coup of 1966, the Brazilian military intervention of 1964, and Chile under Pinochet after 1973.

The fragmentation of the party system, on the other hand, has posed severe difficulties for democratic governments. New democratic governments in Peru and Brazil have faced particularly high risks in launching difficult stabilization measures, and have had considerable difficulty establishing credibility. During the 1980s, state elites in these countries tended to delay stabilization measures, despite the costs in doing so. In both Latin America and Africa, the resurgence of fragmented or polarized party systems clearly increases the risks of unstable coalitions, populist appeals, favoritism, and wide swings in policy.

An important implication of this analysis is that the engineering of the political and electoral system can have important consequences for the stability of electoral and legislative majorities, and thus for their capacity to mobilize support for credible policy initiatives. The key challenge for new democratic governments is to organize political conflict in ways that allow successive administrations to organize relatively stable majorities and thus to avoid sharp policy discontinuities.

In the concluding essay, we outline several possibilities for achieving this objective, including social pacts, a system dominated by the center-left, a centrist two-party system, and dominance by the center-right. The viability of any of these models must be assessed on a case-by-case basis, since they are not simply the result of institutional engineering, but of long-standing political traditions. Nonetheless, we conclude that the institutionalization of reform is most likely in party systems that have the following three characteristics. First, a significant segment of competitors within the party system have opportunities to share in governance. Second, they find it in their political interest to reduce the stakes of competition by delegating economic authority to portions of the economic bureaucracy.

Finally, all of the chapters stress a simple, but crucial point: reforms are unlikely to be sustained unless they generate adequate economic payoff to secure at least the acquiescence of broad segments of the electorate.

CONCLUSION: IDEOLOGY, SOCIAL LEARNING, AND ECONOMIC REFORM

In the final analysis, it is entirely possible that neither interest-based explanations nor institutional ones will be entirely satisfactory for explaining how societies cope with the challenges of policy reform and consolidation. Particularly within a democratic framework, consolidation may also require what Kahler calls social learning; the evolution of a broader ideational consensus among leaders, interest groups, party elites and attentive publics that sets some boundaries on the range of economic debate. Such a consensus does not imply stasis or the absence of conflict; distributive struggles will always arise over policy. Nonetheless, it is possible that the long-term sustainability of policy choices will depend on a convergence of thinking about fundamental means-ends relationships in the economy. If so, then the formation of elite preferences, ideas, and ideology, as well as the evolution of public opinion, are potentially important explanatory variables.

The appropriate historical analogy to the present would be to previous periods of fundamental change in economic thinking. In the advanced industrial states, the consolidation of Keynsian policies depended on such a change in discourse, from assumptions about a self-equilibrating market system to the idea that the state had a positive role in correcting market failures. The same set of assumptions took root around import-substituting projects during the period from 1930 through 1960 across a wide range of developing countries. Neither of these new models eliminated policy conflict, but they did present political elites with new policy options and cognitive maps.

The ideological changes of the 1980s may have a comparable impact. Though different groups clearly had different policy preferences, few could argue, as many did in the 1950s, that fiscal imbalances or inflation were not causes for concern. Similarly, there was a growing recognition of the limits of state intervention in markets and of inward-looking development strategies, though substantial debate remained about how far to go in a more liberal direction.

The extent to which such common understandings about cause and effect relationships have emerged among political and economic actors has major implications for the kinds of demands that are made within the political system and the way distributive conflicts are fought out. New ideas do not, as Peter Hall has commented, "simply rest on top of other factors already there. Rather, they can alter the composition of other elements in the political sphere, like a catalyst or binding agent that allows existing ingredients to combine in new ways."[49]

This again raises the question of what determines national receptiveness to different ideas. Interest-based explanations, whether Marxist or pluralist, are likely to emphasize the congruity between orthodox ideas and the interests of newly emergent groups, such as exporters or financial interests. There can be little doubt that liberalizing reforms benefit some groups more than others, but broad changes in the nature of ideological discourse do not appear explicable in terms of new coalitions alone. To the contrary, new ideas often serve as the *basis* on which such coalitions form.

Crises are likely to be crucial to broad social learning, since they reveal fundamental limits on previous ways of thinking. In the 1930s, the depression was felt across class lines, stimulating fundamental changes in the assumptions about the possibilities of state intervention. The hyperinflations and deep depressions of the 1980s may have a similar function, but only if broad segments of the population have reason to believe that orthodox reforms do in fact provide a welfare-improving alternative. For some countries, this may have been proven. For other countries, the weakness of the economic response to date does not rule out countervailing ideological trends that once again call into question the advantages of market-oriented policies.

[49] Peter Hall, "Conclusion: The Politics of Keynesian Ideas," in Hall, ed., *The Political Power of Economic Ideas: Keynesianism Across Nations* (Princeton: Princeton University Press, 1989), p. 367.

PART I

International Constraints

International Influence on Economic Policy: Debt, Stabilization, and Structural Reform

Barbara Stallings

THE THIRD WORLD in the early 1990s is a dramatically different place than it was fifteen years ago. In the 1970s, as many developing economies were booming, the belief was widespread that a powerful state combined with a heavy dose of protection could produce development. Third World governments allied themselves with private bankers—or occasionally public donors—to obtain external financing for development plans, so international constraints no longer appeared to inhibit growth, and direct foreign investment could be restricted to placate nationalistic sentiments. As a result of increased state activities, debt burgeoned, budgets and current accounts ran deep in the red, and inflation soared, but there was little evidence of preoccupation.

By the late 1980s, a sea change had occurred. In the midst of deep recession, governments were taking significant political risks in order to bring budget deficits and inflation under control at the same time that they tried to find ways to meet payments on crushing debt burdens. Even more significant, a massive shift in development strategy was under way. State firms were on the auction block and tariff barriers were tumbling. Foreign corporations were again being courted in hopes of getting access to capital and markets. These trends are continuing, and even accelerating, in the 1990s.

How can we account for these changes in economic policy? If this question had been posed in the 1970s, the answers would have stressed the power of international forces in determining the options of Third World nations. The dependency approach in vogue at the time would have pointed to the role of the International Monetary Fund (IMF) and World Bank, the private commercial banks, and their home governments as the agents that made Third World governments change their preferred policy positions toward the favored orthodoxy. The pressure of debt burdens—which such analysts often saw as having been forced upon Third World

The author would like to thank all members of the research group for their comments on various drafts of the chapter, but special thanks go to Stephan Haggard, Robert Kaufman, and Peter Evans.

governments—would have been portrayed as the leverage that provided the international actors with their power. The more sophisticated of the dependency analysts would have tried to show how these international actors worked with allies in the Third World countries themselves to stimulate policy change in the desired direction.[1]

In the late 1980s, by contrast, the perspective had shifted, and the dominant intellectual paradigm downplayed international variables in favor of domestic politics. The particular type of domestic variables differed by analyst. Some stressed political coalitions,[2] while others focused on the state.[3] The earlier volume of this project reflected this trend. The concluding chapter by Joan Nelson argued the following:

> Broadly, external agencies were less important than domestic political forces in determining the timing and scope of adjustment decisions. Concerted pressure from the international financial institutions, bilateral donors, and commercial banks and the providing or withholding of financial relief play prominent roles in the tales of all our cases. But the degree to which such pressures actually induced decisions that would not otherwise have been taken varied greatly.[4]

> External agencies' financial support and technical guidance facilitated both stabilization and structural change in many of the cases of relatively successful implementation. . . . But since similar guidance and financial support were being offered to the governments that failed to follow through, external support emerges as a sometimes necessary, but far from sufficient, condition for implementation.[5]

Likewise, Miles Kahler says in chapter 2 of this volume that IMF and World Bank conditionality has not been very effective. "This survey suggests that the external agencies have had, overall, limited influence on decisions for and successful implementation of stabilization and structural adjustment programs."

---

[1] On the dependency approach, see especially Fernando Henrique Cardoso and Enzo Faletto, *Dependency and Development in Latin America* (Berkeley: University of California Press, 1979) and Peter Evans, *Dependent Development* (Princeton: Princeton University Press, 1979). A historical analysis of the emergence of dependency theory is found in Gary Gereffi, *The Pharmaceutical Industry and Dependency in the Third World* (Princeton: Princeton University Press, 1983), chap. 1.

[2] For an example of the coalitional approach, see Jeffry Frieden, "Class, Sectors and Foreign Debt in Latin America," *Comparative Politics* (October 1988): 1–20.

[3] The statist approach, in contrast to dependency, is most forcefully argued by Stephan Haggard. See, for example, "The Newly Industrializing Countries in the International System," *World Politics* 38, no 2 (January 1986): 343–70, and *Pathways from the Periphery: The Politics of Growth in the Newly Industrializing Countries* (Ithaca: Cornell University University Press, 1990).

[4] Joan M. Nelson, ed., *Economic Crisis and Policy Choice: The Politics of Adjustment in the Third World* (Princeton: Princeton University Press, 1990), p. 330.

[5] Ibid., p. 347.

I would argue that the older ideas about external influence have been too quickly abandoned. Ironically, just as international variables became especially important in the 1980s, they disappeared as the key factor from theories of development. As often happens, theory is out of phase with reality. The permissive international environment of the 1970s led theorists to deemphasize international variables in the 1980s when international constraints were once again mounting. To be sure, the importance assigned to international factors depends on the questions being asked. If we are trying to discover why a particular government decides to undertake (or not) a particular reform at a particular time, then domestic factors—political and institutional—are likely to dominate. Likewise, it may well be the case that many individual Bank and Fund programs have been failures, either in letter or spirit, so their influence appears small. But, if the question is why the general thrust of Third World economic policy was so different in the 1980s than in the 1970s, then international factors loom large.[6]

My purpose in this chapter is to construct a framework for analyzing the impact of international influence in the Third World and to see how far it can take us in understanding changes in economic policy. I do not believe that international variables can provide a total explanation; domestic variables continued to play an important role, even in the 1980s. My argument is that international factors are crucial in explaining broad shifts in policy, both in contrasting the 1980s with the 1970s and in explaining changes within the decade of the 1980s. They are also useful in accounting for variation across countries, but for that purpose domestic factors are essential too.

The chapter is organized around three main tasks. First, I will reexamine the literature on dependency, whose specific focuses is on international influence on Third World development. This involves tracing the evolution of that literature and also specifying with more precision the mechanisms of influence and the conditions under which they operate. Then, I will turn to three policy areas and look at the experience of a group of countries from Africa, Asia, and Latin America over the course of the 1980s. The objective will be to study the impact of international variables in determining economic stance. Finally, I will conclude by discussing the circumstances under which international factors are particularly influential.

The empirical sections of the chapter concentrate on the three issues that have dominated economic policy-making during the 1980s: debt ser-

[6] A similar point with respect to the role of social classes is made by Erik Olin Wright, "Class and Politics," in Joel Krieger, ed., *Oxford Companion to Politics of the World* (New York: Oxford University Press, forthcoming).

vice, stabilization, and structural adjustment. In each case, there has been a movement toward broadly orthodox policies and market-oriented reforms. I will explore the role of international variables in producing this particular type of change. Each of the three issues represents a cluster of policies. Debt service involves relations with private banks and bilateral creditors as well as multilateral agencies. Stabilization includes policies to deal with both inflation and the balance of payments, but the focus here will be on the latter. Structural adjustment spans an enormous range of activities from trade policy to ownership of assets to institution building; among these the emphasis will be on trade liberalization and privatization. The countries to be examined derive mainly from the case studies in the earlier volume of this project (nine from Latin America, three from Africa, and one from Asia).[7] To broaden the empirical base slightly, two more cases from Asia are added (South Korea and Thailand). Although the fifteen countries do not constitute any kind of scientific sample, they do include cases that vary substantially on each of the variables of concern.

THE RISE AND DEMISE OF DEPENDENCY THEORY

Debates about the role of foreign influence on Third World development have centered on two questions. One is the relative importance of international versus domestic variables (dependency versus statist or coalitional analysis). The second, assuming international variables are crucial, is whether the resulting effects are negative or positive (dependency versus modernization). The two sets of debates are too well known to require extensive recapitulation,[8] but I will outline the basic tenets of the dependency perspective so as to be able to assess its critics and the decline of dependency as a major paradigm of development theory. Only then will we be in a position to ask if the approach still offers some useful insights.

Dependency theory sought to explain why Latin American countries had failed to become industrial societies on the model of the United States and Western Europe. Early versions were fairly simplistic agent-centered approaches, focusing on foreign governments, intelligence agencies, multinational corporations, and international financial institutions. They alleged that these organizations had taken capital out of Latin America, distorted development patterns, and undermined governments and other

[7] The thirteen countries from the earlier volume included Argentina, Brazil, Chile, Colombia, Costa Rica, Dominican Republic, Jamaica, Mexico, Peru, Ghana, Nigeria, Zambia, and the Philippines.

[8] For a summary of the two debates, see Barbara Stallings, "The Role of Foreign Capital in Economic Development," in Gary Gereffi and Donald Wyman, eds., *Manufacturing Miracles: Paths of Industrialization in Latin America and East Asia* (Princeton: Princeton University Press, 1990), pp. 56–59.

groups that tried to limit their power. When structural analyses were put forward, they concentrated on the extraction of surplus in a mechanical and static fashion: profits moving to the metropole from the center areas of the periphery and to the latter from the periphery of the periphery. The bottom-line conclusion was the incompatibility of dependency and development, and the consequent need for a socialist revolution.[9]

Even as the first versions of dependency theory were being published in the United States, a more sophisticated version was being written in Latin America itself. Drawing on the work of an earlier generation of Latin American historians and social scientists, this "historical-structural" version of dependency analysis was an implicit critique of the external-deterministic dependency approach.[10] That is, it focused not on direct links between center and periphery but on intermediaries, specifically groups in Latin America who shared interests with international actors and thus joined forces with them to promote mutual gain often at the expense of other national groups. In addition, historical-structural dependency theory stressed changes in the nature of links between center and periphery during different stages of growth—from colonialism, to raw materials export, import-substitution industrialization, and internationalization of the domestic market. It also pointed to the diversity of socioeconomic-political circumstances among Latin American countries and thus the different types of links within the international economy. Given the diversity, it was argued that some countries could indeed combine dependency and development, although of a particularly unequal type.[11]

Criticisms of dependency came from many directions—from left and right, from theorists and policy analysts, from experts on Latin America and other regions. As suggested above, some critics challenged the mechanisms posited, while others concentrated on the effects of international influence. The debates were confused by the multiplicity of theories that were joined under the label of "dependency." Three main intellectual criticisms can be identified; in addition, there were certain "real world" trends that also contributed to the demise of dependency analysis.

A first criticism, voiced by many if not most critics of dependency, was its lack of specificity, its global scope—its general "fuzziness." How was

[9] The best-known book of this genre is Andre Gunder Frank, *Capitalism and Underdevelopment in Latin America* (New York: Monthly Review Press, 1967). See also Teresa Hayter, *Aid as Imperialism* (Harmondsworth, England: Penguin, 1971) and Cheryl Payer, *The Debt Trap* (New York: Monthly Review Press, 1974).

[10] On the relationship between the two versions of dependency theory, see the comments by Fernando Henrique Cardoso, "The Consumption of Dependency Theory in the United States," *Latin American Research Review* 12, no. 3 (1977): 7–24.

[11] The best works in this approach are Cardoso and Faletto, *Dependency and Development*, and Evans, *Dependent Development*.

dependency to be defined? What were its effects? In particular, what was its relationship to development? Did dependency operate in the same ways everywhere? Did it change over time and, if so, how? What was the opposite of dependency? How could the theory be falsified? Some of this criticism was due to a lack of understanding about the nature of dependency analysis as a framework or paradigm rather than a theory per se.[12] Nevertheless, its adherents often went out of their way to deny the legitimacy of attempts to formulate definitions or typologies of types of dependency, to extract hypotheses from its general propositions, and to use quantitative data to test those hypotheses.[13]

A second set of critiques concerned an alleged overemphasis on international relationships and corresponding neglect of domestic forces. The Marxist left, especially among Latin Americanists, argued that dependency analysts did not pay sufficient attention to social classes and class struggle. The stress on external relations was said to displace attention from domestic conflicts between capital and labor that were more fundamental determinants of underdevelopment.[14] At the same time, experts on East Asia denounced dependency for not realizing that the state was more important than foreign actors in determining development possibilities. One version of this argument said that dependency analysts had mixed up causality relationships: foreign capital did not determine development strategies; rather, development strategies determined the need (or not) for foreign capital. If the state—generally defined in this literature as government bureaucrats—made the proper decisions, it could control foreign capital. The East Asian economies, especially those of South Korea and Taiwan, were offered as examples.[15]

The success of the Asian economies was also related to a third type of criticism of dependency analysis. It harked back to the "modernization" theory that dependency had been a reaction against, arguing that external flows (capital, trade, technology, and ideas) had a *positive* impact on development. The proof usually offered was the East Asian NICs (newly industrializing countries), which had opted for export-oriented development strategies in the 1960s while Latin America had moved on to a

---

[12] A discussion of the theoretical status of the dependency literature is offered by Gabriel Palma, "Dependency: A Formal Theory of Underdevelopment or a Methodology for the Analysis of Concrete Situations of Underdevelopment," World Development 6, no. 7–8 (July/August 1978): 881–924.

[13] For such a criticism, see Cardoso, "Consumption of Dependency Theory."

[14] Examples of this type of criticism are contained in Ronald Chilcote, ed., Dependency and Marxism: Towards a Resolution of the Debate (Boulder, Colo.: Westview Press, 1982) and Ronaldo Munck, The Politics of Dependency in the Third World (London: Zed Books, 1984).

[15] For criticisms of dependency theory by East Asianists, see Haggard, "The Newly Industrialized Countries," and Alice Amsden, "Taiwan's Economic History: A Case Study of Etatisme and a Challenge to Dependency Theory," Modern China 5, no. 3 (1979): 341–79.

more advanced stage of import-substitution industrialization. The Asian economies were not only growing much faster, according to this argument, but they also had more equal income distribution. Furthermore, they had been able to recover much more rapidly from the shocks of the 1970s and early 1980s than had the less open Latin American (or African) economies.[16] A more moderate version of this critique was not as positive about the benefits of openness (and indeed pointed out that the Asian economies were not uniformly open to imports or direct investment), but insisted that explanations must be provided for the great differences among Third World countries all facing similar external conditions.[17]

Beyond these intellectual critiques, there were also political and economic events occurring in the world that helped to undermine the power of dependency analysis. One was the enormous quantity of loans available to Third World governments during much of the 1970s. These loans relieved foreign exchange constraints and increased the power of governments vis-à-vis the multinational corporations that had been seen as the most powerful agents of dependency.[18] Second, an intellectual consensus began to crystalize among leaders of the industrial countries and the international financial institutions around the benefits of open trade regimes and a smaller state. As the 1970s loan binge came to an end in the early 1980s, the power behind the intellectual consensus began to grow as international financial institutions (IFIs)—rather than the private bankers—controlled the available capital.[19] Third, the superior performance of the East Asian economies in comparison to Latin America in the 1980s further reinforced the intellectual consensus about the advantages of openness.[20] A final blow was the fall of socialism in Eastern Europe and the Soviet Union. Marxism, the underpinning for much of the dependency analysis, fell into disrepute. Equally telling, the main examples of noncapitalist development disappeared as did Soviet financial support for Third World governments that opposed orthodox policies.[21]

[16] For a comparative analysis of the external shocks in Third World countries, see Bela Belassa and F. Desmond McCarthy, *Adjustment Policies in Developing Countries, 1979–83: An Update*, World Bank Staff Working Paper No. 675 (Washington, D.C.: World Bank, 1984). A version of this type of criticism also came from the Marxist left; see Bill Warren, *Imperialism: Pioneer of Capitalism* (London: New Left Books, 1980), esp. chap. 7.

[17] See Haggard, "The Newly Industrializing Countries."

[18] On the use of loans to escape from direct investment, see Jeffry Frieden, "Third World Indebted Industrialization," *International Organization* 35 (Summer 1981).

[19] Miles Kahler, "Orthodoxy and its Alternatives: Explaining Approaches to Stabilization and Adjustment," in Joan M. Nelson, ed., *Economic Crisis and Policy Choice: The Politics of Adjustment in the Third World* (Princeton: Princeton University Press, 1990), chap. 2.

[20] Belassa and McCarthy, *Adjustment Policies.*

[21] On the implications of the changes in Eastern Europe and the Soviet Union for socialist ideology, see Adam Przeworski, "What Don't We Know about Capitalism, Socialism, and

The combination of intellectual critiques and reinforcing international trends had a devastating effect on dependency analysis: it is rarely even mentioned today. Nevertheless, the issues dealt with by dependency analysts have not gone away. Indeed they became more serious in the 1980s and will continue to do so in the 1990s. This follows from the outcome of the two debates mentioned earlier. As the predominant view—even in the Third World—has changed toward a more positive evaluation of economic openness, policy has also shifted in that direction. Simultaneously, consensus has emerged on the primacy of domestic variables, and analysts have discarded international ones. Thus, we have a situation in the 1990s where economies are more open to international forces but analysts pay less attention to their impact. As a consequence, theorists and policy makers alike are ill-prepared to understand or cope with many of the problems that now face us.

For those who remain concerned about the effects of international forces on development possibilities, what is to be done? One option is to begin tabula rasa to construct a framework for analysis. My alternative is to try to retrieve the main insights of dependency but to deal with the main intellectual critiques. In particular, two problems must be addressed. On the one hand, there has been a lack of analytical specification of the *mechanisms* whereby international variables influence Third World countries. What are the component parts of dependent relationships, and how do they operate? On the other hand, there has been a lack of attention to the *conditions* under which the different mechanisms are relevant. Is international influence always and everywhere equally powerful? If not, what determines its strength? When should domestic factors be brought in? The remainder of this section will be devoted to an initial attempt to answer these questions in order to construct a framework to be used in analyzing the empirical materials on debt, stabilization, and structural reform policies.

MECHANISMS OF INTERNATIONAL INFLUENCE

In reading the empirical literature on dependency, three main types of relationships appear between external and internal structures and actors. One concerns the operation and impact of international markets that constitute the constraints—and opportunities—within which Third World actors must operate. A second stresses the economic, political, and ideological "linkage" between domestic groups and international actors. The third concentrates on the power relations between international ac-

Democracy," East-South System Transformation Working Paper No. 1, University of Chicago, 1990.

tors and Third World governments, the question of "leverage." In examining the three in turn, it will be necessary not only to be clear about the mechanisms involved but also to specify the characteristics of Third World countries that make the latter vulnerable to them.

Markets

Short-term fluctuations and long-term trends in international markets are important determinants of the availability of external resources that developing country governments require for both economic and political purposes. Shifts in these markets can be positive (providing governments with additional resources and thus greater ability to invest, offer services, and attract political support) or negative (constricting resources and limiting policy options). Industrial countries as well as Third World nations suffer when terms of trade move against them or when recession hits, but there are reasons to think that Third World countries are more vulnerable to these external shocks.

The principal international markets for developing country exports are the advanced industrial countries. The main impact of this factor comes through its influence on the volume of exports a given Third World country can sell. Demand for those exports is a function of level of economic activity; it is also a function of level of protection, whether tariffs or quotas. With a few important exceptions, Third World countries are price takers. Thus, terms-of-trade shifts are determined exogeneously, by levels of international demand in the short run and technical change and habits in the longer term. When the volume of exports declines or when the price is such as to being about a decline in value of exports, especially if this brings about a trade deficit or worsens one, severe economic problems can be created. If finance is not found, imports must be cut, resulting in lower consumption and/or investment.

The importance of financial markets is related to a country's merchandise trade balance but not entirely determined by it. A trade deficit requires financing. High past borrowing may also require new borrowing to service debt and provide for repatriation of profits. Terms of borrowing (interest, fees, maturity) are largely determined exogeneously. The important factor is type of lender: public lenders have softer terms than do private banks. The latter also tend to lend at floating interest rates that vary with market conditions, shifting interest rate risk to the borrower. Lack of access to international financial markets will reinforce economic problems as the burden of adjusting the economy falls on imports. The alternative is to cut debt payments, but this action risks limiting possibilities of obtaining future finance.

Price movements and world demand are always important for Third

World exporters, but attention is paid to them mainly when changes are adverse. Thus much more is said about international constraints than opportunities, and the term "international shock" is generally assumed to be negative. In the postwar period, markets for goods and finance have often moved together in cycles, the 1970s and 1980s constituting an extreme peak and trough. Table 1.1 provides some data on international economic trends for the 1960–89 period. They indicate that real growth rates in the world declined in the 1980s to their lowest level in the postwar era, terms of trade deteriorated for oil-importing Third World countries, and both real and nominal interest rates rose to a postwar peak. These trends were accompanied by a sharp decline in the availability of private commercial lending for Third World borrowers, which was not compensated by a small (nominal) increase in public-sector credit.

These shifts in goods and financial markets profoundly affected the economic policy agenda for most Third World countries. The expansive period of the 1970s provided abundant resources that gave governments

TABLE 1.1
World Economic Indicators, Annual Averages, 1960–1989

	1960–1969	1970–1979	1980–1989
GDP Growth Rates			
World	4.9%	3.8%	2.9%
Industrial Countries	4.9	3.3	2.8
Third World	4.8	5.8	3.4
Non-Oil Third World	4.4	5.7	4.1
Terms of Trade			
Industrial Countries	+0.5	−1.3	+0.6
Third World	+0.7	+7.7	+0.2
Non-Oil Third World	+0.6	−0.7	−0.4
Interest Rates			
U.S. Prime (nominal)	5.3	8.1	11.9
U.S. Prime (real)[a]	2.6	1.0	7.0
Third World Finance (net)			
Private Creditors	n.a.	$22.5bn[b]	$12.2bn[c]
		(40.0)[a,d]	(13.5)[a,d]
Public Creditors	n.a.	15.0[b]	19.4[c]
		(26.6)[a,d]	(21.4)[a,d]

Sources: International Financial Statistics Yearbook, 1990 (for growth rates, terms of trade, and interest rates); World Bank, *World Debt Tables*, various issues (finance).

[a] Deflated by GDP deflator (industrial countries)
[b] 1973–82
[c] 1983–89
[d] 1989 dollars

the ability to invest and simultaneously increase consumption of the population. Large-scale projects, from infrastructure to industrial production facilities, were established in this period. Since the loans went primarily to governments, most of these investments were made by state-owned firms, thus increasing their importance relative to the private sector. Public-sector employment as well as social services were expanded. The end of these bonanzas in the 1980s meant that such expenditures were no longer possible as governments had to retrench.

A growing economy also made it possible to reward supporters, thus making coalition building relatively easy. Distribution could be accomplished without *re*distribution. The absence of resources in the 1980s certainly did not guarantee that governments would fall, but it made it more difficult to maintain political allegiance.[22] It also made certain types of political-economic strategies nonviable. The most obvious example was the decline of populism, attributable at least in part to the absence of external finance.[23] In addition, as will be seen, the constriction of markets provided the conditions for linkage and leverage to become much more potent sources of international influence.

Even within boom or bust periods overall, market trends have differential impact on countries, depending on economic structure. Many characteristics are potentially relevant; two are particularly salient. One set of characteristics are those that determine vulnerability to trade shocks. Openness of the economy (measured by the ratio of exports and imports to GDP) will exacerbate the impact of adverse developments in international markets. In addition, the structure of exports and imports is crucial. Raw materials exports are especially subject to price shocks, while some industrial exports are vulnerable to protection. Recession affects all trade. In general, diversification provides protection against trade shocks, but most Third World countries are less diversified, and therefore more vulnerable, than the advanced industrial countries.[24]

[22] There has been an extensive debate on the relationship between economic crisis and democracy. See especially Karen Remmer, "Democracy and Economic Crisis," in David Felix, ed., *Debt and Transfiguration? Prospects for Latin America's Economic Revival* (New York: M. E. Sharpe, 1990). A comparison for the 1930s and 1980s along these lines is found in Paul Drake, "Debt and Democracy in Latin America, 1920s–1980s," in Barbara Stallings and Robert Kaufman, eds., *Debt and Democracy in Latin America* (Boulder, Colo.: Westview, 1989).

[23] On populism in the 1970s and 1980s, see Robert Kaufman and Barbara Stallings, "The Political Economy of Populism," in Rudiger Dornbusch and Sebastian Edwards, eds., *The Macroeconomics of Populism in Latin Amercia* (Chicago: National Bureau of Economic Research and University of Chicago Press, 1991).

[24] This argument is similar to the literature on interdependence where the distinction is drawn between sensitivity and vulnerability. Sensitivity merely implies that a change in one part of the economic system affects all other parts. Some economies can quickly compensate

A second set of characteristics produces susceptibility to financial market shocks. A low volume of export revenue and/or a low domestic savings rate will increase vulnerability to cutoffs of finance such as occurred in 1982. Problems of debt service will be compounded by interest rate hikes, particularly of debt priced at floating interest rates. Reserves can cushion a country against negative shocks, but such protection is only temporary and at some point reserves must be replenished.

Linkage

Linkage refers to the tendency of certain groups in the Third World to identify with the interests and outlook of international actors and to support coalitions and policies reflecting them. The concept of linkage was particularly stressed in the historical-structural version of dependency analysis. Cardoso and Faletto, the preeminent writers of this genre, say "there is no metaphysical relation of dependence between one nation and another, between one state and another. These relations are made possible through a network of interests . . . that bind some social groups to others, some classes to others."[25] Examples of these interest networks abound, most frequently involving businesspeople, technocrats, the military, and the middle class. In each case, both interest-based and cultural ties link Third World groups to their counterparts in industrial countries.

From the standpoint of policy choice, business groups constitute the most important networks. Externally-oriented business is bound to the industrial countries by both interest and cultural ties. The former is epitomized by managers or other high-level employees of multinational firms operating in the Third World, but such alliances also include looser relationships with suppliers, bankers, and customers abroad. Interest-based ties are often supplemented by educational experiences in an industrial country, by travel, and by consumption patterns that require imported goods. Among businesses, of course, some have closer international ties than others. Two categories that have been suggested to differentiate businesses are exporters versus those producing for the domestic market and liquid versus fixed asset holders.[26] In both cases, the former are more likely to have significant international ties.

Top-level technocrats are likely to have studied abroad. The educational impact of their experience is not simply a general acquaintance with an international lifestyle but specific knowledge relevant to their

---

for these changes so as to protect themselves in all or part. Others still remain severely affected; those are vulnerable rather than just sensitive. See Robert O. Keohane and Joseph Nye, *Power and Interdependence* (Boston: Little Brown, 1977).

[25] Cardoso and Faletto, *Dependency and Development*, p. 173.
[26] Frieden, "Class, Sectors, and Foreign Debt."

profession provided within the paradigms acceptable in the industrial countries. The archetypical example was the "Chicago Boys," the Pinochet economists trained at the University of Chicago on an exchange program with the Catholic University in Santiago, but this project has identified many less extreme cases. Furthermore, many technocrats spend time working for an international organization in the United States or Europe, which tends to further their identification with the policies they espouse.[27]

The Third World military is another group whose hierarchy is likely to have had training abroad. For example, figures gathered by U.S. researchers indicate that over half a million foreign military officers and technicians have received training in the United States or at the U.S. Army School in Panama.[28] Similar experiences in Europe are frequent for Asian and African military officials. Being indoctrinated into the culture of the United States or European military through education is supplemented by purchase of advanced equipment from the same countries.

For substantial sectors of the middle class, the "network of interests" comes mainly through consumption and lifestyle ambitions. Through the media, imported products become known and the perceived necessity to purchase them provides a powerful link with counterparts in the industrial countries. For the wealthier, ownership of goods is supplemented by travel and perhaps education abroad. For the very wealthy, ownership of assets abroad, whether a condominium in Miami or a bank account in Geneva, provides a safety net as well as a tangible stake in the industrial world.[29]

When ruling political coalitions are closely tied to such internationally-oriented groups, they are likely to have different policy orientations than governments based on labor, peasants, marginal urban sectors, or even domestically-oriented business. As I will argue, "internationalist" coalitions are more likely to advocate payment of the foreign debt, budget and wage restraints to bring about macroeconomic balance, and reforms such as liberalization and privatization. This set of policies is the one pushed by influential groups in the industrial countries and favored by the ideological consensus to which the internationalist Third World groups are especially atuned.

How do such coalitions come to exercise power over economic policy? If a country has an electoral system, such coalitions must seek support from voters and will probably rely on appeals to the middle class. In in-

[27] The example of the "Chicago Boys" is very well described in Arturo Fontaine, *Los economistas y el Presidente Pinochet* (Santiago: Zig-Zag, 1988).

[28] Michael Klare and Cynthia Arnson, *Supplying Repression: U.S. Support for Authoritarian Regimes Abroad* (Washington, D.C.: Institute for Policy Studies, 1981), p. 47.

[29] Dale Johnson, ed., *The Middle Class* (Boulder, Colo.: Westview Press, 1985).

stances when a winning electoral coalition could not be formed, and such groups have felt fundamentally threatened, the coalitions have provided support for military coups. For both electoral and military paths, there is also abundant evidence of assistance from international allies, whether governments, parties, unions, or business firms. Short of exercising direct control over policy, of course, such coalitions can use a variety of resources to influence policy in directions that are favorable to them.

Once an internationally-oriented coalition is in power, the orthodox orientation of the technocrats becomes important. Whether as cabinet ministers or merely as advisors or lower-level officials, their influence on policy making is strong. Of course, there is no guarantee that such technocrats will actually be able to persuade their political masters to take politically dangerous measures, but certain conditions that make success more likely can be identified.[30]

The effectiveness of international linkage networks can be expected to vary according to two factors discussed in the previous section on markets. One relates to economic structure. The more open an economy—the more reliant it is on international trade and finance—the more dense will be the international networks. In economies where many small and medium-size firms are engaged in exports, rather than only a few large ones, these contracts will be especially numerous. On the consumption side, openness also provides access to imported goods, which creates a powerful link with the industrial world. Assuming that economic openness extends to communications, the media will further international identifications.

The second factor has to do with the state of the international market and the resulting constraints that Third World countries are facing at a given time. If external constraints are tightly binding or a crisis exists, the influence of technocrats is likely to increase in any type of government. Ministries that are the most internationally oriented—usually the finance ministry and the central bank—will rise in power. In more political terms, an economic crisis may give an edge to a coalition that claims to have special access to international resources.

A review of the governments in office during the 1980s in the fifteen countries under consideration in the chapter suggests that internationally-oriented coalitions did become more prevalent during the decade. Such an analysis is problematic, of course, given the difficulties in labeling coalitions as "international" or "domestic." More interesting are two other categories: governments that were initially backed by domestic coalitions but changed orientation after coming to office and governments that were

---

[30] In chapter 2 of this volume, Kahler discusses several cases where technocrats were not able to deliver on promises of policy change.

backed by domestic coalitions but campaigned on platforms promising orthodox policies. For example, in Argentina, the Peronist government quickly made an alliance with the most internationally-connected groups in the country as a way of dealing with the economic crisis. In Ghana and Nigeria, progressive military governments eventually turned to the IMF and World Bank for economic help. In Chile and Jamaica, less internationally-oriented coalitions were elected but arguably because they promised not to tamper with previous economic policies. The fact that there is no case of an internationalist government shifting in a domestically-oriented direction provides further support for the argument of a move toward orthodoxy in the 1980s.

Leverage

Leverage is a less subtle form of international influence than linkage. It involves the direct use of power, with a promise of reward (or a threat of punishment) for carrying out (or not) a desired policy. Leverage is most effective when resources are scarce, creditors are unified, and the incentives they offer are credible. The best known examples in the economic policy making sphere are the conditionality bargains with the international financial institutions (IMF and World Bank), analyzed by Miles Kahler in chapter 2 of this book. The concept, however, is broader than IMF and World Bank conditionality. It also includes explicit or implicit bargaining with the private banks, bilateral aid agencies, multinational corporations, and (in extreme cases not considered here) intelligence services and even the armed forces.

Because leverage is less subtle than linkage, the mechanisms in principle are easier to identify. The most transparent case is negotiations with the IFIs. Although the details are not normally made public, the outcome is known if an agreement is reached. The general types of economic policy requirements are also well known for the different types of finance offered by the IMF and World Bank. These range from relatively simple demand management policies for an IMF standby through extensive structural reforms for a World Bank structural adjustment loan. If the conditions are agreed to in a credible way, monies will be disbursed in tranches.[31]

Bilateral aid agencies have also been frequent users of conditionality, but often of a more political sort. The U.S. Agency for International Development (USAID) is an extreme case in this sense. It is well known for

[31] For analyses of the role of the IMF and World Bank, under the new circumstances of the 1980s and 1990s, see Catherine Gwin and Richard Feinberg, eds., *Pulling Together: The IMF in a Multipolar World* (New Brunswick, N.J.: Transaction Books, 1989) and Richard Feinberg et al., *Between Two Worlds: The World Bank's Next Decade* (New Brunswick, N.J.: Transaction Books, 1986).

trying to reward friends and punish enemies. The Japanese aid agencies, now the largest donors in the world, operate in a quite different way. Traditionally, they shied away from attaching conditions to loans, but U.S. pressure and their increased activity level have changed that. Rather than impose their own conditions, however, they "piggyback" on IMF and World Bank conditions.[32]

After reappearing on the scene in the 1970s as a major source of finance for the Third World, the private banks disbursed large amounts of loans and attached very few strings to them. In general, they had neither the will nor the capacity to impose conditions. The goal was to turn their new petrodollar deposits into profits, not to reform Third World economies. In fact, they undermined the attempts of the Bank and Fund to do so. When the debt crisis began in 1982, however, the situation rapidly changed. The banks joined forces with the IFIs and with the governments of the industrial countries to reschedule loans in exchange for more orthodox economic policies.[33]

A final actor in the leverage game is the multinational corporation (MNC). MNCs were perhaps the major external actor in dependency analysis. They were viewed as displacing local firms from the most profitable activities, creating unemployment by introducing capital-intensive technology, coercing governments into providing incentives of various kinds, and displacing decision-making to their headquarters country. They were able to wield this power through both carrot and stick: Third World countries' need for investment funds and (if trouble arose) the backing of their home governments.[34] In the 1970s, like the multilateral agencies, the MNCs were on the sidelines. Third World governments were able to get bank loans and make their own investment decisions. A decade later, they too had returned in force as governments clamored to obtain investment and were willing to make policy changes to get it. New foreign investment laws sprung up all over the Third World, from Mexico to Mozambique, as competition for MNC investment increased.

The scope for leverage, then, has varied substantially over the course of the postwar period, depending on the characteristics of creditors. Table 1.2 shows those changes. High-conditionality bilateral loans and direct investment dominated in the 1960s, only to be displaced by uncondi-

[32] On U.S. foreign aid, see Robert Wood, *From Marshall Plan to Debt Crisis: Foreign Aid and Development Choices in the World Economy* (Berkeley: University of California Press, 1986). On the Japanese style of aid, see Robert M. Orr, Jr., *The Emergence of Japan's Foreign Aid Power* (New York: Columbia University Press, 1990).

[33] The banks' style of lending is discussed in Barbara Stallings, *Banker to the Third World: U.S. Portfolio Investment in Latin America, 1900–86* (Berkeley: University of California Press, 1987).

[34] Examples of such activities are discussed in Evans, *Dependent Development*.

TABLE 1.2
Net Flow of Foreign Capital to Third World Countries, 1961–1989

Year	Bilateral	Multilateral	Banks	DFI	Total Amount
1961	31.0%	12.2%	14.2%	42.6%	$4,303 mn (21,302)[a]
1965	35.3	11.3	11.2	42.2	5,851 (25,112)
1970	30.4	9.0	21.8	38.8	9,502 (32,653)
1975	24.1	10.6	35.6	29.7	34,823 (78,964)
1980	20.0	12.7	50.8	16.5	61,331 (92,785)
1985	15.8	30.4	37.6	16.1	40,188 (45,720)
1989	18.7	36.4	8.0	36.8[b]	32,624 (32,624)

Sources: World Debt Tables and Development Cooperation, various issues.
[a] Figures in parentheses are constant (1989) dollars.
[b] On-shore only (excludes tax havens)

tional bank loans in the 1970s. By the late 1980s, high conditionality returned as the multilateral agencies became the largest single source of funds. There were also important shifts in the degree of unity among suppliers of finance. The peak of disunity and competition occurred during the 1970s, as the banks flooded the market with loans. In the 1980s, the situation reversed itself. A new ideological and organizational consensus formed among the industrial countries, and the IMF and World Bank became its lynchpins.

Once again, as with markets and linkage, not all countries are equally susceptible to leverage. Clearly the condition of the international economy, and thus the degree of constraints they face, are fluctuating factors that will be relevant for all countries in determining their bargaining stances. The looser the constraints, the harder the bargain that will be driven. In addition, however, more enduring characteristics, both economic and political, are also important.

In economic terms, if a country has a large market and valuable natural resources, private-sector firms will require fewer incentives to enter. More important is the question of state capacity addressed by Peter Evans in chapter 3 of this book. State capacity is relevant in at least two ways. On the one hand, a high level of state capacity is necessary to be able to negotiate effectively with private investors, whether MNCs or banks. Extensive information on the nature of the markets and the characteristics of individual firms are prerequisites for an advantageous deal in addition to bargaining skills per se. On the other hand, in confronting the multilateral institutions, another type of capacity is relevant—the ability to design an economic program. Those countries without such capacity are left to the mercy of the Bank and Fund to act as substitute ministries of finance; they are extraordinarily vulnerable to this particular kind of leverage.

In the next three sections, I will examine some empirical evidence relating to economic policies on debt service, stabilization, and structural reform in the 1980s. I will show to what extent the mechanisms previously discussed are useful for explaining changes in the three policy areas, both between the decades of the 1970s and within the latter decade.

DEBT SERVICE, REFINANCING, AND ARREARS

Of all the changes confronting the Third World between the 1970s and 1980s, none was more dramatic than the shift in international financial markets. Between 1970 and 1982, Third World countries received a new inflow of $480 billion or an average of $40 billion per year. Even after subtracting interest payments, there was an average annual net transfer to the Third World of $23 billion, about 1.7 percent of GDP. During the rest of the decade, by contrast, net transfers were negative on the order of $21 billion per year, about 1 percent of GDP. For some regions, the figures were far more devastating. In Latin America, net inflows in the earlier period amounted to 1.7 percent of GDP, while the outflows in 1983–89 averaged 2.7 percent.[35]

These changes had tremendous negative effects in virtually all aspects of economic, social, and political life as governments were forced to cope with diminishing resources. The implications for macroeconomic policy and structural reform will be discussed in later sections of the chapter. Here we will concentrate on policies relating to debt management, asking what role international factors played in determining debt policies. The options included full payment of interest and principal as originally scheduled, a mutually-agreed rescheduling of interest and/or principal, or a unilateral moratorium on some or all payments.

The 1970s versus 1980s

In the 1970s, a borrower's market existed during most of the decade. As indicated previously, the main lenders were the world's largest commercial banks. Early in the decade, these banks had begun to look toward Third World borrowers as recession drove their traditional clients out of

---

[35] Calculated from World Bank, *World Debt Tables*, various issues.

the market. The trend was vastly expanded after the first oil shock. Deposits soared for the large banks as the OPEC governments placed their excess revenues there, and the banks in turn had to find borrowers. Simultaneously, Third World oil importers became eager to find resources to meet their expanded oil bills without cutting back on development projects. The mutual interest between them appeared obvious, and money flowed freely.[36]

Several characteristics of the financial flows of this period need to be noted. First was the very large volume of money involved. Gross disbursements to Third World countries averaged $58 billion per year between 1973 and 1982. Some 65 percent of these funds came from the private banks; for the middle-income countries, the share was higher at 80 percent.[37] Second, given the high liquidity of the international financial markets, combined with relaxed monetary policy in the industrial countries, interest rates on these loans were low; real rates were often negative. Maturities were long. The combined effect was that debt service was almost never a problem. It could be easily managed out of new loans with substantial amounts left over for other uses. In the few exceptional cases where debt problems appeared in the 1970s—mainly Peru, Turkey, and Zaire—the banks themselves stepped in to try to resolve the situations.[38] Rather than debt service, then, the debt problem in the 1970s was that the borrower countries were coming to rely on cheap credit and to assume that it would be available indefinitely. On the creditor side, the banks were lending beyond the level of prudence and with little control over how the loans were being used.

The bubble burst on 13 August 1982, when the Mexican minister of finance arrived in Washington to announce that his government could not continue to service its debt as originally contracted. Although a package was quickly put together to aid Mexico, the banks reacted by a generalized cessation of "voluntary" lending. Since borrowers had been counting on new loans to meet debt service payments, the cutoffs extended Mexico's crisis to many other nations. The decline in loans came on top of other negative shocks already under way. Indeed, by late 1982, international markets had generally shifted in ways that significantly tightened constraints on Third World countries. After the second oil shock in 1979–80, reaction in the industrial countries had been different than after the first one. In particular, interest rates were raised to combat inflation and recession resulted. Thus Third World debtors were forced to pay more interest on their debt at the same time that their nonoil export revenues

[36] Stallings, *Banker to the Third World*, esp. pp. 220–40.

[37] Calculated from World Bank, *World Debt Tables*, various issues.

[38] On the banks' attempts at replacing the IMF in the 1970s, see Barbara Stallings, "Euromarkets, Third World Countries, and the International Political Economy," in Harry Makler et al., eds., *The New International Economy* (London: Sage Publications, 1982).

stagnated or declined. In this atmosphere, the shift in access to the financial markets was merely the shock that turned a latent crisis into reality.

The behavior of the markets conformed closely to a model of lending cycles put forth by Charles Kindleberger, based on historical experience.[39] The model has five phases: an exogenous shock leading to "euphoria" among investors, speculation and running up of a high volume of debt, financial "distress" as the euphoria ends, financial crisis when all try to get out of the assets in question, and financial "revulsion" when borrowers cannot regain access to the markets. Kindleberger's basic explanation for the cycles rested on psychology and expectations. An alternative explanation assigns a stronger role to the forces of competition in the relevant markets.[40]

The euphoria and speculative stages certainly matched the situation in the 1970s as banks fought for the mandate to lead the huge (and very lucrative) syndicated loans for Third World governments. Other lenders, especially the IMF, glowered from the sidelines, as Third World governments joined forces with the banks to avoid any loans that placed limits on their spending or conditions on their policies. The Mexican debacle brought on the periods of distress and crisis in the 1980s. The question was the type of response that would be followed. In Kindleberger's model, the outcome depended on whether there was a lender of last resort. To a certain extent, the IMF fulfilled that role in the 1980s, working in close collaboration with the U.S. government. The competition among creditors was ended for a time, and a basic strategy devised to deal with the crisis. It had four main elements: rescheduling of payments, usually with a grace period, new money from the private banks, additional finance from the international institutions, and policies on the part of debtor countries to cut budget deficits and produce trade surpluses.[41]

To carry out this strategy, the banks organized themselves into creditor committees, one for each debtor nation. The committees were composed of about a dozen large banks from the United States, Europe, and Japan; they negotiated on behalf of all creditor institutions. Based on this strategy, three rounds of negotiations took place from 1982 to 1985. During this period, thirty four countries in Africa, Asia, Latin America, and Eastern Europe rescheduled loans with the commercial banks.[42] A key prerequisite for the rescheduling was that the country have a standby

[39] Charles P. Kindleberger, *Manias, Panics, and Crashes* (New York: Basic Books, 1978).

[40] A reformulation of Kindleberger's model suggesting a political-economic rather than psychological approach is found in Stallings, *Banker to the Third World*, esp. pp. 303–10.

[41] An authoritative account of the debt strategy is Martin Feldstein et al., *Restructuring Growth in the Debt-Laden Third World* (New York: Trilateral Commission, 1987).

[42] Maxwell Watson et al., *International Capital Markets: Developments and Prospects*, IMF Occasional Paper 43 (Washington, D.C.: IMF, 1986).

arrangement in place with the IMF. Paris Club reschedulings, especially important for the poorer countries with more debt from public agencies than private banks, were also keyed to IMF agreements. This concerted approach by creditors meant that heavily-indebted governments had little opportunity to improve the terms being offered them since the lenders could not be played off against each other. One way of improving terms would have been the formation of a debtor cartel to confront the creditors' cartel. Although it appeared on several occasions that the Third World nations would organize themselves, such a development never actually came about.[43]

While a consensus about how to deal with debt problems existed among the major creditors in the early 1980s, providing the basis for their power, this consensus had begun to dissolve by the second half of the decade. The first major shift in debt policy was signalled by Treasury Secretary James Baker's announcement of the so-called Baker Plan in September 1985. Responding to widespread criticisms from debtor countries and even some creditors, Baker modified the earlier emphasis on austerity to stress the need for growth. He also called for more money for fifteen heavily-indebted countries, to come from the international financial institutions and the private banks. The governments of the industrial countries were not directly involved, which aroused resentment among the private creditors and began to dilute the consensus. Later, it was further diluted by the introduction of the "menu approach" to give banks more options for dealing with their problem loans. They could either continue to provide more money with each rescheduling or they could take their losses and exit the process.[44]

Although the Baker Plan, as modified by the menu approach, continued to be supported by the executive branch of the U.S. government, congressional alternatives multiplied in the mid-1980s. Likewise the banks began to experiment with alternatives and to take steps to lower their vulnerability to Third World debt. The French and Japanese governments offered their own plans, which were publicly rejected by the United States. Later, some elements were incorporated into the plan announced by Treasury Secretary Nicholas Brady in July 1989. The Brady Plan implicitly recognized that the Third World debt could not be completely repaid by calling for debt reduction, either through exchanging loans for bonds with a lower face value or lower interest rates; an alternative was new lending.

[43] For discussion of the problems in forming a debtor cartel, see Diana Tussie, "The Coordination of Latin American Debtors: Is There a Logic Behind the Story?" in Stephany Griffith-Jones, ed., *Managing Third World Debt* (New York: St. Martin's Press, 1988).

[44] The origins and attempted implementation of the Baker Plan are analyzed in Mary Geske, "The Baker Initiative: An Analysis of Domestic and International Sources of U.S. Foreign Economic Policy" (Ph.D. diss., University of Wisconsin, 1991).

The bonds would be backed by guarantees, partially financed by the IMF, World Bank, and creditor governments. In addition Brady encouraged a more flexible IMF policy to allow disbursement of its funds to governments that still had arrears with the private banks.[45]

Changes during the 1980s

To explore the impact of changing creditor behavior on debtors' policy stance, we need data on the latter. Table 1.3 provides some basic information on debt burden and debt service in the fifteen countries. It also includes data on arrears with respect to interest payments for public-sector long-term debt and on moratoria. Nine of the fifteen countries in the sample had no arrears in the early part of the decade. Those that did— the African countries, the smaller Latin American nations, and the Philippines—had very small amounts of interest payments behind schedule during this period. Moreover, none of the governments in arrears declared them as an explicit policy on nonpayment. In the later 1980s, by contrast, the debtors began going their own way. Table 1.3 shows the increase in arrears, both in number of countries and size of arrears. By the end of the decade, ten countries were behind in payments. Most of those arrears were substantially larger than the beginning of the decade, and four countries had declared unilateral moratoria. While some of the deterioration of the debt-service picture was due to the effects of market conditions, there were also individual country differences deriving from linkage and leverage.

Within the overall pattern, three groups of countries can be identified. First were five countries that never ran up arrears at any point in the decade—Korea, Thailand, Colombia, Chile, and Mexico, although the last two negotiated major debt restructuring during the 1980s. This group included countries with very high debt burdens (Chile and Mexico) so the reason for repayment cannot be ascribed solely to the ability to pay. Rather, these were governments convinced of the value of an international orientation for their economies and the need for international finance in the future. They also had political systems with sufficient centralization that they could enforce the distribution of domestic costs necessary to continue debt payments.

The other ten countries went in several different directions. One group —including Peru, Brazil, Costa Rica, and Zambia—openly declared unilateral moratoria on their debt service. The best known case was Peru, where Alan García used his inaugural address to denounce the IMF and to announce that Peru would devote only 10 percent of its export reve-

[45] For a discussion of the Brady Plan and other initiatives, see U.N. Economic Commission for Latin America and the Caribbean, *Latin America and the Caribbean: Options to Reduce the Debt Burden* (Santiago: ECLAC, 1990).

TABLE 1.3
Debt Indicators: Weight of Debt and Arrears, 1980–1988

	1980–82				1986–88			
	Total Debt	Debt/GNP	TDS/XGS	Arrears	Total Debt	Debt/GNP	TDS/XGS	Arrears
Argentina	$35.5 bn	65.3%	44.3%	$0 mn	$56.6 bn	69.0%	74.5%	$988 mn
Brazil	81.2	32.8	70.1	0	116.8	37.3	46.4	1142[a]
Chile	15.0	57.3	59.7	0	20.7	120.7	34.4	0
Colombia	8.7	24.0	22.5	0	16.5	47.4	44.2	0
Costa Rica	3.2	122.4	25.9	10	4.6	105.8	28.1	198[a]
Dom. Repub.	2.3	35.7	26.0	11	3.8	84.1	20.2	142
Jamaica	2.3	88.9	22.8	0	4.3	173.7	42.1	32
Mexico	73.9	38.4	52.6	0	103.9	72.7	47.9	0
Peru	10.9	47.7	55.1	0	17.6	49.9	16.1	1904[a]
Korea	33.3	50.1	21.3	0	41.5	33.0	25.0	0
Thailand	10.4	30.7	19.8	0	19.9	41.8	25.8	0
Philippines	20.9	55.4	34.1	34	29.3	84.7	35.2	78
Ghana	1.4	33.0	13.6	9	3.0	57.6	47.2	8
Nigeria	11.3	11.9	9.8	6	28.0	94.3	24.0	640
Zambia	3.5	95.4	23.2	33	6.2	320.5	29.1	248[a]

Source: World Debt Tables.
[a] Moratorium in place for at least part of period

nues to debt service in order to give priority to its debt to its own people. A "domestic" coalition par excellance, the García government hoped to begin a large-scale move away from full debt service, thus forcing the creditors to provide relief, but its policies had the opposite effect. Only Zambia followed suit in 1987. The expansionist policies that accompanied García's debt strategy produced massive economic contraction and inflation, thus "inoculating" other countries from following Peru's example.[46]

In a separate and more restricted move, in February 1987 Brazil declared a moratorium on interest payments to commercial banks on medium and long-term debt. The finance minister of the day, Luiz Carlos Bresser Pereira, went to Washington to present a proposal to end the moratorium through a debt reduction of the sort that would later become the focus of the Brady Plan. In 1987, however, the proposal was rejected out of hand. Bresser resigned soon after, and a new finance minister suspended the moratorium. Analysis of the reason varies. While many stress the loss of trade credits resulting from leverage used by bankers, others claim that pressures within the Brazilian government as well as the private sector were the decisive element; the latter is an interesting example of linkage. In any case, Brazil soon began running up arrears again, despite the formal end to the moratorium.[47]

The remaining countries did the same thing; they ran up arrears quietly rather than openly announcing nonpayment as a policy. In some cases, the arrears were the result of a simple inability to pay. In others, they were at least a partial policy. Argentina was a good example of mixed motives. Given the chaotic state of the Argentine economy by the late 1980s, together with the fact that debt service amounted to 75 percent of export receipts, regular debt service was probably impossible. It went in fits and starts, with partial payments being made and new money provided, but consistent policies simply could not be followed. As will be discussed, this situation led to an entirely new approach by 1989.[48]

Role of International Influence

Although the overall changes in debt service burden between the 1970s and 1980s can be explained by market shocks—price and volume shocks

[46] Barbara Stallings, "Autodestruccíon de una iniciativa positiva: la política de la deuda peruana bajo Alan García," in Heraclio Bonilla and Paul Drake, eds., El APRA de la ideología a la praxis (Lima: Editorial Nuevo Mundo, 1989).

[47] See the account of Paulo Nogueira Batista, Jr., Da crise internacional a moratoria brasileira (Rio de Janeiro: Paz e Terra, 1988). See also Luiz Carlos Bresser Pereira, "A Brazilian Approach to External Debt Negotiation," LASA Forum 19, no. 4 (Winter 1989): 1–7.

[48] The Argentine case is discussed in José María Dagnino Pastore, Crónicas económicas: Argentina, 1969–1988 (Buenos Aires: Editorial Crespillo, 1988).

in both the goods and financial markets—other differences followed in their wake. In particular, international leverage reappeared on the scene after having been in decline for the previous decade. Likewise, linkage took on different characteristics in comparison with the 1970s. It is to the latter two variables that I will look to explain the pattern of response to the debt crisis during the 1980s, both the differences in general behavior of debtors between the early and late 1980s and the differences among individual debtors over the course of the decade.

Leverage, the exercise of economic power, was the main explanation for the continued service of the debt during the early years of the debt crisis. During this period, the creditors offered both carrot and stick to the debtors. The latter took the form of threats to cut off trade credits to any debtor that revolted and, ultimately, to embargo bank accounts and goods held in creditor countries. The former involved new loans in the short run, designed to permit interest payments to continue. In the longer run, the promise was renewed access to the international credit markets. The effectiveness of the leverage depended on two requirements being met. On the one hand, the creditors had to present a united front so that one could not be played off against another. On the other hand, the negative sanctions and/or positive incentives had to be credible.

As the evidence indicates, both requirements were met during the first few years of the crisis. Once a strategy had been designed, it was carried out under the leadership of the IMF. The main idea was to keep both debtors and creditors from abandoning the debt negotiations. The IMF managing director called in the leading banks and told them they had to put up additional money in proportion to their outstanding loans; only if they did so would the Fund agree to supervise the debtor governments' economic policies. In this way, the banks' loans would be protected, while the debtors would be provided with some of the money to enable them to pay. Additional funds were provided by the IFIs, and maturing loans were rescheduled. The largest banks, which formed the bank advisory committees, were in charge of pressuring the smaller banks to cooperate; in the event of trouble, the relevant Central Bank would step in to help. As a result of this unified pressure, very few debtors failed to go along.

By mid-decade, however, several elements began to change. The initial expectation had been that the debt crisis could be worked through in a few years. As it became clear that no end was in sight, creditor unity began to break down. The large banks became increasingly annoyed that the governments of the industrial countries were not directly contributing new money; the smaller banks wanted out no matter what the cost. Many people—congressional representatives, foreign governments, even bankers—became convinced that the debt could not be repaid, and schemes were drawn up that implicitly admitted it. Until the Brady Plan, however, the U.S. executive branch would not tolerate such a view. The Brady Plan itself undermined unity by encouraging the IMF to loan to countries in arrears to banks. Moreover, the credibility of both the sanctions and incentives began to fall as the increasing disagreement on the part of creditors was reflected in a lack of action in response to countries that did not keep up on their payments—especially if they were small and they did not announce defiant policies. As governments saw they could get away with arrears, this increasingly came to be seen as a viable option for those who were not determined internationalists. Moreover, even the internationalists became discouraged by the lack of rewards (i.e., new "voluntary" loans) in return for making the sacrifices necessary to keep up on debt payments.

Beyond this overall pattern, two other questions must be addressed. First, why did some countries continue to pay throughout the decade while others fell into arrears and, among the latter, why did some do so in a more confrontational way? Second, why was no debtor cartel formed to match the creditor cartel? Although leverage has some role in answering these questions, linkage plays a more important part. The core of the linkage argument centers on political coalitions.

The five governments that never ran up arrears were prominent examples of internationalist coalitions. Financiers, exporters, and an internationalized middle class formed the core of the coalitions behind them, and economic policy was managed by technocrats with strongly orthodox leanings. In addition, political power in the five countries was sufficiently centralized, although by varying institutional mechanisms, that they could suppress or ignore the political problems caused by shrinking resources. While such a description fits the cases of Korea, Thailand, and Colombia, those countries also had lighter debt burdens than most others when measured by the export revenues available to support debt service. Chile and Mexico, by contrast, had heavy debt-service ratios, thus better demonstrating the importance of coalitional orientation.

At the other extreme were the four countries that openly declared moratoria: Peru, Brazil, Zambia, and Costa Rica. The García government in Peru and the Kaunda regime in Zambia—despite many important differences between them—are both examples of coalitions oriented toward domestic interests. The Sarney government in Brazil was more heterogeneous (including parties of both left and right), so it is not surprising that there were fluctuations in its policy depending on which faction controlled the economic ministries. Finally, the Costa Rican government under Oscar Arias represented a strong social democratic tradition, but its debt policy was part of an overall economic strategy that saw an incompatibility between full debt service and stabilization and gave priority to the latter.

The governments that ran up arrears but without confrontation included a rather heterogeneous group. Some indeed had domestically-based coalitions, which the argument here has identified with a low priority on debt service. In addition, however, they were also weak governments, either because of lack of skills and infrastructure (the African and smaller Latin American nations of Ghana, Nigeria, Dominican Republic, and Jamaica) or serious political problems (Argentina and the Philippines). These domestic political characteristics exacerbated economic problems, leading to the quiet accumulation of arrears as the easiest solution. Such an approach was reinforced by the failure of creditors to impose penalties on countries running up arrears.

Political coalitions also affected the ability of debtor countries to form a cartel. On numerous occasions, observers and even participants predicted that debtors would combine into a cartel to deal with creditors, especially since the latter had organized themselves in such a way. That is, the so-called Bank Advisory Committees, which negotiated with individual countries, did so on behalf of all creditors. Nonetheless, a debtor cartel never emerged, and debtors agreed to creditors' demands that negotiations be handled on a case-by-case basis.

Two types of explanations have been suggested for the lack of a cartel. One relies on leverage and skillful maneuvers on the part of creditors. One participant, for example, has documented a pattern whereby favorable terms were provided to key participants just before important meetings at which joint debtor action was on the agenda.[49] Similarly, an Argentine political scientist has used game theory to analyze "why don't our governments do the obvious?" Side payments to those who refuse to participate in a cartel and sanctions for those who do are part of his answer.[50] Chile and Peru provide extreme examples of countries that were treated well for following creditor rules and poorly for "misbehavior."

Another explanation for the failure to form a cartel relies on linkage-type arguments. Those governments with an internationalist orientation did not want to be associated with such a movement even if there were some short-term economic benefits to be gained. They were more concerned with a long-term reputation for creditworthiness, considered necessary to obtain access to the financial markets. Even governments based on domestic coalitions, which did not place absolute priority on debt service, encountered enough differences among themselves that no agreement was possible. Game theory has also been applied to a debtor-based explanation, stressing lack of leadership and lack of confidence in other players to follow through on agreements to confront creditors jointly.[51]

[49] Tussie, "Coordination of Third World Debtors," pp. 282–307.

[50] Guillermo O'Donnell, "External Debt: Why Don't Our Governments Do the Obvious?" *CEPAL Review* 27 (December 1985).

[51] Laurence Whitehead, "Latin American Debt: An International Bargaining Perspective" (Paper presented at the Annual Conference of the British International Studies Association, Aberystwyth, Wales, December 1987). See also O'Donnell, "External Debt."

BALANCE-OF-PAYMENTS DEFICITS AND STABILIZATION POLICY

The issues of debt service and stabilization are clearly related. For some fifteen years, the two policies moved in tandem. Their patterns across the decades of the 1970s and 1980s were not only very similar, but they were both determined by the same process: the large-scale influx of private bank loans to the Third World during the 1970s. This loan inflow enabled Third World governments to meet debt service obligations, while largely freeing them from the stabilization requirements attached to credits from the international financial institutions. When this permissive international environment turned more restrictive in the early 1980s, international pressures emerged for both debt service and stabilization. By the mid-1980s, however, such pressures began to diverge. While international creditors put high priority on timely debt service in the early part of the decade, but slacked off later, the pattern for stabilization was the opposite. Pressure for stabilization did not let up; if anything, it increased during the decade.

Stabilization has different definitions. In chapter 6 of this volume, Stephan Haggard and Robert Kaufman analyze stabilization as the lowering of inflation. Here I am concerned with stabilization as a problem of balance-of-payments deficits. It is with respect to this latter definition that the IMF has been especially involved since it is unmanageable balance-of-payments deficits that typically have driven countries to the Fund. The latter would provide its own loan and open the door to other sources of finance if it approved of a country's economic policies. The particular type of policies likely to win approval was well known: orthodox measures designed to cut demand by reducing budget deficits, restricting credit, and holding down wages together with a devaluation and a bow toward fewer controls. Such policies would produce a recession that would ease balance-of-payments problems in the short run; they might or might not have any long-run impact. The political problems caused by recession and devaluation were disliked by all governments, although some were more amenable than others as will be discussed below.[52]

The 1970s versus the 1980s

Private bank loans in the 1970s provided a way to finance balance-of-payments deficits *without* any policy changes. As a result, current account deficits increased significantly during the decade when compared to the earlier postwar years. The average current account deficit for nonoil developing countries between 1970 and 1982 as a percentage of GDP was

---

[52] For a discussion of conditionality, see chapter 2 of this volume.

2.6 percent compared to 0.9 percent in the 1950s and 1960s.[53] Given certain assumptions about private-sector behavior, it follows that the loans also permitted large budget deficits, which most economists consider to be a major cause of inflation.[54] Thus the loan influx may have facilitated both balance-of-payments deficits and inflation.

In the 1980s, this situation reversed itself. Liquidity available to the Third World contracted, other negative shocks also appeared, and stabilization could no longer be avoided. The most important transmission agent was the IMF, which became a more influential actor for several interrelated reasons. First, the Fund had gradually increased its own resources, both through quota increases and types of loan facilities, so that its loans came to be significant in themselves, particularly given that commercial lending had evaporated. This can be seen in the rise of the average IMF loan package from $74 million in the 1970s to $217 million in the 1980s.[55] Since GDP was stagnant in this period for troubled Third World countries, the IMF loans as a share of GDP rose substantially. Second, private sources dried up so that IMF loans represented a larger share of available resources. In the 1970s, use of IMF credit amounted to 3.2 percent of all long-term external finance, while in the 1980s the figure increased to 6.7 percent.[56] Third, other creditors reinforced the IMF position rather than undermining it as they had in the 1970s.

These factors explain most of the difference between the lower incidence of stabilization policies in the 1970s compared to the 1980s. Table 1.4 shows the number of IMF programs approved per year during the two decades and the amount of money provided. Totals were 177 programs for $13.1 billion during the 1970s and 269 programs for $58.5 billion during the 1980s. The combination of negative external shocks (and thus more need for foreign exchange), changed composition of external finance, and increased creditor unity provided the conditions for greater use of IMF leverage in favor of stabilization.

Changes within the 1980s

Within the decade of the 1980s, the trend was an increasing, though often reluctant, move toward stabilization. Early in the 1980s, creditors had

[53] Figures for 1970–82 are calculated from World Bank, *World Debt Tables, 1988–89*. Averages for 1950s and 1960s are backward extrapolations, based on Latin American trends as reported in Stallings, *Banker to the Third World*, appendix 3.

[54] The assumption about the private sector is that its saving more or less equals its investment.

[55] Calculated from table 1.4.

[56] Based on disbursement data in World Bank, *World Debt Tables*, various issues. Note, however, that *net* IMF lending was negative for much of the 1980s.

TABLE 1.4
International Monetary Fund Programs Approved, 1971–1990

Year[a]	No. of Programs	Amount (mn)	Amount (mn 1990)
1971	18	502	1,725
1972	13	289	932
1973	13	297	908
1974	15	1,156	3,266
1975	14	319	806
1976	20	1,257	2,850
1977	20	4,474	936
1978	18	1,058	2,046
1979	18	1,228	2,209
1980	28	2,488	4,126
1981	32	8,169	12,359
1982	24	9,463	13,143
1983	31	12,801	16,582
1984	27	4,185	5,148
1985	24	3,283	3,871
1986	19	2,684	3,053
1987	32	3,765	4,151
1988	30	2,084	2,224
1989	24	3,389	3,508
1990	26	8,629	8,629
Avg. 1971–80	17.7	1,307	1,980
Avg. 1981–90	26.9	5,845	7,267

Source: IMF Annual Report, 1990.

[a] Years ending April 30

assured debtors that the crisis would be short-lived if they would reduce their deficits and continue servicing their debts; by mid-decade it was clear this was not true. One of the consequences was an increased emphasis on structural adjustment, but this was a complement to, not a substitute for, stabilization. Within the general trend toward stabilization, however, differences in timing and degree of commitment can be found.

Table 1.5 presents a rough chronology of when relatively long-lasting stabilization measures were undertaken in the fifteen countries. There were also abortive attempts, of which the most interesting were the three heterodox packages instituted by Argentina, Brazil, and Peru in 1985–86. the table shows that a small number of countries negotiated stabilization programs early in the decade. Not surprisingly, there was an overlap between this group and the "good debtors" described above. The early stabilizers included Korea, Thailand, and Mexico. The Monge government in Costa Rica might also be put in this category. On their own, without much outside pressure, these governments believed that their future eco-

TABLE 1.5
Periodization of Stabilization Measures, 1980–1990

Early Stabilizers (1980–82)	Middle Stabilizers (1983–84)	Late Stabilizers (1985–88)	Late-late Stabilizers (1989–90)
Korea	Philippines	Chile	Argentina
Thailand	Ghana	Colombia	Brazil
Mexico	Jamaica	Nigeria	Peru
Costa Rica	Dom. Republic		
		[Argentina]	Zambia (?)
		[Brazil]	
		[Peru]	
		[Zambia]	

[   ] = Failed heterodox program

nomic performance depended on eliminating inflation and deficits. Their policies were a response to international shocks, and they were supported by international finance, but they were not brought about by international leverage.

For a second group of countries, stabilization occurred a bit later in this period—around 1983–84—but it was the result of heavy pressure from the international agencies. The Philippines was a case in point. By 1984, Marcos was forced to implement stabilization policies after the IMF discovered that he had been doctoring the books to hide the true policies being followed. Another very important case was Ghana, whose new government began a major program with the IMF and World Bank in 1983. This program—now the principal success story in Sub-Saharan Africa—came about when the Soviet Union and Libya refused to provide finance to the populist-nationalist Rawlings government. Desperate for foreign exchange, Rawlings was finally forced to make a deal with the international agencies. Zambia, the Dominican Republic, and Jamaica also came under heavy pressure from the IMF and USAID and instituted austerity measures by 1983. Of these, only the Jamaican program proved relatively durable.

For other countries, stabilization was yet more controversial and did not take place until the economic situation had further deteriorated later in the decade. In these countries, serious domestic interests opposed politically unpopular measures such as devaluation, cutting fiscal expenditure, and raising taxes. This was especially the case in countries that had new democratic governments or were in the process of a transition to democracy. African examples included Nigeria, where Shehu Shagari briefly presided over a civilian government in the early 1980s. In Latin America, Peru returned to democracy in 1980, while the military in Argentina and Brazil were trying to appeal to the populace as a prior step to return to civilian rule. Far from stabilizing, many of these governments began expansions, as did Betancur in Colombia.

An especially interesting case in this context was Chile. Between 1973 and 1981, Chile had not only implemented a successful stabilization program, which eliminated an enormous fiscal deficit and cut inflation to the low double digits, but it had also carried out the purest version of free-market policies in the Third World. Nevertheless, in the late 1970s and early 1980s, Chile ran up a large current account deficit as the exchange rate became overvalued and private-sector borrowers acquired large amounts of foreign-currency loans to finance an import binge. Believing that private-sector indulgence was not the same as similar activity by the public sector, the government refused to stabilize the former. In addition, after the economy entered into crisis in 1982, the government found itself forced to nationalize much of the country's banking sector together with the nonperforming firms that the banks had repossessed. Ultimately, at the insistence of the international banks, it was even forced to take over responsibility for the foreign debt of the financial sector. Although a standby agreement had been negotiated with the IMF in late 1982, it was quickly violated by the bank nationalization in 1983. An attempt to return to the targets was partially successful in later 1983, but political pressures led the military government to install a finance minister who ran an expansionary policy until early 1985. So, in spite of Chile's strong inclinations toward cooperation with the international system, it deviated during several crucial years. Not until early 1985 did the economy return to its earlier track.[57]

In the second half of the decade, as many governments were beginning to fall behind on debt service, those same governments came to regard stabilization as more important. Although the process was far from smooth, and some programs were more effective and consistent than others, almost all governments had at least initiated policies to restore macroeconomic balance by the end of the 1980s. The single exception was Zambia, where the Kaunda government continued in power with little authority to maintain any consistent economic strategy.

Most of the early stabilizers continued their policies, although there was some backsliding and shift of policies in certain periods (e.g., Jamaica, Costa Rica, Dominican Republic). The more common response, however, was to tighten up policies. Chile in 1985 returned to a restrictive monetary and fiscal stance after its brief bout with expansionism and backed it with an extended fund facility (EFF) agreement with the IMF.

[57] On Chile, see Barbara Stallings, "Politics and Economic Crisis: A Comparative Study of Chile, Peru, and Colombia," in Nelson, *Economic Crisis and Policy Choice.*

Colombia also changed its policy direction by 1985. In the case of Colombia, antipathy toward the IMF was such that a special shadow agreement had to be negotiated, but many argued that it was more stringent than a normal standby would have been.

In Africa, likewise, there was a trend toward orthodox stabilization. In the African cases, the IMF and World Bank played a much more important role than in Latin America, both in persuading governments to undertake the policies and even in designing them. Ghana continued and intensified its program begun in 1983. Nigeria began a program in 1985, under a new military government that had mixed success. Even Zambia, which had fitfully undertaken stabilization policies in the early 1980s, began a major push in 1985. It was abandoned in 1987, but continued pressures—especially from European governments—are likely to produce a new program.[58]

Some countries initially sought to avoid orthodoxy. In 1985–86, three Latin American countries—Argentina, Brazil, and Peru—announced so-called heterodox stabilization policies. Domestic factors both enabled them to try an alternative approach (high reserves, high state capacity necessary to design alternative policies) and gave them special need to do so (political pressures on new democracies). The characteristics of the three packages varied somewhat. Argentina's was more conservative, but all involved the use of controls to arrest price rises rather than relying on demand management, and all were unwilling or unable to sustain fiscal and monetary discipline. The common aim was to cut inflation without provoking a recession. Even after several attempts to adjust and modify the packages, all three ultimately resulted in massive failure.[59] By the end of the decade, the heterodox experiments had led to such deterioration in their economies that their leaders felt obliged to act. Argentina, Brazil, and Peru all had four-digit inflation, contracting production, and serious balance-of-payments problems. Shock programs were introduced by new leaders elected in 1989–90. As will be discussed, all three stabilization programs were combined with proposals to open the economies and reduce the role of the state. Their success, however, remains very much an open question.[60]

[58] On the African cases, see Thomas Callaghy, "Lost between State and Market: The Politics of Economic Adjustment in Ghana, Zambia, and Nigeria," in Nelson, *Economic Crisis and Policy Choice.*

[59] On the various heterodox plans, see Persio Arida, ed., *Inflación cero* (Bogotá: Oveja Negra, 1986). A direct comparison is made in José Pablo Arellano, "Comparación de los planes de estabilización de Argentina, Brasil y Perú," *Apuntes* (Lima) 20 (1987): 3–13.

[60] The most spectacularly successful case of stabilization in Latin America in this period is not among the countries being discussed here. Using an orthodox policy package, Bolivia cut inflation from 12,000 percent in 1985 to only 15 percent in 1987. On the Bolivian experience, see Juan Antonio Morales and Jeffrey Sachs, "Bolivia's Economic Crisis," in

These experiences themselves became part of the process that led to the wider adoption of orthodox policies at the end of the decade. An interesting feature to note was the speed with which the heterodox packages failed. International constraints had become so much tighter that populist policies that would probably have been sustainable in the 1970s became rapid disasters in the 1980s. The lack of international finance, including the negative effects of capital flight, imposed a discipline that would not have existed to nearly the same extent earlier.[61]

Role of International Influence

Stabilization was the policy area where domestic political and economic variables played the greatest role. In this sense, debt and stabilization were quite different. Servicing debt removed resources from the country but the process was less visible and, correspondingly, less politicized, although open opposition to debt service did exist. Stabilization, by contrast, embodied policies on government expenditure, credit, wages, and prices that were highly visible and therefore much more politically controversial. It was against these policies, then, that labor, business, and other interest groups organized strikes, protests, and behind-the-scenes pressure campaigns.

Despite the strong role for domestic variables, international influence was also significant; in terms of explaining variation in stabilization efforts between the 1970s and 1980s, it was fundamental. Negative shocks reintroduced stabilization onto the agenda in 1982 after the availability of finance had mitigated its incidence substantially for a decade. Shocks included recession in the industrial countries, high interest rates, and deteriorating terms of trade. In particular, however, there was the end to "voluntary" lending after 1982. In order to reschedule debt or get new "involuntary" loans, an agreement with the IMF was required. Debt reduction under the Brady Plan also carried an IMF agreement as a prerequisite as did rescheduling of bilateral debt through the Paris Club.

Linkage and leverage again helped to account for differences in behavior across countries. For Korea, Thailand, Mexico, and Costa Rica, the early stabilizers, little pressure was required, although financial assistance—especially in the case of Mexico—was important. Korea, Thailand, and Mexico, also among the countries that never ran up arrears,

Jeffrey Sachs, ed., *Developing Country Debt and the World Economy* (Chicago: University of Chicago Press, 1989) and Juan L. Cariaga, "Bolivia," in John Williamson, ed., *Latin American Adjustment* (Washington, D.C.: Institute for International Economics, 1990).

[61] Reasons for the decline in populism in the 1980s are discussed in Robert Kaufman and Barbara Stallings, "The Political Economy of Populism," in Rudiger Dornbusch and Sebastian Edwards, eds., *Populism in Latin America* (Chicago: University of Chicago Press, 1991).

have already been characterized as being controlled in the 1980s by co-alitions with strong internationalist links. They also had sophisticated technocratic teams with extensive foreign training and experience who strongly believed in the value of macroeconomic balance. Such a coalition and team returned to power in Mexico with the election of de la Madrid in 1982 and was reinforced by the ascent of Chun Doo Hwan in Korea in 1980; in Thailand similar forces were already in place. Costa Rica is more complex. It had not only run up arrears but also declared a moratorium on its debt service. The latter came in 1986, after a successful stabilization program from 1982 to 1984, and was instituted by a more liberal presi-dent. The moratorium was seen as a requirement for effective stabiliza-tion, however, not as a way of escaping it.[62]

In addition to the early stabilizers, there were two other countries where linkage played an important role. The delayed timing of stabili-zation in Chile and Colombia, the other two countries with clean debt records, was a consequence of domestic political processes. The period 1982–84 was an anomaly in both countries in the context of recent polit-ical-economic history. For reasons too lengthy to explain here, both had financial leaderships that pursued expansionary policies despite the gen-eral tendency in the two governments toward a more restrictive stance. These policies led to imbalances of a relative sort (high in comparison to the past but not to neighboring countries) that were used as an excuse to replace the ministers and change the policies. The IMF and World Bank helped nudge the governments in this direction, but political leaders were already inclined to move.[63]

Leverage was more extensive in other cases. Sometimes it was success-ful, other times not, depending on market conditions and linkage. The heterodox programs could be seen as a reaction against leverage. The Pe-ruvian program was based on the theory that the IMF programs had mis-understood the economy and actually made problems worse. The official international institutions had nothing to do with the Peruvian policies and strongly opposed them—although a different group of international experts played a major role in designing them. The Brazilian program was designed at home, while the IMF was more involved in the Argentine policies as reflected in their more conservative bent. Even after these countries switched to an orthodox direction, they still designed their own programs although with more collaboration with the international insti-tutions. In the small Latin American countries, pressure was successful early in the decade, but attempts to bring about followup had little im-

---

[62] On Costa Rica, see Joan Nelson, "The Politics of Adjustment in Small Democracies: Costa Rica, the Dominican Republic, and Jamaica," in Nelson, *Economic Crisis and Policy Choice*.

[63] Stallings, "Politics and Economic Crisis."

pact. Domestic politics stood firmly in the way, especially since public opinion in these countries seemed to consider that the population had sacrificed enough already.

For other countries, international influence had more lasting impact. In the Philippines, the IMF and U.S. government—once they resolved their conflicting interests with the Marcos government—intervened to force a stabilization program in 1984–85. In Colombia, the need for international finance (for investment projects rather than debt service) and the perceived inability to obtain it without a change in policy stance, led to the turnabout in 1984–85. Both the IMF and the World Bank were closely involved in the negotiations, despite the lack of a formal IMF agreement. Even in Chile, IMF pressure to abandon the expansionist measures of 1984 had an impact although many in the government wanted to move in the same direction.

As usual, it was in the African cases where foreign influence was the greatest. The World Bank, for example, had over forty missions in Ghana in 1987 alone; its policies were largely designed by outsiders. In Zambia, the Bank and Fund conducted the analysis, established the framework, and guided the negotiations for the 1985–87 orthodox push. A Zambian official described the situation as "The IMF and World Bank have become the Ministry of Finance in Zambia."[64] In Nigeria as well, close collaboration took place with the World Bank although the policy package was presented as the government's own.

STRUCTURAL ADJUSTMENT: LIBERALIZATION AND PRIVATIZATION

The most fundamental policy changes in the 1980s went beyond stabilization and debt to structural changes in economic structure and development strategy. This shift was especially apparent in the last couple of years of the decade as government after government, including those that had been elected on entirely different platforms, lined up to declare themselves advocates of export promotion, liberalization, and privatization. It is too early for proponents to declare the victory of these policies, since implementation is much more difficult than simple pronouncements, but the change in direction is greater than any time since the 1930s.

The new interest in structural reform did not come from efforts by domestic interest groups. While there were groups favoring such policies (probably strongest in Mexico), they were weak and had never had much success in advocating these policies before. Rather, a panoply of international factors constitute the prime explanation for the new emphasis. Most important, perhaps, was the negative international outlook and dim prospects for rapid movement. Access to finance was likely to depend

[64] Callaghy, "Lost between State and Market," p. 292.

increasingly on adherence to orthodox economic policies, both short and long-term. Those governments and other groups favoring heterodox preferences were put in a particular bind by the decline of the socialist countries, which had provided both development assistance and ideological support. Finally, most of the nations that were doing well economically had adopted orthodox strategies, and the self-declared heterodox ones had all ended in dismal failure. The lessons that could reasonably be drawn from these experiences were not always clear, but they were nonetheless hard to resist.

The 1970s versus 1980s

As with the other issue areas, two different timing comparisons should be examined. One is the near absence of orthodox structural reform in the 1970s as contrasted to the 1980s. Second is the change within the 1980s. Like debt policy and different from stabilization, there was a fairly clear distinction in movements toward structural change over the course of the 1980s; most occurred near the end of the decade.

The comparison across decades shows that all three types of international variables help to explain the difference. The permissive economic context in the 1970s provided no reason to change from the import-substitution industrialization strategy that most Third World governments followed. Nor was there any ideological consensus around such a shift, and thus little or no leverage was exerted in that direction. Under these circumstances, domestic groups favoring change had no special entrée to policy-making circles. Only two countries of the fifteen made any significant moves toward structural reform in the 1970s. Chile took very controversial steps to liberalize and privatize its economy in the years following the installation of a particularly brutal military government in 1973. Tariffs were lowered to a uniform 10 percent, and a large number of state enterprises were privatized. In terms of export promotion, of course, Korea also had moved toward structural change very early—in the 1960s—but it did not open its borders to imports or reduce the role of the state as Chile did.[65]

Changes within the 1980s

Within the 1980s, a similar picture emerges. There was little inclination toward structural reform in the first half of the decade, despite the sharp

[65] On the early Korean and Chilean structural reforms, see Stephan Haggard and Richard Cooper, "Policy Reform in Korea," in Robert Bates and Anne O. Kreuger, eds., *The Political Economy of Structural Adjustment* (London: Basil Blackwell, forthcoming) and Barbara Stallings and Philip Brock, "The Political Economy of Structural Reform in Chile, 1973–90," in the same volume.

deterioration in the international economic context. On the one hand, it was still not high on the agenda of international creditors. Not until the announcement of the Baker Plan in September 1985 did structural adjustment become a major focus of creditor policy. On the other hand, it was not yet clear to most Third World governments that something beyond macroeconomic stabilization might be required to deal with the new international political economy.

Since structural change threatens so many entrenched interests in society, most governments will not initiate it without an overwhelming number of factors pushing it forward. The lack of short or even medium-term finance is not sufficient. The long-term economic outlook must be perceived as extremely bleak without a major change in development strategy as well as macroeconomic policy. Strong international pressure—both financial and ideological—is also required. Only under these extreme circumstances will political leaders take the risks inherent in opting for structural change. Since these two elements emerged only over the course of the decade, extensive structural change would not have been expected until they were in place in the latter part of the 1980s. Even then, of course, the implementation process ultimately may be unsuccessful. As of the early 1990s, only a small number of cases of structural change had been implemented; the rest were still mainly declarations of intention.

Table 1.6 provides an idea of the time track of structural adjustment policies by use of World Bank adjustment lending, both macro structural

TABLE 1.6
World Bank Adjustment Loans, 1980–1989 (millions)

	1980–85	1985–89
Argentina	None	3 SECAL ($1150)
Brazil	2 SECAL ($655)	1 SECAL ($500)
Chile	None	3 SAL ($750)
Colombia	None	3 SECAL ($850)
Costa Rica	1 SECAL ($25)	2 SAL ($180)
Dom. Republic	None	None
Ghana	1 SECAL ($40)	2 SAL, 3 SECAL ($585)
Jamaica	3 SAL, 1 SECAL ($228)	3 SECAL ($90)
Korea	2 SAL ($550)	1 SECAL ($220)
Mexico	1 SECAL ($352)	8 SECAL ($3315)
Nigeria	1 SECAL ($250)	2 SECAL ($952)
Peru	None	None
Philippines	2 SAL, 1 SECAL ($652)	3 SECAL ($800)
Thailand	2 SAL ($325)	None
Zambia	None	4 SECAL ($222)

Sources: World Bank, *Report on Adjustment Lending II: Policies for the Recovery of Growth* (1990).

adjustment loans (SALs) and sectoral loans (SECALs). This indicator is not entirely satisfactory, since loan agreements can be signed with little intent to carry them out and some change certainly occurs without Bank support, but it gives a broad overview of when the main adjustment thrust took place. With very few exceptions, structural adjustment—even more than stabilization—was absent from the Third World agenda in the early 1980s. This fact is reflected in the pattern of structural adjustment loans over the decade. The majority of countries received far more adjustment credits in the 1985–89 period than in 1980–85; the overall totals for the fifteen countries were $3.1 billion (seventeen loans) in the earlier period versus $9.2 billion (thirty-eight loans) in the later one.

Within this general pattern, three groups can again be identified. First are those countries that made structural adjustments early in the decade—especially Korea and Thailand, but also Jamaica, whose new prime minister elected in 1980 favored a greater role for the private sector even if he initially resisted austerity policies. These countries received the bulk of their structural adjustment loans in the first half of the 1980s, but all three continued their efforts throughout the decade. Thus Korea accelerated the liberalization of its trade system and began a major financial reform. The latter included divestiture of the commercial banking sector and easing of restrictions on foreign banks.[66] Jamaica, after a period of acrimonious relations with its creditors, made substantial progress on tariff reform and privatization.[67] Thailand also continued some reforms, but its economic boom and renewed access to the private credit markets lowered its incentives to adjust.[68]

A second group began a move toward structural adjustment around the middle of the decade and pushed continuously, if sometimes fitfully, up to the present. In Asia, such a pattern was found in the Philippines. A relatively successful stabilization had been forced on Marcos during 1984–85, but very little if anything in terms of structural change had been undertaken. When Marcos was overthrown, his successor managed to push liberalization and privatization as anti-Marcos reforms and therefore politically progressive, despite their very different connotation elsewhere in the Third World.[69]

In Latin America, several governments, including Mexico, Chile, and

[66] On Korean stabilization and structural change in the 1980s, see Bijan B. Aghevli and Jorge Marquez-Ruarte, *A Case of Successful Adjustment: Korea's Experience during 1980–84*, IMF Occasional Paper 39 (Washington, D.C.: IMF, 1985).

[67] Nelson, "The Politics of Adjustment."

[68] Chaipat Sahasakul, Nattapong Thongpakde, and Keokam Kraisoraphong, "Thailand," in Paul Mosley, Jane Harrigan, and John Toye, eds., *Aid and Power: The World Bank and Policy-Based Lending in the 1980s* (London: Routledge, 1990).

[69] Stephan Haggard, "The Political Economy of the Philippine Debt Crisis," in Nelson, *Economic Crisis and Policy Choice.*

Costa Rica, enacted structural reforms throughout the latter half of the 1980s as a followup to earlier stabilization policies. In the case of Mexico, despite the statements of President de la Madrid from the beginning of his term in December 1982, the real decision to pursue structural reform came in 1986. The oil crisis in 1985–86 was perhaps the key factor in the change of approach. The crisis made it clear that Mexico had to diversify exports, that macroeconomic stabilization alone was insufficient to resolve the problems the country faced. The decision to join the GATT in 1986 was a turning point since even the industrialists who had torpedoed a similar proposal the previous decade no longer opposed it.[70]

For Chile, the second half of the decade saw a return and intensification of the privatization and liberalization policies of the previous decade. Some of the privatization was simply returning to the private sector the banks and firms acquired during the crisis period in 1982–83. In addition, however, new firms that had not been on the list for privatization were added as part of a political strategy to gain support for the Pinochet government and to limit the room for maneuver of a new government, whenever one might come to power. These aims dictated the particular form of privatization: selling shares in small blocks so as to increase the stake of a wide gamut of the population in protecting the right to private property.[71] In Costa Rica, too, there were some fairly serious attempts to rationalize public firms even if little outright privatization took place.[72]

In the African cases, partly because of the all-encompassing nature of the crises on that continent and partly because of the intimate role played by the IMF and World Bank, stabilization and structural change tended to be combined from the beginning rather than occurring in stages. Thus in the mid-1980s Nigeria, and especially Ghana, initiated policies designed to remove price controls, cut back on government involvement in the economy such as marketing boards, and liberalize trade. These measures were components of broad packages to deal with inflation and deficits but also to make the economies more efficient for future growth.[73]

A third group of countries did not move toward structural change (or stabilization) until the end of the decade. In fact, the ongoing efforts of the countries already mentioned paled by comparison to the rush toward privatization and liberalization after 1988. Most of this change occurred in Latin America, the bastion of closed economies and strong states in the postwar period. (It was reinforced by events in Eastern Europe, which is not covered here.) The most dramatic cases involved leaders who, either

---

[70] Robert Kaufman, "Stabilization and Adjustment in Argentina, Brazil, and Mexico," in Nelson, *Economic Crisis and Policy Choice*.

[71] Stallings, "Politics and Economic Crisis,"

[72] Nelson, "The Politics of Adjustment."

[73] Callaghy, "Lost between State and Market."

individually or through their parties, had stood for completely different policies. In Argentina, for example, Peronist president Carlos Menem not only deviated from his own electoral campaign platform but from the entire tradition of the party to announce that his government would sell off the major state enterprises (including the oil industry) and lower tariffs and other trade barriers.[74] In Venezuela, Carlos Andrés Pérez, who as president from 1974 to 1978 had been the individual most responsible for the growth of Venezuela's public sector, announced policies to privatize and liberalize after being reelected in 1988.[75]

Brazil's new president, Fernando Collor de Mello, who was inaugurated in March 1990, actually campaigned on a platform of stabilization and structural change. He tried to implement his proposals but has run into very strong opposition in the congress.[76] Peru's new direction is even more recent. Like Menem and Pérez, the new president, Alberto Fujimori, campaigned against orthodox economic measures. Indeed, his victory was due to his lack of support for such policies, which were openly advocated by his main opponent, the novelist Mario Vargas Llosa. Once in office, however, Fujimori announced a "shock program" at least as severe as Vargas Llosa had proposed. Most of it centered on stabilization, but there were also promises to lower protection and rationalize the public sector.[77]

In the case of Mexico, the election of Carlos Salinas in 1988 led to an intensification of structural change already begun by his predecessor. Salinas has sold off a number of major state firms, including the airlines, telephones, and even mineral industries such as copper. The banks taken over by López Portillo in 1982 are also being reprivatized. His trade mea-

[74] On Peronist unions' dismay about Menem's policies, see *Latin American Weekly Report* (hereafter *LAWR*), 6 July 1989, p. 1, and 20 July 1989, pp. 2–3. On the policies per se, see *LAWR*, 6 July 1989, pp. 2–3 and 28 September 1989, pp. 2–3. A review of the privatization program is found in *LAWR*, 13 September 1990, p. 9.

[75] On Carlos Andrés Pérez's initial "shock program" and the response, including riots, see *LAWR* 19 January, p. 2; 9 February 1989, p. 11; and 9 March 1989, p. 1. On the evolving structural adjustment measures, see *LAWR*, 4 May 1989, p. 10 (on tariffs); 7 September 1989, p. 9 and 12 April 1990, p. 9 (privatization); and 15 February 1990, p. 11 (foreign investment regulations).

[76] On Collor's initial proposals for stabilization and structural change, see *LAWR*, 29 March 1990, p. 2. On implementation problems, see *LAWR*, 31 May 1990, p. 11, and 5 July 1990, pp. 4–5. For an analysis of the stabilization policy, see Luiz Carlos Bresser Pereira, "Hyperinflation and Stabilization in Brazil: The First Collor Plan," in Paul Davidson and Jan Krugel, eds., *Economic Problems of the 1990s* (London: Edward Elgar, 1991).

[77] On Fujimori's campaign program, see *LAWR*, 29 March 1990, p. 9, and 19 April 1990, p. 2. It is interesting to note that his victory was seen as going against the trend toward greater privatization and liberalization in Latin America; see *LAWR*, 21 June 1990, p. 1. Fujimori's actual policies are described in *LAWR*, 23 August 1990, p. 1; 11 October 1990, pp. 10–11; and 18 July 1991, p. 10.

sures have been even more far reaching.While de la Madrid lowered tariffs, Salinas has proposed a free trade area between Mexico and the United States. A crucial goal of a free trade area would be to attract large amounts of foreign investment to modernize Mexican industry. Again, these measures go against decades of policy by the ruling party.[78]

Finally, there is a group of countries in Latin America where changes of government have occurred in the last few years and where a shift away from liberalization and privatization might have been expected. The main examples are Chile (with its return to a civilian government based on a center-left coalition) and Jamaica (where Michael Manley, who fostered a nationalist and statist program in the 1970s, was returned as prime minister). In both cases, however, the new governments have indicated that they intend to continue with the basic policies of their predecessors while trying to pay more attention to distributional issues. The new Chilean finance minister has even announced that Chile, like Mexico, is interested in establishing a free trade area with the United States.[79] Lastly, in Colombia, whose governing elite had not previously thought the country needed much structural change given its relatively successful macroeconomic performance, the new president has begun to talk about privatization and renewed emphasis on nontraditional exports.[80]

The Role of International Influence

The rush to privatization and liberalization in the 1980s, especially in the latter half of the decade, is prima facie evidence that external forces were operating. It is hard to construct an argument suggesting that domestic forces just happened to coincide in so many dissimilar countries to bring about such similar policy decisions. This is not to say that domestic political and economic variables had no role in the initial decisions, and it is most certainly not to deny that they will be crucial in the attempts to implement these policies. But the pathbreaking changes in development strategy—the turn away from inward-oriented, state-dominated import substitution industrialization toward outward-oriented, private-sector-dominated export-led growth—resulted largely from international mar-

[78] On Mexico's structural adjustment measures, which accelerated after the debt agreement was finalized, see *LAWR*, 7 September 1989, pp. 8–9; 5 October 1989, p. 9; 22 March 1990, pp. 8–9; and 17 May 1990, pp. 4–5. A summary of Mexico's privatization program is found in *LAWR*, 7 March 1991, pp. 4–5. On the free trade negotiations, see *LAWR*, 12 April 1990, pp. 4–5; 7 June 1990, p. 4; and 29 April 1991, p. 4.

[79] On the economic policies advanced by the Aylwin campaign, see *LAWR*, 5 October 1989, p. 12. On government policies, especially interest in a free trade agreement with the United States, see *LAWR*, 20 December 1990, p. 12.

[80] On the position of the current Colombian government, see *LAWR*, 6 September 1990, p. 10.

ket shifts, linkage, and leverage. The role of international ideological currents has also been extremely important.

The market shocks that occurred in the late 1970s and early 1980s have already been extensively described in earlier sections of the chapter, but one point must be added: there was a growing perception that these shocks were not temporary deviations. With the benefit of hindsight, in fact, it seemed more likely that the 1970s were the deviation and the 1980s the trend of the future. This was not an obvious conclusion in the early 1980s. Even the creditors believed that adjustment would be relatively swift.

Since the decision to change development strategy is such a fundamental one, it will never be made lightly. Certainly there was no need for such a decision in the 1970s when financial support existed for continuation of the old policies. The exceptions prove the rule. The Koreans made such a decision in the 1960s, under the threat of being cut off from U.S. aid, the major underpinning of their economy. The Chileans made a similar decision a decade later in the wake of one of the most traumatic political-economic experiences in postwar history. The success of these two cases in terms of economic growth has provided support for other countries to follow suit, but such examples were not enough without many other factors pushing in the same direction.

If international market trends were fundamental in accounting for policy changes toward the package that came to be known as "structural adjustment," they were complemented and reinforced by other international factors as well. One was greater use of leverage. While the IMF increased it role in coordinating debt service policies and promoting stabilization in the 1980s, the World Bank also increased its resources and broadened its mandate. In particular, with the announcement of the Baker Plan in 1985, the World Bank was brought into the center of activity in Third World economic policy. Baker's plan emphasized structural adjustment, and the World Bank became the lead organization for such activities through increased concentration of SALs and SECALs. The quid pro quo for these large loans was economywide or sectoral adjustment programs. The loans were the embodiment of the new ideological consensus that had been building for some time among economists and governments in the industrial countries, together with the international finance institutions. That consensus stressed the value of liberalization and privatization; the loans were a mechanism for bringing them about.[81]

Finally, linkage was increasingly effective in furthering structural adjustment in the late 1980s when compared to earlier periods. On the one

[81] The World Bank structural adjustment loans are discussed in Feinberg et al., esp. chaps. 1–2.

hand, technocrats who had long argued for more open economies and a bigger role for the private sector suddenly found increased backing from the outside. They could count on political support from the United States and other advanced industrial countries, intellectual reinforcement from the IMF and World Bank, and empirical evidence of successful performance from countries that had followed an open-economy model. On the other hand, economic and political groups in Third World countries also found a more receptive audience for their longstanding positions in favor of economic liberalism. One reason was an increase in the number of advocates. As the new economic policies were tried, especially devaluations that made Third World exports more competitive internationally, new groups of exporters emerged and joined the bandwagon for economic openness. The local groups could often turn their international connections into votes at home by promising, explicitly or implicitly, that they could deliver access to international resources to help resolve the economic crises that continued to devastate large parts of the Third World.

Conclusions

The main argument of this chapter is that international influence was crucial in explaining major economic policy changes in the Third World during the 1980s. A first step in the analysis was to use the dependency literature as a basis for identifying a set of mechanisms—markets, linkage, and leverage—whereby this influence was exerted. Then, the role of the three mechanisms was examined in the context of case studies on debt management, stabilization, and structural reform. This final section looks back across the case studies to specify the conditions under which international variables were most influential. The conditions can be categorized along four dimensions: (1) time period, (2) stage of policy-making process, (3) issue area, and (4) country characteristics.

Introduction of *time period* makes explicit the point that international influence is not constant. The tighter the economic constraints and the greater the political and ideological consensus, the greater the impact on policy-making of all three mechanisms. In the 1970s, both economic and political variables at the international level were permissive from the perspective of Third World countries. International growth rates were relatively high, and finance flowed freely. Conflict and competition among industrial countries, as well as with the socialist bloc, meant that no orthodoxy reigned and therefore none could be imposed on weaker countries. In the 1980s, by contrast, international conditions—both political and economic—turned restrictive. The world economy slowed, finance dried up, and an international ideological and organizational consensus emerged around the use of market mechanisms as the proper approach to development. When this consensus was strong with respect to a particular issue (debt in the early 1980s, structural reform in the late 1980s, stabilization throughout the decade), Third World countries faced heavy pressure to go along in order to get access to resources.

International influence also varied according to *stage of the policy process*. For the sake of simplification, the process can be divided into decision-making, policy implementation, and resultant economic outcomes. Using these categories, it can be argued that international influence was most powerful at the first and last stages. Making decisions about economic policy involves a relatively small number of people, some with much greater weight than others. Ultimately, the president and a few key advisors are the main decision makers although they must take into account to varying degrees the opinions of other groups.[82] A good deal of international influence, both financial and ideological, can be brought to bear on these decision makers through the mechanisms of linkage and leverage.

When the implementation stage arrives, by contrast, international influence is less effective (see Kahler, chapter 2 of this volume). International actors can help by providing finance to smooth both political and economic problems, and lack of finance can probably derail programs that might otherwise succeed. Even with substantial international finance, however, powerful political opposition forces can undermine policies they disagreed with in the first place. Perhaps more important, lack of state capacity can severely limit the ability to implement a program, especially one involving major structural change as opposed to less fundamental demand management policies.[83] International advisors can be hired, as many governments have done, but hiring an entire bureaucracy is not feasible.

Finally, turning to economic outcomes of the policy process, the international role appears forcefully. Changes in market conditions can make a poorly designed program successful, or they can undermine the most carefully crafted one. The effects of oil price fluctuations have been the most dramatic examples but certainly not the only ones. These outcomes,

[82] The extent to which societal groups must be taken into account depends on the amount of control the government has over the population. This, in turn, depends in part on the type of political regime. A theoretical discussion of some related questions is found in Robert Putnam, "Diplomacy and Domestic Politics: The Logic of Two-Level Games," *International Organization* 42, no. 3 (Summer 1988): 427–60.

[83] On the distinction between the type of support required for stabilization as opposed to structural change, see Joan Nelson, "Conclusions," in Nelson, *Economic Crisis and Policy Change*, pp. 358–59.

in turn, feed back and become an essential component of the next round of decisions.

Issue area is another variable as far as international influence is concerned. The three types of influence discussed here—debt service, stabilization, and structural reform—showed significant differences, both across issue areas as a whole and within issues across time. The brief look at the empirical evidence suggests the following pattern of international effects:

	Early 1980s	Late 1980s
Debt	Strong	Weak
Stabilization	Mixed	Mixed
Structural reform	Weak	Strong

The impact of international factors on debt policy in the early 1980s was strong because the creditors were united, and debtors divided, and the threat of sanctions and promise of rewards were still believed. The impact declined considerably by mid-decade as both of these factors changed. Creditors came to advocate and follow diverse approaches to the debt problem. Governments of the industrial countries also came to favor differing policies. And the links between governments, banks, and multilateral agencies loosened. At the same time, sanctions were not invoked against governments running up arrears, and there was no evidence of a return to the credit markets for model debtors, except in Asia. Thus the incentives did not encourage compliance.

On structural reform, there was little international impact in the early part of the decade because it was not yet a major concern among creditors. Debt and stabilization more than filled the agenda of the industrial countries with respect to the Third World. Only with the shift in U.S. policy as symbolized by the announcement of the Baker Plan in 1985 did structural adjustment become an important goal to be pursued in Third World negotiations. The acceleration of adjustment lending by the World Bank is concrete evidence of the new relevance of the issue after 1985. Even within the 1985–90 period, however, there was a difference. Not until the Bush election victory in November 1988 did it became clear that the emphasis on structural change would not vary substantially.

Finally the evidence regarding stabilization is mixed. Most obviously, international economic shocks, and particularly the decline in lending, set the stage for stabilization to return to a prominent place on the policy agenda in the 1980s. These shocks, in turn, increased the role of technocrats in economic policy-making; in most cases the technocrats were strong supporters of macroeconomic balance. Furthermore, the restrictive market conditions of the decade made leverage more effective. That leverage worked for some countries, especially small ones with weak state capacity, and it was not needed in others. Since stabilization policies have been the most politicized of the three issue areas until now, it is here that the role of domestic variables has been strongest.

Country characteristics constitute a final set of variables that helps to mediate the impact of international influence. A number of domestic characteristics coming out of the first volume of this project—government ideology, regime type, interest group organization and mobilization, and state capacity—result in groups of countries that responded differentially to the three types of international influence. As a consequence, these groups tended to cluster together in the earlier discussions of debt, stabilization, and structural change.

A first group of countries are those for which international leverage was least important while market shocks and international linkage were crucial. They included Korea, Thailand, Chile, Mexico, and perhaps Colombia. In these countries, the governments and important private-sector elites decided early that their interests lay with international economic integration and a strong private sector. They had enough technical expertise to devise policies to follow up on those interests. They also had the political capacity, through various forms of authoritarian governing structures, to implement their chosen policies. While international financial support was useful, especially for Mexico and Chile, trade was at least as important as a means for obtaining foreign exchange. In this situation, access to markets, high levels of demand, and favorable prices became central. For this group of countries, changes in their economic policy stance were overdetermined: both domestic and international variables pushed in the same direction.

In a second group of countries, extremely different from the one just described, international leverage was most prevalent—although not always successful in its aim. They include the African and the less-developed Latin American nations of Ghana, Nigeria, Zambia, Jamaica, Dominican Republic, Peru, and perhaps Costa Rica. In these countries, despite often highly centralized authority through a mix of military governments and authoritarian civilian ones, the technical capacity of the state was so low that international assistance was required to gather statistical information, devise economic policies, and even staff ministries at times. This meant that international actors had great sway in shaping the general direction of economic policy as well as technical details.

Whether these policies were actually implemented, however, depended on the opposition that could be mounted to unpopular policies. In Ghana under Rawlings, opposition was nil; in Jamaica under Seaga, it was also weak. In Nigeria, the Dominican Republic, and especially Zambia, the opposition forces have been more effective in countering government policy although not in proposing effective alternatives. In Peru, by contrast, opposition to the semiorthodox policies followed by the Belaúnde government led to a very different administration under Alan García, which actually instituted a set of heterodox policies, also devised by foreign experts but of a different persuasion than those in most of the international agencies.

A final group of countries consists of three—Brazil, Argentina, and the Philippines—that were and are always on the brink of self-sustaining growth but have yet to make it. They have the technical capacity to match the Koreans and Mexicans, but, as Haggard and Kaufman suggest, this technical capacity has been undermined by weak political institutions and highly personalistic political leadership. During the 1980s, all three underwent a transformation of political structure from authoritarianism to democracy. They have been more vulnerable to international pressure than the other strong state group because of their failure to fully develop their economies. But they can also resist, so policy tends to swing. Most recently, all have faced their vulnerability vis-à-vis the international economy and decided to turn outward rather than inward. Nonetheless, the ability to implement the policies advocated by the current leaders, each of whom is in a precarious position, remains to be demonstrated.

To conclude by returning to the point where this analysis began, in trying to evaluate the effect of international variables, it is important not to miss the overall picture for the details. It is also important to take a broad view of the nature of international influence. The latter is not limited to IMF and World Bank conditionality, the focus of Miles Kahler's chapter in this book. Indeed that kind of leverage may be less relevant than market shocks and linkage between domestic actors and international forces. Furthermore, we need to take a broad view of when international influence has been significant. Kahler uses the strict implementation of IMF or World Bank conditions as his measure, but even very imperfect implementation can create a new dynamic in a country. For example, a stabilization program may not achieve its targets, but if it reduces economic imbalances somewhat and raises consciousness about their relevance, then it cannot simply be written off as one more failure. Likewise, if a program of privatization is introduced but not completely achieved, it still helps bring about a different policy approach. It is this change in dynamic that seems tremendously significant when the 1970s and 1980s are compared—regardless of whether one considers the changes to be positive or negative. The shift is undoubtedly more striking in the Latin American (and Eastern European) context than elsewhere, but it is not limited to those regions. The international environment the Third World had to confront, and the pressures it faced from international actors, played a crucial role in the transformation.

CHAPTER TWO

External Influence, Conditionality, and the Politics of Adjustment

Miles Kahler

THE ARRAY of policy changes that nations undertake to deal with external imbalances has long been of interest to other countries, to the international institutions that represent them, and to private creditors. The bargains struck between these outside agencies—private creditors, national governments, international financial institutions (IFIs)—and national governments have been collectively labeled conditionality. Superficially, conditionality takes a straightforward form: an exchange of policy changes for external financing, whether debt rescheduling or relief, multilateral credits, bilateral loans, or grants.

Given the domestic political costs associated with many of the policy changes demanded, conditionality has been a persistent source of conflict between external creditors and national governments since large scale international financial flows began in the nineteenth century.[1] In earlier periods, such as the interwar years, policy change and external finance were not explicitly linked in conditionality bargains. The missions of Edward Kemmerer in Latin America during the 1920s were advisory and private, despite encouragement by the United States government. Nevertheless, Latin American elites at the time were aware of the underlying exchange: a seal of approval from the "money doctor" meant a much greater likelihood of increased private capital inflows.[2]

Following World War II, the exchange of policy changes for the use of International Monetary Fund (IMF) resources was made explicit at United States insistence, and the concept of conditionality associated

Some portions of this paper have appeared previously in "International Actors and the Politics of Adjustment," in Joan Nelson, ed., *The Fragile Politics of Adjustment* (Washington, D.C.: Overseas Development Council, 1989). The author thanks Jeffry Frieden, John McMillan, John Toye, Clay Moltz, and the other authors in this volume for helpful advice and comments and Denise Norton and Stephen Saideman for their research assistance.

[1] For example, Albert Fishlow, "Conditionality and Willingness to Pay: Some Parallels from the 1890s," in Barry Eichengreen and Peter Lindert, eds., *The International Debt Crisis in Historical Perspective* (Cambridge, Mass.: The MIT Press, 1990).

[2] Paul Drake, *The Money Doctor in the Andes: The Kemmerer Missions, 1923–1933* (Durham, N.C.: Duke University Press, 1989), p. 17.

with IMF standbys was introduced and refined.[3] By the end of the 1950s, the content and principle of conditionality was stirring debate and opposition among the developing countries, a critical stance that has persisted. In the 1980s, that opposition has increased with the scale of the adjustment demanded of many developing countries, particularly the highly indebted ones. At the same time, the notion of conditionality has been formally incorporated into the amendments to the Articles of Agreement of the IMF, and de facto conditionality has become a feature not only of a share of World Bank lending, but of bilateral aid programs as well.[4]

The interests of members in this creditor coalition, often portrayed as converging in the 1980s, do not coincide precisely. For commercial banks and other private creditors, intervention in the politics of adjustment is driven by a desire for repayment, which requires oversight of core economic policies central to any government's economic strategy and political standing. National governments are also creditors and have developed intergovernmental institutions such as the Paris Club to coordinate their rescheduling negotiations. Their economic interests as creditors, however, are often subordinated to foreign policy goals; their behavior cannot be modeled as simply as private creditors.

These mixed national goals are reflected in turn in the actions of IFIs, in particular the IMF and the World Bank. Their aims in policy oversight are broader than those of the other actors. Repayment drives them in part: the IMF needs to ensure the revolving nature of its resources, available to all of its members; the World Bank, dependent on its standing in the private credit markets, must also be attentive to arrears in repayment. Both organizations also have strong interests in lending as well, which complicates their bargaining stance. More important, however, are the policy goals delegated to these institutions by their most powerful members. For the IMF, those tasks include surveillance of exchange rate policies (and by extension, macroeconomic policies) and ensuring that national adjustment policies do not conflict

---

[3] Conditionality had not been part of the original Bretton Woods agreement; for its early history, see Sidney Dell, *On Being Grandmotherly: The Evolution of IMF Conditionality* (Princeton, N.J.: Princeton University, International Finance Section, Princeton Studies in International Finance, 1981), p. 4–7.

[4] The literature on conditionality is vast. A particularly useful brief review of Fund practice is Andrew Crockett, "Issues in the Use of Fund Resources," *Finance and Development*, June 1982: 10–15; for recent restatements, Constantine Michalopoulos, "World Bank Programs for Adjustment and Growth," and Manuel Guitian, "Adjustment and Economic Growth: Their Fundamental Complementarity," in Vittorio Corbo et al., *Growth-Oriented Adjustment Programs* (Washington, D.C.: IMF/World Bank, 1987), pp. 15–94.

with the broader purposes of the organization. The Bank has developed policy-based lending in the form of structural adjustment loans (SALs) and sectoral adjustment loans (SECALs) to ensure a stable macroeconomic environment for its traditional project lending, directed toward poverty alleviation and infrastructure development. In addition, both the IMF and the World Bank were tied in the 1980s to a debt strategy that directed their lending toward ensuring repayment of private creditors.

The conditionality bargain—external financial assistance for economic policy change—has been criticized, not only for the content of the policies recommended, but also, from differing perspectives, for its lack of efficacy. As the record I review demonstrates, the ability of conditional financing to produce reliably either positive economic outcomes or policy change has been challenged by critics in the developing countries as well as academic investigators. Despite these criticisms and doubts, however, the use of conditional financing as a policy instrument is likely to grow. Already a new form of joint conditionality linking the IMF and the World Bank has appeared in Policy Framework Papers that are required of those low-income countries participating in the Structural Adjustment and Enhanced Structural Adjustment Facilities. The latest phase of the debt crisis, emphasizing debt reduction, might argue for a future of less severe adjustment for indebted countries as their debt burdens decline. All proposals for debt reduction, however, even those more radical than the Brady Plan, envisage continuing oversight of debtor economic policies to ensure that the remaining debt is serviced.[5] Although considerable attention is given in these proposals to the gains and losses of different players in debt reduction scenarios, no suggestions are offered for improving the efficacy and efficiency of conditionality.

More sweeping in their implications are the end of the Cold War and the changes that are rapidly reshaping the political landscape of Eastern Europe and the Soviet Union. United States support for a lead role on the part of the IMF and the World Bank (as a means of leveraging limited American financial resources) suggests that conditionality in one form or

[5] Benjamin J. Cohen, for example, suggests that "creditors would be permitted to withdraw all concessions on such matters as interest rates if IDRA [International Debt Restructuring Agency] determined that a debtor was not complying with its policy commitments." (*Developing Country Debt: A Middle Way* [Princeton, N.J.: Princeton University International Finance Section, 1989], p. 34.) Jeffrey Sachs argues in his proposal that "participation will require adherence to the strict conditionality of the IMF and World Bank." (*New Approaches to the Latin American Debt Crisis* [Princeton, N.J.: Princeton University, International Finance Section, Princeton Studies in International Finance, 1989], p. 37.)

another will feature in the financing arrangements that are made to further economic reforms in the region. Eastern Europe will test assumptions that conventional forms of conditionality will work effectively during rapid political change, in a region where economic reforms and creditworthiness have not been closely related in the past.

Finally, in an international system in which military threats may prove less and less useful as a means for influencing the behavior of other states, the effectiveness of conditionality offers a measure of one instrument of financial power. The European Community, awarded a lead role in organizing Western assistance to Eastern Europe, is a purely economic entity; Japan, whose considerable military power is constrained domestically and internationally, could wield enormous financial influence.[6] Conditionality offers one window for estimating the range of financial or economic influence that may be exerted internationally during the next decade.

CONDITIONALITY AS INFLUENCE

Conditionality is unlikely to fade as an issue in international policy; it can be used to deepen understanding of strategies of international influence, a subject of central importance to international relations. Much of the attention devoted to such strategies has come from specialists in security relations and has dealt with coercive bargaining and deterrence theory. Alexander George and Richard Smoke recently restated criticisms of classical deterrence theory that they first made over fifteen years ago, arguing against its single-minded emphasis on the use of threats (particularly military threats) to change an adversary's behavior. Instead they argue for embedding deterrence in a broader theory of international influence, one that "encompasses the utility of positive inducements as well as, or in lieu of, threats of negative sanctions." Deterrence in this view "must be viewed as only one of a number of different instruments of foreign policy."[7]

"Third wave" critics of classical deterrence theory have followed

---

[6] An advisory panel to the Japanese Ministry of Finance recently recommended that Japan's large trade surpluses be maintained and used to spur growth in the developing countries. Press reports note the implications for the content of conditionality, supplanting American emphasis on a reduced government role with a model more congenial to government-business collaboration. ("Tokyo Panel Asks Wider Japan Help to Poorer Nations," *New York Times*, 4 June 1990, sec. A1, col. 4.)

[7] Alexander L. George and Richard Smoke, "Deterrence and Foreign Policy," *World Politics* 41, no. 2 (January 1989): 182, 181. The argument was originally made in *Deterrence in American Foreign Policy* (New York: Columbia University Press, 1974), p. 605.

George and Smoke in emphasizing the importance of offering inducements to adversaries in an effort to avoid a conflict spiral that leaves both
sides worse off than before their bargaining began.[8] Although contentious
methodological debate continues to surround deterrence theory, firm
conclusions regarding the appropriate mix and sequencing of sanctions
and inducements have not yet been drawn. Robert Jervis recently
summed up the unsatisfactory state of the argument: "Threats and con-
ciliation generally need to be combined, but their optimal mixture and
timing is extremely difficult, in part because it depends on the adversary's
goals and perceptions, which are hard for the state to discern."[9]

Investigations of the conditions for international cooperation have
provided a second set of contributions to a broader theory of international influence. Robert Axelrod's treatment of the iterated Prisoner's Dilemma game suggests that a strategy of reciprocity, and, more specifically,
Tit-for-Tat, is a robust means for achieving and maintaining cooperative
outcomes under certain conditions.[10] Such a strategy begins with an
opening cooperative move and then simply imitates the other player's
moves. Others have argued the utility of such a strategy even in situations
whose underlying structure is not clearly a Prisoner's Dilemma game.[11]
The appropriate mix and sequencing of accommodating and sanctioning
moves in a broader strategy of reciprocity, however, remains indetermi-
nate. Axelrod argues that "the precise level of forgiveness that is optimal
depends on the environment."[12] Lack of attention to contextual issues
can result, for example, in an undesirable spiraling or extension of conflict.[13]

The construction of a theory of influence that bridges issue areas in
international relations and a theory of statecraft that offers more carefully specified counsel on appropriate strategies to ensure cooperative
outcomes still lies in the future.[14] By embedding conditionality—defined

[8] The typology of "waves" in deterrence theory is developed by Robert Jervis, "Deterrence Theory Revisited," *World Politics* 31, no. 2 (January 1979): 289–324.

[9] Robert Jervis, "Rational Deterrence: Theory and Evidence," *World Politics* 41, no. 2
(January 1989): 198.

[10] Robert Axelrod, *The Evolution of Cooperation* (New York: Basic Books, 1984).

[11] Kenneth A. Oye, "Explaining Cooperation under Anarchy: Hypotheses and Strategies," *World Politics* 38, no. 1 (October 1985): 14–15.

[12] Axelrod, *Evolution*, p. 120.

[13] Robert Axelrod and Robert O. Keohane, "Achieving Cooperation under Anarchy:
Strategies and Institutions," *World Politics* 38, no. 1 (October 1985): 245.

[14] David Baldwin's critique of conventional approaches to economic statecraft is a partial
exception, but Baldwin continues to emphasize the threat/punishment instruments of economic statecraft rather than the promise/reward dimensions of economic bargaining. David
Baldwin, *Economic Statecraft* (Princeton: Princeton University Press, 1985). For a review

as a promise of financial support in exchange for specified policy changes—in a larger class of external strategies to influence state policy, its practice, and outcomes may contribute to this enterprise. Framing conditionality in this way permits its often arcane technical vocabulary (performance criteria, prior conditions) and specific conventions to be situated in a larger class of international phenomena. Conditionality, however, needs to be disaggregated and examined in light of several contrasting approaches to the exercise of international influence. In the discussion that follows, the influence of external agencies—primarily the international financial institutions (the World Bank and the IMF)—will be considered in two contrasting ways. The first theoretical approach, drawn from treatments of international borrowing that use dynamic contract theory, treats credit relationships as repeated bargaining games. The second approach, developed primarily as an explanation for international cooperation and the evolution of international institutions, is the theory of social learning and consensual knowledge.

Each of these models of external influence over policy choice emphasizes a different facet of the relationship between IFIs and national governments. The bargaining model centers on the core exchange of financial support for policy change, rewarding compliance with continued finance in the next round, punishing slippage with suspension of that support. The social learning model focuses not on the leverage that finance provides over national behavior but on the tacit and explicit alliances across the negotiating table that are created by policy dialogue, technical assistance, and other avenues of influence in the policy process.

These models of external influence are too simplified in their treatment of the strategies of external actors, the coordination problems of those actors, and, above all, the domestic politics of adjustment that interact with external influence attempts. Incorporating these political dimensions serves to strengthen and refine the models. In addition to testing their explanatory power, revised versions of these models may also offer prescriptions for improving the record of collaboration between external actors and developing country governments.

The need for such prescriptions stems from the widely held view that conditionality (and related efforts to influence economic policy choice) are failures. Before reexamining conditionality outcomes in the light of these two models, it is worth reviewing aggregate and case studies that have evaluated the record of external policy intervention by the IFIs.

---

of recent treatments of economic sanctions, see Stefanie Ann Lenway, "Between war and commerce: economic sanctions as a tool of economic statecraft," *International Organization* 42, no. 2 (Spring 1988): 397–426.

DOES CONDITIONALITY WORK?

Most existing studies of IMF and World Bank conditionality are less interested in the issue of influence over policy change than the effects of conditionality and IFI programs on economic outcomes: growth, current account deficits, and inflation. Such studies are designed to confront the often heated debate over the economic consequences of external advice and policy prescriptions without closely scrutinizing intervening variables.

Early efforts at measuring the effects of Fund or Bank conditionality (and many popular and journalistic efforts today) make simple before and after comparisons: Did economic performance improve by some measure after acceptance of a Fund standby or a World Bank structural adjustment loan? As John Williamson has pointed out, this standard is clearly biased against the international financial institutions, since it assumes that the prior economic trajectory could be sustained in the absence of policy changes urged by the external agencies.[15]

To deal with the weaknesses of the before-and-after approach, at least three other designs have been used to determine the effects of Fund programs: a comparison of economic performance in countries with Fund programs and a control group of nonprogram countries; comparison of actual performance in a Fund program and the program's targets; and a comparison of simulations using "IMF policies" and other sets of policies.[16] Mohsin Khan's summary of these results suggests modest economic effects at best: greatest on the balance of payments and the current account, negligible on the rate of inflation, and uncertain on the growth rate. Distributional effects have been examined less frequently than other economic outcomes: Manuel Pastor's analysis of Fund programs in Latin America, however, points to significant declines in the labor share of national income under IMF conditionality.[17]

As Khan notes, even the most sophisticated of these studies omit "the

---

[15] John Williamson, "On Judging the Success of IMF Policy Advice," in John Williamson, ed., *IMF Conditionality* (Washington, D.C.: Institute for International Economics, 1983), p. 132.

[16] For an excellent account of these approaches and a summary of recent studies of the effects of Fund conditionality, see Mohsin S. Khan, "The Macroeconomic Effects of Fund-Supported Adjustment Programs: An Empirical Assessment," IMF Working Paper (23 December 1988), p. 3.

[17] Ibid., p. 13. Khan does argue, on the basis of additional modified control-group studies that lengthening the period of evaluation strengthens the positive effects of Fund programs and that programs have had markedly more effect on the external balance in the 1980s than in the 1970s (p. 26). Manuel Pastor, Jr., *The International Monetary Fund and Latin America* (Boulder, Colo.: Westview Press, 1987), pp. 88–89.

degree of implementation of the policies agreed to between the Fund and the country." In other words, "Fund countries" (or "Bank countries") are considered a homogeneous group, even though the degree of actual policy change varies widely. This bias in the sample could be interpreted as likely to improve the record of implemented Fund programs. There is, of course, a prior question that he sidesteps: the degree of implementation itself may be a legitimate measure of Fund success. It is that record that is of greatest interest here, since it permits measurement of the degree of external influence over policy change during adjustment. Following Williamson, the best measure of influence is the degree to which external actors change the trajectory of national policy from what it would have been in the absence of their intervention.

One can argue that the ultimate influence of the IFIs and other external actors over economic outcomes extends beyond their ability to influence the economic policy trajectory of a country. Goldstein and Montiel note two other effects: a program supported by the IMF or World Bank may increase the overall level of confidence in the country's economy, affecting capital inflows in particular. An economic program supported by external agencies might also increase the effectiveness of any given policy change by altering the expectations of agents in the economy.[18] Although it is possible that simply negotiating a program with international lending agencies would produce these supplementary effects, they are probably dependent on changed government behavior as well: external and internal economic actors will assess a government's actions rather than its rhetoric.

Studies of the effects of conditionality that undertake to examine the first, and most political, question of whether policy trajectories change under external influence point to a record of mixed implementation, at best. Reviews of program implementation before 1982, when financial constraints on developing countries tightened and IFI bargaining power increased, suggest that conditionality had a weak impact. Tony Killick's review of IMF programs, based on IMF program data and case studies, suggests that "the Fund has experienced considerable difficulty in ensuring that its programmes are implemented." As Killick notes, the IMF itself has assigned a large measure of the failure to implement to "political constraints" and "weak administrative systems."[19] Stephan Haggard's study

---

[18] Morris Goldstein and Peter Montiel, "Evaluating Fund Stabilization Programs with Multicountry Data: Some Methodological Pitfalls," IMF Staff Papers 33, no. 2 (June 1986): 310.

[19] Tony Killick et al., The Quest for Economic Stabilization (London: Heinemann, 1984), pp. 251–55, 260–61. Killick goes on to question the association of observance of perfor-

of Extended Fund Facility agreements with the IMF also remarks on a dismal record of implementation: of the thirty cases studied, twenty-four were not implemented in their original form and sixteen of these were cancelled.[20] In a study of African adjustment programs supported by the IMF in 1980–81, the record in reducing the fiscal deficit and restraining growth of net domestic credit was poor: most countries failed to achieve their fiscal target; only about half reached their credit objectives.[21]

The change to tougher international economic conditions and shrinking sources of alternative finance in the 1980s did not at first change the record dramatically. The first World Bank study of SALs and SECALs in fifteen developing countries showed an overall compliance rate of about sixty percent (with full implementation of conditions as the criterion for success); over eighty percent if "substantial progress" on conditions is employed. One pattern that clearly emerges in the World Bank study is variation across policy areas: manipulation of prices meets with greater success and those areas that are not politically sensitive and do not require institution-building also display higher compliance.[22] A second World Bank evaluation of policy-based lending indicates a much more positive record of implementation, and most significantly, an increase in implementation rates during the 1980s, "both for countries that had adjustment lending since the early 1980s and for countries that started more recently."[23]

Two recent collaborative research efforts have analyzed the issue of change in policy trajectory and subsequent patterns of implementation through fine-grained case studies of IMF and World Bank involvement in the politics of adjustment. Each of these projects uses a somewhat less precise means of evaluating IFI influence; necessarily so in the case of IMF programs, since the Fund does not publish data on country implementation of its programs. Neither finds evidence of significantly higher IFI in-

---

mance criteria with overall implementation of programs, and observance of performance criteria with improvement in economic indicators (such as the balance of payments).

[20] Stephan Haggard, "The Politics of Adjustment: Lessons from the IMF's Extended Fund Facility," in Miles Kahler, ed., *The Politics of International Debt* (Ithaca, N.Y.: Cornell University Press, 1986), pp. 157–86.

[21] Justin B. Zulu and Saleh M. Nsouli, *Adjustment Programs in Africa: The Recent Experience* (Washington, D.C.: International Monetary Fund, 1985), p. 13. It is worth noting that the period examined by Zulu and Nsouli was one of very loose conditionality by comparison to the pattern after 1981. Also, these measures of compliance were not wholly under the government's control.

[22] *Adjustment Lending: An Evaluation of Ten Years of Experience* (Washington, D.C.: The World Bank, 1988), pp. 60–61.

[23] *Report on Adjustment Lending II: Policies for the Recovery of Growth* (Washington, D.C.: World Bank, March 1990), p. 6.

fluence through conditionality than the studies just mentioned. The first of these projects, centered on the politics of both stabilization and broader economic policy change in developing countries, has attempted to estimate the independent effects of external agencies on government decisions to undertake such programs (both IMF and World Bank) and on government implementation of those programs. The study divided programs between those that stopped at stabilization measures and those that carried out a broader program of policy change, whether orthodox or heterodox.[24]

In general, significant influence by external agencies on decisions to undertake stabilization programs (uniformly of an orthodox variety) was limited to a small number of governments in the sample, those delicately balanced or deeply divided cases in which external agencies did seem to tilt decisions on economic program in favor of stabilization. The Philippines under Marcos in late 1984, the Dominican Republic under Jorge Blanco, also in 1984, and Zambia under Kaunda in 1985 were divided regimes, and for them the Bretton Woods institutions represented lenders of last resort. In Ghana in 1982–83, after years of economic disaster, the need for external finance reinforced the arguments of a coherent economic team that initiated and then broadened an orthodox stabilization and adjustment program.[25] Even in these cases, in which the external agencies were able to forge a temporary alliance with only one part of the government, subsequent implementation was decidedly mixed. In implementing both stabilization and neo-orthodox structural adjustment programs, the IMF and the World Bank were deeply involved, and their impact was highest in the case of smaller countries and those with limited state capabilities, where the technocratic team was stretched to the limit. Ghana, Jamaica, and Zambia were clear examples of such intervention in implementation. Overall, however, any connection between deeper involvement by external agencies and success in implementation is difficult to discern in this sample of country cases.

A second study of World Bank policy-based lending is confined to a smaller number of country cases (nine), but its narrower focus on one IFI permits a more precise estimation of the influence of conditionality on policy change.[26] The compliance estimates made by those completing

[24] Joan Nelson, ed., *Economic Crisis and Policy Choice: The Politics of Adjustment in Developing Countries* (Princeton, N.J.: Princeton University Press, 1990). This collaborative effort covers the experience of thirteen developing countries (nineteen governments); results are summarized in appendix table A2.1.

[25] For a summary, ibid., p. 330; on the Ghana case, Thomas Callaghy, "Lost between State and Market," ibid., pp. 274–75.

[26] Paul Mosley, Jane Harrigan, and John Toye, *Aid and Power: The World Bank and Policy-based Lending* (London: Routledge, 1991).

country cases studies are somewhat lower on average than the World Bank figures cited above (about 54 percent), with a wide dispersion about this mean score.[27]

This survey suggests that external agencies overall have had limited influence on decisions for and successful implementation of stabilization and structural adjustment programs. The studies cited, while demonstrating the importance of heightened financial constraints in particular cases, do not demonstrate a consistent pattern of greater influence in the 1980s. A study of Latin American programs that extends to 1984 argues that the power of the Bretton Woods institutions has been inflated:

> To describe the IMF as a 'poverty broker,' as does the title of a recent book, or to charge the Fund with undermining democracy is to engage in hyperbole. The power of the IMF remains a useful myth for governments seeking a scapegoat to explain difficult economic conditions associated with severe balance-of-payments disequilibria, but the ability of the IMF to impose programs from the outside is distinctly limited.[28]

Two peculiarities in the samples employed by the IFIs and by outside researchers may reduce this estimate of influence even further. Defenders of IMF or World Bank conditionality often argue that simple before-and-after comparisons do not take into account the adverse selection represented in the sample of countries turning to the Fund or the Bank: their economic plight is far worse than most developing countries. Two other clusters of countries may more than countervail this bias in the sample. The political explosions that often surround the entry of the IMF or the World Bank into the adjustment process may convince countries not to come to the IFIs because of the political consequences: Brazil and Venezuela fell into that category during much of the 1980s. An interesting counterfactual is raised: Would countries that have broken with the IFIs have pursued economic policies that produced better outcomes with access to external economic policy advice and, most important, the finance that could be mobilized by the IFIs? A second group of countries, which I will consider more fully, raises the obverse issue of selection: they seemed to undertake their change of economic course in advance of any intervention by the IMF or the World Bank, although, in some cases, financial support may have been significant in sustaining their policy changes.

This record of limited external influence leads to the question that is central to the rest of this chapter: Why, in a decade when the role of the

---

[27] Ibid., vol. 1, p. 136.

[28] Karen Remmer, "The politics of economic stabilization: IMF standby programs in Latin America," *Comparative Politics*, October 1986, p. 21.

IFIs has been so prominent and the alternative sources of finance so slender, has their ability to influence government policies not been greater? The proximate answer to this question is simply the existence of powerful sources of conflict between the policy strictures of the external actors and the political interests of many developing country governments. That political conflict can erupt along at least three dimensions. First, conflict may center on the *content* of the programs and even the model of how the economy works. A second and more significant source of political conflict has been *nationalist resentment* at the intervention that is implied by conditionality. Governments will seek to preserve their policymaking autonomy against external directives; the appearance of subordination to such directives may lower their legitimacy and therefore their ability to implement chosen policies. Finally, conditionality and the policy changes it entails will affect the economic interests and political standing of groups inside and outside government in different ways. One prediction is certain: some will perceive themselves as losers in the adjustment process and will react to that threat of loss. Government employees resist layoffs and pay freezes; politicians oppose the dismantling of state enterprises that provide them with patronage; import-competing industries argue against trade liberalization. If these changes are coupled with economic stagnation, then the list of losers will grow longer.[29] Even if a political elite sees its policies as aligned with those of the external actors, the political costs of conditionality may induce resistance to agreement and a collapse of implementation.

These dimensions of political conflict surrounding conditionality and adjustment can pull governments toward a failure to undertake negotiations with the IFIs and noncompliance with agreements reached. Nevertheless, the prevalence of these features of the political landscape and the wide dispersion of performance over national cases raises the possibility that the influence strategies and their failure to take into account the politics of adjustment may explain the pattern of influence outlined above.

In evaluating the strategies of external actors and explanations for their success and failure, the array of cases examined will be those employed in the studies of Nelson and Mosley et al. (see appendix tables A2.1 and A2.2 for a summary of those cases). To avoid a possible sample bias toward "problem" cases, in which the adjustment experience involved considerable conflict with external agencies and a mixed record, at best, in

---

[29] For a more systematic treatment of political institutions and economic interests in the politics of adjustment, see Stephan Haggard and Robert Kaufman, "The Politics of Stabilization and Adjustment," in Jeffrey D. Sachs, ed., *Developing Country Debt and Economic Performance* (Chicago: University of Chicago Press, 1989), pp. 209–54.

implementing policy changes, an additional case, Indonesia, is included as well, although without the detail of the other country cases. Although this rough-and-ready assembling of cases leaves much to be desired in terms of sampling, the shortage of fine-grained data on the relations between external actors and national governments during adjustment makes this the only feasible, albeit second-best, strategy.

The Bargaining Model and Conditionality

Official rhetoric at the Fund and the Bank often emphasizes that relations with borrowing governments are apolitical, consensual, and noninterventionist. Programs are designed by governments to meet their own needs; if they also meet the criteria of the Fund and the Bank, then they will be supported financially. In the words of one experienced World Bank staff member, "the word *leverage* does not occur in the Bank's lexicon":

> The Bank's policy assistance has been essentially a cooperative venture with the recipient countries. Successful country programs must be homegrown and cannot be standardized or externally imposed; they should be designed and perceived as central to the countries' own interests. The Bank plays a supplemental role, backing up and helping to implement sound policy initiatives.[30]

Despite this official distaste for the notion that IFI financial support is a lever that can be used to enforce policy changes, such a model of IFI intervention in adjustment captures at least part of the influence strategy of external actors. Casting IFI strategies in this way also situates them in a rich literature on bargaining that has evolved to explain the behavior of private financial institutions and markets.

Dynamic contract theory has been used by economists to deal with the poor fit between the conventional model of borrowing and the pattern of syndicated bank lending (and rescheduling) in the 1970s and 1980s. Financial markets in these models are not perfectly competitive: a small number of lenders and borrowers elicits strategic behavior. The core problem that is addressed is the difficulty in enforcing contracts between lenders (in most examples, banks or consortia of banks) and borrowers who are sovereign states. Enforcement through explicit contracts is difficult, costly, or impossible in these circumstances; sanctions (such as attachment of assets) are uncertain or puny in comparison to the risks (and gains) of default. These models therefore assume implicit contracts of two sorts—internal and external. The effective threat that enforces an internal

---

[30] Barend A. de Vries, *Remaking the World Bank* (Washington, D.C.: Seven Locks Press, 1987), pp. 64, 66.

implicit contract is the threat of ending the lending-borrowing relation-ship, or, in Crawford's words, "continuation of the relationship must have value for both parties relative to their next-best alternative." An ex-ternal implicit contract is enforced in part by the anticipated response of those outside the parties immediately bargaining and contracting. Cross-conditionality, in which lending by one set of creditors (such as commer-cial banks or a bilateral aid donor) is made dependent on the lending decisions of another (such as the IMF) is one example of an effort to cre-ate such an external implicit contract. A final assumption that is central in many dynamic contract models are asymmetries of information: one party or both possess private information that shapes the bargaining out-come.[31]

The immediate application of these austere models to the IFIs (or gov-ernmental actors) is rendered difficult by the more complex goals of these actors as compared to commercial banks: simple repayment, as noted, does not capture the continuing interest that they have in developing country policy trajectories. These differences between the IFIs and the commercial banks are based in their internal organization. The behavior of the IFIs (or aid agencies) is not profit-seeking, rather it satisfies the goals of their principals, particularly the largest industrial states, who have both economic and strategic interests in particular developing coun-tries. The developing countries themselves sit on both sides of the bar-gaining table: they are (in a small way) shareholders and principals in the IFIs as well as being their clients. In addition, the internal organizational incentives of the IFIs point them toward renewal of lending: careers are made in managing programs successfully and "moving loans," not, by and large, in standing aside, even from developing countries with poor reputations. In the World Bank, continued lending is necessary to main-tain its profitability and the solvency of its borrowers; the inhibitions within the organization to saying "no" are therefore high.

[31] An excellent summary is given by Vincent P. Crawford in *International Lending, Long-Term Credit Relationships, and Dynamic Contract Theory* (Princeton, N.J.: Princeton Uni-versity, International Finance Section, Princeton Studies in International Finance, March 1987). Also Crawford, "Dynamic Games and Dynamic Contract Theory," *Journal of Con-flict Resolution*, 29, 2, June 1985, 195–224; early treatments can be found in Jonathan Eaton and Mark Gersovitz, *Poor-Country Borrowing in Private Financial Markets and the Repudiation Issue* (Princeton, N.J.: Princeton University, International Finance Section, Princeton Studies in International Finance, June 1981) and Jeffrey Sachs, *Theoretical Issues in International Borrowing* (Princeton, N.J.: Princeton University, International Finance Section, Princeton Studies in International Finance, 1984). Also, Kenneth M. Kletzer, "Asymmetries of Information and LDC Borrowing with Sovereign Risk," *The Economic Journal* 94 (June 1984): 287–307. The emphasis on the reputational basis for lending has recently been challenged by Jeremy Bulow and Kenneth Rogoff, "A Constant Recontracting Model of Sovereign Debt," *Journal of Political Economy* 1989: 97, 1, 155–78.

All of these qualifications suggest that the IFIs' preferences and bargaining behavior will point to a higher cost assessment of terminating a lending relationship, a greater unwillingness to punish a defector, than the conventional view would predict. Nevertheless, a bargaining model of creditor-developing country relationships that draws on the insights of dynamic contract theory can be applied with profit to the IFIs. Paul Mosley's treatment of World Bank-developing country bargaining over the conditionality attached to Structural Adjustment Loans is an example of a model that takes into account many of the problems presented by implicit contracts.[32] Mosley makes the simplifying assumption that the World Bank (by implication, any IFI) will attempt to use conditionality as "a bargaining counter in a game in which the donor (the Bank) seeks to influence economic policy in the manner desired by it, whereas the recipient resists all such attempts at influence which do not harmonise with its own political priorities." The utility function of the developing country government is relatively easy to model: it seeks to obtain as much finance as possible for as few politically burdensome conditions. The IFI utility function, however, taking into account the complex motivation noted, includes a desire to maximize policy change while also spending its budget.[33]

Using the country cases in this sample, the bargaining model of external influence can be tested. Crude expectations of consistent and heightened IFI influence during the 1980s—belied by the record of decision and implementation given above—are not met for reasons that are illuminated by the dynamic contract model: the inability of the IFIs to deliver reliably a mix of financial support and conditionality that is acceptable to the "median" developing country; counterproductive and often ineffective efforts to control alternative sources of finance (cross-conditionality); declining usefulness of the scapegoat or lightning rod role in bargaining; and perhaps most important, asymmetries in information that pose difficult selection and monitoring problems for the IFIs.

Finance and the Reputation for Compliance

Dynamic contract models of international lending are driven by reputational considerations: a government will not default (or defect from an IMF or World Bank program) because doing so would endanger future lending from the source reneged upon. The IFIs enhance this sanction by

---

[32] Paul Mosley, *Conditionality as Bargaining Process: Structural Adjustment Lending, 1980–86* (Princeton, N.J.: Princeton University, Internation Finance Section, Princeton Essays in International Finance, October 1987) and Mosley, Harrigan, and Toye, *Aid and Power*, vol. 1, chap. 3.

[33] Mosley et al., *Aid and Power*, vol. 1, p. 71.

tranching their lending: the borrower is not awarded the full amount of a standby or SAL at the beginning of the agreement; it is parcelled out, conditional on the completion of successive policy changes. As Paul Mosley has noted, this system may limit losses, but it leaves the cynical borrower in a strong position after receipt of the last tranche, and, with perfect foresight, would lead to no policy-based lending at all.[34] The absence of perfect foresight is not the principal bar to defection on the part of borrowers, however; future agreements (and finance) that might be foregone with repeated defection (slippage) from the policy conditions are a key incentive to staying in the conditionality game.

How heavily that future is discounted depends on two calculations regarding future finance: the availability of alternative nonconditional finance in the absence of compliance (considered below with cross-conditionality) and the ability of the IFIs to mobilize the finance "promised" if conditionality is implemented.

Incentives for compliance were often distorted for the heavily indebted countries in the 1980s by the inability of the IFI "seal of approval" to mobilize other sources of external finance. As a result, the financial incentives for persisting in difficult adjustment programs were often lacking: future cooperative relations with the IMF and World Bank were heavily discounted. In certain cases, the IFIs were unable to guarantee a level of bilateral aid that would ease the political costs of adjustment for beleaguered politicians. Among these cases, the Zambian program that was aborted in May 1987 is often cited as an example of failure because of inadequate funding. In part, donor wariness resulted from Zambia's past record of erratic implementation; in part, the Zambian program was too early for new measures of support (the SAF and ESAF) that were designed for low-income, heavily indebted countries. In any case, the Zambian elite saw inadequate financial incentives in its future to justify accepting rising political costs.[35] Guyana was another case in which the World Bank did not offer a SAL large enough to overcome the political risks perceived in policy changes and was unable to mobilize a large inflow from aid donors.[36] In Nigeria, the Structural Adjustment Program put in place under Babangida was greeted with a weak response from both domestic and international investors that deepened the political controversy surrounding the program.[37]

[34] Paul Mosley, *Conditionality as Bargaining Process*, p. 15.

[35] Callaghy, "Lost between State and Market," in Nelson, *Economic Crisis*, pp. 299–300; Christopher Colclough, "Zambian Adjustment Strategy—With and Without the Fund (Brighton, U.K.: Institute for Development Studies, 1987), p. 11.

[36] Jane Harrigan, "Guyana," in Mosley et al., *Aid and Power*, vol. 2, pp. 385–86.

[37] Callaghy, in Nelson, *Economic Crisis*, p. 316.

For another group of developing countries, the heavily indebted middle-income countries, the value of future cooperation with the IFIs has been reduced by the changed relationship between IFIs and private creditors, particularly the commercial banks. One of the incentives to cooperation with the IFIs in the past had been the value of their seal of approval in providing a reputational asset for developing countries in the private financial markets. In the course of the 1980s, the ability of the Fund and the World Bank to exercise their catalytic role on private capital flows declined. Foreign direct investment to heavily indebted countries undertaking adjustment programs did not pick up markedly. In successive phases of the debt crisis, although additional bank lending could be mobilized through "concerted lending," the commercial banks did not produce the net "new money" that had been promised that was a key part of the incentives for adjustment, much less a return to the credit markets by the debtors[38] (see figures 2.1, 2.2, and 2.3).[39] IMF influence on the banks was even lower in the cases of the smaller Latin American borrowers and surprisingly ineffectual with official lenders (such as export credit agencies).[40] Even "model" debtors, such as Chile, were forced to rely on multilateral and bilateral assistance to support their onerous repayments to the commercial banks.[41]

The costs to the IFIs were even higher than the erosion of the value of their seal of approval. IFI collaboration with private creditors has skewed the incentives against adjustment in perverse ways. As Jeffrey Sachs has argued most forcefully, the burden of debt servicing serves as an effective tax on adjustment: any gains made are siphoned off to the benefit of outside creditors, rather than redounding to the benefit of the domestic economy and its citizens.[42] Given the political costs of adjustment, this structure offers few incentives for persisting in an adjustment program: lending over and above the debt servicing flows recedes, like a mirage, into the future. The structure itself also raises the political costs, since political opponents can argue that adjustment measures are being under-

---

[38] Jeffrey D. Sachs, "Conditionality, Debt Relief, and the Developing Country Debt Crisis," in Sachs, *Developing Country Debt*, 262–63.

[39] In figures 2.1, 2.2, and 2.3, multilateral net tranfers equal the sum of net transfers from the World Bank and the International Development Association combined with the amount of purchases minus the amount of repurchases from the IMF.

[40] C. David Finch, *The IMF: The Record and the Prospect* (Princeton, N.J.: Princeton University, International Finance Section, Princeton Studies in International Finance, 1989), p. 17.

[41] Patricio Meller, "Chile," in John Williamson, editor, *Latin American Adjustment: How Much Has Happened?* (Washington, D.C.: Institute for International Economics, April 1990), p. 70.

[42] Sachs, *New Approaches*, p. 28.

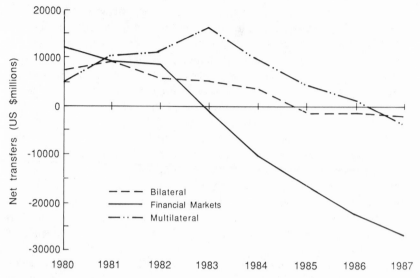

Figure 2.1. Trends in Net Transfers to All Developing Countries, 1980–1987
Source: World Debt Tables: External Debt of Developing Countries, 1988–89 ed. (Washington, D.C.: The World Bank, 1988).

Note: For figures 2.1, 2.2, and 2.3, the term *multilateral* refers to the sum of net transfers from the World Bank, the International Development Association, and the amount of repurchases from the International Monetary Fund.

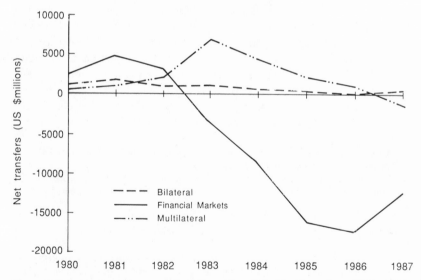

Figure 2.2. Latin American and Caribbean Trends in Net Transfers, 1980–1987
Source: World Debt Tables: External Debt of Developing Countries, 1988–89 ed. (Washington, D.C.: The World Bank, 1988).

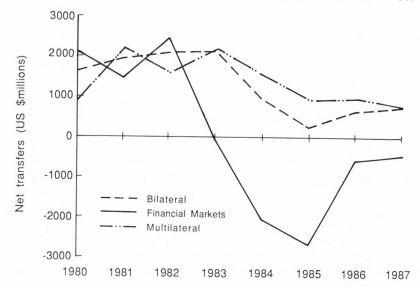

Figure 2.3. Sub-Saharan African Trends in Net Transfers, 1980–1987
Source: World Debt Tables: External Debt of Developing Countries, 1988–89 ed. (Washington, D.C.: The World Bank, 1988).

taken only for foreigners. In the past, one basis for an alignment of interests between the IFIs and at least a portion of a developing country government was the role that the international institutions played in coaxing financial support from skeptical creditors, public and private. Now, these institutions were increasingly seen not as the agents of developing country members but as bill collectors for a creditor cartel. Levels of trust and cooperation inevitably declined.

In short, the financial incentives that are part of conditionality bargaining have declined for many developing countries in the 1980s; the costs of defection or no agreement with the IFIs have therefore declined. At the same time, the IFIs have tried to adjust the other side of the contract—policy changes—in ways that heighten the political costs for some governments. Conditionality has been made more stringent in at least three ways. The simple number of policy conditions required for a particular financial package rose in the 1980s, although there are signs that the World Bank began to reduce its lengthy lists later in the decade (the ratio of conditions/finance increased). Second, the phasing of financial support was shifted, particularly in IMF programs, against "front-loading" and toward more equal tranches over the life of the program or even "back-loading" finance toward the end of the program. Finally, many have argued that conditionality became tougher, a concept that might be estimated as the product of the number of conditions in a program multiplied by the ratio of political costs to conditions (e.g., more devaluations demanded, more severe budget cuts).

The data for evaluating these supposed changes in conditionality are not available—the record of implementation for specific measures in IMF programs or even the content of the programs are not published. Even more intractable is a measurement of the political costs that would make conditionality more or less "tough." Paul Mosley has analyzed a sample of World Bank SALs on the dimension of "tightness," which he measures by number of conditions.[43] He finds no correlation between slippage (failure to implement agreed conditions) and tightness of conditionality. Equally significant, in terms of the incentives facing a developing country, Mosley could detect no clear relationship between implementation of earlier SAL programs and tightness of conditionality or availability of later SALs. In other words, a reputation for compliance seemed to produce little additional lending from the World Bank. Instead the tightness of conditionality was linked to the bargaining position of the recipient country: those countries most dependent on World Bank finance received the most stringent conditions.[44]

Evidence of any clear association between intensity of conditionality and success in implementation is also difficult to find in the country cases examined. Table 2.1 has been constructed using those cases for which some evidence is available of conditionality "toughness" in IMF and World Bank programs, as well as a rough indication of the scale of finance relative to other countries of the same size. Estimates on both the conditionality and financial dimensions are necessarily approximate. A number of the cases in the table are also ambiguous: Chile enjoyed relatively generous support from the IFIs, but that support only offset the large negative transfers to the commercial banks. Nevertheless, a number of patterns are evident; even more important are the patterns that are *not* evident.

The northeast cell strongly suggests that tough conditionality, even exercised in situations in which the developing country had few financial alternatives, was not successful without adequate financial incentives for the governments in question. None of the governments implemented more than a stabilization program (with the partial exception of the Babangida government in Nigeria); in general, this is a cell of collapsed programs. In those cases in which successful stabilization programs were carried out, the wielding of conditionality and finance did approach the

[43] Mosley argues that number of conditions also seems to be associated with conditionality that is "politically and administratively most demanding." (Mosley et al., *Aid and Power*, vol. 1, p. 125.)

[44] Mosley, *Conditionality as Bargaining Process*, pp. 24–26; Mosley et al., *Aid and Power*, vol. 1, p. 125.

TABLE 2.1
Conditionality, Finance, and Policy Change

	Finance	
Conditionality	High	Low
Tough	Jamaica, 1984–85[a]	Ecuador SAL
	Costa Rica, 1982–88[a]	Jamaica, 1986–89[a]
	Chile, 1982–88[a]	Guyana SAL
	Ghana, 1983–88[a]	Zambia, 1982–87
	Mexico, 1982–88[a]	Peru, 1983–84
	Malawi SAL[a]	Dominican Republic, 1984–86[a]
	Kenya SAL	Nigeria, 1986–88[a]
		Colombia, 1984–86[a]
		Philippines, 1984–86[a]
Soft or none	Jamaica, 1980–83	Brazil, 1985–88
	Philippines, 1980–84	Colombia, 1982–84
	Phillippines, 1986–87 (and SAL)[a]	Venezuela
	Turkey, 1980–85 (and SAL)[a]	Peru, 1985–87
	Thailand SAL[a]	Argentina, 1985–87
	Indonesia (1980s)[a]	

[a] Indicates successful implementation of a stabilization program or a program of broader economic reform; in the case of SALs, implementation of more than 50% of conditions; data from appendix tables A2.1 and A2.2.

crude bargaining model. In the Dominican Republic, the divided Jorge Blanco government was tilted toward stabilization by external financial pressure, but could not be pressed into more extensive reforms; by strengthening technocrats within the Marcos government after 1983, external creditors were able to force a harsher stabilization program on the Philippines than any in the past twenty years.[45]

The southeast cell could be labeled the heterodox cell, a collection of large and midsize Latin American countries that chose to embark on their own (mildly) heterodox economic programs. With the exception of Peru and Venezuela, the results were not catastrophic, although the gains that might have been made with a combination of increased external finance and IFI conditionality are difficult to estimate. This cell could have been expanded greatly by including those countries in table A2.1 that implemented no coherent economic program.

The two cells on the left of the diagram strongly suggest the dominance of a "finance" effect over a "conditionality" effect. In instances of relatively tight conditionality and the mobilization of large-scale finance, the independent effect of conditionality was often ambiguous. Conditionality in Jamaica and Costa Rica "affect[ed] the timing and design of many re-

[45] Stephan Haggard, in Nelson, *Economic Crisis*, p. 240; Paul Mosley, "The Philippines," in Mosley et al., *Aid and Power*, vol. 2, pp. 52–53.

forms" but could not force reform in the face of strong domestic opposition.[46] Although Ghana accepted apparently strong conditionality, John Toye argues that it was not "particularly harsh or coercive"; when slippage occurred the World Bank typically renegotiated rather than impose a financial penalty.[47] Strong external financial support often resulted in a relatively successful record of implementation even under conditions of "soft" conditionality (the southwest cell). There were exceptions: the Marcos government in the Philippines before 1983 and the early years of the Seaga government were instances of governments that "took the money and ran." The explanation for most of the successful cases, however, is not finance alone. As Joan Nelson concluded after examining the array of cases in appendix table A2.1:

> [The] level of financial support, measured either as concessional aid or as net capital flows (relative to the size of the recipients' economies or populations), bears no consistent relationship to extent of implementation of reforms. Financing for governments that pursued broad reforms varied from large to modest (or negative, in terms of net capital flows for some cases). And some countries that got very heavy financial support, like Costa Rica, made only modest progress on structural reforms.[48]

The Philippines represents almost a quasiexperiment that demonstrates this point. IMF and World Bank involvement in structural adjustment had been persistent since the late 1970s, but the Marcos government did little that was not simultaneously undercut by the dynamics of its crony capitalist base. After 1983, tightened conditionality and straitened financial circumstances forced the government into a draconian stabilization program, but could not force broader policy changes. The Aquino government was able to move ahead with a partial program of economic reforms that Marcos had failed to implement, even though it enjoyed the same combination of generous external finance and soft conditionality that had produced little under the previous government. Domestic political parameters had changed, not the level of World Bank or IMF involvement. The Aquino government was able to overcome resistance to the reforms in part by portraying them as a break with the Marcos era and an attack on crony capitalism.[49]

One possible explanation for some of the variation in cases of relatively generous external finance is the failure of external agencies to control access to alternative sources of finance. It is to that hypothesis that we now turn.

[46] Joan Nelson in Nelson, *Economic Crisis*, p. 205.
[47] John Toye, "Ghana," in Mosley et al., *Aid and Power*, vol. 2, p. 196.
[48] Joan Nelson, "Conclusion," in Nelson, *Economic Crisis*, p. 19.
[49] Haggard, in Nelson, *Economic Crisis*, pp. 248–49.

External Implicit Contracts: Cross-Conditionality

The availability of nonconditional finance was a disincentive for compliance with IFI conditionality and reappeared as some developing countries returned to the financial markets after the mid-1980s. By reducing the need for future conditional finance (or even the expectation of such a need), financial windfalls, such as recurrent commodity booms, no-questions-asked aid, or private credit reduces the likelihood of continued cooperation with the IFIs. Typically, the borrower will exploit the conditional lender, agreeing to policy changes only to obtain a seal of approval that will increase its access to other sources of finance. The Philippines under Marcos in the 1970s epitomized this pattern. Bolivia in the late 1970s is another example: "There was no politically right time to undertake adjustment, until the government no longer had access to foreign loans. As long as these loans could be used, all governments, stable or not, could and would postpone unpopular measures to raise domestic savings."[50]

Even in the 1980s, when private financial flows to most developing countries declined sharply, the ability to find alternative sources of finance often reduced compliance abruptly. Both Turkey and Thailand, which already enjoyed relatively soft conditionality—Thailand's SALs, for example, were not tranched—broke off conditional borrowing from the World Bank because of their reentry into the private financial markets. Mosley argues that this ability to find financial alternatives in the late 1980s was "one of the major limitations on the Bank's bargaining power" with middle-income countries.[51]

Since alternative, low-conditionality finance weakened the bargaining power of the IFIs and reduced their influence on the economic policies of borrowers, any ability to tie the lending behavior of other creditors or donors to IFI criteria would, in theory, increase their influence. One technique that seemed likely to shore up the position of creditors during the 1980s was the development of cross-conditionality—a clear attempt to convert internal contracts into external contracts by involving parties outside the IFI-developing country bargain in its financial future. The fact that other creditors would rely on the IFI conditionality contracts for reputational information seemed likely to deter developing country governments from overturning their agreements with the World Bank and the IMF.

In its narrowest version, cross-conditionality requires the collaboration

[50] "Power and the IMF: the Example of Bolivia," *Euromoney* (January 1982): 107.

[51] Chaipat Sahasakul et al., "Thailand," and Mosley, "Ecuador," in Mosley et al., *Aid and Power*, vol. 2, chaps. 13 and 19.

of the IMF and the World Bank in their bargaining with developing country governments. Although formal cross-conditionality has been denied by the IMF and the World Bank in their lending for standbys and SALs, the convergence of the institutions on "structural" issues of economic management (in contrast to their past concentration on short-run balance of payments disequilibrium and project lending, respectively) has necessarily produced behavior that appears as cross-conditionality.

Richard Feinberg has labeled three variants of de facto cross-conditionality, all of which were apparent in the 1980s. Consultative cross-conditionality makes the lending of one institution in a country dependent on the other: all World Bank SALs in the first half of the 1980s and nearly all SECALs were made to countries that had also negotiated an IMF program.[52] By the end of the decade, however, this close association had broken down: only four-fifths of SALs and three-fifths of SECALs were made to IMF program countries. This divergence of the Bretton Woods organizations led to a 1989 agreement reinstating the earlier convention of World Bank lending only to countries with an IMF agreement. The World Bank could still claim that cross-conditionality did not exist in the narrow sense, however, since cancellation of a Fund program or failure to meet IMF targets would not lead to suspension of World Bank loans.[53] Feinberg describes two other variants of de facto cross-conditionality: the use of similar criteria of judgment by the two organizations (interdependent cross-conditionality) and the failure to meet targets of one organization because of the suspension of lending by the other (indirect financial linkage).[54] The introduction of the Structural Adjustment and Enhanced Structural Adjustment Facilities introduced a formal cross-conditionality for those (poorer) developing countries who borrowed from the facility: the Policy Framework Paper required in SAF/ESAF programs was approved by both the Bank and the Fund as well as the country government.

Cross-conditionality with other actors also demonstrated the same weakening during the 1980s. Formal linkage of USAID bilateral programs to IMF or World Bank conditionality was prohibited after 1985 by the Kemp-Kasten amendment. Although direct reference to the Bretton Woods organizations was eliminated, however, USAID's judgments continued to run parallel to the IFIs and informal coordination continued.[55]

[52] Richard Feinberg, "The Changing Relationship Between the World Bank and the International Monetary Fund," *International Organization* 42, no. 3 (Summer 1988): 554; Mosley et al., *Aid and Power*, vol. 1, p. 96.

[53] *Report on Adjustment Lending II*, pp. 47–48.

[54] Feinberg, "The Changing Relationship," 555–57.

[55] General Accounting Office, Report to the Administrator, Agency for International Development, *Foreign Assistance: U.S. Use of Conditions to Achieve Economic Reforms* (August 1986), pp. 17–18.

Paris Club rescheduling (the renegotiation of official loans and credits) remains dependent on the existence of an IMF stand-by arrangement. The close collaboration of the IFIs and the commercial banks, described earlier, began to fray as concerted lending from the banks became less significant and the Bretton Woods organizations became more willing to lend in the absence of an agreement with the banks to clear arrears.

Cross-conditionality was limited in its application by the individual costs that were perceived by creditors, despite the possibility for joint gains in bargaining power. The IMF and the World Bank often jockeyed over their institutional prerogatives or simply disagreed over the correct strategy to pursue. World Bank lending to Argentina in 1988 (with United States support) was perhaps the most significant example of such unwillingness to achieve joint gains against a borrowing country. Other creditors, particularly industrialized country governments, could pressure the IFIs to reach an agreement with a particular country (often a large debtor) because of concern over national financial institutions or foreign policy objectives. Although Mosley did not find easier initial bargains for clients of the United States in his study of World Bank SALs, those clients were treated more leniently when slippage occurred.[56] Developing country governments also played upon the conflicting interests of creditors. Jamaica's "Fresh Look" initiative in 1985–86 may have been an effort to develop a new approach to adjustment, but it could also be read as an attempt to drive a wedge between the United States, the World Bank, and the IMF. Zaire's Mobutu extended better terms to certain creditors, manipulating and dividing the coalition that he confronted.[57]

Implicit cross-conditionality also imposed other costs on the relationship between IFIs and developing country governments. Additional players served to add "noise" to reputational readings by sending conflicting signals to the country in question: compliance was more difficult to monitor when a government could choose to respond to the requirements of one bargain and not another. The smaller, aid-dependent countries in which implicit cross-conditionality was most likely were also those with the weakest capacities to bargain with the IFIs and to implement their programs. Efforts to coordinate creditor bargaining positions without explicit joint action only served to overload the handful of top negotiators who, as one participant described it, had to listen to the same arguments three times. Most damaging to the level of compliance, however, was indirect financial linkage, which was also most damaging for smaller countries. In Costa Rica and Jamaica, implementation of programs became an

[56] Mosley et al., *Aid and Power*, pp. 128, 165.

[57] Winsome J. Leslie, *The World Bank and Structural Transformation in Developing Countries: The Case of Zaire* (Boulder, Colo.: Lynne Rienner, 1987), pp. 134–36.

excessively intricate process in which no part could advance without the others and in which a brief delay in funding with one creditor could force renegotiations or suspension with another. The Guyana SAL epitomized this type of linkage: the IMF would not lend without a level of external support that would permit successful stabilization, but those other flows were dependent on a Fund program. The Fund essentially handed over its lead role to the World Bank, but the Bank's seal of approval was not credible enough to induce the necessary assistance: the program was judged a failure.[58]

Among the cases surveyed, coordination among creditors did increase bargaining power and compliance in certain cases: the cross-conditionality of World Bank, aid donors, and the IMF in Malawi increased the leverage of the World Bank in its structural adjustment loan; other smaller countries probably moved more rapidly along the path of structural change because aid donors in particular acted in concert with (or at least not in opposition to) the IFIs. Other cases, however, can be marshalled to demonstrate the costs of cross-conditionality to the long-term relationship between IFIs and national governments, through institutional overload, misleading or conflicting signals, and misguided financial linkage. It seems unlikely that lack of creditor coordination fully explains the record of decision and implementation in these episodes of economic policy change.

Asymmetric Information: Selection and Monitoring

The dependence of cooperation on repetition and self-enforcement is rendered more difficult when the behavior (reputation) on which compliance is judged is obscured by "noise" and difficult or impossible to monitor.[59] The IFIs face a difficult problem of adverse selection in those countries that are candidates for assistance, since governments rarely turn to finance coupled with policy conditionality unless their economic plight is critical (which often implies weak commitment to policy change). One pattern of successful IFI intervention does emerge from these cases: the "order of play" in the conditionality game is central. Table 2.2 demonstrates a fairly clear-cut pattern: prior commitment and policy action (taken before external support is offered) is a good predictor of successful implementation. Successful influence is more likely if governments first

[58] Harrigan, "Guyana," in Mosley et al., *Aid and Power*, vol. 2, p. 386.

[59] David M. Kreps, "Corporate Culture and Economic Theory," in James E. Alt and Kenneth A. Shepsle, editors, *Perspectives on Positive Political Economy* (Cambridge: Cambridge University Press, 1990), p. 105. John McMillan has noted that "noise" in IFI transactions is likely to be a more severe problem than in the case of commercial bank agreements, since simple repayment is not the only criterion for fulfillment of the contract.

TABLE 2.2
Government Commitment and Program Outcomes

Program Implementation	Level of Government Commitment before External Support[a]	
	High	Low
High	Costa Rica, 1982–84[b]	Philippines, 1984–86[b]
	Nigeria, 1986–88[b]	Dominican Republic, 1984–86[b]
	Philippines, 1986–87 (and SAL)[b]	Jamaica, 1984–89 (+ SAL)[b]
	Ghana, 1983–88 (and SAL)[b]	Kenya SAL
	Chile, 1982–88[b]	Mexico, 1982–88[b]
	Thailand SAL[b]	Costa Rica, 1984–88[b]
	Turkey, 1980–85 (and SAL)[b]	Colombia, 1984–86[b]
	Indonesia (1980s)[b]	
	Malawi SAL[b]	
Low	Heterodox cases (Brazil, Peru, Argentina)	Jamaica, 1980–83
		Dominican Republic, 1978–82
		Costa Rica, 1979–82
		Ecuador SAL
		Kenya SAL
		Guyana SAL
		Peru, 1983–84
		Zambia, 1983–84

[a] Level of commitment is measured by policy implementation before external financial support.

[b] Indicates successful implementation of a stabilization program or a program of broader economic reform; in the case of SALs, implementation of more than 50% of conditions; data from tables A2.1 and A2.2.

commit themselves to an adjustment program and *only then* are supported financially by the IFIs. The pattern would be even clearer if a stringent behavioral definition of commitment had not been used: significant policy change before external financial support. The northeast cell seems to belie the close association between prior commitment or "ownership" of a program and later success. Two observations heavily qualify the appearance of successful and "uncommitted" governments, however. A number of cases in that cell—Mexico and Jamaica—could be argued post hoc to have demonstrated strong commitment to a program as domestic political pressures mounted (another test), but could not be said to have instituted major policy changes in advance of external assistance. The northeast cell also contains several relatively successful stabilization programs (Colombia, Philippines, Dominican Republic) that were not transformed into broader programs of policy change. Some of these cases were marked by a delicate balance of internal political forces that was influenced by the IFIs in the direction of stabilization. This cell suggests that the requirement of clear prior commitment may be less necessary in the case of short-term stabilization programs than it is in programs of extensive policy change. By putting together the findings in tables 2.1 and 2.2, the association of successful initiation and implementation with a sequencing of governmental commitment plus generous financial support becomes even clearer.

The evidence from particular cases of successful implementation supports these findings. Thailand and Indonesia lie at one end of the commitment spectrum. Thailand's Structural Adjustment Loan was part of a clear Fifth Plan policy framework and was preceded by specific government actions; the policy "downpayment" of Thailand was substantial, since the Thai government had initiated more than one-half of the measures before agreement with the Bank.[60] Indonesia from the late 1960s through the 1980s exhibited a similar pattern of endogenous policy change (particularly in its large devaluations) that was supported by large amounts of external finance mobilized by the IFIs.[61] Turkey offers another example in the 1980s. Some have argued that the level of finance provided makes Turkey an exceptional case—that "these massive capital inflows virtually ensured the success of the adjustment effort."[62] Equally important, however, was the commitment made by the Turkish government to their economic program in 1980—before substantial outside involvement or bargaining with external agencies. In Africa, Ghana, which has undertaken a sweeping and orthodox program, was the third largest recipient of World Bank IDA funds in 1987 (after India and China); its concessional aid per capita in 1988 was twice the average for the rest of Africa. Nevertheless, the IFIs did not spring immediately to support the Ghanaian program; the Jerry Rawlings government launched its program in 1983 with relatively low levels of support before external sources of finance were willing to endorse its political commitment.[63] At the other end of the spectrum, several prominent failed programs were the result of a misreading of commitment by the external actors: the Seaga government's first years and Zambia (in which Kenneth Kaunda's support for the program was overestimated) are two examples.

Drawing on these experiences, a number of observers of IFI conditionality have also endorsed this sequencing of external influence on adjustment programs. David Finch has argued that many of the failures in IMF support for country programs are related to the "pressures to undertake

[60] Chaipat Sahasakul, Nattapong Thongpakde, and Keokam Kraisoraphong, "Thailand," in Mosley et al., *Aid and Power*, vol. 2, p. 102.

[61] Interview, Washington, D.C., October 1989.

[62] Ahmed Abdallah, "Discussion," in Vittorio Corbo, Morris Goldstein, and Mohsin Khan, eds., *Growth-Oriented Adjustment Programs* (Washington, D.C.: IMF and World Bank, 1987).

[63] John Toye suggests that the Rawlings government could not have formulated its economic program without "a great deal of informal assistance provided by the Fund and the Bank." (Toye, "Ghana," in Mosley et al., *Aid and Power*, vol. 2, p. 158.)

programs before the political conditions necessary to support them are in place"; Peter Kenen urges that "governments should be encouraged to change their policies before they apply for Fund credit."[64] Jeffrey D. Sachs has argued for "requiring more prior actions on the part of the borrowing government, so that the government proves its resolve to carry through on the negotiated program (and is forced to build the domestic political base for the policy changes)."[65] The World Bank itself has emphasized the need for government ownership of a program as one of the determinants of successful policy change.[66]

Endorsing governmental commitment does not alleviate the difficult task of outsiders in *reading* that commitment, a task that becomes central to the success of external influence through finance. If government commitment followed by financial support produces cooperative and successful adjustment outcomes, the informational obstacles to successfully implementing such a strategy remain formidable. Governments have strong incentives to argue that they are committed to such programs, even when they are not; the external lender must design selection and screening procedures to determine which of those governments are in fact intending to implement policy change along desired lines.

For reasons discussed earlier, the IFIs are constrained in the amount of selection that they can carry out, but several techniques have been employed to deal with information asymmetries that obscure a government's level of commitment. For the IMF, prior actions—required before a program is approved by the Fund and often including politically costly measures—serve as a hurdle and a test of true intentions. The reputation measure of the "track record" of a country in past adjustment episodes is also used as a means of predicting future action, particularly for multiple-year programs.

A third selection criterion runs counter to a reliance on reputation, however, and is suggested by case studies in the politics of adjustment. Although the connection between adjustment success and type of political regime (democratic vs. authoritarian, for example) is relatively weak, association between a strengthened commitment to policy change and a change of government or regime appears to be closer. Haggard and Kaufman argue that political business cycles are apparent in many developing countries and that the timing of adjustment in those cycles may be key:

[64] C. David Finch, *The IMF: The Record and the Prospect* (Princeton, N.J.: Princeton University, International Finance Section, September 1989), p. 20; Peter Kenen, "The Use of IMF Credit," in *The International Monetary Fund in a Multipolar World: Pulling Together* (Washington, D.C.: Overseas Development Council, 1989), p. 84.

[65] Sachs, "Conditionality, Debt Relief, and the Debt Crisis," in Sachs, *Developing Country Debt and Economic Performance*, p. 269.

[66] *Report on Adjustment Lending II*, pp. 55–56.

"If the period prior to elections is likely to be characterized by expansionary policies and resistance to stabilization, the period following elections will allow governments more leeway to introduce reforms." This is particularly the case when a new government succeeds an antecedent administration whose economic policies are perceived as a failure and when it confronts a divided opposition.[67] New regimes present a mixed set of signals: they may present a reinforced version of the new government pattern described; on the other hand, transitional regimes (authoritarian to democratic) often find it difficult to institute stabilization programs on taking power.[68] A number of new regimes or governments are among the cases enacting successful stabilization or economic reform programs: Costa Rica under Monge, Mexico under de la Madrid, the case of Turkey, the Philippines under Aquino.[69]

A further difficulty in selecting for commitment is the interactive effect of IFI finance and government willingness to commit to policy change. Even in those cases in which finance followed commitment, prior communication between IFIs and governments had made clear that substantial financial support was available for a credible economic program—this was, for example, the case in Turkey in 1980. Cases of "pure" or autonomous commitment exist—both Chile and Rumania carried out harsh adjustment programs with relatively little external financial support (when transfers to private creditors are taken into account)—but knowledge of resource availability is likely to influence a government's turn toward economic policy change.

Each of these selection or screening devices adds to the reliable information possessed by external principals about their prospective counterparts in the adjustment bargain. None of them, however, provides a high level of confidence about the intentions and political standing of their interlocutors in every case. In certain cases, the ambiguity about intentions is deep even for expert observers of a country's politics. In Ghana, for example, two readings were made of the "revolutionary" Provisional National Defense Council under Rawlings: that the government was dominated by "patient revolutionaries" who would overturn the ERP af-

[67] Stephan Haggard and Robert Kaufman, "The Politics of Stabilization and Structural Adjustment," in Jeffrey D. Sachs, ed., *Developing Country Debt and Economic Performance*, vol. 1 (Chicago: University of Chicago Press, 1989), pp. 242–43; also Joan Nelson, "Conclusions," in Nelson, *Economic Crisis*, p. 312.

[68] Compare the findings of Karen L. Remmer, "The Politics of Economic Stabilization," p. 21, with Haggard and Kaufman, "Politics of Stabilization," pp. 243–44; see also chapter 6 by Haggard and Kaufman in this volume.

[69] Paul Mosley argues, based on the case studies of SALs, that "the arrival in power of a new government has often facilitated reform—by reducing the number of vested interests that need to be confronted—but is neither an essential nor an adequate precondition for effective reform." (Mosley et al., *Aid and Power*, vol. 1, p. 161.)

External Influence · 119

ter stabilization or that the government was "schizophrenic," genuinely divided between populist radicals and market-oriented pragmatists. The government's rhetoric and its actions could be read to fit with either interpretation.[70] In such situations of high uncertainty, other mechanisms of monitoring and control are required.

Even in cases in which commitment is high and the model of external intervention approaches that in the IFIs own rhetoric—not leverage but support for indigenous economic policy change—conditionality is not wholly irrelevant. Political resistance to programs may create roadblocks to implementation for even a highly committed government. Commentary on the generally successful programs in Turkey from 1980–85 suggests that political incentives for fiscal laxness might have been offset by continued external conditionality. All is not harmony with committed governments: conflicts of interest exist on particular measures. Also, generous and "guaranteed" external finance can create its own incentives for slippage, a pattern detected by Joan Nelson in the case of small countries such as Costa Rica and Jamaica.[71]

For all of these reasons, IFIs and other external actors attempt to monitor government implementation of adjustment programs. Those who undertake monitoring face problems of hidden information and hidden action similar to that often confound efforts to select governments on the basis of commitment. Monitoring has become more difficult as conditionality has broadened: macroeconomic policy change has been linked to a host of structural adjustment measures, such as trade liberalization, public sector rationalization, and agricultural price reform. As Mosley points out, this broadening has increased the lag between the expected policy action and the outcome that will be used to measure compliance.[72] Monitoring also has higher political costs than the manipulation of incentives: it is often more intrusive and more likely to arouse nationalist resentment.

Finally, certain monitoring mechanisms are not available to external actors seeking to exercise influence across national boundaries. McCubbins and Schwartz have argued in the context of domestic politics that "fire alarm" mechanisms may be more efficient than "police patrols" in monitoring the actions of bureaucratic agents.[73] The contrast between the two is fairly simple: Police patrol mechanisms involve direct surveil-

---

[70] Callaghy in Nelson, *Economic Crisis*, pp. 276–77.

[71] Nelson, "Politics of Adjustment in Small Democracies," in Nelson, *Economic Crisis and Policy Choice*, p. 206.

[72] Mosley, *Conditionality as Bargaining*, p. 2.

[73] Matthew D. McCubbins and Thomas Schwartz, "Congressional Oversight Overlooked: Police Patrols versus Fire Alarms," *American Journal of Political Science* 23, no. 1 (February 1984): 165–79.

lance to detect hidden action that deviates from the monitor's interests. Fire alarm mechanisms use interested third parties to produce the desired information; citizen complaint procedures, hearings, and legal standing are all examples of fire alarm mechanisms. The IFIs are constrained from using fire alarm monitoring devices by the conventions of national sovereignty. The citizens and organized groups of a country are the likeliest participants in a fire alarm system of oversight; however, the national government is the gatekeeper to its own population. (The IMF has met with groups outside the government on rare occasions, but only at the invitation of the government.) Other national governments play a minor role in ringing fire alarms when the policies of another government create externalities that impinge on its own economic well-being, but many economic policy measures taken by a government do not directly affect the interests of other states, and foreign policy interests may deter other governments from reaching for the alarm switch.

Bargaining for Commitment: External Actors as Political Targets

Political resistance to adjustment from groups that will suffer costs poses the knottiest issues for those outside a country who are attempting to further the resisted changes. Even if a political elite is unified in its endorsement of the desired policy changes, even if incentives and monitoring work effectively, unexpected political resistance can overturn the adjustment program. We are now in the realm of what Robert Putnam has labeled "involuntary defection": "Voluntary defection refers to reneging by a rational egoist in the absence of enforceable contracts. . . . Involuntary defection instead reflects the behavior of an agent who is unable to deliver on a promise because of failed ratification."[74]

The distinction between a government that is forced to defect from an agreement by political resistance and one that chooses to do so after calculating the costs and benefits to its future relations with external creditors is a slippery one. Consider a government that returns to the IMF or World Bank pleading that the recently agreed standby or SAL is on the rocks because of obstreperous opposition in the legislature (or the military or the labor unions). In short, the agreement "cannot be ratified." How does the outsider know that this is indeed the case, that the resistance is genuine? How does the outsider know that the politician in question is investing his political capital to ensure that the agreement is ratified?

---

[74] Robert D. Putnam, "Diplomacy and Domestic Politics: The Logic of Two-Level Games," *International Organization* 42, no. 3 (Summer 1988): 438.

The second question is usually more difficult, although the use of domestic political opposition for bargaining advantage makes the first pertinent in many cases. It raises a profound issue of moral hazard: Should external agencies regard politics as analogous to the weather, a set of random events that are not subject to the control of the government. Clearly not: on the one hand, the political leadership is not simply a calculating machine adding and subtracting political vectors; on the other hand, in the short run at least, some political constraints are relatively fixed.

At least two extreme strategies could be pursued by the external agent. One taken in the past, at least rhetorically, by the IMF and the World Bank, would regard political obstacles as entirely under the control of the political elite. Removing them in this view is simply a question of political will that is not included in the conditionality bargain. An alternative is to regard the political costs associated with adjustment as real costs that must be included in the compensation structure of conditionality. Mosley, for example, argues that the World Bank should explicitly offer compensation for the losers in adjustment, since politicians are likely to provide compensation in any case, in a far more inefficient way. As Terry Moe suggests, the coinage of compensation for bureaucrats and politicians could be some version of fiscal slack, the difference between the actual costs of government and the budget. Slack provides the politician with resources to meet the political costs of adjustment. Of course, it offends the emphasis on efficiency that motivates the IFIs and other external creditors, as does the notion of compensation. But the issue is more profound than ideological queasiness. The external actors *should* expect that the politician will invest some share of his political capital in overcoming the resistance to policy change; it is unrealistic to expect him to invest all of it, to the point of losing power.

One principle that could be employed is compensation, but only partial compensation, a sharing of the risks of political resistance between the external providers of finance and the political leadership of the country.[75] Adopting the principle of partial compensation, however, leaves a considerable burden of information gathering to be able to cross-check the estimates of resistance offered by the politicians. Here, the IFIs may have been negligent. The institutional memory of the IFIs regarding the politics of adjustment episodes is very short; there is little systematic attention to collecting or making available to their staffs the political lessons of particular programs. The IFIs could also make more of an effort to test the political waters of a country beyond the technocratic circles with which they typically bargain.

[75] This principle is also embodied in the device of insurance policy deductibles.

A final strategy of influence that is designed to deal with political resistance is in effect another form of political compensation. It is time-honored, although now regarded with disfavor: the external agencies as lightning rods or scapegoats. This strategy works only if the politicians of a country have a peculiar ordering of political costs and benefits: the political costs of appearing responsible for an adjustment program are ranked higher than the costs of appearing subservient to external agencies. (This peculiar ordering of costs may explain why certain national elites have not used the IFIs in this way.) Recently, the IFIs have become more reluctant to accept this role as their own preferred strategies have changed. The IFIs had regarded the core of their approach as devising a set of incentives and monitoring devices that would serve to induce program implementation whatever the real interests of a nation's political leadership. Now selection and commitment seems to loom larger: publicly demonstrated ownership of a program becomes a key piece of information for the external agencies. In two recent cases, Zambia and Venezuela, the managing director of the IMF, Michel Camdessus, publicly refused to accept the role of lightning rod, passing responsibility for the program back to national political leaders. In his exchange of letters with President Pérez of Venezuela that were made public, Camdessus clearly signaled the change of course: "It is a prerogative of sovereign states to decide themselves what measures are required for recovery, however unpleasant those measures may be. And it does them honor if they take responsibility for policies in the eyes of their people, even in the most adverse circumstances."[76]

Although the emerging orthodoxy on selection for commitment is supported by successful cases of implementation, there may be cases in which the IFIs, while not accepting the role of lightning rod or scapegoat, may opt for "creative conditionality" to lower the costs to politicians of their presence. Two instances of such successful creativity can be found among these cases. The Babangida government in Nigeria found itself unable to turn to the IMF without paying high domestic political costs. The enterprising World Bank staff in Lagos, viewed with much less nationalist distrust, was able to assist the government in devising an economic program that met many of the IFIs stipulations but could be portrayed as the government's own program (and that later led to an IMF standby).[77] When Colombia decided to turn to the IMF under external financial pressure, it received an unusual arrangement that permitted an IMF seal of approval

[76] "Fund Will Support Venezuela's Well-Conceived Measures," *IMF Survey* 18, no. 6 (20 March 1989): 82.

[77] Callaghy, "Lost between State and Market," in Nelson, *Economic Crisis*, p. 307.

without traditional conditionality.[78] In each of these cases, the IFIs were not made scapegoats, but their willingness to maintain a low political profile became part of the underlying bargain.

The bargaining model directs attention to several key aspects of the relations between IFIs and the developing countries and does explain part of the pattern of limited influence that was apparent in the 1980s. Inadequate finance, confused and often burdensome cross-conditionality, and difficulties in selecting for and monitoring commitment contribute to understanding why, under conditions of acute financial distress in many developing countries, IFI influence was not greater.

The model cannot explain, however, the apparent increase in economic policy change over the course of the 1980s. In light of the trends in net transfers illustrated in figures 2.1–2.3, the bargaining model would predict that IFI influence would peak in the early to mid-1980s, when alternative sources of finance declined unexpectedly and repayments to the IFIs had not yet increased. The pattern of implementation of policy changes, however, does not match the "arc of influence" illustrated in these diagrams. The latest World Bank report on adjustment lending suggests that implementation has improved steadily over the course of the 1980s. A recent study of Latin American economies suggests policy convergence on a centrist "Washington consensus" represented in part by the IFIs.[79] The bargaining model and the flaws that it illuminates in IFI strategies of influence would not have predicted this sort of convergence or progress in implementation. To understand this record, one must turn to another model of influence based on social learning.

LEARNING AND TRANSNATIONAL COALITIONS: INFLUENCE THROUGH DIALOGUE

The bargaining model described to this point, based on models of international lending characteristic of the 1970s and 1980s, assumes fixed or stable preferences and strategies (IFIs seek economic policies that will lead to external adjustment; governments seeks as little economic policy change as possible given political risks) and unitary actors. The second model of influence—social learning—questions these assumptions. In particular, the beliefs of those bargaining externally and determining policy internally become important elements in any explanation of cooperative outcomes. The hierarchy of goals pursued is no longer assumed to be fixed; it can change through the introduction of new information or

[78] Barbara Stallings, "Politics and Economic Crisis," ibid., pp. 157–58.

[79] John Williamson, "The Progress of Policy Reform in Latin America," in Williamson, *Latin American Adjustment*, pp. 400–407.

new cognitive maps. Influence operates not only through bargaining but through persuasion or "debate" (to use Anatol Rapaport's term): efforts to align interests more closely through changing the definition of those interests.

Models based on cognitive change and social learning confront a number of serious obstacles. First is a level-of-learning problem. Theories of organizational learning have had to account for the transfer of individual cognitive change to the organization itself; such theories emphasize "encoding inferences from history into routines that guide behavior."[80] Social or political learning requires a similar encoding beyond a single organization. Few accounts of learning deal with the process of such transfer from the individual to larger social units in other than a murky way.

Connected to this lack of clarity about process is the demanding empirical task of demonstrating that a particular behavioral change is the result of a clearly specified cognitive alteration at one level or another. The investigation of shared beliefs is not an impossible empirical task but, once again, it has rarely been attempted in a rigorous fashion. Nor have alternative explanations for policy change been carefully compared to an explanation based on change in ideology or beliefs. A first step in such empirical investigation is obviously the definition of those cognitive or ideational elements that are presumed to have an influence on the policies in question.

A final conundrum concerns the depth and permanence of learning that occurs. Most models of organizational or social learning include more than one type of learning: the variants are usually divided by the degree of cognitive, organizational, or political change that is implied. Argyris and Schön, for example, distinguish between "single-loop" learning that does not challenge the "norms, objectives, and basic policies" of the organization from "double-loop" learning that alters organizational norms.[81] Peter Hall delineates first-order (change in policy instrument settings), second-order (change in policy instruments and their settings), and third-order (change in the first two as well as "the hierarchy of goals behind the policy") learning.[82]

These competing yet parallel classifications raise the issue of permanence in social learning. Learning can be reversed or superseded; if change in beliefs is rapid or repeated, the changes in question may not

[80] Barbara Levitt and James G. March, "Organizational Learning," *Annual Review of Sociology* 14 (1988): 320.

[81] Chris Argyris and Donald A. Schön, *Organizational Learning: A Theory of Action Perspective* (Reading, Mass.: Addison-Wesley Publishing Company Inc., 1978), pp. 18–19, 21–22.

[82] Peter A. Hall, "Policy Paradigms, Social Learning and the State: The Case of Economic Policy-making in Britain," *Comparative Politics*, forthcoming.

represent social learning. The notion of encoding changes in organizational and political theories, ideologies, or policy paradigms suggests that learning (at least of the "higher" orders) is not likely to be a frequent event. If its frequency matches poorly the policy variations that are of interest, then its explanatory usefulness may be limited.

Despite the knotty problems encountered in using this approach, it does approach the issue of external influence from a different angle: if policy change can be related to learning, external actors, such as the IFIs, may be able to influence or accelerate such learning. The IFIs themselves, as organizations, may also be characterized as learning.

The IFIs and other external agencies have a strong interest in shaping the process of learning by national governments in directions that will lead to greater alignment with external policy preferences. Consensual knowledge, agreement on the underlying features of the national economy and on the policy prescriptions best suited for adjustment, may explain the likelihood of cooperative outcomes between national governments and the IFIs. Richard Cooper, for example, has recently argued that international policy cooperation is more likely when there is agreement on the underlying model of the issue space that policy is attempting to address.[83]

Certainly agreement on the model and the policy prescriptions flowing from it strengthened the record of implementation in the country cases examined: in all of the cases that successfully implemented broader reforms of a neo-orthodox variety, the IFIs and the political principals in the country were in broad ideological agreement. Only the Rawlings government in Ghana is a partial exception to the generalization—Rawlings once commented, "I don't understand all these theories, all this economic blah blah blah." Even in that instance, the military regime did not have to overcome a well-organized ideological opposition.[84] In the case of Chile, the Pinochet regime was hyperaligned: it pursued policies to reorient the Chilean economy that exceeded external conditionality. External influence in such cases seemed superfluous.[85]

In other cases, notably Zambia, Guyana, and Turkey pre-1980, attachment to socialist or statist ideology produced program collapse. In the case of short-run stabilization programs, model agreement seemed less essential: an extreme case is Romania, which implemented a "stabilization" program far harsher than that recommended by the IFIs during the

---

[83] Richard N. Cooper, "International Cooperation in Public Health as a Prologue to Macroeconomic Cooperation," in Richard N. Cooper, ed., *Can Nations Agree?* (Washington, D.C.: The Brookings Institution, 1989), p. 240.

[84] Callaghy, in Nelson, *Economic Crisis*, p. 275.

[85] See Ricardo Ffrench-Davis, "Adjustment and Conditionality in Chile, 1982–83" (Corporacion de Investigaciones Economicas para Latinoamerica, June 1989), pp. 15, 17.

1980s while continuing to organize its economy along lines antithetical to the market orientation of the IMF. (In certain respects, Ceausescu was a neo-Stalinist Pinochet).[86]

One of the key instruments employed by the IFIs in efforts to construct a common base of consensual knowledge is the policy dialogue. The shortcomings of the bargaining model of influence and its apparent failure to shift national policies have lent support to those who argue for a model of Fund and Bank relations with developing countries that is less dependent on oversight and monitoring and linked to persuasion and joint problem-solving. In this view, policy dialogue would improve the record of program negotiations and implementation in two ways. Policy dialogue, however, seems unlikely to induce more than first- or second-order learning in the absence of efforts to ally more directly to those in national governments who share the underlying intellectual maps of the IFIs.

Even if the interests of a government appear to conflict with the interests of external actors such as the IFIs, dialogue with a government may assist the IFIs in finding such individuals: allies within the government whose interests *are* aligned more closely with the policy preferences of the IFIs. Such a strategy of learning through technocratic alignment seems to support another set of arguments concerning learning and cooperation: the importance of transnational epistemic communities who share a common set of "cause-and-effect beliefs" and appropriate control over policy in a particular issue-area.[87]

In negotiation and implementation of adjustment programs the key transnational community is technocratic, particularly those trained as economists at American or European universities.[88] At times of economic and political uncertainty, politicians (or heads of organizations) consult with and empower a new or wider range of specialists. These specialists may in turn lead the government to "learn" through defining its interests and strategies in new ways and forging new alliances with international

---

[86] On the case of Ghana, Thomas Callaghy, "Lost between State and Market," in Nelson, *Economic Crisis and Policy Choice*, p. 275; on Romania, Anne Henderson Dannenbaum, "The International Monetary Fund and Eastern Europe: The Politics of Economic Stabilization and Reform" (Paper presented at the 1989 American Political Science Association Annual Meeting), 21.

[87] For an example of this sort of analysis, Peter Haas, "Do Regimes Matter? Epistemic Communities and Mediterranean Pollution Control," *International Organization*, 43, no. 3 (Summer 1989): 377–403; Haas, *Saving the Mediterranean* (New York: Columbia University Press, 1989); and a forthcoming special issue of *International Organization*, edited by Haas, *Epistemic Communities and International Policy Coordination*.

[88] Whether the transnational network of mainstream professional economists is an epistemic community that shares not only causal beliefs but a common policy project is not of concern here.

actors. James Sebenius has noted that transnational epistemic communities, although portrayed as engines of social learning, can also be incorporated in more conventional bargaining models, as a " '*de facto natural coalition*' seeking to build a 'winning coalition' of support behind its preferred policy choice."[89]

In selecting allies—fellow members of an epistemic community attached to particular economic diagnoses and prescriptions—the IFIs and other adjustment-seeking external actors seem to employ two criteria. One, described above, is agreement on a model of the economy that matches mainstream economics. The other is bureaucratic position: accounts by both the critics and supporters of the Bank and the Fund suggest that technocrats within agencies responsible for macroeconomic and budgetary oversight (typically the finance ministry and the central bank) are often closely aligned with proadjustment pressure from the outside. In many cases, the career paths of these allies had socialized them further:

> By the 1980s, in almost all developing countries some senior economic officials (and/or influential private economists) had spent some time as staff members of the IMF, the World Bank, or the regional international development banks. . . . Often, alumni of the international financial institutions played key roles in the dual political game of adjustment. They interpreted external pressures and attempted to persuade their colleagues in domestic decision-making circles, and they interpreted internal constraints and attempted to persuade their former associates in dialogue with external agencies.[90]

Close alignment between a cadre of national economic technocrats and the IFIs seems to have been a prerequisite for agreement in this sample of cases, whether middle-income countries with highly developed bureaucratic structures or low-income states with weak authoritarian regimes. In Mexico, close relations between the IFIs and anti-inflationary technocrats in the central bank and the Treasury dated to the late 1940s; the long tenure of key officials lent considerable stability to the alliance.[91] In Zaire, a state deeply penetrated by political influence, a group of officials managing relatively insulated parastatals provided the World Bank's "small constituency of Zairian technocrats who support [its] efforts" in the country, reinforcing its relatively weak leverage.[92] Zambia was one of the rare instances in which the technocratic cadre was so weak that the

---

[89] James K. Sebenius, "Bargainers with Shared Beliefs: Negotiation Analysis and Epistemic Communities," forthcoming, *International Organization* (Winter 1992).

[90] Joan Nelson, "Conclusions," in Nelson, *Economic Crisis*, pp. 330–31.

[91] Robert R. Kaufman, *The Politics of Debt in Argentina, Brazil, and Mexico* (Berkeley, University of California: Institute of International Studies, 1988), pp. 63–65.

[92] Winsome J. Leslie, *The World Bank and Structural Transformation in Developing Countries: The Case of Zaire* (Boulder, Colo.: Lynne Rienner, 1987), p. 128.

program was essentially designed by the external agencies, which became the Ministry of Finance in the eyes of many Zambians.[93]

Unfortunately, although the strategy of social learning through technocratic alignment often produced initial agreement, it was unable to sustain that agreement in many cases. National learning through technocratic empowerment failed when learning did not extend up (to the political principals), laterally (to the implementing agencies), and down (to a trained civil service). Many failures, particularly in weak authoritarian states, resulted from a failure to assess the relationship of technocratic interlocutors to the political principals in the system. As Haggard and Kaufman describe in distinguishing between weak and strong authoritarian regimes, the political leadership may delegate considerable autonomy to economic technocrats: determining the limits of that autonomy may be extremely difficult for external actors.[94] Political elites may choose to revoke that autonomy, even after a lengthy period of bureaucratic hegemony. In the 1970s, for example, central bank and Treasury technocrats in Mexico lost their position of dominance under the presidencies of Echeverría and López Portillo.[95]

Efforts to assess the degree of technocratic autonomy have confronted two types of information manipulation on the part of national players. Politicians may use technocrats to win the confidence and financial support of the IFIs and aid donors, while carefully segmenting authority over economic decisions and circumscribing their power. The master at this game may have been Ferdinand Marcos in the Philippines. As described by Haggard, Marcos used "liberal" technocrats, such as Laya and Virata, to legitimate the regime in the eyes of foreign lenders, while carefully retaining a dualistic decision-making structure that protected the crony capitalism of his political allies. The strategy worked (in the sense of ensuring adequate finance and relatively low conditionality) until the discovery in late 1983 that the central bank had been manipulating the statistics that it offered the IMF. That breach of trust produced a much tougher approach to conditionality on the part of creditors and forced Marcos into a tough stabilization program that contributed to his political downfall.[96] In Zaire, Mobutu would frequently appoint trusted technocrats to strategic positions in order to attract more lending, and then abruptly remove them after additional financing had been committed.[97] In other cases, failure to implement an agreed program derived less from

[93] Callaghy, in Nelson, *Economic Crisis*, p. 292.

[94] Haggard and Kaufman, "Politics of Stabilization and Adjustment," pp. 235–36.

[95] Kaufman, *Politics of Debt*, p. 80.

[96] Stephan Haggard, "The Political Economy of the Philippine Debt Crisis," in Nelson, *Economic Crisis*, pp. 225, 230, 240.

[97] Leslie, *The World Bank*, pp. 136–37.

conscious manipulation of the technocrats than a misjudgment of their power vis-à-vis their political masters: Hasting Banda, as Minister of Agriculture in Malawi overrode his technocrats' agreement with the World Bank; Kenneth Kaunda in Zambia was much less committed to orthodox adjustment than his economic team.

Reliance on technocratic allies also founders on their limited powers vis-à-vis other bureaucratic players. Neoorthodox finance ministers often cannot carry their colleagues in the planning and "spending" ministries. Even in the Indonesian government, the power of the technocrats, with their training in economics, has come under challenge from the "technicians," who are more nationalist in their orientation and not aligned with the IFIs.[98] The power of technocrats allied to the IFIs may be artificially inflated: a bureaucratic interlocutor has every incentive to portray his power over economic policy as greater than it is; external actors once again confront a nearly intractable problem of hidden information. Case studies of World Bank SALs demonstrate the importance of involving implementing ministries in the policy dialogue. An able and energetic technocratic team in Kenya was unable to exercise much control over policy instruments outside the "push-button" instruments of the Finance Ministry and Central Bank.[99] In Ecuador as well, the young technocratic team did not involve the Agriculture Ministry in its negotiations despite the significance of agricultural reforms in the Bank's structural adjustment conditionality.[100]

External actors have sometimes found it impossible to rely on technocratic agents because there are simply too few of them. In several of the smaller developing countries in the sample—Ghana, Costa Rica, Jamaica, Zambia—weakness in bureaucratic capabilities at the lower levels was a significant barrier to implementation. Both the World Bank and the IMF have programs of technical assistance designed to create interlocutors. Directed through the Fiscal Affairs and Central Banking Departments at the IMF, technical assistance is "consumer-oriented": it is kept separate from Fund conditionality and dependent upon requests from member governments.

In other cases, the need for reliable personnel to carry out policy formulation and monitoring has led to the "reexpatriatization" of economic decision-making in these instances: external actors ensure alignment of interests by parachuting individuals of their choosing into key positions.

[98] Wing Thye Woo, and Anwar Nasution, "Indonesian Economic Policies and Their Relation to External Debt Management," in Jeffrey Sachs and Susan Collins, eds., *Developing Country Debt and Economic Performance* (Chicago: University of Chicago Press, 1991), vol. 3, book 1.

[99] Paul Mosley, "Kenya," in Mosley et al., *Aid and Power*, vol. 2, p. 301.

[100] Paul Mosley, "Ecuador," ibid., vol. 2, p. 430.

Even a trusted agent on the spot, however, requires minimal cooperation by the government to carry out his mission. In Zaire, expatriate advisors were cut off from necessary sources of information; civil servants were encouraged to regard the expatriates with suspicion, as "agents" (literally) furthering the "recolonization of Zaire."[101] The Economic Recovery Program in Ghana has been characterized by an even greater influx of expatriate advisers and consultants. Their presence has created nationalist resentment and a belief that they are principal beneficiaries of the ERP.[102]

Apart from these political shortcomings in a strategy of governmental learning through technocratic alignment, technocratic strengthening has produced increased conflict rather than alignment in certain cases. Carlos Diaz-Alejandro noted a decade ago that the "import substitution of economists" in Argentina, Brazil, and Chile had led to a decline in IMF influence in those countries.[103] The heterodox experiments in Latin America during the 1980s were, by and large, designed by economists with North American training and professional connections. Even in a poorer country, such as Malawi, IMF and World Bank efforts to support a group of technocrats who could analyze alternative policy options produced resistance from those same technocrats in the Ministry of Agriculture during negotiations for SAL III: the new "allies" of the IFIs simply disagreed with their prescriptions for agricultural pricing.[104]

Although the presence of technocratic allies may be a necessary condition for successful influence in most developing countries, this strategy of induced national learning has clear limits. In middle-income developing countries, interlocutors may share common training and discourse with IFI staff, but their ideological preferences and bureaucratic positions may make them adversaries rather than allies. In low-income countries, the creation of a technocratic core, short of reliance on expatriates, has become a major obstacle to the creation of a firm transnational alliance. And in many cases, the technocratic allies of external actors are in vulnerable political positions, despite their importance for a government's reputation and its access to external finance.

If learning at a deeper and more permanent level is to take place, it must include key members of the political elite, the principals who ultimately decide economic policy. In many cases, given the policy trajectory of the past, the elite is being asked to undergo a shift in policy paradigm and, as Peter Hall argues, such a shift is unlikely to take place purely within the

---

[101] Leslie, *The World Bank*, pp. 137–38.
[102] Callaghy, "Lost between State and Market," in Nelson, *Economic Crisis*, p. 38.
[103] In Williamson, *IMF Conditionality*, p. 345.
[104] Jane Harrigan, "Malawi," in Mosley et al., *Aid and Power*, vol. 2, chap. 15.

state.[105] Social learning, if it is to be consolidated, will involve a wider political debate. It may also require (following Thomas Kuhn's account of scientific paradigm shifts) the actual replacement of particular elites through a change in government or regime. The results described previously, in which new government and regimes seemed more likely to institute broader programs of economic change, match this model of deeper and more permanent social learning. External actors, and particularly the IFIs, are likely to have little influence over the course of such learning or its consolidation, which appears to be highly dependent on endogenous political change. External actors may, however, provide important external legitimation to those endorsing a new template for policy.

VIRTUOUS AND VICIOUS CYCLES OF INFLUENCE

The instruments used by external actors to exert influence over economic policy change—whether bargaining over finance and conditionality or exercising suasion through policy dialogue and transnational coalitions—often appear ineffectual means of exerting influence on national economic policies. Nevertheless, instances of successful collaboration that have produced improved economic prospects are also apparent in this review of cases. Indonesia and Turkey, for example, suggest a virtuous cycle of influence, in contrast to the vicious cycles that characterize many other developing countries in their relations with the IFIs. In such a virtuous cycle, both IFIs and national governments delivered on their repeated conditionality bargains and both sides benefited from joint gains that reinforced the bargain. The national governments took risky adjustment measures in advance of financial support from the outside; the external players delivered or catalyzed large amounts of foreign assistance in the form of IFI programs, foreign aid, and debt rescheduling. Skeptics argue that conditionality and even external advice were superfluous in these cases: alignment of interest was so close that external influence was hardly required. A closer reading of the cases, however, suggests a close working relationship with the IFIs, one in which genuine dialogue appears to take place.

What has occurred in these cases—more clearly in Indonesia than in Turkey—is a cycle of influence, sustained over time, in which reputation breeds cooperation, which attracts resources, which reinforces the policies desired. Donors get the policy changes that they want, by and large; the government gets reinforcement among its constituents through improved economic performance; constituents become willing to take a longer view given the credibility of the government's policies built up over

[105] Hall, "Policy Paradigms," pp. 19–20.

time. Such a cycle is shorthand for creating and sustaining governmental commitment (and credibility) in following a particular policy trajectory.

External actors can help to create (in a modest way) such commitment, although their efforts are highly dependent on the internal politics of adjustment and economic policymaking. The two models of influence, however, present starkly different prescriptions for inducing commitment. The bargaining model points to the need for credibility on the part of the IFIs, both in delivering financial support and in terminating the lending relationship when governments fail to implement promised policy changes. Both promise and threat have been less than credible during most of the 1980s. The model also suggests that creditor collaboration could be used to strengthen IFI bargaining power: in reality, when such collaboration has been achieved, its costs to the IFI relations with the country often outweighed the putative bargaining advantage. The bargaining model also suggests that compensation to losers from policy change may be a low-cost way of creating commitment on the part of governments. Finally, and most important, the emphasis on government commitment points to greater selection and fewer programs.

The prescriptions of a social learning model often run counter to these recommendations. The learning model emphasizes suasion and coalition-building as means to political commitment. Rather than credible threats to terminate a borrowing relationship, it emphasizes maintaining relations, as a means of estimating changes in commitment and widening the range of alternatives considered by an equivocating government. It accepts the need and the value for division of labor among creditors, for reasons of domestic political sensibilities as well as organizational comparative advantage; the appearance of a monolithic creditor coalition may be counterproductive. Rather than displaying a tough and inflexible bargaining position, the learning model suggests that the IFIs themselves must change as they reassess national and international conditions and that one of the costs of empowering their technocratic allies may be more serious debate over the correct policy line. Finally, the learning model would derive from the 1980s the lesson that reliance on a small island of technocrats for implementing wrenching economic reforms is a risky strategy. Learning must be extended from technocrats to political principals and to implementing agencies. Perhaps the best prescription for such broader and deeper social learning is patience rather than intervention.

The use of conditionality in its broadest sense is likely to widen during the 1990s. More actors—the European Community and Japan, in particular—will be wielding more financial power in a world in which the United States is barely first among equals. These efforts to shape national policies will be undertaken in societies, such as Eastern Europe, whose political features and adjustment paths differ significantly from those on which past lessons, however limited, have been built. The next step in evaluating the exercise of influence is a more refined analysis of the circumstances in which strategies based on the bargaining model or the learning model are more successful. Agencies may need to be redesigned in order to separate policies based on these competing images of international interaction. Only a process of continuous learning in this larger sense on the part of external agencies and donor governments is likely to produce a ratio of virtuous cycles of influence to vicious cycles that exceeds the mediocre record of the last decade.

TABLE A2.1
Adjustment Decisions and Implementation: A Rough Typology

Government	Periods to which Table Refers	No Coherent Program	Stabilization	Structural Change		
				Partial, Little Strategy	....	Broad, Clear Strategy
Limann (Ghana)	Sep. 1979–Dec. 1981	X				
Guzman (Dominican Republic)	Aug. 1978–Jul. 1982	X				
Carazo (Costa Rica)	Mid-1979–Apr. 1982	X				
Belaúnde (Peru)	Jan. 1983–Mar. 1984		C			
	Apr. 1984–Jul. 1985	X				
Kaunda (Zambia)	Jan. 1980–Nov. 1982	X				
	Dec. 1982–May 1987		C			C
	May 1987–end 1988[a]	X				
Sarney (Brazil)	Feb. 1986–Jan. 1987	(moratorium)	C[b]			
	Feb. 1987–Mar. 1988	X				
Jorge Blanco (Dominican Republic)	Aug. 1982–Jun. 1984		I			
	Jul. 1984–Apr. 1986	(mildly expansionist program)				
Betancur (Colombia)	Jul. 1982–Jun. 1984		I			
	Jul. 1984–Jun. 1986	X				
Marcos (Philippines)	1980–Jul. 1984	X				
	Aug. 1984–late 1985		I			
	Late 1985–Feb. 1986	X				
Babangida (Nigeria)	Sep. 1985–May 1986	X				
	Jun. 1986–end 1988[a]		I	M		
Monge (Costa Rica)	Jun. 1982–Feb. 1984		I			
	Mid-1983–Apr. 1986			M		

Arias (Costa Rica)	Jun. 1986–end 1988[a]			
Alfonsin (Argentina)	Dec. 1983–late 1984		(expansionist program)	M
	Jun. 1985–mid-1987	I[h]		M
Seaga (Jamaica)	Oct. 1980–Dec. 1983			M
	Apr. 1984–Oct. 1985	I		
	Oct. 1985–Feb. 1989			I
Aquino (Philippines)	Feb. 1986–Jul. 1987			I
Rawlings (Ghana)	Jan. 1982–Mar. 1983		X	I
	Apr. 1983–end 1988[a]	I		I
de la Madrid (Mexico)	Dec. 1982–Dec. 1988	I		I
Pinochet (Chile)	Mid-1975–mid-1982	I		I
	Mid-1982–Mar. 1984	I		
	Apr. 1984–Feb. 1985		(retrenchment of some market-oriented measures)	
	Feb. 1985–end 1988[a]			I
García (Peru)	Mid-1985–mid-1987	C[h]		C[h]

Source: Economic Crisis and Policy Choice: The Politics of Adjustment in the Third World, ed. by Joan M. Nelson (Princeton: Princeton University Press), 1990.

Key: X = No coherent program
C = Program largely or wholly collapsed
M = Mixed record of implementation
I = Program substantially implemented
h = Heterodox program
a = Program still under way as of late 1988

TABLE A2.2
World Bank Policy-based Lending Cases

	Implementation of Conditionality (% of conditions implemented on all SALs and SECALs at end of loan period)
Turkey	95
Thailand	70
Jamaica	63
Philippines	62
Ghana	58
Malawi	55
Kenya	38
Ecuador	28
Guyana	15

Source: Paul Mosley, Jane Harrigan and John Toye, *Aid and Power: The World Bank and Policy-based Lending* (London: Routledge, 1991), vol. 1, table 5.2.

PART II

The State and the Politics of Adjustment

The State as Problem and Solution: Predation, Embedded Autonomy, and Structural Change

Peter Evans

POSTWAR DEVELOPMENT theorizing began in the 1950s and 1960s with the assumption that state apparatuses could be used to foster structural change. The state's principal charge was to accelerate industrialization, but it was also expected to play a role in modernizing agriculture and providing the infrastructure necessary for urbanization. Experience during subsequent decades undercut the state's image as the preeminent change agent, generating instead a mirror image of the state as the principal obstacle to development. In Africa, even sympathetic observers could not ignore the cruel parody of postcolonial hopes being enacted by most states on the continent.[1] Bloated state apparatuses were equally obvious targets for Latin Americans trying to understand the roots of the crisis-ridden stagnation that confronted them.[2]

The new image of the state as the problem arose partly because it had

This paper represents the latest presentation of a set of ideas on the comparative analysis of the Third World state that orginally appeared as Working Paper 11 in the series on Comparative Development put out by Brown University's Center for the Study of Comparative Development in 1989. A more abbreviated version (minus India, Korea, and Taiwan) was published in the special issue on Comparative National Development of *Sociological Forum* (4, no. 4 [December 1989]: 561–88) edited by Alejandro Portes and A. Douglas Kincaid. A reformulated version of the material on developmental states appeared in *The Korean Journal of Policy Studies* 4 (1989): 129–46. Along the way a large number of debts have been acquired. I would like to acknowledge the support of a Guggenheim Fellowship and a fellowship from the Center for Advanced Study in the Behavioral Sciences (funded by NSF Grant #BNS8700864) without which this article could not have been written. I am also grateful to Pranab Bardhan, Robert Bates, Jeffry Frieden, Mark Granovetter, Albert Hirschman, Evelyne Huber, Atul Kohli, Kathleen Much, Ben Schneider, Ian Shapiro, Barbara Stallings, John Stephens, Charles Tilly, Steven Topik, Robert Wade, John Waterbury, and two anonymous reviewers for having provided useful substantive commentaries on an earlier version. This version has benefited substantially from the thoughtful and thoroughgoing editorial work of Stephan Haggard and Brian Folk.

[1] See, for example, Piotr Dutkiewicz and Gavin Williams, "All the King's Horses and All the King's Men Couldn't Put Humpty-Dumpty Together Again," *IDS Bulletin* 18, no. 3 (July 1987).

[2] Hernando de Soto's *The Other Path: The Invisible Revolution in the Third World* (New York: Harper and Row, 1989) is probably the best known indigenous manifesto of disillusionment.

failed to perform the tasks set out by the earlier agenda, but it was not only that. In at least some cases the state had, in fact, fostered substantial structural change, opening the way toward greater reliance on local industrial production. The salient definition of structural change had also changed. As Stallings (chapter 1) emphasizes, the downturn in the growth of world trade in the 1970s, coupled with the dramatic rise in real interest rates in the late 1970s and the drying up of commercial loans at the beginning of the 1980s, forced developing countries to focus anew on adjusting to the constraints imposed by the international environment; hence structural change became defined primarily in terms of "structural adjustment."

Real shifts in the development agenda and negative appraisals of past performance interacted with changes in the ideological and intellectual climate to bring to the forefront of the developmental debate the question of whether the state should even try to be an active economic agent. Minimalist theories of the state that emphatically limited the scope of effective state action to the establishment and maintenance of private property relations returned to prominence, bolstered by an impressive "neoutilitarian" analytic apparatus. Moreover, neoutilitarian theories of the state fit well with orthodox economic prescriptions for managing problems of structural adjustment. By the mid-1980s the combination was hard to resist.

Like most policy currents and intellectual fashions, the surge of neoutilitarian orthodoxy was self-limiting.[3] Problems in the implementation of structural adjustment programs and new doubts about whether structural adjustment was sufficient in itself to insure future growth led to rethinking the role of the state once again. By the end of the 1980s a third wave of thinking on the role of the state was beginning to crystalize.

To begin with, analysts like Kahler pointed out that orthodox policy prescriptions, despite their disdain for the wisdom of politicians, contained the paradoxical expectation that the state (the root of the problem) would somehow be able to become the agent that initiated and implemented adjustment programs (become the solution). It was not that this expectation was empirically unrealistic. As Waterbury (chapter 4) and others have emphasized, insofar as liberalization, privatization and other policies associated with structural adjustment have in fact been undertaken, state managers have played a vanguard role in initiating them. Nonetheless, it was not consistent with the rent-seeking behavior predicted by the neoutilitarian theory of the state.

Like it or not the state remains central to the process of structural

---

[3] See Miles Kahler, "Orthodoxy and its Alternatives: Explaining Approaches to Stabilization and Adjustment" in Joan Nelson, ed., *Economic Crisis and Policy Choice: The Politics of Adjustment in the Third World* (Princeton: Princeton University Press, 1990), pp. 33–61.

change, even when change is defined as structural adjustment. Recognition of the state's centrality inevitably leads back to questions of state capacity. It is not just a question of being able to recognize correct policies. The consistent pursuit of any policies, whether they are aimed at "getting prices right" or implanting local industry, requires the enduring institutionalization of a complex set of political machinery and, as Samuel Huntington pointed out forcefully a generation ago, such institutionalization can by no means be taken for granted. By the end of the 1980s, even former bastions of orthodoxy like the World Bank were disposed to consider the possibility that their clients' problems may arise, not just from bad policies, but from institutional deficiencies correctable only in the long term.[4] Dismantling the state is not the answer. It must be reconstructed.

Recognition of the importance of state capacity, not simply in the sense of the prowess and perspicacity of technocrats within the state apparatus but also in the sense of an institutional structure that is durable and effective, is characteristic of the third wave of thinking about the state and development. The unrealistically optimistic expectations concerning the state as an instrument of development that characterized the first wave have been exorcised, but so have the utopian visions that the state's role could be limited to patrolling to prevent violations of property rights. Among those writing about problems of adjustment, Callaghy is a good example of this third wave.[5] His analysis of the adjustment process assumes that the ability to deal with specific problems like stabilization and adjustment is rooted in diffuse general characteristics of the state apparatus and its relation to surrounding social structures and that these in turn are consequences of long term processes of institution change.

The analysis that follows is an attempt to contribute to the third wave. Its empirical base is not the analysis of the relation between state capacity and successful implementation of programs of structural adjustment. Instead it reexamines the state's role in the earlier developmental agenda—industrial transformation—and tries to provide an analytical portrayal of the institutional characteristics that separated states which were more successful at this task from those that were less successful.

The strategy of taking a step back and looking at earlier patterns of industrial transformation should not be taken as an assertion that the definition of effective state institutions is invariant across economic agen-

---

[4] Thomas Callaghy cites the World Bank's 1989 report on adjustment lending as example of the new emphasis on institution building in "Toward State Capability and Embedded Liberalism in the Third World: Lessons for Adjustment," pp. 115–38, in Joan Nelson, ed., *Fragile Coalitions: The Politics of Economic Adjustment* [Overseas Development Council U.S.–Third World Policy Perspectives No. 12] (New Brunswick, N.J.: Transaction Books, 1989), p. 133.

[5] Callaghy, "Toward State Capability," pp. 117, 131–32.

das. Some of the institutional characteristics that facilitated the growth of local industry may well be dysfunctional to the pursuit of an agenda of stabilization and adjustment. Nonetheless, there is a crude correlation between state performance around an agenda of industrial transformation and performance around an agenda of adjustment. African states that failed to implant local industries have been equally unsuccessful in securing growth through a program of structural adjustment. The East Asian cases that were most successful in implementing programs of industrial transformation have also been most successful at dealing with issues of adjustment. Latin American states lie somewhere in between in their performance on both agendas. Noting this crude correlation is a long way from demonstrating that there are important institutional features which facilitate both sets of tasks. Still, it suggests that an understanding of industrial transformation may not be irrelevant to the eventual construction of an analysis of the state's role in successful adjustment.

The crude correlation of state performance across tasks also suggests questioning neoutilitarian conceptualizations that portray the institutional requirements of implementing orthodox economic prescriptions as antithetical to those required to foster local industrialization. If better theoretical foundations are needed, it may make sense to review the classic institutionalist perspectives of Weber, Gerschenkron, Hirschman, and others rather than relying only on the "new institutionalism."

Conceptual reconsideration and comparative historical analysis will both be undertaken here. First, I examine some of the inconsistencies in the neoutilitarian vision of the state. I then probe some of the insights of the classic comparative institutionalist literature for clues that might help in building an analysis of effective state structures. The bulk of the chapter is an inductive comparative analysis of more and less successful states. The focus of this comparative analysis is not on stabilization and adjustment in the 1980s but rather on efforts to promote industrial transformation over the course of the post-World War II period. Several cases are examined. Zaire under Mobutu is taken as an example of an almost purely predatory state. Three East Asian cases—Japan, Taiwan and Korea—are used to explore the characteristics of the developmental state. These cases are then compared with two states that have achieved considerable success in some sectors and during some time periods but failed to be consistently developmental—Brazil and India. Finally, I will try to extract some analytical lessons from this comparative analysis and speculate on their relevance to problems of stabilization and adjustment.

PERSPECTIVES ON THE STATE

Antipathy toward the state as an institution has many roots, as anyone who has ever waited endlessly in line at a licensing agency or confronted an intransigent public servant is well aware. The second wave attack on the state drew support from such antipathies as well as from the obvious evidence of poor performance. The evolution of theoretical perspectives on the state also played an important role in generating the second wave.

Even theories of development that privilege the market as an institution have always recognized that "the existence of the state is essential for economic growth,"[6] but the essential state was a minimal one, "restricted largely, if not entirely, to protecting individual rights, persons and property, and enforcing voluntarily negotiated private contracts."[7] In its minimal neoclassical form, the state was treated as an exogenous black box whose internal functionings were not a proper or worthy subject for economic analysis. Neoutilitarian political economists, however, became convinced that the negative economic consequences of state action were too important to leave the black box closed. To unravel its workings, they applied the "standard tools of individual optimization" to the analysis of the state itself.[8]

The exchange relation between incumbents and supporters is the essence of state action. Incumbents require political supporters to survive and the supporters, in turn, must be provided with incentives sufficient to prevent their shifting support to other potential officeholders. Incumbents may either distribute resources directly to supporters, through subsidies, loans, jobs, contracts, or the provision of services, or use their rule-making authority to create rents for favored groups by restricting the ability of market forces to operate. Rationing foreign exchange, restricting entry through licensing producers, and imposing tariffs or quantitative restrictions on imports are all ways of creating rents. Incumbents may also exact a share of the rent for themselves. Indeed, it is hypothesized that "com-

---

[6] Douglas North, *Structure and Change in Economic History* (New York: Norton, 1981), p. 20.

[7] James M. Buchanan, Robert D. Tollison, and Gordon Tullock, eds., *Toward a Theory of the Rent-Seeking Society* (College Station, Tex.: Texas A&M University Press, 1980), p. 9.

[8] T. N. Srinivasan, "Neoclassical Political Economy, the State and Economic Development," *Asian Development Review* 3, no. 2 (1985): 38–58, 41. Among public choice theorists Nobel Laureate James Buchanan and his collaborators Tollison and Tullock are best known (see Buchanan, Tollison and Tullock, *The Rent-Seeking Society*). Others would include William A. Niskanen, *Bureaucracy and Representative Government* (Chicago: Aldine-Atherton, 1971); Richard D. Auster and Morris Silver, *The State as Firm: Economic Forces in Political Development* (The Hague: Martinus Nijhoff, 1979). The recent re-emergence of neoclassical political economy represents a similar, though usually less extreme, perspective. See David C. Colander, ed., *Neoclassical Political Economy: An Analysis of Rent-seeking and DUP Activities* (Cambridge, Mass.: Ballinger, 1984). Elements of the neoutilitarian view are also present in collective action perspectives, e.g., Mancur Olson, *The Rise and Decline of Nations* (New Haven, Conn.: Yale University Press, 1982), and the new institutional economics, which emphasizes property rights, e.g., Douglas North, *Structure and Change in Economic History*.

petition for entry into government service is, in part, a competition for rents."[9] In the economy as a whole, high returns from "directly unproductive profit-seeking" make investment in productive activities less attractive. Efficiency and dynamism decline.

In order to escape the deleterious effects of state action, the state's sphere should be reduced to the minimum, and bureaucratic control should be replaced by market mechanisms wherever possible. The range of state functions considered susceptible to marketization varies but some authors even speculate on the possibility of using "prizes" and other incentives to induce "privateers" and other private citizens to provide at least partially for the national defense.[10]

It would be foolish to deny that the neoutilitarian vision captures a significant aspect of the functioning of most states, perhaps the dominant aspect of the functioning of some states. Rent seeking, conceptualized more primitively as corruption, has always been a well-known facet of the operation of Third World states. Some states' apparatuses consume the surplus they extract, encourage private actors to shift from productive activities to unproductive rent seeking, and fail to provide collective goods. They have no more regard for their societies than a predator does for its prey and are legitimately called "predatory."[11]

Because it reintroduces politics, the neoutilitarian view should even be considered an improvement on the traditional neoclassical vision of the state as neutral arbiter. Indeed, the assumption that state policies "reflect vested interests in society" partially recaptures some of Marx's original insights into the biases that characterize state policy.[12] As an explanation of one pattern of the incumbent behavior which may or may not dominate in a particular state apparatus, neoutilitarian thinking is a useful contribution. As a monocausal master theory applicable to states gener-

[9] Anne O. Krueger, "The Political Economy of the Rent-Seeking Society," *American Economic Review* 64, no. 3 (June 1974): 291–303, 293.

[10] Auster and Silver, *The State as Firm*, p. 102.

[11] It is important to note that this vernacular way of conceptualizing the predatory state is quite different from the way the term is used by it advocates. Deepak Lal, *The Hindu Equilibrium: Cultural Stability and Economic Stagnation, India c. 1500BC–AD1980*, vol. 1 (Oxford: Clarendon Press, 1988), and Margaret Levi, *Of Rule and Revenue* (Berkeley: University of California Press, 1988) both equate predatory behavior with revenue maximizing behavior. In Levi's use states may maximize revenue in ways that promote development or in ways that impede it. Thus, the term *predatory* in her usage has no necessary developmental implications. States that others call developmental could easily be labeled predatory under Levi's definition. Lal is more convinced of the negative relation between revenue maximization and development. For him, as for the neoutilitarians, the alternative to the predatory state is the minimal nightwatchman state and there is no analytical space for a developmental state.

[12] Colander, *Neoclassical Political Economy*, p. 2.

ically, which the neoutilitarian view tends to become in the hands of its more dedicated adherents, the neoutilitarian model is problematic.

To begin with, it is hard to explain why, if officeholders are primarily interested in individual rents, they do not all "freelance." Neoutilitarian logic provides little insight into what constrains individual incumbents to work together as a collectivity at all. If we postulate that somehow the state solves its own collective action problem, there is no reason, within the logic of neoutilitarian arguments, for those who have a monopoly on violence to rest content being nightwatchmen and every reason for them to try to expand rental havens. In short, strict adherence to a neoutilitarian logic makes the existence of the state difficult to explain and the night-watchman state almost a theoretical impossibility.[13]

At the same time, the neoutilitarian assumption that exchange relations are natural, that is epistomologically prior to other kinds of social relationships, is not well supported by empirical evidence. Detailed studies of real processes of exchange (as opposed to analytical summaries of their results) find that markets operate well only when they are supported by other kinds of social networks.[14] An efficient system of property relations is not enough. The smooth operation of exchange requires the dense, deeply developed medium of trust and culturally shared understandings, summarized by Durkheim under the deceptively simple heading of the "noncontractual elements of contract."

For better or worse, markets are always inextricably embedded in a matrix that includes both cultural understandings and social networks composed of polyvalent individual ties. In some cases support for exchange relations may be generated by informal interaction. In other cases, formal hierarchical organizations may "internalize" exchange relations.[15] If markets must be surrounded by other kinds of social structures in order to operate, then neoutilitarian attempts to free the market from the state may end up destroying the institutional underpinnings that allow exchange to operate. This is, of course, the position of the classic tradition of comparative institutionalist scholarship which emphasized the essential complementarity of state structures and market exchange, particularly in the promotion of industrial transformation.

This tradition has always been critical of the proposition that exchange

[13] It is important to note that this critique is intended to highlight some of the problems inherent in the thinking that supported the radical second wave approach to the state, not as a review of the wide variety of literature on the state that has emerged under the general rubric of rational choice. For one such review see Levi, *Of Rule and Revenue*, appendix.

[14] See Mark Granovetter, "Economic Action and Social Structure: The Problem of Embeddedness," *American Journal of Sociology* 91, no. 3 (November 1985): 481–510.

[15] Cf. Oliver E. Williamson, *Markets and Hierarchies: Analysis and Antitrust Implications* (New York: Free Press, 1975).

was a natural activity that required only the most minimal institutional underpinnings. Forty years ago Polanyi argued, "The road to the free market was opened and kept open by an enormous increase in continuous, centrally organized and controlled interventionism."[16] From the beginning, according to Polanyi, the life of the market has been intertwined not just with other kinds of social ties, but with the forms and policies of the state.

Looking at established market societies, Weber carried this line of reasoning further, arguing that the operation of large scale capitalist enterprise depended on the availability of the kind of order that only a modern bureaucratic state could provide. As he put it: "Capitalism and bureaucracy have found each other and belong intimately together."[17] Weber's assumption of the intimate relation was, of course, based on a conception of the bureaucratic state apparatus that was the mirror image of the neo-utilitarian view. Weber's bureaucrats were concerned only with carrying out their assignments and contributing to the fulfillment of the goals of the apparatus as a whole. Use of the prerogatives of office for maximizing private interests was, for Weber, a feature of earlier prebureaucratic forms.

For Weber, the state was useful to those operating in markets precisely because the actions of its incumbents obeyed a logic quite different from that of utilitarian exchange. The state's ability to support markets and capitalist accumulation depended on the bureaucracy being a corporately coherent entity in which individuals see furtherance of corporate goals as the best means of maximizing their individual self-interest. Corporate coherence requires that individual incumbents be to some degree insulated from the demands of the surrounding society. Insulation, in turn, is enhanced by conferring a distinctive and rewarding status on bureaucrats. The concentration of expertise in the bureaucracy through meritocratic recruitment and the provision of opportunities for long-term career rewards was also central to the bureaucracy's effectiveness. In short, Weber saw construction of a solid, authoritative framework as a necessary prerequisite to the operation of markets.

Later observers extended Weber's vision of the state's role. The ability to implement rules predictably, however necessary, is not sufficient. Gerschenkron's work on late developers complements Weber by focusing on the specific contributions of the state apparatus to overcoming problems created by a disjunction between the scale of economic activity required

[16] Karl Polanyi, *The Great Transformation* (Boston: Beacon Press, 1957), p. 140.
[17] Max Weber, *Economy and Society*, ed. Guenter Roth and Claus Wittich (New York: Bedminster Press, 1968), p. 1395, n. 14.

for development and the effective scope of existing social networks.[18] Late industrializers confronting production technologies with capital requirements in excess of what private markets were capable of amassing were forced to rely on the power of the state to mobilize the necessary resources. Instead of simply providing a suitable environment, as it did in Weber's model, the state was now actively organizing a crucial aspect of the market. Gerschenkron's argument also raises a new issue—the problem of risk taking. The crux of the problem faced by late developers is that institutions that allow large risks to be spread across a wide network of capital holders do not exist, and individual capitalists are neither able nor interested in taking them on. Under these circumstances the state must serve as surrogate entrepreneur.

Hirschman takes up this emphasis on entrepreneurship as the missing ingredient for development in much more detail. Based on his observations of the "late late" developers of the twentieth-century Third World, Hirschman argues that capital, in the sense of a potentially investable surplus, is not the principal ingredient that is lacking in developing countries. What is lacking is entrepreneurship in the sense of willingness to risk the available surplus by investing it in productive activities, or in Hirschman's own words, "the perception of investment opportunities and transformation into actual investments." If "maximizing induced decision-making" is the key as Hirschman argues it is, then the state's role involves a high level of responsiveness to private capital.[19] It must provide disequilibrating incentives to induce private capitalists to invest and at the same time be ready to alleviate bottlenecks that are creating disincentives to investment.

States that succeed in undertaking the tasks that Gerschenkron and Hirschman outline, as well as those set out by Weber, are legitimately called "developmental."[20] They extract surplus but they also provide col-

[18] Alexander Gerschenkron, *Economic Backwardness in Historical Perspective* (Cambridge, Mass.: Belknap, 1962).

[19] Albert Hirschman, *The Strategy of Economic Development* (New Haven, Conn.: Yale University Press, 1958), pp. 35, 44.

[20] The term *developmental state*, like predatory state, is used with a variety of meanings. Piotr Dutkiewicz and Gavin Williams, "All the King's Horses," for example, apply the term to any state that professes an interest in development, regardless of whether there is a plausible argument that state actions have had any positive developmental consequences, or for that matter whether there is a plausible argument that the professed interest is more than rhetorical. Thus, Dutkiewicz and Williams' developmental states are analytically indistinguishable from predatory states. My use of the term is similar to that of the IDS group, e.g., Gordon White and Robert Wade, "Developmental States and Markets in East Asia: An Introduction," in White, ed., *Developmental States in East Asia* (London: Macmillan, 1988) and Chalmers Johnson, and also bears a family resemblance to what Raymond Duvall and John Freeman call entrepreneurial states in "The Techno-bureaucratic Elite and the Entre-

lective goods. They foster long-term entrepreneurial perspectives among private elites by increasing incentives to engage in transformative investments and lowering the risks involved in such investments. They may not be immune to rent-seeking or to using some of the social surplus for the ends of incumbents and their friends rather than those of the citizenry as a whole. Yet, on balance, the consequences of their actions promote rather than impede economic adjustment and structural transformation.

The existence of developmental states is generally recognized. In fact, some would argue that they have been the essential ingredient in "late" or "late late" development. White and Wade argue, for example, that "the phenomenon of successful 'late development' . . . should be understood . . . as a process in which states have played a strategic role in taming domestic and international market forces and harnessing them to a national economic interest."[21] Identifying the structural features that allow these states to be developmental is, however, a more controversial task.

The Gershenkronian/Hirschmanian vision makes the relationship between state capacity and insulation (or "autonomy") more ambiguous than a strictly Weberian perspective or, for that matter, a neo-Marxist one.[22] For the insulated state to be effective, the nature of a project of accumulation and the means of implementing it must be readily apparent. In a Gerschenkronian or Hirschmanian scenario of transformation, the shape of a project of accumulation must be discovered, almost invented, and its implementation demands close connections to private capital. A Prussian-style bureaucracy might well be effective at the prevention of force and fraud, but the kind of surrogate entrepreneurship that Gerschenkron talks about or the kind of subtle triggering of private initiative that Hirschman emphasizes would demand more than an insulated, corporately coherent administrative apparatus. It demands accurate intelligence, inventiveness, active agency and sophisticated responseness to a changing economic reality. Such arguments demand a state that is more embedded in society than insulated.[23]

Whatever the structural features that underlie state capacity, argu-

preneurial State in Dependent Industrialization," *American Political Science Review* 77 (1983): 569–87.

[21] White and Wade, "Developmental States," p. 1.

[22] Neo-Marxist arguments for the necessity of relative autonomy from the particularistic demands of individual capitalists reinforce the idea of a positive relation between capacity and autonomy. Cf. Dietrich Rueschemeyer and Peter Evans, "The State and Economic Transformation: Toward an Analysis of the Conditions Underlying Effective State Intervention," in Peter Evans, Dietrich Rueschemeyer, and Theda Skocpol, eds., *Bringing the State Back In* (New York: Cambridge University Press, 1985), pp. 44–77.

[23] Cf. Granovetter, "Economic Action and Social Structure," for a discussion of embeddedness.

ments for the central role of the state apply most strongly to situations in which structural transformation is the order of the day. Industrialization, which is the focus of the case studies that follow, is the classic example of this kind of transformation, but structural adjustment also requires more than incremental movement. It is also when transformation is on the agenda that the contrast between predatory and developmental states comes into sharpest relief. As Callaghy points out, the potential existence of a positive state role creates no logical necessity of the potential being realized. Societies and economies that "need" developmental states don't necessarily get them, as the case of Zaire amply demonstrates.

ZAIRE: AN EXEMPLARY CASE OF PREDATION

Since Joseph Mobutu Sese Seko gained control over Zaire in 1965, he and his coterie within the Zairian state apparatus have extracted vast personal fortunes from revenues generated by exporting the countries impressive mineral wealth. Over the next 25 years Zaire's GNP per capita *declined* at an annual rate of 2 percent a year, gradually moving the country toward the very bottom of the world hierarchy of nations and leaving the country's population in misery as bad or worse than that which they suffered under the Belgian colonial regime.[24] Zaire is, in short, a textbook case of a predatory state in which the preoccupation of the political class with rent-seeking has turned society into its prey.

Following Weber, Callaghy emphasizes the patrimonial qualities of the Zairian state; the mixture of traditionalism and arbitrariness that Weber argued retarded capitalist development.[25] True to the patrimonial model, control of the state apparatus is vested in a small group of personally connected individuals. At the pinnacle of power is the "presidential clique," which consists of "50-odd of the president's most trusted kinsmen, occupying the most sensitive and lucrative positions such as head of the Judiciary Council, secret police, Interior Ministry, President's office and so on."[26] Next is the "presidential brotherhood" who are not kin, but whose positions still depend on their personal ties with the president, his clique, and each other.

One of the most striking, and ironic, aspects of the Zairian state is the extent to which market relations dominate administrative behavior, again almost as a caricature of the neoutilitarian image of how rent-creating

[24] World Bank, *World Development Report, 1991* (New York: Oxford University Press, 1991), p. 204.

[25] Thomas Callaghy, *The State-Society Struggle: Zaire in Comparative Perspective* (New York: Columbia University Press, 1984), pp. 32–79.

[26] David Gould, "The Administration of Underdevelopment," in Guy Gran, ed., *Zaire: The Political Economy of Underdevelopment* (New York: Praeger, 1979), p. 93.

state apparatuses are likely to work. A Zairian archbishop described it as follows:

> Why in our courts do people only obtain their rights by paying the judge liberally? Why do the prisoners live forgotten in prisons? They do not have anyone who can pay the judge who has their dossiers at hand. Why in our office of administration, like public services, are people required to return day after day to obtain their due? If they do not pay the clerk, they will not be served.[27]

President Mobutu himself characterized the system in much the same way saying: "Everything is for sale, everything is bought in our country. And in this traffic, holding any slice of public power constitutes a veritable exchange instrument, convertible into illicit acquisition of money or other goods."[28]

The prevalence of such a thoroughgoing market ethic might at first seem inconsistent with what Callaghy characterizes as an "early modern absolutist state,"[29] but it is in fact quite consistent. Personalism and plundering at the top destroy any possibility of rule-governed behavior in the lower levels of the bureaucracy. Moreover, the marketization of the state apparatus makes the development of a bourgeoisie oriented toward long-term productive investment almost an impossibility by undermining the predictability of state action.

The persistence of the regime itself might be taken as evidence that Mobutu has managed to at least construct a repressive apparatus with the minimal amount of corporate coherence necessary to fend off potential competitors. It is not clear that even this is the case. As Gould puts it bluntly: "The bureaucratic bourgeoisie owes its existence to past and continued foreign support."[30] Aid from the World Bank as well as individual Western nations has played an important role, but French and Belgian troops at critical moments (e.g., in Shaba in 1978) have been the sine qua non of Mobutu's remaining in power.[31] Thus, Mobutu provides only a weak test of the limits to which rent seeking can be allowed to prevail without undermining even the repressive apparatus necessary for regime survival.[32]

[27] Cited in Callaghy, The State-Society Struggle, p. 420.

[28] Crawford Young, "Zaire: The Unending Crisis," Foreign Affairs 57, no. 1 (Fall 1978): 172.

[29] Callaghy, The State-Society Struggle.

[30] Gould, "The Administration of Underdevelopment," p. 93.

[31] Galen Hull, "Zaire in the World System: In Search of Sovereignty," in Gran, The Political Economy of Underdevelopment, pp. 263–83.

[32] Obviously, a full analysis of both the original character of the regime and its persistence would require more careful attention to the nature of Zaire's social structure. For a general approach to the question of the state and development which begins with an analysis of social structure see Joel Migdal, Strong Societies and Weak States: State-Society Relations

Zaire confirms clearly that it is not the bureaucracy that impedes development so much as the *absence* of a coherent bureaucratic apparatus. The "kleptopatrimonial" Zairian state is an amalgam of personalism and a thoroughly marketized administrative apparatus.[33] It is precisely the kind of exchange-dominated state that the neoutilitarians postulate and fear, but it is not only rampant rent seeking and distorted incentives that are produced. Weakness at the center of the political-economic system undermines the predictability of policy required for private investment. The state fails to provide even the most basic prerequisites for the functioning of a modern economy: predictable enforcement of contract, provision and maintenance of infrastructure, and public investment in health and education.

Zaire also poses some problems for conventional views of the importance of state autonomy in formulating coherent adjustment and growth strategies. On the one hand, since the state as a corporate entity is incapable of formulating coherent goals and implementing them, and since policy decisions are up for sale to private elites, the state might be seen as completely lacking in autonomy. This lack of autonomy is what permits pervasive rent seeking to prevail. At the same time, however, the Zairian state is strikingly unconstrained by society. It is autonomous in the sense of not deriving its goals from the aggregation of societal interests. This autonomy does not enhance the state's capacity to pursue goals of its own, but rather removes critical social checks on arbitrary rule. The Zairian case suggests that the relationship between capacity and autonomy needs rethinking. This becomes even more evident in looking at the developmental states of East Asia.

DEVELOPMENTAL STATES

While states like Mobutu's were providing practical demonstrations of the perversions predicted by neoutilitarian visions of the state, a different set of nations halfway around the world were writing historical records that confirmed insitutionalist expectations. By the end of the 1970s, the economic success of the major East Asian newly industrialized countries (NICs), Korea and Taiwan, was increasingly interpreted as depending on

and State Capabilities in the Third World (Princeton, N.J.: Princeton University Press, 1988).

[33] The conjunction of leviathan and the invisible hand is not as contradictory as it might seem but is, in fact, quite common. It does take different forms in different states. For example, in the less traditionally corrupt military regimes of Argentina and Chile, brutal, leviathan-like control over political dissension was combined with fierce imposition of market logic on the surrounding society.

the active involvement of the state,[34] even by observers with a neoclassical bent.[35] The East Asian cases are not only important in understanding the developmental role of the state in general. They are also important because they suggest that the institutional underpinnings of the earlier agenda of local industrial transformation may not be irrelevant to the successful execution of an agenda of adjustment. These states are, after all, the paradigmatic cases of both rapid local industrialization and effective adjustment to changing international markets.

The Japanese Model

Looking for institutional bases on which to build rapid industrialization, the East Asian NICs drew on the regional model of the active state—Japan. Analyses of the Japanese case provide a nice starting point for understanding of the developmental state. Chalmers Johnson's account of the golden years of the Ministry of International Trade and Industry (MITI) provides one of the best pictures of the developmental state in action.[36] His description is particularly fascinating because it corresponds so neatly to what a sophisticated implementation of ideas from Gerschenkron and Hirschman might look like in practice.

In the capital-scarce years following World War II, the Japanese state acted as a surrogate for weakly developed capital markets, while inducing transformative investment decisions. State institutions from the postal saving system to the Japan Development Bank were crucial in getting the needed investment capital to industry. The state's centrality to the provision of new capital, in turn, allowed MITI to aquire a central industrial policy role. Given its role in the approval of investment loans from the Japan Development Bank, its authority over foreign currency allocations for industrial purposes and licenses to import foreign technology, its ability to provide tax breaks, and its capacity to articulate "administrative guidance cartels" that would regulate competition in an industry, MITI was in a perfect position to "maximize induced decision-making."[37]

Some might consider Johnson's characterization of MITI as "without doubt the greatest concentration of brainpower in Japan" an exaggeration, but few would deny the fact that until recently, "official agencies

[34] Alice Amsden, "Taiwan's Economic History: A Case of Etatisme and a Challenge to Dependency Theory," *Modern China* 5, no. 3 (1979): 341–80.

[35] For example, Leroy Jones and Sakong Il, *Government, Business and Entrepreneurship in Economic Development: The Korean Case. Studies in Modernization of the Korean Republic, 1945–1975* (Cambridge, Mass.: Harvard University Press, 1980).

[36] Chalmers Johnson, *MITI and the Japanese Miracle: The Growth of Industrial Policy, 1925–1975* (Stanford, Calif.: Stanford University Press, 1982).

[37] See, for example, Johnson's description of MITI's nurturing of the petrochemical industry in the 1950s and 1960s, *MITI and the Japanese Miracle*, p. 236.

attract the most talented graduates of the best universities in the country
and positions of higher level official in these ministries have been and still
are the most prestigious in the country."[38]

There is thus clearly a Weberian aspect to the Japanese developmental
state. Officials have the special status that Weber felt was essential to a
true bureaucracy. They follow long-term career paths within the bureaucracy and operate generally in accordance with rules and established
norms. These characteristics vary somewhat across the Japanese bureaucracy, but the less bureaucratic, more clientelistic agencies like the Ministry of Agriculture are generally viewed as "pockets of conspicuous inefficiency."[39] If Japan confirms Weberian pronouncements regarding the
necessity of a coherent, meritocratic bureaucracy, it also indicates the necessity of going beyond such prescriptions. All descriptions of the Japanese state emphasize the indispensability of informal networks, both internal and external, to the state's functioning. Internal networks,
particularly the *gakubatsu*, or ties among classmates at the elite universities from which officials are recruited, are crucial to the bureaucracy's
coherence.[40] These informal networks give the bureaucracy an internal
coherence and corporate identity that meritocracy alone could not provide. The fact that formal competence, rather than clientelistic ties or traditional loyalties, is the prime requirement for entry into the network,
makes it much more likely that effective performance will be a valued
attribute among loyal members of the various *batsu*. The overall result is
a kind of "reinforced Weberianism," in which the "nonbureaucratic elements of bureaucracy" reinforce the formal organizational structure in
the same way that Durkheim's "noncontractual elements of contract" reinforce the market.[41]

External networks connecting the state and private are even more important. As Chie Nakane puts it, "the administrative web is woven more
thoroughly into Japanese society than perhaps any other in the world."[42]
Japanese industrial policy depends fundamentally on the ties that connect
MITI and major industrialists.[43] Ties between the bureaucracy and private powerholders are reinforced by the pervasive role of MITI alumni,

[38] Johnson, *MITI and the Japanese Miracle*, pp. 26, 20. Johnson reports that in 1977 only
thirteen hundred out of fifty-three thousand passed the higher-level Public Officials Examination and cites an overall failure rate of 90 percent for the years 1928–43 (p. 57).

[39] Daniel I. Okimoto, *Between MITI and the Market: Japanese Industrial Policy for High
Technology* (Stanford, Calif.: Stanford University Press, 1989), p. 4.

[40] In 1965 an astounding 73 percent of higher bureaucrats were graduates of Tokyo University Law School.

[41] Cf. Rueschemeyer and Evans, "The State and Economic Transformation."

[42] Cited in Okimoto, *Between MITI and the Market*, p. 170.

[43] Okimoto, *Between MITI and the Market*, p. 157, estimates that the deputy director of
a MITI sectoral bureau may spend the majority of his time with key corporate personnel.

who through *amakudari* (the "descent from heaven" of early retirement), end up in key positions not only in individual corporations but also in the industry associations and quasi-governmental organizations that comprise "the maze of intermediate organizations and informal policy networks, where much of the time-consuming work of consensus formation takes place."[44]

The centrality of external ties has led some to argue that the state's effectiveness emerges "not from its own inherent capacity but from the complexity and stability of its interaction with market players."[45] This perspective is a necessary complement to descriptions like Johnson's, but it runs the danger of setting external networks and internal corporate coherence as opposing alternative explanations. Instead internal bureaucratic coherence should be seen as an essential precondition for the state's effective participation in external networks. If MITI were not an exceptionally competent, cohesive organization, it could not participate in external networks in the way that it does. If MITI were not autonomous in the sense of being capable of independently formulating its own goals and able to count on those who work within it to see implementing these goals as important to their individuals careers, then it would have little to offer the private sector. MITI's relative autonomy is what allows it to address the collective action problems of private capital, helping capital as a whole to reach solutions that would be hard to attain otherwise, even within the highly organized Japanese industrial system.

This embedded autonomy is the mirror image of the incoherent absolutist domination of the predatory state and constitutes the organizational key to the effectiveness of the developmental state. Embedded autonomy depends on an apparently contradictory combination of Weberian bureaucratic insulation with intense immersion in the surrounding social structure. How this contradictory combination is achieved depends, of course, on both the historically determined character of the state apparatus and the nature of the social structure in which it is embedded, as a comparison of Japan with the East Asian NICs illustrates.

Korea and Taiwan

Korea and Taiwan have different state structures linked to different social bases of support, different patterns of industrial organization, and different policy strategies.[46] Nonetheless, they share crucial features. In both, the policy initiatives that facilitated industrial transformation was rooted

[44] Okimoto, *Between MITI and the Market*, p. 155.

[45] Richard J. Samuels, *The Business of the Japanese State: Energy Markets in Comparative and Historical Perspective* (Ithaca, N.Y.: Cornell University Press, 1987), p. 262.

[46] Cf. Tun-jen Cheng, "The Politics of Industrial Transformation: The Case of the East Asia NICs" (Ph.D. diss., Department of Political Science, University of California, 1987).

in coherent, competent bureaucratic organization. Though both of the East Asian NICs look more autonomous than the Japanese state, both reveal elements of the embedded autonomy that was crucial to Japan's success.

In comparing the Korean bureaucracy to Mexico's, Kim Byung Kook points out that while Mexico has yet to institutionalize exam-based civil service recruitment, meritocratic civil service examinations have been used for recruiting incumbents into the Korean state since A.D. 788, more than a thousand years.[47] Despite Korea's chaotic twentieth-century political history, the bureaucracy has been able to pick its staff from among the most talented members of the most prestigious universities. Data on the selectivity of the Higher Civil Service Examinations are almost identical to the data offered by Johnson for Japan. Despite a sevenfold increase in the annual number of recruits to the higher civil service between 1949 and 1980, only about 2 percent of those who take the exam are accepted.[48]

Along with similar recruitment patterns comes the inculcation of a particular corporate culture. Choi's discussion of the Economic Planning Board, for example, notes the same kind of confidence and esprit de corps that characterize MITI in Johnson's description.[49] Finally, as in Japan, meritocratic recruitment via elite universities and the existence of a strong organizational ethos creates the potential for constructing *batsu*-like solidary interpersonal networks within the bureaucracy. Looking at those who passed the civil service examination in 1972, Kim found 55 percent were graduates of Seoul National University and of these, 40 percent were graduates of two prestigious Seoul high schools.[50]

While the Korean bureaucracy seems an archetype, Korea's experience also shows the insufficiency of a bureaucratic tradition. In the 1950s under Rhee Syngman, the civil service exam was largely bypassed, with only about 4 percent of those filling higher entry level positions entering via the civil service exam. Nor were those who entered the higher civil service able to count on making their way up through the ranks via a standard process of internal promotion. Instead higher ranks were filled primarily on the basis of politically-driven "special appointments."[51]

The character of bureaucratic appointment and promotion under Rhee

[47] Kim Byung Kook, "Bringing and Managing Socioeconomic Change: The State in Korea and Mexico" (Ph.D. diss., Department of Government, Harvard University, 1987), pp. 101–2.

[48] Kim, "Bringing and Managing Socioeconomic Change," p. 101.

[49] Choi Byung Sun, "Institutionalizing a Liberal Economic Order in Korea: The Strategic Management of Economic Change" (Ph.D. diss., Kennedy School, Harvard University, 1987).

[50] Kim, "Bringing and Managing Socioeconomic Change," p. 101.

[51] Ibid., pp. 101–2.

is, of course, quite consistent with the character of his regime. While Rhee presided over a certain amount of import-substituting industrialization, his regime was more predatory than developmental. Massive U.S. aid, in effect, financed substantial government corruption. Rhee's dependence on private sector donations to finance his political dominance made him dependent on clientelistic ties with individual businessmen and, not surprisingly, "rent-seeking activities were rampant and systematic."[52]

Without a deep, thoroughly elaborated, bureaucratic tradition, neither the Park regime's reconstruction of bureaucratic career paths nor its reorganization of the economic policy making apparatus would have been possible. Without some powerful additional basis for cohesion in the upper ranks of the state, the bureaucratic tradition would have remained ineffectual. Without both in combination it would have been impossible to transform the state's relationship to private capital.

Only with the ascension to power of a group with strong ideological convictions and close personal and organizational ties was the state able to "regain its autonomy."[53] The junior officers involved in the coup led by Park Chung Hee were united by both reformist convictions and close interpersonal ties both on service experience and close *batsu*-like network ties originating in the military academy.[54] The super-imposition of this new brand of organizational solidary sometimes undercut the civilian state bureaucracy as military men were put in top posts but, in general, the military used the leverage provided by their own corporate solidarity to both strengthen and discipline the bureaucracy. Under Park the proportion of higher entry-level positions filled with Higher Civil Service examinees quintupled and internal promotion became the principal means of filling all ranks above them, with the exception of the highest political appointments.[55]

One of the features of the revitalized state bureaucracy was the relatively privileged position held by a single pilot agency, the Economic Planning Board (EPB). Headed by a deputy prime minister, the EPB was chosen by Park to be a "superagency" in the economic area.[56] Its power to coordinate economic policy through control of the budgetary process is enhanced by mechanisms like the Economic Ministers Consultation Committee and by the fact that its managers are often promoted into leadership positions in other ministries.[57] As in the Japanese case the ex-

---

[52] Cheng, "The Politics of Industrial Transformation," p. 200.

[53] Ibid., p. 203.

[54] See for example Kang's (1988) description of the Hanahoe club, founded by members of the eleventh military academy class.

[55] Kim, "Bringing and Managing Socioeconomic Change," pp. 101–8.

[56] Ibid., p. 115.

[57] For example, according to Choi, "Institutionalizing a Liberal Economic Order," p. 50,

istence of a pilot agency does not mean that policies are uncontested within the bureaucracy. The EPB and the Ministry of Trade and Industry (MTI) are often at loggerheads over industrial policy.[58] Nonetheless, the existence of a given agency with generally acknowledged leadership in the economic area allows for the concentration of talent and expertise and gives economic policy a coherence that it lacks in a less clearly organized state apparatus.

When the Park regime took power its goal seemed to be not just insulation from private capital but complete dominance over it. Criminal trials and confiscation were threatened and the leaders of industry were marched through the street in ignominy as corrupt parasites. This soon changed as Park realized that he needed to harness private entrepreneurship and managerial expertise to achieve his economic goals.[59] Over time, and particularly in the 1970s, the ties between the regime and the largest chaebol (conglomerates) became so tight that visiting economists concluded that "Korea, Inc." was "undoubtedly a more apt description of the situation in Korea than is 'Japan, Inc.' "[60]

As in the case of Japan, the symbiotic relationship between the state and the chaebol was founded on the fact that the state had access to capital in a capital scarce environment.[61] Through its ability to allocate capital the state promoted the concentration of economic power in the hands of the chaebol, and "aggressively orchestrated" their activities.[62] At the same time, the Park regime was dependent on the chaebol to implement

"four out of five Ministers of the Ministry of Trade and Industry between December 1973 and May, 1982 were former Vice-Ministers of the EPB."

[58] Cheng, "The Politics of Industrial Transformation," p. 231–32, claims that the MTI rather than the EPB dominated industrial policy making in the early 1970s, but clearly by the late 1970s the EPB was again dominant.

[59] See Kim Eun Mee, "From Dominance to Symbiosis: State and Chaebol in the Korean Economy, 1960–1985" (Ph.D. diss., Department of Sociology, Brown University, 1987); Kim Myoung Soo, "The Making of the Korean Society: The Role of the State in the Republic of Korea (1948–1979)" (Ph.D. diss., Department of Sociology, Brown University, 1987).

[60] Mason et al., The Economic and Social Modernization of the Republic of Korea (Cambridge: Harvard University Press, 1980), cited in Bruce Cumings, "The Origins and Development of the Northeast Asian Political Economy: Industrial Sectors, Product Cycles and Political Consequences," in F. Deyo, ed., The Political Economy of the New Asian Industrialism (Ithaca, N.Y.: Cornell University Press, 1987), p. 73.

[61] The importance first of foreign aid and then of foreign loans, both of which were channeled through the state and allocated by it was a cornerstone of the state's control over capital. See Kim, "From Dominance to Symbiosis"; Woo Jung-en, Race to the Swift: State and Finance in Korean Industrialization (New York: Columbia University Press, 1991); and Barbara Stallings, "The Role of Foreign Capital in Economic Development," in Gary Gereffi and Donald L. Wyman, eds., Manufacturing Miracles: Paths of Industrialization in Latin America and East Asia (Princeton: Princeton University Press, 1990), pp. 55–89.

[62] Robert Wade, Governing the Market: Economic Theory and the Role of Government in East Asian Industrialization (Princeton: Princeton University Press, 1990), p. 320.

the industrial transformation that constituted its primary project and the basis for its legitimacy.

The embeddedness of the Korean state under Park was a much more top-down affair than the Japanese prototype, lacking the well-developed intermediary associations and focused on a much smaller number of firms. The size and diversification of the largest *chaebol* did give them interests that were relatively "encompassing" in sectoral terms so that the small number of actors did not limit the sectoral scope of the shared project of accumulation.[63] Still, the Korean state could not claim the same generalized institutional relation with the private sector that the MITI system provided and never fully escaped the danger that the particularistic interests of individual firms might lead back in the direction of unproductive rent seeking. This, at least, was the perception of the Young Turk technocrats in the EPB at the beginning of the 1980s who felt that it was past time that the state begin to distance itself from resource claims of the largest *chaebol*.[64]

Korea is pushing at the limit to which embeddedness can be concentrated in a few ties without degenerating into particularistic predation. The opposite risk, of weak links to private capital threatening the state's ability to secure full information and count on the private sector for effective implementation, is represented by the region's second prominent pupil of the Japanese model, Taiwan.

In Taiwan, as in Korea, the state has been central to the process of industrial accumulation, channeling capital into risky investments, enhancing the capacity of private firms to confront international markets, and taking on entrepreneurial functions directly through state-owned enterprises. In Taiwan, as in Korea, the ability of the state to play this role depended on a classic, meritocratically-recruited, Weberian bureaucracy, crucially reinforced by extra-bureaucratic organizational forms. As in the case of the Korean state, the Kuomintang (KMT) regime is built on a combination of longstanding tradition and dramatic transformation, but differences in the historical experience of the two states led to very different patterns of relations with the private sector and, in consequence, very different patterns of state entrepreneurship. The transformation of the Kuomintang state following its arrival on Taiwan is as striking as the changes in Korea between the Rhee and Park governments. On the mainland the KMT regime had been largely predatory, riddled with rent seeking and unable to prevent the particular interests of private speculators from undermining its economic projects. On the island, the party remade

[63] Cf. Mancur Olson, *The Rise and Decline of Nations*.

[64] See Stephan Haggard and Chung-in Moon, "Institutions and Economic Policy: Theory and a Korean Case Study," *World Politics* 42, no. 2 (January 1990): 210–37.

itself. Freed of its old landlord base, and aided by the fact that the "most egregiously corrupt and harmful" members of the capitalist elite did not follow Chiang Kai Shek to the island,[65] the KMT was able to completely rework its ties with private capital. A corrupt and faction-ridden party organization came to approximate the Leninist party-state that it had aspired to be from the beginning,[66] thus providing the state bureaucracy with a reinforcing source of organizational cohesion and coherence more powerful and stable than could have been provided by military organization alone.

Within the reinforced governmental apparatus, the KMT put together a small set of elite economic policy organizations similar in scope and expertise to Japan's MITI or Korea's EPB.[67] The Council on Economic Planning and Development (CEPD) is the current incarnation of the planning side of the economic general staff. It is not an executive agency but "in Japanese terms lies somewhere between MITI and the Economic Planning Agency."[68] The Industrial Development Bureau (IDB) of the Ministry of Economic Affairs is staffed primarily by engineers and takes a more direct role in sectoral policies. Both of these agencies, like their counterparts in Korea and Japan, have traditionally been successful in attracting the best and the brightest. Staff members tend to be both KMT members and graduates of the country's elite Taiwan National University.[69]

Without negating the fundamental transformation in the character of the Kuomintang apparatus, it is also noteworthy that as in the case of Korea, the existence of a long bureaucratic tradition gave the regime a foundation on which to build. Not only was there a party organization that provided political cohesion at the top, but there was also an economic bureaucracy with considerable managerial experience. For example, the National Resources Commission (NRC), founded in 1932, had a staff of twelve thousand by 1944 and managed over one hundred public enterprises whose combined capital accounted for half of the paid-up capital of all Chinese enterprises. It was an island of relatively meritocratic recruitment within the mainland regime and its alumni eventually came to play a major role in managing industrial policy on Taiwan.[70]

The punishing experience of being undercut by the particularistic inter-

---

[65] Tom Gold, *State and Society in the Taiwan Miracle* (New York: M.E. Sharpe, 1986), p. 59.

[66] Cheng, "The Politics of Industrial Transformation," p. 97.

[67] The discussion that follows draws primarily on Wade, *Governing the Market*.

[68] Wade, *Governing the Market*, p. 198.

[69] Ibid., p. 217.

[70] According to Wade, *Governing the Market*, pp. 272–73, the pool of NRC technocrats provided among other leading economic bureaucrats eight out of fourteen Ministers of Economic affairs.

ests of private speculators on the mainland led the political leadership of the KMT as well as the alumni of the NRC to harbor a fundamental distrust of private capital and to take seriously the anticapitalist elements of Sun Yat Sen's ideological pronouncements. These predilections were reinforced by the pragmatic fact that strengthening private capitalists on Taiwan involved increasing the power of an ethnically distinct, politically hostile private elite. It is therefore hardly surprising that instead of turning Japanese properties over to the private sector as its American advisors recommended, the KMT retained control, generating one of the largest state-owned sectors in the non-Communist world.[71] What is surprising is that Taiwan's state-owned enterprises (SOEs), in contrast to the pattern of inefficiency and deficit financing that is often considered intrinsic to the operation of such firms, were for the most part both profitable and efficient.[72]

On Taiwan, SOEs have been key instruments of industrial development. In addition to the banking sector, which was state-owned as in post-Rhee Korea, state-owned enterprises accounted for the majority of industrial production in the 1950s[73] and, after falling off a bit in the 1960s, their share expanded again in the 1970s.[74] SOEs are particularly important in basic and intermediary industries. China Steel, for example, has enabled Taiwan to successfully outcompete all Organization for Economic Cooperation and Development (OECD) steel exporters in the Japanese market.[75] The state enterprise sector not only makes a direct entrepreneurial contribution, but is also a training ground for economic leadership in the central state bureaucracy.[76] Thus, economic policy formation in Taiwan grows out of "a little understood but apparently vigorous policy network which links the central economic bureaus with public enterprises [and] public banks."[77]

What is striking in comparing Taiwan with Korea and Japan is the extent to which the Taiwanese private sector has been absent from economic policy networks. Even though the current trend is to "expand and institutionalize decision-making inputs from industrialists, financiers and

[71] See Cheng, "The Politics of Industrial Transformation," p. 107; Wade, *Governing the Market*, p. 302.

[72] Cf. Waterbury, chapter 4.

[73] Wade, *Governing the Market*, p. 78. Even in the 1980s, the state accounted for almost half of Taiwan's gross domestic capital formation and state enterprises accounted for two-thirds of the state's share (Cheng, "The Politics of Industrial Transformation," p. 166).

[74] Wade, *Governing the Market*, p. 97.

[75] P. Bruce, "World Steel Industry: The Rise and Rise of the Third World," *Financial Times* (London, 22 November 1983), cited in Wade, *Governing the Market*, p. 99.

[76] According to Wade, *Governing the Market*, p. 275, "most Ministers of Economic Affairs have had management positions in public enterprises."

[77] Wade, *Governing the Market*, p. 295.

others,"[78] historical relations between the KMT state and private (mainly Taiwanese) capital have been sufficiently distant to raise the question of whether embeddedness is really a necessary component of the developmental state.

The Taiwanese state unquestionably operates effectively with a less dense set of public-private network ties than the Korean or Japanese versions of the developmental state. Nonetheless, its lack of embeddedness should not be exaggerated. It is hardly isolated from the private sector. Gold has shown the close relations that existed between the government and the nascent textile sector in the 1950s, as well as the key intermediary role the government played in the development of the semiconductor industry in the 1970s. Wade notes that IDB officials spend a substantial portion of their time visiting firms and are engaged in something very much like MITI's "administrative guidance."[79] He provides a revealing example of the state's close interaction with private capital in his discussion of negotiations between raw materials producers and textile companies in the synthetic fiber industry. While the formal negotiations involved the downstream industry association (Manmade Fibers Association) and the upstream domestic monopolist (a state-MNC joint venture), state managers were continuously involved.[80] By engaging in this kind of negotiation state managers ensure that neither the country's efforts at backward integration into intermediary products nor the export competitiveness of its textile producers is threatened by unresolved private conflicts. Informal public-private networks may be less dense than in the other two cases, but they are clearly essential to Taiwan's industrial policy.

In addition to defining the limits to which embeddedness can be reduced, the Taiwanese case highlights the symbiotic relationship between state autonomy and the preservation of market competition. The role of state autonomy in preserving market relationships is also crucial in Korea and Japan, but it is most apparent in the case of Taiwan.[81]

The evolution of the textile industry offers the best illustration.[82] In the early 1950s, K. Y. Yin, ignoring the American-trained economists advising his government, decided that Taiwan should develop a textile indus-

---

[78] Ibid., p. 293.

[79] Ibid., p. 284.

[80] Ibid., p. 281.

[81] Cf. Stephan Haggard, *Pathways from the Periphery: The Politics of Growth in the Newly Industrializing Countries* (Ithaca, N.Y.: Cornell University Press, 1990), pp. 44–45.

[82] Cf. Peter Evans and Chien-kuo Pang, "State Structure and State Policy: Implications of the Taiwanese Case for Newly Industrializing Countries" (Paper presented at the International Conference on Taiwan: A Newly Industrialized Country, National Taiwan University, 3–5 September 1987).

try. The result was the textile entrustment scheme that, by providing an assured market and raw materials, minimized the entrepreneurial risk involved in entering the industry and successfully induced the entry of private capital. In this initial phase, the state was supportive in a classic Hirschmanian way, inducing investment decisions and stimulating the supply of entrepreneurship.[83]

The entrustment scheme in itself is unusual only in the lengths to which the state was willing to go in order to ensure that entrepreneurship was forthcoming; otherwise it was very similar to the policies of most Latin American countries in the initial phases of industrialization. What is unusual is that the entrustment scheme did not become the instrument of the entrepreneurs it had created. Instead, the KMT regime progressively exposed its "greenhouse capitalists" to the rigors of the market, making export quotas dependent on the quality and price of goods, gradually shifting incentives toward exports, and finally diminishing protection over time.[84] Thus, the state was able to enforce the emergence of a free market rather than allowing the creation of rental havens. Without the autonomy made possible by a powerful bureaucratic apparatus, it would have been impossible to impose the unpleasantness of free competition on such a comfortable set of entrepreneurs.

The example reinforces the point made earlier in relation to embeddedness and autonomy in Japan. Private capital, especially private capital organized into tight oligopolistic networks, is unlikely to be a political force for competitive markets. Nor can a state that is a passive register of these oligopolistic interests give them what they are unwilling to provide for themselves. Only a state that is capable of acting autonomously can provide this essential collective good. Embeddedness is necessary for information and implementation, but without autonomy embeddedness will degenerate into a supercartel, aimed, like all cartels, at protecting its members from changes in the status quo.

A final, equally important characteristic of the developmental state is also well illustrated by the Taiwanese case. While the government has been deeply involved in a range of sectors, the Taiwanese state is extremely selective in its interventions. The bureaucracy operates in Wade's

[83] See Gold, *State and Society in the Taiwan Miracle*, p. 70; Pang Chien Kuo, "The State and Economic Transformation: The Taiwan Case" (Ph.D. diss., Department of Sociology, Brown University, 1987), pp. 167–69.

[84] The same strategy continues to be used. Wade, *Governing the Market*, pp. 207–8, recounts the IDB's efforts to induce local VCR production at the beginning of the 1980s. Two local companies were at first given a monopoly, but when, after a year and a half, they were still not producing internationally competitive products, Japanese firms were allowed to enter the market (with local joint venture partners) despite the protests of the original entrants.

words as a "filtering mechanism," focusing the attention of policy makers and the private sector on products and processes crucial to future industrial growth.[85] Like most of the KMT's Taiwan strategy, selectivity was in part a response to previous experience on the mainland; having experienced the disasters of an overextended state apparatus, the KMT was determined to husband its bureaucratic capacity in its new environment.[86] Selectivity would, however, seem to be a general feature of the developmental state. Johnson describes how the Japanese state, having experimented with direct and detailed intervention in the pre-World War II period, limited itself to strategically selected economic involvement after the war,[87] and Okimoto goes so far as to note that in terms of its overall size, the Japanese state could be considered "minimalist."[88]

The Dynamics of Developmental States

The salient structural features of the development state should now be clear. Corporate coherence gives them the ability to resist incursions by the invisible hand of individual maximization by bureaucrats; internally, Weberian characteristics predominate. Highly selective, meritocratic recruitment and longterm career rewards create commitment and a sense of corporate coherence. Developmental states have benefited from extraordinary administrative capacities, but they also restrict their interventions to the strategic necessities of a transformative project, using their power to selectively impose market forces. The sharp contrast between the prebureaucratic, patrimonial character of the predatory state and the more closely Weberian character of developmental states should give pause to those who attribute the ineffectiveness of Third World states to their bureaucratic nature. Lack of bureaucracy may come closer to the correct diagnosis.

At the same time, the analysis of the East Asian cases has underlined the fact that the nonbureaucratic elements of bureaucracy may be just as important as the non-contractual elements of contract.[89] Historically deep, informal networks, or tightknit party or military organization have enhanced the coherence of the East Asian bureaucracies. Whether these ties are based on commitment to a parallel corporate institution or performance in the educational system, they reinforce the binding character

[85] Wade, *Governing the Market*, p. 226.

[86] Johnson notes in his discussion of the Japanese case how the state apparatus, having attempted with very mixed success detailed and direct intervention in the pre-War period, limited itself to strategically chosen interventions after the war.

[87] Johnson, *MITI and the Japanese Miracle*.

[88] Okimoto, *Between MITI and the Market*, p. 2.

[89] Cf. Rueschemeyer and Evans, "The State and Economic Transformation."

of participation in the formal organization structure rather than under-cutting in the way that informal networks based on kinship or parochial geographic loyalties do in the predatory pattern.

Having successfully bound the behavior of incumbents to its pursuit of collective ends, the state can act with some independence in relation to particularistic societal pressures. The autonomy of the developmental state is, however, of a completely different character from the aimless, absolutist domination of the predatory state. It is not just relative auton-omy in the structural Marxist sense of being constrained by the generic requirements of capital accumulation. It is an autonomy embedded in a concrete set of social ties which bind the state to society and provide in-stitutionalized channels for the continual negotiation and renegotiation of goals and policies.

In order to understand how this felicitous combination of autonomy and embeddedness emerged, it is necessary to set the developmental state in the context of a conjuncture of domestic and international factors. East Asian developmental states began the post-World War II period with leg-acies of long bureaucratic traditions and considerable prewar experience in direct economic intervention, in Korea and Taiwan under Japanese co-lonialism. World War II and its aftermath provided all these states with unusual societal environments. Traditional agrarian elites were deci-mated, industrial groups were disorganized and undercapitalized, and ex-ternal resources were channeled through the state apparatus. The out-come of the war, including, ironically, American occupation in Japan and Korea, qualitatively enhanced the autonomy of these states vis-à-vis pri-vate domestic elites.[90] The combination of historically accumulated bu-reaucratic capacity and conjuncturally generated autonomy, placed them in an exceptional historical position.

At the same time, the state's autonomy was constrained by the inter-national context, both geopolitical and economic. These states were cer-tainly not free to make history as they chose. The international context excluded military expansion, but generated clear external threats. Eco-nomic expansion was not only the basis for shoring up legitimacy, but for maintaining defensive capabilities in the face of these threats. American hegemony on the one side and expansionary Asian communism on the other left them little choice but to rely primarily on private capital as the instrument of industrialization. The environment conspired to create the conviction that rapid, market-based industrialization was necessary to re-gime survival. Their small size and lack of resources made the place of export competitiveness in successful industrialization obvious.

[90] See Johnson, *MITI and the Japanese Miracle*; Pang, "The State and Economic Trans-formation."

Commitment to industrialization motivated these states to promote the growth of local industrial capital. Their exceptional autonomy allowed them to dominate (at least initially) the formation of the ties that bound capital and the state together. Out of this conjuncture the kind of embedded autonomy that characterized these states during the most impressive periods of their industrial growth emerged: a project shared by a highly developed bureaucratic apparatus and a relatively organized set of private actors who could provide useful intelligence and decentralized implementation.

Recent developments suggest that embedded autonomy is not a static characteristic of the developmental state. In contrast to the absolutist domination of the predatory state, which seems self-reinforcing, embedded autonomy has been, to a surprising extent, its own gravedigger. The very success of the developmental state in structuring the accumulation of industrial capital has changed the nature of relations between capital and the state. As private capital has become less dependent on the resources provided by the state, the state's relative dominance has diminished. MITI influence in the 1980s cannot be compared to the golden era of the 1950s and early 1960s. Korean *chaebol* can now tap international capital markets directly[91] and the state's ability to veto their projects has correspondingly eroded.[92]

The capacity of state apparatuses to command the loyalties of the most talented graduates of the best universities has also begun to erode as private careers become more rewarding. For example, Wade notes that the proportion of Masters and Ph.D.s entering government service in Taiwan has dropped substantially while the share entering the private sector has risen,[93] which is not surprising given the increasing salary differentials between the public and private sector. Whether the bureaucracy's traditional esprit de corps and corporate coherence can be preserved in the face of these trends remains to be seen. Even more fundamentally, the achievement of higher standards of living has made it more difficult to legitimize a national project justified solely on grounds of its contribution to the growth of GNP. Resurgent distributional demands, both political and economic, do not fit comfortably with the elite networks and bureaucratic structures which fostered the original project of industrial accumulation.[94]

[91] See Woo, *Race to the Swift*.

[92] See, for example, Kim, "From Dominance to Symbiosis," on the interaction of the state and the *chaebol* in the auto industry in the early 1980s.

[93] Wade, *Governing the Market*, table 7.1, p. 218.

[94] As Rueschemeyer and Evans, "The State and Economic Transformation," p. 53, argue, the state capacity required to implement distributional policies is likely to be significantly

There is no reason to presume that the developmental state will persist in the form that has been described here. Nor can we presume that if these state apparatuses persisted in their present form they would promote the satisfaction of future societal goals. They proved themselves formidable instruments for instigating the accumulation of industrial capital but, in all likelihood, they will have to be transformed in order to deal with the problems and opportunities created by the success of their initial project.

BRAZIL AND INDIA: "INTERMEDIATE" CASES

Having developed the contrast between the embedded autonomy of the East Asian developmental state and the incoherent absolutism of the predatory Zairian regime, it is time to look at how elements from these two ideal types can be combined in different ways to produce results that are neither purely predatory nor consistently developmental. Brazil and India provide ample illustration of how elements from the developmental ideal type may be combined with characteristics that negate Weberian insulation and undercut embeddedness.

Both states have fostered significant transformation. An impossibly fissiparous country, the home of a huge population of desperately poor agriculturalists whose resource base is rapidly eroding, India nonetheless achieved substantial industrialization and very respectable growth rates in the 1950s and early 1960s. After faltering in the 1970s, the country has again grown rapidly in the 1980s. Brazil has sustained high growth rates over the course of the postwar period and experienced a miraculous burst of industrialization in the 1970s. The deterioration of the "Brazilian miracle" in the 1980s undercut its claim to being a developmental state, but Korea could well envy the massive trade surpluses that its industry continued to produce at the end of the 1980s.

Brazil

A plethora of historical and contemporary research make the differences between Brazil and the ideal typical developmental state clear.[95] The dif-

---

higher than that required to implement policies aimed at accumulation, further complicating prospects for success.

[95] Among historical studies those by Jose de Carvalho Murilo, "Elite and State-building in Brazil" (Ph.D. diss., Department of Political Science, Stanford University, 1974); and Fernando Uricoechea, *The Patrimonial Foundations of the Brazilian Bureaucratic State* (Berkeley: University of California Press, 1980) are particularly relevant to this discussion. Important recent contemporary studies include Sergio Abranches, "The Divided Leviathan: The State and Economic Policy Making in Authoritarian Brazil" (Ph.D. diss., Department of Political Science, Cornell University, 1978); Michael Barzelay, *The Politicized Market Economy: Alcohol in Brazil's Energy Strategy* (Berkeley: University of California Press,

ferences begin with the simple question of how people get government jobs. Barbara Geddes chronicles the unusually extensive powers of political appointment and the corresponding difficulty Brazil has experienced in instituting meritocratic recruitment procedures.[96] Ben Schneider points out that while Japanese prime ministers appoint only dozens of officials and American presidents appoint hundreds, Brazilian presidents appoint thousands.[97] It is little wonder that the Brazilian state is known as a massive *cabide de emprego* (source of jobs), populated on the basis of connection rather than competence.

The negative consequences of patronage are exacerbated by the character of the career patterns that such a system encourages. Instead of being tuned to the longterm gains via promotions based on organizationally relevant performance, Brazilian bureaucrats face staccato careers, punctuated by the rhythms of changing political leadership and periodic spawning of new organizations. A 1987 survey by Schneider of 281 Brazilian bureaucrats found that they shifted agencies very four or five years. Since the top four or five layers of most organizations are appointed from outside the agency itself, long-term commitment to the agency has only a limited return and construction of an ethos and of agency- and policy-relevant expertise is difficult. There is thus little to restrain strategies oriented toward individual and political gain.[98]

Unable to transform the bureaucracy as a whole, Brazilian leaders have tried to create pockets of efficiency (*bolsoes de eficiencia*) within the bu-

---

1986); Frances Hagopian, "The Politics of Oligarchy: The Persistence of Traditional Elites in Contemporary Brazil" (Ph.D. diss., Department of Political Science, MIT, 1987); Barbara Geddes, *Economic Development as a Collective Action Problem: Individual Interests and Innovation in Brazil* (Ann Arbor, Mich.: University of Michigan Microfilms, 1986); Silvia Raw, "The Political Economy of Brazilian State-Owned Enterprises" (Ph.D. diss., Department of Economics, University of Massachusetts, 1986); Ben R. Schneider, "Politics within the State: Elite Bureaucrats and Industrial Policy in Authoritarian Brazil" (Ph.D. diss., Department of Political Science, University of California, 1987); Ben R. Schneider, "Framing the State: Economic Policy and Political Representation in Post Authoritarian Brazil," in John D. Wirth, Edson de Oliveira Nunes, and Thomas E. Bogenschild, eds., *State and Society in Brazil: Continuity and Change* (Boulder, Colo.: Westview Press, 1987); Helen Shapiro, "State Intervention and Industrialization: The Origins of the Brazilian Automotive Industry" (Ph.D. diss., Department of Economics, Yale University, 1988); and Eliza J. Willis, "The State as Banker: The Expansion of the Public Sector in Brazil" (Ph.D. diss., University of Texas at Austin, 1986). The discussion that follows draws especially on Schneider.

[96] Geddes, *Economic Development as a Collective Action Problem.*

[97] Schneider, "Politics Within the State," pp. 5, 212, 644.

[98] Ibid., p. 106. As Schneider points out, there are positive as well as negative features to this pattern. It discourages organizationally parochial perspectives and generates a web of inter-organizational ties among individuals. The main problem with these career patterns is that they provide insufficient counterweight either to the idiosyncratic decision-making from the top political leadership or to the tendencies toward individualized rent seeking.

reaucracy,[99] modernizing the state apparatus incrementally rather than through a broader transformation.[100] The National Development Bank (BNDE), favored especially by Kubitschek as an instrument of his developmentalism in the 1950s, was, until recently, a good example of a pocket of efficiency.[101] Unlike most of Brazil's bureaucracy, the BNDE offered "a clear career path, developmental duties and an ethic of public service."[102] Early in its institutional life (1956) the BNDE started a system of public examinations for recruitment. Norms grew up against arbitrary reversal of the judgments of the bank's technical personnel (*opiniao do tecnico*) by higher-ups. A solid majority of the directors was recruited internally, and a clear esprit de corps developed within the bank.[103]

Agencies like the BNDE are, not surprisingly, more developmentally effective than the traditional parts of the Brazilian bureaucracy.[104] According to Geddes those projects in Kubitschek's Target Plan that were both under the jurisdiction of executive groups or work groups and under the financial wing of the BNDE fulfilled 102 percent of their targets whereas those projects that were the responsibility of the traditional bureaucracy achieved only 32 percent.[105] Because the BNDE was a major source of long term investment loans, its professionalism was a stimulus to improving performance in other sectors.[106] Tendler notes, for example, that the necessity of competing for loan funds was an important stimulus to the improvement of proposals by Brazil's electrical power-generating companies.[107]

Unfortunately, the pockets of efficiency strategy has a number of disadvantages. As long as pockets of efficiency are surrounded by a sea of

[99] Geddes, *Economic Development as a Collective Action Problem*, p. 105.

[100] See Philippe Schmitter, *Interest Conflict and Political Change in Brazil* (Stanford, Calif.: Stanford University Press, 1971); Schneider, "Politics Within the State," p. 45.

[101] The BNDE later became the BNDES (National Bank for Economic and Social Development). Its history is discussed by both Geddes and Schneider, but the fullest discussions are Luciano Martins, *Estado Capitalista e Burocracia no Brasil Pos64* (Rio de Janeiro: Paz e Terra, 1985), and Willis, "The State as Banker."

[102] Schneider, "Politics Within the State," p. 633.

[103] Willis, "The State as Banker," pp. 96–126.

[104] Among the agencies highlighted by Geddes, *Economic Development as a Collective Action Problem*, p. 117, are the BNDES, CACEX, SUMOC, DASP, Itamaraty, Kubitscheks Executive Groups and Work Groups and the foreign exchange department of the Bank of Brazil.

[105] Geddes, *Economic Development as a Collective Action Problem*, p. 116.

[106] According to Willis, "The State as Banker," p. 4, the bank has "virtually monopolized the provision of long term credit in Brazil, often accounting for as much as 10 percent of gross domestic capital formation."

[107] Judith Tendler, *Electric Power in Brazil: Entrepreneurship in the Public Sector* (Cambridge, Mass.: Harvard University Press, 1968). See also Schneider, "Politics Within the State," p. 143.

traditional clientelistic norms, they are dependent on the personal protection of individual presidents. Geddes, for example, chronicles the decline in the effectiveness of the Departmento Administrativo de Servico Publico (DASP) established by Vargas in 1938 as part of the Estado Novo once Vargas' protection was no longer available.[108] Willis emphasizes the dependence of the BNDE on presidential support, both in terms of the definition of its mission and in terms of its ability to maintain its institutional integrity.[109]

Incrementalism, or reform by addition, is likely to result in uncoordinated expansion and make strategic selectivity much more difficult to achieve. Having entered power with the intention of shrinking the state by as much as two hundred thousand positions, the Brazilian military ended up creating "hundreds of new, often redundant, agencies and enterprises" and expanding the federal bureaucracy from seven hundred thousand to 1.6 million.[110] Trying to modernize by piecemeal addition also undercuts the organizational coherence of the state apparatus as a whole. As new pieces are added, a larger and ever more baroque structure emerges. The resulting apparatus has been characterized as "segmented,"[111] "divided,"[112] or "fragmented."[113] It is a structure that not only makes policy coordination difficult, but encourages resort to personalistic solutions.

Just as the internal structure of the Brazilian state apparatus limits its capacity to replicate the performance of the East Asian developmental states, the character of its embeddedness makes it harder to construct a project of industrial transformation jointly with industrial elites. While the Brazilian state has been an uninterruptedly powerful presence in the country's social and economic development since colonial times, it is important to keep in mind that, as Fernando Urichochea, Jose Murilo de Carvalho and others have emphasized, "the efficiency of government . . . was dependent . . . on the cooperation of the landed oligarchy."[114] Despite the increasing weight of industrial capital in the economy, the persistent legacy of rural power continues to shape the character of the state. Hagopian argues that contemporary rural elites have turned increasingly to trying to use the state as an instrument for reinforcing their traditional

[108] Geddes, *Economic Development as a Collective Action Problem*, p. 97.
[109] Willis, "The State as Banker."
[110] Schneider, "Politics Within the State," pp. 109, 575, 44. This was the goal of Roberto Campos (p. 575).
[111] Barzelay, *The Politicized Market Economy.*
[112] Abranches, "The Divided Leviathan."
[113] Schneider, "Politics Within the State."
[114] Uricoechea, *The Patrimonial Foundations*, p. 52.

clientelistic networks.[115] Thus, rather than being able to focus on its relationship with industrial capital, the state has always had to simultaneously contend with traditional elites threatened by the conflictful transformation of rural class relations.

At the same time, relations with industrial capital have been complicated by the early and massive presence of transnational manufacturing
capital in the domestic market.[116] The threat of domination by transnational corporations (TNCs) created an atmosphere of defensive nation-
alism and made it more difficult to discipline domestic capital. It is much
harder to force industrial capital to confront the market, as K. Y. Yin did
with the Taiwanese textile industry, when transnational capital is the
probable beneficiary of any gale of creative destruction.

Problems created by divisions in dominant economic elites were reinforced by the nature of state structures. The lack of a stable bureaucratic
structure also made it harder to establish regularized ties with the private
sector of the administrative guidance sort and pushed public-private interaction into individualized channels. Even the military regime, which
had the greatest structural potential for insulation from clientelistic pressures, proved unable to construct an administrative guidance relationship
with the local industrial elite.[117] The regime was "highly legitimate in the
eyes of the local bourgeoisie, yet unconnected to it by any well-institu-
tionalized system of linkages."[118] Instead of becoming institutionalized,
relationships became individualized, taking the form of what Cardoso
called "bureaucratic rings": small sets of individual industrialists connected to an equally small sets of individual bureaucrats, usually through
some pivotal office holder.[119] As Schneider points out, the ad hoc, person-

---

[115] Hagopian, "The Politics of Oligarchy."

[116] See Peter Evans, *Dependent Development: The Alliance of Multinational, State and
Local Capital in Brazil* (Princeton: Princeton University Press, 1979); for a discussion of the
consequences of foreign capital in Brazil, "Reinventing the Bourgeoisie: State Entrepreneur-
ship and Class Formation in Dependent Capitalist Development," *The American Journal of
Sociology* 88 (Supplement 1982): S210–47. For a more general contrast between Latin
America and East Asia see Peter Evans, "Class, State and Dependence in East Asia: Some
Lessons for Latin Americanists," in F. Deyo, ed., *The Political Economy of the New Asian
Industrialism* (Ithaca, N.Y.: Cornell University Press, 1987); Stallings, "The Role of Foreign
Capital in Economic Development."

[117] As a very cohesive corporate group whose lack of combat opportunities brought tech-
nocratic (i.e., educational) criteria for internal mobility to the fore, the Brazilian military
approximated a KMT-style institutional reinforcement to the state's bureaucracy. See
Alfred Stepan, *The Military in Politics: Changing Patterns in Brazil* (Princeton: Princeton
University Press, 1971), and especially Geddes, *Economic Development as a Collective
Action Problem*, chap. 7.

[118] Evans, "Reinventing the Bourgeoisie," p. S221.

[119] Fernando Henrique Cardoso, *Autoritarismo e Democratizacao* (Rio de Janeiro: Paz e
Terra, 1975).

alized character of these linkages makes them both undependable from the point of view of industrialists and arbitrary in terms of their outcomes.[120] They are, in short, quite the opposite of the sort of state-society ties that are described by Samuels and others in their discussions of the developmental state.

Overall, this reading of the internal structure and external ties of the Brazilian state is consistent with Schneider's lament that "the structure and operation of the Brazilian state should prevent it from fulfilling even minimal government functions."[121] But it is important to underline that despite its problems the Brazilian state has been entrepreneurially effective in a variety of industrial areas, and that these areas have undoubtedly contributed to its long-term growth and industrialization. These successes are, as we would expect, found in areas where the relevant state organizations had exceptional coherence and capacity. These coherent state organizations, in turn, also rested on a more institutionally effective set of linkages with the private sector, the precise pattern visible in the developmental states of East Asia.

Shapiro's discussion of the role of the Grupo Executivo para Industria Automobilistica (GEIA) in the implantation of Brazil's auto industry during the late 1950s and early 1960s is a good example. She concludes that overall "the Brazilian strategy was a success" and that the planning capacity and subsidies provided by the state through the GEIA were crucial to inducing the required investments.[122] The GEIA served as a sectorally specific minipilot agency. Because it combined representation from all the different agencies that needed to pass on plans, it "could implement its program independently of the fragmented policy-making authority" that plagued the government as a whole.[123] Its ability to provide predictable timely decisions was critical to risk reduction as far as the TNCs that were being asked to invest were concerned. In addition, again much like MITI or the IDB, the GEIA "played a critical coordinating role between the assemblers and the parts producers."[124]

The later development of the petrochemical industry exhibited an even more potent variant of embedded autonomy.[125] Trebat concludes that state-led investment in the petrochemical industry saved foreign

[120] Schneider, "Framing the State," pp. 230–31.
[121] Schneider, "Politics Within the State," p. 4.
[122] Shapiro, "State Intervention and Industrialization," p. 57.
[123] Ibid., p. 111.
[124] Ibid., p. 58.
[125] See Evans, *Dependent Development*; "Reinventing the Bourgeoisie"; "Class, State and Dependence in East Asia"; and "Collectivized Capitalism: Integrated Petrochemical Complexes and Capital Accumulation in Brazil," in Thomas C. and Philippe Faucher Bruneau, eds., *Authoritarian Brazil* (Boulder, Colo.: Westview, 1981).

exchange[126] and was economically reasonable given the prevailing opportunity costs of capital.[127] At the heart of the initiative was Petrobras, the most autonomous and corporately coherent organization within the state enterprise system. Equally crucial to the explosive growth of Brazil's petrochemical capacity in the 1970s, however, was the dense network of ties that were constructed to link the Petrobras system to private capital, both domestic and transnational.

Out of these sectoral examples a clear overall difference between the Brazilian state and the archetypal developmental state emerges. Embedded autonomy is a partial rather than a global attribute, limited to certain pockets of efficiency. The persistence of clientelistic and patrimonial characteristics has prevented the construction of Weberian corporate coherence. Brazil's complex and contentious elite structure makes embeddedness much more problematic. It is hardly surprising that embedded autonomy remains partial.

India

The Indian state is even more ambiguously situated in the space between predatory and developmental than the Brazilian one. Its internal structure, at least at the apex, resembles the Weberian norm, but its relation to the country's convoluted social structure more thoroughly undercuts its capacity to act. Its harsher critics see it as clearly predatory and view its expansion as perhaps the single most important cause of India's stagnation.[128] Others, like Pranab Bardhan, take almost the reverse point of view, arguing that state investment was essential to India's industrial growth in the 1950s and early 1960s and that the state's retreat from a more aggressively developmental posture has been an important factor in India's relatively slow growth in the 1960s and 1970s.[129]

At the time of independence the Indian Civil Service (ICS) was the apex of a venerable bureaucracy. It was the culmination of a tradition that stretched back at least to the Mughal empire.[130] Its eleven hundred members formed a prestigious elite, providing "the steel frame of empire" for two hundred years.[131] Its successor, the Indian Administrative Service

[126] Thomas Trebat, *Brazil's State-Owned Enterprises: A Case Study of the State as Entrepreneur* (Cambridge, England: Cambridge University Press, 1983).

[127] See Evans, "Collectivized Capitalism."

[128] E.g., Lal, *The Hindu Equilibrium.*

[129] Pranab Bardhan, *The Political Economy of Development in India* (Oxford: Basil Blackwell, 1984).

[130] See Lloyd I. Rudolf and Susanne Hoeber Rudolf, *In Pursuit of Lakshmi: The Political Economy of the Indian State* (Chicago, Ill.: University of Chicago Press, 1987).

[131] Richard P. Taub, *Bureaucrats Under Stress: Administrators and Administration in an Indian State* (Berkeley: University of California Press, 1969), p. 3.

(IAS) has carried on the tradition. Entry is primarily via a nationwide examination which, historically at least, has been as highly competitive as its East Asian counterparts.[132] While educational training is not concentrated in a single national university in the way that it is in East Asia, solidary networks are enhanced by the fact that each class of recruits spends a year together at the National Academy of Administration.[133]

Despite an historically deep tradition of solid state bureaucracy, the colonial traditions that the IAS inherited were by no means an unambiguous asset from the perspective of development. Assimilation of imperial culture and a humanistic training was an important criteria of acceptance into the ICS. Even after the English had departed, IAS exams still had three parts, English, English essay, and general knowledge.[134] An intelligent generalist might, of course, perform well, if career patterns provided the opportunity for the gradual acquisition of relevant technical knowledge and skills. Unfortunately, career patterns do not generally afford this kind of opportunity. Careers are characterized by the same kind of rapid rotation of people in jobs that characterize the Brazilian bureaucracy. Rudolf and Rudolf report, for example, that chief executives in the petrochemical industry have an average tenure in office of about fifteen months.[135] In addition to the problems of the IAS tradition itself, the extent to which the "steel frame" has remained uncorroded is questionable. The Rudolfs argue that there has been an "erosion of state institutions" at least since the death of Nehru.[136] Contemporary fieldstudies have found corruption not just endemic but overwhelming.[137] Erosion may be due in part to problems internal to the bureaucracy, but the difficulties of building connections to the surrounding social structure seem the more serious source of difficulty. In a "subcontinental, multinational state" like India state-society relations are qualitatively more complex than in the East Asian cases.[138] Given the diseconomies of scale inherent in administrative organizations, it would take a bureaucratic apparatus of truly extraordi-

[132] Taub, Bureaucrats Under Stress, p. 29, reports that in 1960 eleven thousand college graduates competed for one hundred places.

[133] An example of the solidary created is the statement by one of Taub's (Bureaucrats Under Stress, p. 33) informants that he could "go anywhere in India and put up with a batch mate [member of his IAS class]," a possibility that the informant considered unheard of in terms of normal relations with nonkin.

[134] Take, for example, the question cited by Taub (Bureaucrats Under Stress, p. 30): "Identify the following: Venus de Milo, Mona Lisa, the Thinker, William Faulkner, Corbusier, Karen Hantze Susman, Major Gherman Titov, Ravi Shanker, Disneyland."

[135] Rudolf and Rudolf, In Pursuit of Lakshmi, p. 34.

[136] Ibid., chap. 2.

[137] E.g., Robert Wade, "The Market for Public Office: Why the Indian State Is Not Better at Development," World Development 13, no. 4 (1985): 467–97.

[138] Rudolf and Rudolf, In Pursuit of Lakshmi.

nary capacity to produce results comparable to what can be achieved on an island of twenty million people or a peninsula of forty million. Class, ethnic, religious, and regional divisions compound administrative difficulties.

From the time of independence, the political survival of Indian regimes has required simultaneously pleasing a persistently powerful rural landowning class and a highly concentrated set of industrial capitalists. The shared interests of larger landowners and the millions of "bullock capitalists" in the countryside give this group daunting political weight.[139] At the same time, the large business houses like the Tatas and Birlas must be kept on board.[140] Since business houses and landowners share no encompassing developmental project, the divided elite confronts the state in search of particularistic advantage. They comprise in Bardhan's terms, "a flabby and heterogeneous dominant coalition preoccupied in a spree of anarchical grabbing at public resources."[141]

The micropolitics of state-private interactions further diminish the possibility of the state leading a coherent developmental project. Historically, the stereotypical IAS veteran was an anglophile Brahman of Fabian socialist ideological leanings. The private capitalists with whom he was dealing were likely to be of lower caste, different cultural tastes, and opposing ideology. While these stereotypes have gradually changed over time, shared discourse and common vision, on the basis of which a common project might be constructed, are often still lacking, leaving the exchange of material favors as the only alternative to hostile stalemate. Policy networks that allow industry experts from within the state apparatus to collect and disseminate information, build consensus, tutor, and cajole are missing. Nor do we find sectorally specific networks comparable to the one that binds together the state and private capital in the Brazilian petrochemical industry. Unlike the developmental states, the Indian state cannot count on the private sector either as a source of information about what kind of industrial policy will fly or as an effective instrument for the implementation of industrial policy.

It would be unfair and incorrect to say that the Indian state has made

[139] Ibid.

[140] Dennis Encarnation, *Dislodging the Multinationals: India's Strategy in Comparative Perspective* (Ithaca, N.Y.: Cornell University Press, 1990), p. 286.

[141] Bardhan, *The Political Economy of Development in India*, p. 70. It is interesting to contrast this vision with a quite different social structural dilemma, equally difficult for a would-be developmental state. In Maurice Zeitlin and Richard E. Ratcliff's *Landlords and Capitalists: The Dominant Class of Chile* (Princeton: Princeton University Press, 1988), analysis of Chile they found not a split elite but one which united agrarian and industrial interests, thus ensuring that the elite as a whole would resist transformation of the agrarian sector and the kind of single-minded focus on industrialization that characterized East Asian cases.

no developmental contribution. State investment in basic infrastructure and intermediate goods was a central element in maintaining a respectable rate of industrial growth in the 1950s and early 1960s. Even Deepak Lal admits that infrastructural investments and the increase in the domestic savings rate, both of which depended largely on the behavior of the state, were "the two major achievements of post-Independence India."[142] State investment in basic agricultural inputs, primarily irrigation and fertilizers, played an important role in increasing agricultural output. The state has invested effectively, if not always efficiently,[143] in basic and intermediate industries like steel and petrochemicals and even in more technologically adventurous industries like electrical equipment manufacture.[144]

Unfortunately, these are largely accomplishments of the past, of the 1950s and early 1960s. Increasingly, lack of selectiveness in state intervention has burdened the bureaucracy and helped propel the erosion of state institutions. The "license, permit, quota raj" has attempted to enforce detailed control over the physical output of a broad range of manufactured goods.[145] At the same time, the state is directly involved in production of a variety of goods greater than even relatively expansive states like Brazil have attempted. Indian SOEs produce not only computers but also televisions, not only steel but also automobiles.[146] The state-owned share of corporate assets moved from one-sixth to a half between 1962 and 1972,[147] as the number of state enterprises grew from five in 1951 to 214 in 1984.[148] Given the overwhelming demands created by the sheer task of supplying even minimalist governance, unselective state involvement is simply unsustainable.

Relative to Brazil, it might be argued that India suffers from excessive autonomy and inadequate embeddedness and consequently has more difficulty in executing the kind of sectoral projects that are the focus here.

[142] Lal, *The Hindu Equilibrium*, p. 237.

[143] For a good discussion of problems in the inefficiency of state investments in terms of extraordinarily high capital output ratios etc., see Isher Judge Aluwalia, *Industrial Growth in India: Stagnation since the Mid-Sixties* (Delhi: Oxford University Press, 1985).

[144] Ravi Ramamurti, *State-owned Enterprises in High Technology Industries: Studies in India and Brazil* (New York: Praeger, 1987).

[145] See Encarnation, *Dislodging the Multinationals*.

[146] This lack of selectivity is not always evident in aggregate comparisons. For example, the distribution of public enterprises in Korea and India looked quite similar when Leroy Jones and Edward S. Mason, "Role of Economic Factors in Determining the Size and Structure of the Public-Enterprise Sector in Less-developed Countries with Mixed Economies," in Jones, ed., *Public Enterprise in Less-developed Countries* (New York: Cambridge University Press, 1982), p. 22, considered manufacturing a single sector rather than disaggregating it.

[147] Encarnation, *Dislodging the Multinationals*, p. 283.

[148] Lal, *The Hindu Equilibrium*, p. 257.

At the same time, the degree to which the "steel frame" still retains some residual coherence may help account for India's ability to avoid the disastrous excesses that Brazil has fallen prey to.

Given their continental scale, Brazil and India may appear as *sui generis*, and of limited comparative relevance. Yet their states share many of the same problems, both with one another and with many of the middle-income developing countries as well. Their bureaucracies, which are not patrimonial caricatures of Weberian structures as in the predatory case, still lack the corporate coherence of the developmental ideal type. Consistent career ladders that bind the individual to corporate goals while simultaneously allowing him to acquire the expertise necessary to perform effectively are not well institutionalized. India has a more thoroughly Weberian organizational structure, but lacks the ties that might enable it to mount a shared project with social groups interested in transformation.

With less well-developed bureaucratic capacity, these intermediate apparatuses must nevertheless confront more complex and divided social structures. Their ability to construct a project of industrialization is specifically complicated by the continuing social power of agrarian elites. In the Brazilian case the problem is complicated even further by the historical importance of foreign firms at the core of the industrial establishment. In the Indian case it is exacerbated by the cultural divergence between state managers and private capitalists. In both countries the state has tried to do too many things; it has been unable to strategically select a set of activities commensurate with its capacity. Lesser capacity and a more demanding array of tasks combine to make embedded autonomy impossible.

STATE STRUCTURES AND ADJUSTMENT

This comparative analysis strongly reinforces the idea that policy-makers as well as theorists can benefit from the third wave of thinking on states and development. The comparative evidence argues strongly in favor of focusing more on state capacity as an important factor in policy choice and outcomes and helps clarify the structures and processes that underlie capacity. Most specifically, this analysis challenges the tendency to equate capacity with insulation. It suggests instead that transformative capacity requires a combination of internal coherence and external connectedness that can be called embedded autonomy.

The first and most obvious lessons to be extracted from these cases is that bureaucracy is in *under-*, not over-, supply. This is not only a problem in the post-colonial societies of the sub-Sahara. Even in countries like Brazil that enjoy relatively abundant supplies of trained manpower and a long tradition of state involvement in the economy, predictable, coherent, Weberian bureaucracies are hard to find. The standard perception to the contrary flows from the common tendency for patrimonial organizations to masquerade as Weberian bureaucracies. There is an abundance of rule-making or administrative organizations, but most have neither the capability of pursuing collective goals in a predictable, coherent way nor an interest in doing so. Weber misled his successors by insisting that bureaucracy would naturally sweep all other forms before it. Just as markets are less natural than Smith would have had us believe, so bureaucracies need more nurturing than Weber led us to expect.

The second lesson is an extension of the first. The state's ability to perform administrative and other functions must be treated as a scarce good. Early visions of the developmental state seemed to assume that the resources necessary to undertake new tasks would be automatically generated by the performance of the tasks themselves, just as expanding firm sales generate resources for new production. The analogy is false. Unjudicious expansion of the menu of tasks leads too easily to a vicious cycle. State capacity grows more slowly than tasks expand. Administrative and organizational diseconomies of scale and scope lead to declining performance. Inadequate performance undercuts legitimacy and makes it hard to claim the resources necessary to increase capacity. The gap between capacity required and capacity available yawns wider until even the effective execution of nightwatchman duties is threatened.

Almost all Third World states try to do more than they are capable of doing. The contrasting balance of capacity and tasks that separates India and Brazil from the East Asian developmental states illustrates the point. The developmental states not only had higher levels of capacity but exercised greater selectivity in the tasks they undertook. They focused on industrial transformation and their strategies of promoting industry were designed to conserve administrative resources.

The call for selectivity jibes nicely with the arguments made in the literature on stabilization and adjustment. One of the prime virtues of adjustment programs is that they are very selective in the capacity they demand. Because they focus on the recalibration of a relatively small number of macroeconomic variables, they obviate the need for the massive regulatory apparatus that is required by less market-conforming strategies, to say nothing of the institution building required by state attempts to take on a directly productive role.

At the same time, however, a good deal of the literature on adjustment shares the second wave perspective's suspicion of state capacity, an implicit fear that increased state capacity will lead to expanding the state's role and is therefore a bad thing in itself. The argument advanced here is quite different. It assumes that even if the state accepts a more limited repetoire, demands for state action will exceed what existing capabilities can deliver. Even with greater selectivity, strengthening capacity is necessary. Reconstruction, not dismantling, is the order of the day.

The argument that has been developed here must also be distinguished from arguments in the literature on stabilization and adjustment that focus on insulation.[149] Stress on insulation implies that in the absence of political pressure technically trained incumbents will make and implement economically correct policy decisions and that such decisions are sufficient basis for successful stabilization and adjustment. Providing technocrats with protection from their political constituencies is presented as the sine qua non of effective action. Implicitly, incumbent technocrats are assumed to have both sufficient knowledge to make the right policy choices as well as the incentives to do so.

Emphasizing corporate coherence and autonomy gives the argument a different flavor. What is at stake is building a self-orienting organization that generates sufficient incentives to induce its individual members to pursue collective goals and assimilate enough information to allow it to choose goals worth pursuing. Capacity implies organizations capable of sustained collective action, not just freedom for individual decision makers to follow the objective logic of the economic situation.

This analysis offers then a complement to Waterbury's discussion of "change teams" (chapter 4). Waterbury focuses primarily on the emergence and survival of the change team. If we project the agenda of adjustment moving forward on a longer term basis however, the question of state capacity must enter the picture. Once it achieves hegemony, a change team must have an apparatus to effect the required policy transformation. The experience of African technocrats suggests that a team without an apparatus is unlikely to be effectual beyond the short term. Conversely, the experience of the East Asian NICs certainly suggests that Weber was not entirely wrong in seeing bureaucratic capacity as fungible across different policy orientations. Apparatuses that were effective in implementing local industrial transformation proved (after, to be sure, varying degrees of internecine struggles) useful instruments in the implementation of an agenda of adjustment.

Autonomy and corporate coherence, like insulation, are well within the Weberian tradition. Emphasis on embeddedness as the necessary complement to autonomy not only contradicts the notion that insulation is the most important feature of capacity, it also departs from a Weberian perspective. Embeddedness represents a different solution to the shortage of capacity. Embeddedness is necessary because policies must respond to the perceived problems of private actors and rely in the end on private actors

---

[149] See Haggard and Kaufman, Introduction to this volume.

for implementation. A concrete network of external ties allows the state to assess, monitor, and shape private responses to policy initiatives, prospectively and after the fact. It extends the state's intelligence and enlarges the prospect that policies will be implemented. Admitting the importance of embeddedness turns arguments for insulation on their head. Connections to civil society become part of the solution rather than part of the problem.

The obvious question is: Why doesn't embeddedness devolve into clientelism, corruption and undermining the effectiveness of the state? Most of the answer lies in the fact that embeddedness is assumed to have value only in the context of autonomy. In the absence of a coherent, self-orienting, Weberian sort of administrative structure, embeddedness will almost certainly have deleterious effects. Since most failed cases in the stabilization literature lack the requisite bureaucratic structures it is hardly surprising that the stabilization literature stresses insulation. When subordination to clientelistic ties is standard administrative operating procedure, achieving greater insulation is a legitimate priority. It is the *combination* of embeddedness and autonomy that works, not either on its own.

The efficacy of embedded autonomy depends on the nature of the surrounding social structure as well as on the internal character of the state. As Migdal notes, connecting the state apparatus, even a coherent one, to a fragmented set of powerholders with no interest of their own in transformation is unlikely to enhance its ability to enact change.[150] As the earlier discussion of the historical dynamics of developmental states indicated, states and social structures must be analyzed together. Without appropriate private interlocutors, building ties with civil society is likely to be a fruitless task, but the state is more than a passive component in the interaction of state and social structure.

Class structure must be seen, at least in part, as the product of state action. It was not simply fortuitous that entrepreneurial groups in Japan, Korea, and Taiwan emerged in a way that made embedded autonomy effective. The contemporary industrial classes of the developmental states are in good measure products of state action. They would no more have assumed their current form in the absence of the state than the state would have been able to realize its goals without them.

In much of the stabilization literature, the role of the state in shaping the character of capital is recognized only in the negative sense. It is assumed that the state can corrupt capital by creating opportunities for rental havens, but, in the absence of state-induced distortions, local capital is expected to respond as Schumpterian entrepreneurs, taking risks,

---

[150] Joel Migdal, *Strong Societies and Weak States*.

making long term investments in productive activities, and seizing on the opportunities inherent in international markets. If this were the case, an insulated state apparatus might be sufficient, but, as World Bank laments over the "slow supply response" suggest, it is generally an unrealistic portrait. Most nascent industrial classes require more active state support and involvement, which is to say some form of embedded autonomy rather than simply insulation.

A stylized reprise of K. Y. Yin and the textile entrustment scheme mentioned earlier should help make these arguments concrete. The creation of a group of textile entrepreneurs depended on a coherent, autonomous state apparatus capable of taking initiative. Without a group of potential capitalists the scheme could not have succeeded, but without the state's initiative and support these potential capitalists would not have filled this particular industrial niche. The second stage, exposing these newly created industrialists to the cold winds of international competition required autonomy in the sense of insulation, just as stabilization programs do. Pressure to preserve a comfortable haven had to be resisted. But there is also the third stage of the process, which is described best in the Taiwanese case by Wade.[151] Entrepreneurs willing to confront the cold winds of competition need information, advice and occasional strategically applied succor in order to survive. This is also what is required to stimulate the supply response in an adjustment program. Embeddedness, not insulation, is what makes this last stage work.

Again there is an interesting intersection between these arguments and those raised by Waterbury in chapter 4. He notes that the "prestructural-adjustment" configuration of economic interests in the cases he examines may well prove less resistant to the forces of change than previous analyses of rent-seeking coalitions have assumed. Obviously, however, the success of an adjustment agenda will require more than the collapse of the old coalition. Insofar as change teams manage to unseat existing industrial elites, this will be in itself a dramatic example of the way in which states reshape social structures, but as time goes on the similarity between the project of Waterbury's change teams and the projects that have been described here should increase. The task of reconstructing an entrepreneurial elite that is able not just to survive but to prosper in a more open environment must take center stage, and this task is likely to bear some strong resemblances to the old project of industrial transformation.

One serious problem remains with the notion of embeddedness as it has been presented here. Because the exclusionary East Asian states have been used as the empirical base for developing the concept, it has been

---

[151] Wade, *Governing the Market*.

defined too narrowly. There is no reason in principle why the kind of networks that connect the state and capital in the East Asian cases could not be constructed in relation to labor and other social groups. Indeed, there is good reason to suspect that such construction may be a necessity in most countries.

Exceptional growth, not just of output but also of real wages, allowed narrow embeddedness to masquerade as a kind of Gramscian hegemony in East Asia. Other states cannot expect the same results. Even effective structural adjustment will not produce East Asian growth rates in most countries of the Third World. In the absence of such growth, legitimacy is harder to come by. In hard times when distributional issues are less easily subordinated to accumulation, more broadly based embeddedness, like that portrayed by Katzenstein[152] in his analysis of the small Western European democracies, may be a better bet.[153] Here again, however, it must be emphasized that embedded autonomy is a relational concept. State structures and strategies require complementary societal counterparts. Constructing the parties and labor movements that form the basis of a broader embedded autonomy is an even more difficult project than constructing a Schumpeterian industrial class.

Implementing the diagnosis that flows from a comparative analysis of states and structural change is clearly more troublesome than implementing second wave prescriptions. As long as the focus is simply on less state intervention, goals and means are straightforward. By comparison, reconstructing the state is an amorphous and frustrating task, a project of decades if not generations. Nonetheless, enhanced state capacity remains a requirement of effective economic policy, including sustained structural adjustment. Pretending otherwise would be a dangerous form of utopianism. Transforming the state from problem to solution must be a central item on any realistic Third World policy agenda.

[152] Peter J. Katzenstein, *Small States in World Markets: Industrial Policy in Europe* (Ithaca, N.Y.: Cornell University Press).

[153] Cf. Joan Nelson, "Introduction: The Politics of Adjustment in Developing Nations," in Nelson, ed., *Economic Crisis and Policy Choice: The Politics of Adjustment in the Third World* (Princeton: Princeton University Press, 1990), pp. 3–32.

CHAPTER FOUR

The Heart of the Matter? Public Enterprise and the Adjustment Process

John Waterbury

THE BASIC QUESTION addressed in this chapter is how states, and those in charge of making state policies, go about reforming themselves. The public enterprise sector, I argue, is at the heart of this process, to the extent that it takes place, because it is within that sector that entitlements and resources devised and allocated by state actors to favored constituencies are concentrated. Thus, I am seeking to explain endogenous and painful change in well established patterns of resource allocation, and I see the public sector as the focal point for such change.

In the countries I will examine, and in scores of other less-developed countries (LDCs), the established patterns of resource allocation were the result of the adoption of strategies of import-substituting industrialization (ISI). These in turn were sustained by the intervention of the public sector in markets and in the direct production of goods and the provision of services. The public sector may be defined broadly as all agencies of government (including the military and sometimes even the official party), but I will concentrate more narrowly on those financial, manufacturing, extractive, and service enterprises owned wholly or effectively controlled by the state.

The reform of the public sector, and particularly of the state-owned enterprises (SOEs), may be carried out without challenging the prevailing growth strategy, although in the last decade of this century that is an increasingly infrequent occurrence. However, as we shall see, both India and Egypt come close to that logic. On the other hand, the determination to liquidate or sell off state enterprises will almost always be part and parcel of a strategic shift toward a strengthening of market forces in allocating resources, toward stimulating private enterprise, and toward greater competitiveness in international markets. The shift in emphasis from public sector reform to privatization will encapsulate a far broader shift in fundamental economic strategy. Analytically and in practice the challenge is to explain how this shift can come about, and how it can be sustained.

My basic argument is as follows:

1. The reform, liquidation, or privatization of SOEs is driven by fiscal crisis of varying intensity. The perception of fiscal crisis, as Kaufman and Haggard point out, is a necessary but not sufficient cause of these changes.
2. The SOE sector in developing countries is the major cause of the public deficit, which in turn fuels inflation, reduces international creditworthiness, crowds out private borrowers, and impedes export promotion.
3. The SOE sector is the lynchpin of a reputedly powerful coalition of beneficiaries with well-established claims to public resources.
4. Much of the "dirty work" of SOE reform and privatization is done in the broader process of structural adjustment through cuts in public expenditures, hiring freezes, and labor shedding.
5. While major economic interests are at stake, and the beneficiaries of reform and privatization remain unorganized, resistance to change will be reduced by the severity of the crisis, the coherence of technocratic policy change teams, and the opportunism of adversely affected interests. When under assault, these typically resort to tactics of *sauve qui peut* rather than cross-coalitional alliances.[1]

THE CASE FOR THE CASES

The argument relies primarily on empirical evidence from four countries; Egypt, India, Mexico and Turkey. The first two have done the least to alter their growth strategies and use of public resources and will thus serve as a kind of control group against which to measure the extent of strategic change and resource reallocation in Mexico and Turkey.

All are large, highly diversified LDC economies that share several specific characteristics. First, until the last decade, they have followed development strategies based on ISI in which state enterprise has played the leading role. India has only marginally modified that strategy in recent years; Egypt has talked a great deal about a major strategy overhaul but so far has done little to implement it. Turkey, and then Mexico, have moved resolutely toward export-led growth, deregulation, and privatization.

The state enterprise sectors of all four are relatively old. In Turkey the SOE sector dates from the late 1920s and the 1930s, in Mexico from the 1930s, in India from the late 1940s and 1950s, and in Egypt from about 1954 on. Thus, relative to most LDCS, we find in these countries the max-

---

[1] For greater detail see John Waterbury, "The Political Context of Public Sector Reform and Privatization in Egypt, India, Mexico and Turkey," in Ezra Suleiman and John Waterbury, eds., *The Political Economy of Public Sector Reform and Privatization* (Boulder, Colr Westview Press, 1990), pp. 293–318; and Henry Bienen and John Waterbury, "The Political Economy of Privatization in Developing Countries," *World Development* 17, no. 5 (1989): 617–32.

imum possibility for the formation of coherent managerial elites in the public sector, for the development of dependent, privileged labor organizations, and for enterprise longevity and tradition. We may hypothesize that in these countries the defense of the public sector is likely to be relatively stronger, the resistance to reform more pronounced, and the range of vested interests affected by reform and privatization broader than elsewhere in the developing world. Hence, if we find major change in the structure of the public sector, we should be able to say with some confidence what forces stood in its way and what elements allowed it to go forward.

The state in each of the countries has been interventionist along a broad front. There has been an attempt at multiyear planning, far-reaching regulation of all economic activity, administered pricing, and efforts to guide market forces, quantitative trade restrictions, and substantial if not total control of banking and other financial institutions by the public sector. They all maintain plan organizations, draw up four- or five-year plans, and see the state as coordinator of all major economic activities.

Each of the four has a private sector of varying strength. The states in question, however, attributed to their private sectors two common characteristics. First, existing private sectors were for some time depicted as weak, given to speculation and profiteering, and prone to sell out the national good through alliances with foreign capital. Much of the rationale for heavy state intervention in the economy has been to protect the poor from private greed and to undertake what shortsighted, unskilled, and undercapitalized private actors could not. Second, each radical ideology held out the prospect that some day a truly nationalist, enlightened, farsighted entrepreneurial bourgeoisie might emerge—one however that would play a supporting role in strategies laid down by the state.

The policy makers and leaders of all four countries have, in the last decade or so, expressed disappointment with the way in which ISI has proceeded and in the performance of SOEs. The pathology of statism is familiar: chronic loss-making SOEs, privileged labor aristocracies, burgeoning domestic deficits, inflation, and mounting external debt. Something approaching crisis, especially in external accounts, was manifest by the middle 1970s, to some extent driven if not caused by the external oil shocks.[2] The initial response was an attempt to streamline and rationalize the statist experiments, to replace redistributive state socialism with cost-effective state capitalism.

The four countries differ in the course of adjustment after the first attempt to deal with the mid-1970s crisis. Mexico and Egypt, increasingly

---

[2] All four countries had shown signs of crisis well before the oil shocks; Mexico in 1954, Turkey in 1959–60, India in 1964–66, and Egypt in 1965–66.

fat with oil and external rents (workers remittances, tourism), abandoned the stabilization-cum-structural adjustment programs with which they briefly flirted in 1976 and 1977. Mexico was driven back to the reform agenda in the early 1980s by the exigencies of servicing its enormous external debt. The Egyptian regime faced cost-of-living riots when in January 1977 the government tried to reduce consumer subsidies. It abandoned the reform agenda at that time and has continued to avoid far-reaching adjustment due to its ability to attract foreign aid based on its strategic position.[3] India never really entered into crisis. Supplemented by the discipline of the emergency period, 1974–77, it managed through careful fiscal and trade policy to protect its fundamental ISI and statist strategy. Turkey, on the other hand, dealt with its severe domestic and external accounts crisis of 1978–79 through a military takeover, the authoritarian implementation of a structural adjustment program and a shift to export-led growth.

Schematically, then, there are two cases of systems maintenance—India and Egypt—in which SOE reform has been designed to prolong the viability of existing arrangements, and two cases of systems transformation—Mexico and Turkey—in which privatization is supposed to alter profoundly the coalitional base of the ISI era. With the exception of Turkey, the process of change, whether structural or marginal, has been carried forward by incumbent elites.

How Change Comes About

The spread of ISI itself as a growth model may provide some clues as to how strategic change is initiated and sustained. It was intended to, and in fact did represent fundamental change in the economies of the periphery and semiperiphery in the interwar years. It was sometimes, although not always, initiated by new political incumbents; that was the case in all four countries under examination here.[4] It was not designed by Western donors or commercial banks, although it eventually received ample support from them, as well as from multinational corporations. Like the neoclassical frameworks now being urged upon the developing world, ISI bore the intellectual imprimatur of a host of development economists.

[3] By way of example, between 1975 and 1990, U.S. assistance to Egypt totaled $29.4 billion, of which nearly $13 billion came as military assistance (Cairo: U.S. Embassy, 1989).

[4] I have in mind the incumbencies of Nasser of Egypt, Nehru in India, Calles and Cárdenas in Mexico, and Atatürk in Turkey. Cárdenas, it should be noted, was primarily the promoter of state intervention in the economy rather than ISI per se. Self-conscious ISI came under the *sexenios* of his immediate successors. See Otto Granados Roldán (1988) "Estado y Rectoría del Desarrollo en México; une Perspectiva Política," in Roldán et al., *México: 75 Años de Revolución: I, Desarrollo Económico* (México: D.F., Fondo de Cultura Economica, 1988), pp. 1–76.

ISI was not the end result of structural imperatives within the societies adopting it. It was not the logical outcome of some unfolding of class forces, although it was, of course, a partial response to the challenge of predominant agricultural sectors with low productivity and low per capita incomes. This notwithstanding, the constituency for ISI was no more structured than are the groups that today advocate reform of its legacy in the public sector. It was a response to the collapse of world trade and primary commodity markets in the 1930s, although the response could be pragmatic and piecemeal, as in Mexico,[5] or comprehensive and strategic, as in Turkey. To varying degrees, the proponents of ISI had to create their own constituencies. These came to be lodged in the military, the state sector itself, protected private interests sometimes dependent on state business, and the state-employed salariate.

At least three explanatory variables can be extracted from the change wrought by the introduction and application of ISI. First the international context provided an impetus for change. Second regnant strategies and policies for economic growth were seen by domestic elites to be deficient. Third, the initiation of new strategies, as in all four countries under scrutiny here, came as the result of sharp discontinuities with previous political arrangements.

Regarding the first point, there is a body of literature (see Stallings in chapter 1 of this volume) that stresses the place of economies in international markets and financial flows.[6] Change in basic economic arrangements is seen as resulting from the pressures to contain trade imbalances, service debt, maintain access to external credit and promote exports. It was, after all, the deterioration in the terms of trade for primary product exporters in the 1930s that led to the first elaborations of the ISI strategy. Today, the intelligentsias of many developing countries see the changes

[5] See Robert Kaufman, "How Societies Change Developmental Models or Keep Them: Reflections on the Latin American Experience in the 30's and the Postwar World," in Gary Gereffi and Don Wyman, eds., *Manufacturing Miracles: Patterns of Development in Latin America and East Asia* (Princeton: Princeton University Press, 1990), pp. 110–38.

[6] For example in two articles, David Cameron seeks to explain why several industrialized economies of western Europe have witnessed a marked increase in the scope of state activities since the Second World War (see Cameron "The Expansion of the Public Economy: A Comparative Analysis," *American Political Science Review* 72 (1978): pp. 1243–61; and "Distributional Coalitions and Other Sources of Economic Stagnation: On Olson's Rise and Decline of Nations," *International Organization* 42, no. 4 (1988): 561–604). In a critique of Mancur Olson's *The Rise and Decline of Nations* (New Haven, Conn.: Yale University Press, 1982) Cameron also seeks to explain why some advanced economies grow faster than others. In both instances, for Cameron the crucial variables relate to a country's "place in the world economy" (1988, p. 597) and the policy responses that flow therefrom. Cameron, however, does not show why countries situated similarly in the world economy perform differently (e.g., Mexico vs. India) or handle external crises differently (e.g., Egypt vs. Turkey).

adumbrated in the form and scale of state economic intervention as being wrung from unwilling and beleaguered policy makers by a powerful alliance of international creditors and academic ideologues.

The economic crises that provide external creditors their leverage also serve to focus and bring to the fore critical analyses formulated by domestic policy makers themselves. This simultaneity of external pressure and internal "paradigmatic shift" is particularly striking in Mexico after 1982.[7] By contrast, in India, despite the existence of an abundant literature critical of the state sector by reputable Indian scholars and policy makers,[8] there has been no crisis sufficient to promote far-reaching policy change. And, for the time being, external creditors have little leverage within the Indian economy.

Another set of propositions on the dynamics of strategic change is derived from Marxist class analysis. It has been argued that the emergence of large public sectors in the developing world should be seen as a way station in the building of capitalism, a stage during which an inexperienced petite bourgeoisie learns the entrepreneurial skills that will allow the state to divest itself of many of its assets.[9]

Divestiture or the retreat of the state may be the outcome, but it is not the maturation of a class, after an apprenticeship in managing public assets, that explains it. While it goes well beyond the scope of this chapter, it would be hard to argue that the four states examined here were the agents of a would-be bourgeoisie. Nor, despite the fact that their bourgeoisies have matured during the years of ISI, can the move toward reform and divestiture be seen as the result of this maturation. Indeed, India's is in most respects the most developed of the four private sector bourgeoisies; aside from Egypt, however, it has done the least to reduce the level of state intervention in the economy and in direct ownership. Further, in all four countries it is precisely the private interests that formed under protective ISI regimes, in which the public sector and its banks acted as risk absorber of last resort, that have seen the least attraction in market-oriented reforms, the lowering of protective tariffs, and the sale of public assets.

By contrast, I argue that the narrow elites that instituted ISI and vested broad ownership rights of assets in the state were under little domestic pressure to divest so long as respectable rates of growth in the economy were maintained. Once they had organized their functional constitu-

---

[7] Bienen and Waterbury, "Privatization in Developing Countries."

[8] E.g., L. K. Jha, *Economic Strategy for the 80s* (New Delhi: Allied Publishers, 1980); and Sharad Marathe, *Regulation and Development: India's Policy Experience of Controls over Industry* (New Delhi: Sage, 1986).

[9] I have explored some of the relevant literature in John Waterbury, "Twilight of the State Bourgeoisie?" *International Journal of Middle East Studies* 23, no. 1 (1991a): 1–17.

ents—including significant parts of the large-scale private sector itself—the nonstate bourgeoisie was not able to change statist policies. The collapse of statist experiments and entrenched coalitions in Eastern Europe, in the absence of any capitalist class, compel us to look beyond class for an explanation of change.

From different disciplinary origins there has been a conflation of assumptions about the likely behavior of public bureaucracies that yields powerful insights into their pathologies but little that would explain why they might change. The main streams of analysis flow from the property rights, the rent seeking, the distributional coalition, and the predatory or revenue-maximizing state approaches.[10] The intersection of these streams has been labeled "the new political economy," and it dwells on the perverse economic effects of state action.

Each of the central propositions involved bears directly upon how one should understand the scope and nature of state economic intervention and hence, for my purposes, of the management and performance of public sector enterprise. Summarizing crudely, the incentive structures involved in public property are likely to reduce the efficiency with which factors are used; the "iron law" of revenue maximization will starve the nonstate economy of needed resources;[11] entrenched interest groups will increasingly shift public resources away from production and into distribution; and entrepreneurial efforts will be devoted to competition for transfers artificially created by public policies (for example, tariffs, franchises, licenses, etc.). Implicitly, none of the proponents of these understandings could envisage an enlightened state apparatus acting in the long-term interests of a nascent capitalist class. Evans' analysis of the developmental state in this volume deals with an empirical reality in Northeast Asia that flies directly in the face of models of the perverse state.

The goodness of fit of these propositions is debatable, but the more important question is that they do not contain any rigorous explanations of the process by which the equilibria they predict will break down. Olson

[10] For a brief summary see Douglass North, *Institutions, Institutional Change, and Economic Performance* (Cambridge, New York: Cambridge University Press, 1990); and "The Approaches to the Study of Institutions," in David Colander, ed., *Neo-Classical Political Economy: The Anaylsis of Rent-Seeking and DUP Activities* (Cambridge, Mass.: Ballinger, 1984), pp. 33–40. Some seminal contributions are to be found in Colander's *Neo-Classical Political Economy*; Jagdish Bhagwati, "Directly Unproductive Profit-Seeking (DUP) Activities," *Journal of Political Economy* 90, no. 5 (1982): 988–1002; Anne Krueger, "The Political Economy of the Rent-Seeking Society," *American Economic Review* 64, no. 3 (1974), pp. 291–303; Olson, *Rise and Decline of Nations*, and T. N. Srinivasan, "Neoclassical Political Economy, the State and Economic Development," *Asian Development Review* 3, no. 2 (1985): 38–58.

[11] Margaret Levi, *Of Rule and Revenue* (Berkeley, Calif.: University of California Press, 1988).

foresees economic decline; Levi, declining state revenues over time; Bhagwati or Krueger, large deadweight losses for the economy. But because all actors are seen essentially as maximizing their own utilities, there appears to be no self-correcting mechanism, only crisis, economic collapse, and overthrow.[12] Certainly Eastern Europe's tribulations would seem to bear this out.

It is the case, however, that today we are confronted with several regimes that have initiated potentially far-reaching change in deeply-rooted patterns of public resource utilization. Those that are easiest to explain are regimes in which there has been some sharp political disjuncture or break in continuity. Among the four countries under consideration here, only Turkey, through the military coup of 1980, has had such a break.

I hypothesize that in those situations in which incumbents undertake politically dangerous reforms, it is the depth of the economic crisis itself that constitutes the major disjuncture with the immediate past.[13] Nowhere is this more striking than in the contrast in Mexico between the halcyon days of López Portillo up to 1982, and the economic disaster that greeted de la Madrid upon his taking office in the same year. It is highly significant that Mexico is saddled with an old conglomeration of distributional coalitions, a developed domestic bourgeoisie threatened by the abandonment of protection, well-trodden paths of rent seeking, and regime continuity more than five decades old. Nonetheless, profound structural change is under way.

The Adjustment Process in the Public Sector

In terms both of policy-making and of the political and economic effects of policies, the reform and privatization of state-owned enterprises cannot be separated analytically from the broader policy process built around structural adjustment. The concern for reform is part and parcel of the broader concern for deficit reduction, the search for increased tax revenue, and the containment of inflationary pressures. Privatization it-

[12] Merilee Grindle, "The New Political Economy: Positive Economics and Negative Politics," *Working Papers*, PPR (Washington, D.C.: World Bank, December 1989); North, *Institutional Change*, p.89.

[13] Even on this point the evidence is mixed. Measures taken in mild crises, such as Mexico's devaluation of 1954, may be hard to sustain, and in that case union pressure led to offsetting wage increases. See Leopoldo Solís, "A Monetary Will o' the Wisp: Pursuit of Equity through Deficit Spending," Research Program in Development Studies Discussion Paper No. 77, Princeton University, 1976. On the other hand Jeffrey Herbst has argued that in Zimbabwe, the depth of the crisis is such that leaders will not undertake partial reforms in the SOE sector because they see them as too puny to alleviate the crisis. See Jeffrey Herbst, "Political Impediments to Economic Rationality: Explaining Zimbabwe's Failure to Reform its Public Sector," *Journal of Modern African Studies* 27, no. 1 (1989): 81.

self is not primarily driven by a search for new revenue through asset sales, as has been the case in Europe, but rather by the effort to reduce public outlays and to generate new investment.

Two characteristics of reform and privatization flow from this. First their costs become part of economywide costs resulting particularly from stagnant labor markets and increasing unemployment. Organized labor finds itself fighting on several fronts, only one of which involves employment practices in SOEs and privatization. Privatization and reform are, in a sense, lost among several measures of retrenchment and austerity, and thus do not become the lightning rod for opposition by entrenched coalitional interests. Second, relatively scarce public talent is spread over several policy domains; tax reform, debt and money supply management, investment selection, and price and credit policy. Public sector reform and privatization is technically demanding and intensive in its use of technical personnel. Given competing demands for its use, the implementation of reform and privatization may be difficult to sustain.

The transition from the reform of SOEs to their privatization is likely to be sequential. I will show that reform efforts were contemplated well before the externally-stimulated crises of the late 1970s, but that the hopes that they could lead to greatly enhanced performance diminished over time. Defenders of the public sector tend to lose credibility (as well as consumer tolerance), and those who advocate using scarce technical and administrative personnel to liquidate or privatize have their day in court.

The sequence is paralleled by one in which the political leadership initially adjusts costs and benefits *within* existing coalitions and then moves to attempt to reconstitute the coalitions themselves. The Turkish military executed this shift after 1980, while President Salinas is beginning it in Mexico today.

The single most important catalyst to this sequential shift is the persistence of large government deficits to which, in the LDCs, state economic entities contribute a far greater share than in industrialized nations. In the late 1970s, on average the size of SOE deficits in developing countries was 4 percent of GDP as opposed to 1.75 percent in advanced industrial economies.[14] When privatization becomes a priority policy issue it is primarily because it is seen as a quick way to reduce the public deficit. Similarly, SOE expenditures as a proportion of GDP tend to be much higher in developing countries than in postindustrial nations (43 percent vs. 30 percent over the period 1980–85),[15] so that efforts to reduce public outlays

[14] Robert Floyd et al., *Public Enterprise in Mixed Economies: Some Macroeconomic Aspects* (Washington, D.C.: IMF 1984), pp. 144–45.

[15] World Bank, *World Development Report, 1988* (New York: Oxford University Press, 1988), p. 47.

may fall heavily on the SOEs. Increasingly privatization is also seen as a vehicle for generating new flows of investment which states, undergoing the financial rigors of adjustment, cannot generate themselves.

The sequential shift, if it is to proceed, will be managed by what I will call a change team. It will consist in technocrats with few or no links to the political arena although their prominence in the realm of macrostrategy may lead to such links. But in their capacity as the brain trust of the political leadership they will be politically isolated and utterly dependent upon the head of state. Conversely, for the team to move an agenda will require the visible and consistent support of the head of state. Such teams were frequently crucial in carrying forward the ISI project in its initial stages, and one thinks of the tandem of Nehru and Mahalanobis in India or of Gamal Abd al-Nasser and Aziz Sidqy in Egypt.[16]

The crucial factor is the public backing of the team by the head of state. In Egypt, President Mubarrek has remained aloof from the few ministers who might be sympathetic to structural reforms, while in Turkey President Özal has been so preoccupied with coalition management that since 1987 his attention to reform has drifted.

It is also important that there be considerable consistency in views and the setting of priorities among the team's members, although it is in the nature of political leadership to want to have a variety of views at its disposal and to balance contending camps. For that reason, and because turnover in change teams tends to be high, it is hard for them to maintain momentum. In Mexico, Finance Minister Pedro Aspe is clearly the driving force of the change team, but he has rivals in other ministries, the Banco de Mexico, and in the Presidency itself. In Turkey, Özal's team of young, foreign-trained technocrats ("two-passport Turks," as the local press sometimes describes them) has seen a number of members fall from grace or move off into the private sector (or, for one, return to the Wharton School).

Change teams are to varying degrees shielded from the groups whose interests will be gored in the reform process. They will be dealing with facets of a crisis that is felt throughout society, but by the very severity of which the populace has been numbed or rendered indifferent to the policy process itself (see Joan Nelson in chapter 5 of this volume). Defenders of old policies can no longer mount a coherent or coordinated defense. It will be clear, then, that policy initiatives originate within the state appa-

---

[16] Interesting discussions of change teams in major policy shifts are to be found in John P. Lewis, *Essays in Indian Political Economy*, Woodrow Wilson School, Princeton University, 1990 draft, who analyses the remaking of Indian agricultural policy in the mid-1960s; and Sylvia Maxfield, *Governing Capital* (Ithaca: Cornell University Press, 1990), who examines López Portillo's team of structuralists who engineered the nationalization of the Mexican banking sector in 1982.

ratus itself and only infrequently can be seen as the result of domestic lobbying.[17]

In examining the initiation of ISI as well as the initiation of neoclassical reforms, it is possible to isolate an important dynamic that inheres in the delegation process. Political leaders may have a few general preferences and targets that they seek to realize. They select among available experts a team that shares those preferences and that is technically competent to pursue them. The head of state, I shall argue, is a pragmatic problem solver, wedded to some extent to the status quo. The team she or he selects, however, may develop an ideological and programmatic approach to the problems it has been charged to solve. In Egypt in the early 1960s, Nasser, whom I see as a trial-and-error statist, put the organization of the economy in the hands of subordinates who wanted to build socialism. In Mexico today, an equally pragmatic de la Madrid and a marginally less so Salinas have set loose technocratic teams in pursuit of an internally consistent neoclassical blue print. Pragmatic problem solving has given way to programmatic transformation. If the top leadership becomes alarmed at the zeal with which the transformation is being pursued, it may disperse the team thereby jeopardizing even pragmatic change. If it stands by the team, we may witness a process of cascading reform.[18]

Coalitions

Top-down change without the support of organized constituencies probably cannot be sustained (see the introduction to this volume). The authors of ISI experiments were generally successful in organizing such support. Most of their success lay in the fact that ISI created many jobs, it was redistributive in its effects (leaving aside the rural sector), and inclusivist in that it could promise benefits to a wide range of interests.

From this inclusivism, ISI regimes fashioned the coalitions that sustained their rule. The coalitions in turn asserted, or were granted, legitimized claims to public resources. Any attempts to alter these entitlements would be resisted and likely defeated by the coalitions. Yet, as noted, this does not appear to have been the case in those instances where incumbents have initiated change, and even less so where new leaders have been brought to or seized power. The evidence is not unambiguous. For example, Egyptian labor, for a time at least, was able to paralyze any steps

[17] See the introduction to this volume; for earlier examples, see Albert Hirschman, *Journeys toward Progress: Studies of Economic Policy-Making in Latin America* (Garden City, N.Y.: Anchor Books, 1965), p. 309.

[18] For the British case see Victor Keegan, "Sold Down the River," *Manchester Guardian Weekly*, 31 December 1989.

toward privatization,[19] and in India Rajiv Gandhi's early efforts to dereg-
ulate the domestic market and liberalize the trade regime were thwarted
by the Congress Party.[20] Mexico's first attempt to join the General Agreement on Tariffs and Trade (GATT), at the end of Lopez Portillo's *sexenio*,
was successfully thwarted by private and public business interests.

By and large, however, resistance has proven to be remarkably feeble.
I believe there are two major reasons for this. First, the defenders of old
arrangements have lost much of their credibility and legitimacy in the
popular mind. Second, many of the nominally entrenched interests did
not win their entitlements through organization and concerted lobbying,
but rather, initially at least, through acts of state. They have not acquired,
therefore, the organizational ethos and sinews that come from self-gen-
erated growth and struggle. By the same token, because the policies of
SOE reform and privatization are not the product of well-organized interests within society, there may be few such interests willing to defend
the policies if they are accompanied by low rates of growth, business failures, inflation, and unemployment. In fact, in contrast to the ISI experiments, the new strategies are not likely in the medium term to improve
income distribution, create many new jobs, appeal to a broad range of
functional interests in society.[21] The factors that facilitate the initiation of
reform and privatization may well make the process difficult to sustain.

What political leadership has going for it is hesitancy and disarray
among the members of old coalitions and a general mood of disillusion
and cynicism among the populace at large. This is leadership's window
of opportunity. In it, new, narrow coalitions can be formed. Parts of the
private sector, especially in the export sector, will benefit from macropol-
icies and from targeted credit and tax breaks. The commercial agricultural sector, especially that part engaged in exports, may well benefit. Mi-
grant workers will enhance the local value of their foreign earnings
through devaluation. Parts of the small-scale and informal sectors may
benefit from deregulation—a striking example is the deregulation of
Mexican trucking. The list is short, and the interests of these groups are
by no means convergent.

In the absence of strong support from domestic actors, the reforms will

[19] Robert Bianchi, "The Corporatization of the Egyptian Labor Movement," *Middle East Journal* 40, no. 3 (1986): 429–44.

[20] Atul Kohli, "Politics of Economic Liberalization in India," *World Development* 17, no. 3 (1989): 305–28.

[21] In interviews with private entrepreneurs in all four countries, I encountered a common theme: they were not particularly interested in privatization but rather in credible state policy regulating relations between public and private enterprise and in opening the entire econ-
omy to private investment. If any of the four private sectors is able to break its symbiotic
ties to the SOEs and public banks it would be India's, yet it has not campaigned for privatization.

live or die by their ability to deliver some real growth. If there is growth, as there has been in Turkey since the early 1980s, then the state can engage in selective compensation for some of the many victims of curtailed public expenditures, layoffs, and inflation.[22]

But the Turkish example also points to a dynamic in which the processes of structural adjustment and SOE privatization may diverge. The maintenance of the SOE sector has become a major instrument for partially compensating organized labor and managers who face some combination of wage erosion, due to inflation, and growing unemployment. My judgement is that the privatization drive in Turkey has lost its attractiveness to the extent that it would impede the state from using the SOEs to ease the pain of other components of the structural adjustment process. By contrast, in Mexico, where between 1982 and 1989 GNP growth was either low or negative, much of the cost of adjustment was passed on directly to society as a whole without compensation. That the costs of adjustment have to some extent already been paid may explain why Salinas appears less concerned with protecting the core of his SOE sector.

The need for compensatory flows produces a variant of Miles Kahler's "orthodox paradox".[23] Because resources available for compensation are necessarily limited, the political authorities must concentrate more discretionary powers in their hands so as to be able to direct the flows where and when they want. Enhanced discretionary powers fly in the face of the logic of the macro-reforms which is to promote automaticity in economic transactions. In the wrong hands or in the wrong context, enhanced discretionary powers at the disposal of the top political leadership can produce a renaissance of rent seeking and perhaps the formation of new entitlements.

OVERHAULING THE PUBLIC ENTERPRISE SECTOR

I have argued that there is a policy sequence in the efforts to improve the economic performance of SOEs, and that the sequence is embedded in the

[22] See John Waterbury "The Political Management of Economic Adjustment and Reform," in Joan Nelson, ed., *Fragile Coalitions: The Politics of Adjustment* (Washington, D.C.: Overseas Development Council, 1989), pp. 39–57 and "Export-led Growth and Coalition-Building in Turkey," *Comparative Politics*, forthcoming. In sharp contrast to Mexico over the same period, Turkey was able to deliver real growth during the 1980s. That in turn was in substantial measure contingent upon large flows of external financing from the G-7 and the World Bank (see Merih Celâsun and Dani Rodrik, "Debt, Adjustment and Growth: Turkey," NBER Project on Developing Country Debt, draft, November 1987). Mexico did not have access to similar levels of external financing of reform.

[23] Miles Kahler, "Orthodoxy and its Alternatives: Explaining Approaches to Stabilization and Adjustment," in Joan Nelson, ed., *Economic Crisis and Policy Choice: The Politics of Adjustment in the Third World* (Princeton: Princeton University Press, 1990), p. 55.

policy context of structural adjustment. Within a decade or so of the state capturing the commanding heights of the economy, the major shortcomings in performance (low productivity, idle capacity, high levels of indebtedness, import dependency, and inability to export, for example) have been identified and to some extent made public. In Egypt and India, for instance, the first domestic questioning of the assumptions of state-led ISI was formulated in the middle 1960s. There then ensued the first of a long series of attempts to change the organizational and monitoring context in which SOEs operate, and the attempts gained urgency as the economies were subjected to external shocks in the 1970's and early 1980's.

The four countries under examination divide in two in terms of this sequence. Egypt and India remain in the first phase of organizational tinkering, although the issue of privatization is openly debated. Mexico and Turkey have entered the second phase and are using many of their best and brightest to engineer the liquidation or sale of a good part of the states' assets.

Public Sector Reform

The challenge of reform is partially determined by the size of the sector itself. In table 4.1 there is a snapshot of the relative claims on public resources of the government sector writ large and of the SOE sector in terms of expenditures to GDP.

The rank ordering of the scale of state intervention carries across a number of other dimensions (employment, investment, fixed capital formation, etc.) not presented here. Egypt is, on all counts, the biggest, and

TABLE 4.1
General Government and State-owned Enterprise Expenditures as a Proportion of GDP: Egypt, India, Mexico, and Turkey (percent)

	Year	General Government Expenditures/GDP	SOE Expenditures/ GDP	Total
Egypt	1988–89	44.0	17.3 (1987)	61.3
India	1985	9.0	15.5	24.5
Mexico	1988	27.0	12.0	39.0
Turkey	1988–89	21.0	28.0	49.0

Sources: Egypt, Middle East Economic Digest (14 December 1989, p. 5), and unpublished World Bank and USAID estimates; India: Review of Public Enterprises 2, no. 7294-IN (Washington, D.C.: World Bank, 12 October 1988). Indian figures do not include outlays at the state level; Mexico, René Villareal, Mitos y Realidades de la Empresa Pública (Mexico City: Editorial Diana, 1988), p. 147, and World Bank figures; Turkey, unpublished World Bank figures.

is an outlier relative to all LDCs.[24] Because I have stressed the importance of deficit reduction in moving the privatization agenda, I have assembled some recent deficit figures for the four countries to give an idea of the magnitudes involved.

In this respect Egypt is in a universe by itself, but Turkey and Mexico run SOE deficits that are proportionately as large as the total public deficit of the United States. The case for privatization might thus seem the most compelling in Egypt, but to date all that has resulted from the country's fiscal imbalances have been ineffectual attempts to reform public enterprise.

THE FUTILITY OF REFORM?

The problems habitually associated with the performance of SOEs probably inhere in the public property regime itself. They involve the multiple and often contradictory tasks assigned to the firms by the political controllers, the lack of managerial autonomy, the lack of incentives for

TABLE 4.2

Public Sector and Public Enterprise Deficits: Egypt, India, Mexico, and Turkey

	Year	Public Sector Deficit % GDP	Primary Deficit % GDP	Public Enterprise Deficit % GDP
Egypt	1986–87	26.3		9.0
India	1988–89	10.4	6.3	3.2
Mexico	1987	14.0	6.0	2.0
Turkey	1990	6.1		2.7

Sources: World Bank, *Egypt: Review of the Finances of the Decentralized Public Sector 1: EMANA Region Report* No. 6421-EGI, (Washington, D.C.: World Bank, 12 March 1987), p. 12; USAID, Cairo, *Public Enterprise Development and Performance in Egypt,* typescript 1989(?), tables 1.0 and 1.1; *India: Review of Public Enterprises 2,* no. 7294-IN (Washington, D.C.: World Bank, October 1988), p. 18; *India: An Industrializing Economy in Transition,* WB Country Study (Washington, D.C.: World Bank, 1989), pp. 60, 63, 75; N. A. Sarma, "Central Government's Budget for 1990–1991," *Business Standard* (April, 1990), pp. 6–15; Bureau of Public Enterprises, *Public Enterprise Survey, 1988–1989* (New Delhi, 1989); *India: Trends, Issues and Options* (Washington, D.C.: World Bank, 1990); Ernesto Zedillo de Leon, "Mexico's Recent Balance of Payments Experience and Prospects for Growth," *World Development* 14 (1986): 963–91; Cuadernos de Renovación Nacional, *Restructuración del Sector Paraestatal,* Mexico City, 1988; Government of Mexico, Poder Ejecutivo Federal, *Plan Nacional de Desarrollo 1989–1994* (Mexico City, Secretaríat of Budget and Program, 1989); Miguel de la Madrid, *Criterias Generales de la Política Económica* (Mexico City, 1986); Osman Ulagay, "The Public Sector Deficit, the Interest Burden, and Inflation," *Cumhuriyet,* 16 March 1990, p. 13 (in Turkish).

[24] *World Development Report 1988,* pp. 44–49.

anyone, including the nominal owners, to monitor performance and hold management accountable, the attentiveness of firms to bureaucratically determined targets rather than to market signals, the tendency toward monopoly or oligopsony in publicly owned firms, the accommodating atmosphere of the soft budget constraint, and the near impossibility of liquidation or bankruptcy.[25]

Large SOE sectors entail the partial deprivatization of the private sector itself as it learns to play the same games as the SOEs in obtaining foreign exchange, credit, raw materials, licenses and markets from the agencies and financial institutions of the state sector. The dilemma of the private sector firm is nearly identical to that of its public sector counterpart. Its rational goal is to seek greater macroeconomic efficiency in all sectors while preserving for itself all the special deals and risk reducing devices that have cushioned it against the costs of greater firm-level efficiency. If every firm, public and private, pursued its narrow interests, macroefficiency could not be achieved. It is the role of public policy through adjustment reforms to restructure these incentives.

It follows that public sector managers, private owners, and organized labor, while more or less cognizant of the macroinefficiencies holding back the economy as a whole, will have a second-best preference for the status quo that protects their acquired privileges and deals. The logic of this argument follows that of the new political economy and of the perverse effects of state intervention. Reform, I argue, will more often than not fall victim to distributional coalitions.

I will state it as axiomatic that specific SOEs, but not an entire SOE sector, can be turned around. These successes cannot spread to entire SOE sectors, as that would defeat the logic of the system as a whole. Consider four factors that all managers of turnarounds cite as crucial: autonomy from political interference, elimination of redundant personnel among workers and managers, pay differentials tied to productivity, and

---

[25] This litany is the subject of a vast literature and an ongoing debate. See, at a minimum, Joseph Stiglitz et al., *The Economic Role of the State* (Oxford: Basil Blackwell, 1989); E. S. Savas, *Privatization: The Key to Better Government* (Chatham, N.J.: Chatham House Publishers, 1987); Wlodzimierz Brus and Kazimierz Laski, *From Marx to Market: Socialism in Search of an Economic System* (Oxford: Clarendon Press, 1989); Janos Kornai, "The Hungarian Reform Process: Visions, Hopes and Reality," in Victor Nee and David Stark, eds., *Remaking the Economic Institutions of Socialism: China and Eastern Europe* (Stanford, Calif.: Stanford University Press, 1989); Mahmood Ali Ayub and Sven Hegstad, *Public Industrial Enterprises: Determinants of Performance*, Industry and Finance Series, vol. 17 (Washington, D.C.: World Bank, 1986); Yair Aharoni, *The Evolution and Management of State-owned Enterprises* (Cambridge, Mass.: Ballinger, 1986); Leroy Jones and Edward Mason, "Why Public Enterprise?," in Leroy Jones and Edward Mason, eds., *Public Enterprise in Less-Developed Countries* (Cambridge: Cambridge University Press, 1986), pp. 17–66.

the ability to generate profits. The SOEs are what they are precisely because they are subjected to political control. Their objectives and the criteria by which they are judged must remain politically determined, otherwise there would be no compelling reason to retain them under public ownership. Likewise, if profits, or some other indicator of real returns to factors, were the predominant measure of success, it would be better to encourage the activity through private enterprise, or at least through contracting with private providers. Finally, shaping the workforce in terms of real markets, and structuring salaries and wages to reflect productivity would cut deeply into the social equity goals typically assigned to SOEs. It would also, of course, cut deeply into entitlements. Finally, such reform would limit the latitude of political authorities to use the SOEs as vehicles for compensatory payments to select constituents in times of adjustment reforms.[26] I believe these factors would hold in any economy in which the public sector plays a substantial role.

With these skeptical observations in mind, I turn now to an examination of the reform efforts of Egypt and India, two countries that have yet to move beyond the reform phase. What these two cases demonstrate are the limits to reform both in terms of the logic of principal-agent relations in the public sector and in terms of the claims placed on SOE sectors by broad-based coalitional interests.

EGYPT

The leadership in Egypt has never disowned its faith that the SOE sector can be made to work efficiently. Since the middle 1960s it has tinkered with the organizational context of the sector at the juncture of the supervisory apparatus (i.e., the level at which the state exercises its ownership rights) with aggregates of firms. The slogan invoked is "the separation of management from ownership." This is typical of most SOE reform processes in which attempts to promote fundamental changes *within* the firm are eschewed. Instead uniform employment, wage, and incentive practices are applied across the sector regardless of the performance of individual firms.

When Egypt's SOE sector first took shape, with the nationalization of British and French interests in the wake of the 1956 Suez War, public firms were grouped under a holding company, known as the Egyptian Development Organization. Within three years, Egypt added another two holding companies, this time with firms taken over from the Egyptian private sector or created by the state itself. The unique feature of these holding companies was the diversity of their assets and the expectation that they would compete with one another. The model was Italy's IRI.

---

[26] Waterbury, "Export-led Growth."

Between 1961 and 1963, however, as Egypt's self-proclaimed socialist transformation reached its apogee, the system was entirely overhauled. The public sector had been greatly expanded after the extensive nationalizations of July 1961 (the so-called Socialist Decrees) followed by smaller takeovers in the next three years. The new arrangement was to organize SOEs by sector. Each sector became homogeneous in its product or service (e.g., textiles, metals, engineering, chemicals, food processing, or trade), and each sector was put under the supervision of a General Organization which in turn answered to a specific ministry (e.g., Industry, Agriculture, Supply, or Defense). The four large nationalized banks were attached to specific sectors. The General Organizations were charged with preparing sectoral plans, developing budget projections, procuring raw materials and financing, and identifying senior management.

There was no competition among them as each sector constituted a quasimonopoly with only partially overlapping markets. Their investment and production strategies were to be worked out in conjunction with the five year plan. All of this "rationalization" was accompanied by unified pay scales and personnel procedures, and promotion by seniority. The whole structure was shielded by high tariff walls and quantitative trade restrictions.

While substantial GNP growth was achieved over the first plan period, 1960–65, Egypt's trade imbalance grew alarmingly and external financing depended on the good will of the Soviet Union and of the United States. The culprit was the SOE sector with its demands for imports, its high cost production, and its inability to export. Moreover, the General Organizations had begun to interfere in all aspects of firm management so that the managers shoved all decisions up to the General Organization level and awaited orders. If none was forthcoming, they did nothing.[27]

War in 1967 and 1973 diverted attention from SOE performance, but in a sweeping move in 1975 (Law 111), the General Organizations were abolished. It was said the company heads would now be free to act like entrepreneurs. The supervisory ministries would set broad targets and help with financing but otherwise leave the companies (some 350 of them by this time) to their own devices, subject only to post hoc review. This move came one year after President Sadat launched the "open-door policy" (infitah) to encourage foreign investment and to force the public sector to compete for domestic markets.[28]

Neither enhanced performance nor a more competitive market was fully achieved. Foreign investment flowed primarily into tourism and

[27] S. Farid, *Top Management in Egypt: Its Structure, Quality and Problems* (Santa Monica, Calif.: Rand Corp., 1970), pp. 36–37.
[28] John Waterbury, *The Egypt of Nasser and Sadat: The Political Economy of Two Regimes* (Princeton: Princeton University Press, 1983), pp. 57–122.

banking, while the ministries absorbed all the tasks of the General Orga-nizations without relinquishing the right to interfere in day-to-day man-agement of the firms. Successful managers were those who pursued joint ventures with foreign investors, in some ways gutting their own SOEs in the process. Due primarily to the objections of organized labor, the initial surge in the formation of joint ventures petered out by 1980.[29]

In 1983, Egypt came nearly full circle in its reform efforts. Law 97 of that year essentially restored the sectoral General Organizations, now called Authorities. Sectoral homogeneity and noncompetitivity were maintained. What had changed most significantly in the intervening years was that the nationalized banks had been freed from the obligations to specific sectors, and in 1981 the National Bank for Investment was cre-ated to undertake SOE financing in conformity with the national plan. At the same time, the SOE budgets were taken off the state budget, thus artificially reducing the budget deficit.

Since the middle 1960s, Egypt has moved from an espousal of state socialism to an ineffective form of state capitalism. The goal is to preserve the state sector, but relegitimize it by making it profitable and responsive to the demands of consumers. Two documents capture this spirit and identify the interests involved. In 1982, the presidentially-appointed Na-tional Specialized Councils issued a two-volume report on the public sec-tor.[30] Its recommendations were of two kinds. First, it sought legal equal-ity for SOEs with companies set up under Law 43. Regarding tariffs, the report recommended that high walls be maintained for locally-produced goods, that tariffs on capital and intermediate goods not be higher than on finished products, and that the state purchase goods and services from the SOEs at their real cost and compensate consumers through subsidies. Second, it urged the reestablishment of sectoral holding companies and, in 1983, got its wish. At the same time it invoked the need to encourage the real autonomy of firm managers, and to link wages to productivity. Such invocations have a nearly liturgical quality to them.

In all of this, the open-door policy was mentioned only insofar as it could impede the flourishing of the SOEs. It was a tract written by the managerial class. Its tone was unsparing toward labor, which would be subjected to flexible hiring and productivity-linked wages, toward the bu-reaucrats who would have their monitoring powers curtailed, and toward

[29] Joint ventures were established under Law 43 of 1974 and its successor Law 32 of 1977. Both stipulated that any joint venture established with a public sector partner would automatically be considered part of the private sector regardless of the distribution of equity between the partners. Labor would not necessarily share in profits nor have representation on the board, as was the case in the public sector. The joint ventures set up in the late 1970s are the closest Egypt has come to privatization.

[30] *Strategic Supports of Industry: Egypt to the Year 2000* no. 17, parts 1, 2 (Cairo: Na-tional Specialized Councils, 1982).

the private sector, which was depicted as the source of unfair competition. Six years later, the Institute of National Planning issued its own investigations of the SOE sector, and its recommendations followed closely on those of the National Specialized Councils.[31] When and if the top political leadership decides to accelerate the adjustment agenda, these state interests may collapse easily, but that leadership may not move with much conviction.

Since 1987, Egypt's economic crisis has deepened. Falling petroleum revenues (until the summer of 1990) and worker remittances were coupled with continued huge public deficits, high inflation, and accumulating arrears on over $50 billion in external debt. Pressure from the donor community focused primarily on interest rates, consumer subsidies, and energy pricing, but there was accompanying urging, especially on the part of the United States Agency for International Development (USAID), to move toward privatization.

Egyptian policy makers in essence stalled. There was no obvious public support for any of the reform measures being urged. The cabinet contained only one figure, the minister of tourism, who openly advocated privatization. There was no technocratic team in place to pursue the reform agenda, and the President was decidedly ambivalent about the whole process. However, in late 1990, he intimated that much more ambitious measures might be in the offing and talked of a "one thousand-day" program to remake the Egyptian economy. In April of 1991 Egypt was, once again, on the verge of signing a long-term stabilization agreement with the IMF that would unify exchange rates, raise interest rates, bring energy prices up to world levels over five years, raise taxes (through a sales tax), eliminate most consumer subsidies over five years, pursue privatization, and reduce the budget deficit to 5 to 6 percent of GDP.

The lesson of the Egyptian example is that the kind of crisis that triggered structural reform in Turkey and Mexico has been postponed because of Egypt's ability to collect strategic and other rents. In that context the coalitional entitlements built up since 1956 have been protected, and existing arrangements defended especially by organized labor, the top bureaucrats, and the military. The obvious performance failures of SOEs have been dealt with through organizational tinkering at the principal-agent level which has tended to come full circle.

INDIA

In its detail, the Indian SOE sector is more complex than Egypt's, due above all to the federal system and a broad array of state-level enterprises. The focus here will be on the federal, or central SOEs (some 239 firms in

[31] *The Future of the Public Sector in Egypt*, in Arabic (Cairo: Institute of National Planning, May 1988).

1989). Like Egypt, India has tried to improve SOE performance mainly through periodic revisions of principal-agent linkages, although some individual firms have carried out significant internal reforms.

In general the evolution of India's SOEs has followed a calendar closely resembling Egypt's. Three five-year plans carried Indian public enterprise into the mid-1960s when the inefficiencies in factor utilization became manifest. These were coupled with severe balance of payments problems that lead to a devaluation of the rupee in 1966. The following year, the Administrative Reform Commission stressed that central SOEs are legally commercial entities and that the government of India should treat them as such.[32]

What distinguishes India most strikingly from Egypt and many other LDCs that followed ISI strategies is the prudence with which it managed its monetary and fiscal policies and its external accounts. Government spending, until the mid-1980s, was carefully controlled, inflation remained low, the rupee was not significantly overvalued, and the external debt and the balance of payments remained within tolerable limits. The monsoon failures of the mid-1960s and early 1970s, the military confrontations with the People's Republic of China (PRC) and Pakistan, and the second oil shock provoked crises that seem mild compared to those of the other three countries. Consequently until the present time the depth of economic crisis has not been such as to push Indian policy makers or politicians to call into question the strategy they have followed for nearly four decades.

Indira Gandhi, who took responsibility for the 1966 devaluation, did not follow consistent policies in dealing with the public sector. On the one hand, she promoted its expansion through the nationalization of most private banks in 1969, the nationalization of the coal sector, and the take over of numerous failing ("sick" in Indian parlance) private enterprises, especially in the textile sector. On the other hand, during the Emergency, 1975–77, she cracked down hard on strikes and agitation among organized labor, and India briefly entered a phase of authoritarian state capitalism. It was not, however, until her return to power in 1980 that public sector reform and economic liberalization were given real prominence.[33]

A leading figure in this effort, and a close advisor to the prime minister, was L. K. Jha, a career civil servant and economic generalist who achieved prominence as an advisor to Prime Minister Shastri in 1964. He became the driving force behind the liberalization measures launched by Indira

[32] *India: Review of Public Enterprises*, Report No. 7294-IN, vol. 2, main text, and vol. 3, appendices and annexes (Washington, D.C.: World Bank, October 1988).

[33] In general, see Baldev Raj Nayar, *India's Mixed Economy: The Role of Ideology and Interest in its Development* (Bombay: Popular Prakashan, 1989).

Gandhi and continued, after 1984, by her son Rajiv Gandhi. The broad lines of what he set out to achieve are contained in his 1980 book, and he recruited a younger group of economists and technocrats to work out detailed plans.

The groundwork was done between 1980 and 1984, but the liberalization program really took off in 1984–85 in the run up to the seventh five-year plan. The main thrust was the easing of the highly restrictive regulatory regime of private enterprise in place since the middle 1950s, but strengthened under Indira Gandhi through the Monopoly and Restrictive Trade Practices law. Deregulation opened up restricted sectors of the economy to private investment, raised investment levels that required licensing, delicensed some twenty-five industries, and allowed for certain kinds of capacity expansion and the introduction of new production lines without official approval. The asset limit above which MRTP legislation would be applicable was raised substantially. In addition, the importation of ca. 1000 items, mostly not produced locally, was delicensed. In order to encourage exports, the rupee was allowed to devalue over the seventh plan period by 40 percent.[34]

During these same years a great deal of attention was focused on improving the performance of the SOEs. Significantly, two of the major high-level reviews were never made public. The first report was produced by a committee set up in September 1984 and chaired by Arjun Sen Gupta who was special secretary to the Prime Minister. The Sen Gupta Report was built around two familiar themes. First, it sought to increase firm-level managerial autonomy by setting up holding companies.[35] The government ministries would undertake overall strategic planning. Through the holding companies memoranda of understanding would be drawn up with individual companies as well as between the holding companies and the ministries. A third theme was peculiar to India; to wit that parliamentary prying into the affairs of SOEs should be limited, as is the case in the U.K., by a "self-denying ordinance."[36] The Sen Gupta report did not address the issue of privatization.

A few years later another high level committee drafted a white paper on the SOE sector. After two years of review and amending, it finally reached the cabinet in late 1988.[37] This report was in most respects an

[34] *India: Trends, Issues and Options* (Washington, D.C.: World Bank, March 1990); see also Kohli, "Liberalization in India."

[35] Unlike Egypt, India had not resorted to holding companies for SOEs with a few notable exceptions such as SAIL and the National Textile Corporation.

[36] Report summarized and critiqued in Prajapati Trivedi, "Sen Gupta Report on Public Enterprises: Eloquent Fuzziness at Best," *Economic and Political Weekly* 22, no. 22 (1987): pp. 55–66.

[37] *India Today*, 30 April 1989, p. 67.

extension of the Sen Gupta document. It too stressed managerial autonomy, and the authorization of corporate and sectoral planning by companies or holding companies. The draft white paper went beyond the earlier report in suggesting that some unviable firms be liquidated or sold
and that SOEs float public share offerings with priority for employees.
The white paper aroused some opposition in the cabinet, and Rajiv Gandhi, who supported it, was persuaded to hold it in abeyance until after
the elections. Congress lost the elections, and the white paper has not
been disinterred.

In the absence of any broadly-conceived approach to SOE reform, the
government of India nonetheless undertook some important specific measures. At the beginning of the seventh five-year plan, Rajiv Gandhi recognized an impending fiscal crisis by announcing that during the plan
period the SOEs would have to generate most of their own investment
resources, either through commercial borrowing or retained earnings.
Some SOEs, such as the National Thermal Power Corporation, were au-
thorized to issue bonds and debentures, but the public response was not
encouraging. By the end of the plan period, it was clear that SOEs in
general continued to rely heavily on budgetary transfers.

The Indian government has instituted the use of memoranda of understanding on a fairly broad scale. These were inspired by the French experience with *contrats plans* begun in the mid-1960s. The object is to
draw up multiyear performance contracts between the government and
the firm by which the government commits itself to specified levels of
financing and prices in exchange for the firm's achieving targets in production or delivery of services within agreed-upon cost parameters. The
contract framework would thus liberate firm management to pursue its
targets with considerable flexibility.

In India the memorandum of understanding implies something less
binding on the two parties. The object is not so much to realize specific
targets but rather to develop, firm by firm, a set of performance indicators
and performance signals that will guide the level of resources provided by
the government. Management is granted greater latitude in committing
funds and making strategic decisions. The first two memoranda were
signed with Steel Authority of India, Ltd. (SAIL) and the Oil and Natural
Gas Commission, and by 1990 had been extended to eighteen other
SOEs.

The memoranda have revealed several drawbacks. They are drawn up
yearly and stipulate that firms provide quarterly reports on performance.
They have tended to function as monitoring devices for the annual budget
of the firm. There are no clear consequences for the failure of either party
to meet its obligations, but the problem is particularly difficult if the government reneges on commitments. In Mexico, where similar memoranda

have been used for some years, a manager remarked to the author that they are a device by which managers and government officials lie to each other.[38]

India illustrates perhaps better than any of the other three the cleavage between the upper level civil administration and the management of the SOEs. The Indian bureaucrats (pejoratively known as the *babus*) are those who exercise ownership rights through financing, taxing, regulating, pricing, monitoring, auditing, and planning. The civil service elite, as well as the politicians, have little interest in promoting the autonomy of the SOEs, which would reduce the need for monitoring and the possibility of political interference. Neither support the dilution of SOE equity through public share offerings, which might lead to challenges to government representatives on SOE boards. The memoranda of understanding are attractive to the administration because they are designed by the Bureau of Public Enterprise which remains largely under their control.[39] Privatization is the least desirable reform because it reduces, perhaps irreversibly, the scope of administrative controls.

To date India's policies of economic liberalization have not included any significant steps toward privatization. At the same time tariff protection for both public and private enterprise remains high. As the World Bank noted: "The import substitution bias of the trade regime has actually increased."[40] In contrast to the other three countries, new SOEs are being added to the public sector at both the state and federal levels on a regular basis.

In India there has been no fiscal, balance-of-payments, or external debt crisis of sufficient magnitude to drive a process of thorough economic

---

[38] For the Indian government view of the memoranda and the texts of some, see Bureau of Public Enterprises, *Public Enterprises Survey, 1988–89* (New Delhi, 1989). The World Bank, *Review of Public Enterprises*, pp. 102–8, provides a thorough critique; also Raj K. Nigam, "Indian Public Sector at the Crossroads," in Waris Kidwai and Baldeo Sahai, eds., *Dynamics of Management of Public Enterprises* (New Delhi: SCOPE, 1989), p. 77. John Nellis, *Contract Plans and Public Enterprise Performance*, World Bank Working Paper No. 118 (Washington, D.C.: World Bank, October 1988), and Mary Shirley, "Evaluating the Performance of Public Enterprises in Pakistan," Policy, Planning and Research Working Paper No. 160 (Washington, D.C.: World Bank, March 1989), evaluate *contrats plans* and memoranda of understanding as they have been applied in several countries.

[39] The BPE constituted a high level committee to draw up individual memoranda and to monitor performance annually. Its members are: the cabinet secretary, the finance secretary, the expenditure secretary, the Planning Commission secretary, the chairman of the Bureau of Industrial Costs and Prices, the chairman of the Public Enterprise Selection Board and the additional secretary of the BPE. In a different context, one SOE manager referred to such officials as "the high priests of the bureaucracy" (P. C. Luthar, "Interface Relationship of Public Enterprises with the Government and the Parliament," in Kidwai and Sahaio, eds., *Dynamics of Management* [New Delhi: SCOPE, 1989], pp. 222–56).

[40] World Bank, *Trends, Issues and Options*, p. 51.

restructuring. The beneficiaries of allocational practices dating back to the early 1950s have accepted the need to improve the performance of the SOE sector, and have backed principal-agent reforms that for the most part do not call into question existing entitlements. Above all the civil service elite has been successful in protecting its supervisory and auditing role vis-à-vis the SOE sector. Change has taken place primarily through industrial deregulation and a limited amount of trade liberalization. Both Indira and Rajiv Gandhi lent some direct support to these policies and, through L. K. Jha, put together a fragile change team that fell foul of strong interests within the Congress party.

Privatization

Privatization and/or liquidation of SOEs will be pursued as the result of a combination of factors involving unsatisfactory attempts at improving SOE performance, the need to reduce the public deficit and generate new investment quickly, and the longer term objective of reducing the state's responsibilities for setting the standards of and safeguarding the socio-economic welfare of the bulk of the citizenry. If it is sustained, it will generally be part of a major strategic shift from ISI to a more open trade regime and perhaps to an export-led growth strategy founded on private enterprise. It will mark the disillusionment with efforts to make old arrangements work better and the determination to transform existing patterns of resource utilization. A head of state committed to an insulated change team will be necessary both to initiate and to sustain the process of transformation.

TURKEY

Under this rubric, Turkey is a pioneer, not only because its strategic shift was begun in 1980, but because there was an earlier episode after 1950. It was in that year that the probusiness Democrat Party came to power having promised to sell off many state enterprises. For various reasons, including the limited purchasing capacity of the Turkish private sector, the promise was not fulfilled. To the contrary, the Democrat Party discovered the political advantages of the public sector and sponsored a significant expansion of the SOEs ("vote factories" as they became known) and a doubling of the managerial corps.[41] Today the lineal descendant of the Democrat Party, the True Path Party, has opposed privatization and set itself up as the guardian of an inward-oriented symbiosis of public and private enterprise.

[41] Feroz Ahmad, *The Turkish Experiment in Democracy, 1950–1975*, Royal Institute of International Affairs (RIIA) (London: Hurst and Co., 1977), pp. 128–30.

In the 1960s and 1970s, Turkey undertook a number of high-level reviews of the SOE sector, yielding recommendations that are similar to those already discussed with respect to Egypt and India.[42] The last came in 1982, when Turgut Özal, Turkey's current president, was briefly out of power. When he returned to the prime ministry in 1983, he ignored the recommended reforms and launched Turkey's privatization drive. He called in foreign consultants, including Morgan Bank, which drew up a privatization master plan in 1986. He recruited a small team of Turkish economists, mainly with foreign training, to design the export and privatization strategies. Özal claimed authorship frequently and publicly for the changes under way.

The privatization drive was part of the more far-reaching shift toward deregulation, trade liberalization, and export-led growth. With something on the order of $12 billion in fresh funds from 1979 to the mid-1980s, Turkey was able to pursue its new strategy without sacrificing real growth in the economy.[43] It was this level of funding, both multilateral and bilateral, more than the policy of constant real devaluation of the Turkish lira, that enabled Turkey to sextuple the value of its exports during the 1980s.[44] The principal instruments for the export drive were large private conglomerates in manufacturing and engineering, represented by trading houses fashioned after the Korean model.[45] The drive was fueled by export tax rebates, duty-free imports of inputs for manufactured exports, and subsidized credits. The SOEs played only a minor role in the drive, and by the end of the 1980s the SOEs were running a $5 billion trade deficit while the private sector registered a $2.4 billion surplus.[46]

The economic cost of Turkey's strategy was in the form of high rates of inflation resulting from high levels of public outlays, the price effects of devaluation, and a growing external debt representing more than half of GDP. As long as real growth in the economy was maintained, there were sufficient resources to invest and redistribute on a selective basis. As

[42] Bertil Walstedt, *State Manufacturing Enterprise in a Mixed Economy: The Turkish Case*, World Bank (Baltimore: Johns Hopkins Press, 1980); Cevat Karataş, "Public Economic Enterprises in Turkey: Reform Proposals, Pricing and Investment Policies," *METU Studies in Development* 13, nos. 1–2 (1986): 135–69; Waterbury, "Export-led Growth."

[43] The funds were committed when the last civilian governments tried to engineer IMF stabilization programs and were accelerated after the military took over in September 1980. The principal sources were the G-7, the World Bank through five SALs, and the IMF.

[44] Celâsun and Rodrik, "Adjustment and Growth."

[45] Ziya Öniş, "Organization of Export-Oriented Industrialization: The Turkish Foreign Trade Companies in Comparative Perspective," Center of International Studies, Princeton University, draft, 1989.

[46] Tüsiad, *The Turkish Economy '89* (Istanbul: Turkish Industrialists and Businessmen's Association, 1989), p. 81.

long as the export drive continued, Turkey could continue to borrow abroad.

The abrupt strategic shift after 1980 was engineered in the wake of a military coup. The generals leading the coup justified their action on the grounds that Turkey was slipping into political anarchy, if not civil war, and that national security required that the military act. But the generals wasted little time in launching the policies that constituted the export drive, and their principal advisor was Özal, who was a civilian engineer with experience in the World Bank before he became prime minister in 1983. During the period of military rule, old political parties were banned, militant trade unions shut down and their leaders arrested, and the universities purged of radical professors on both the left and the right. The fragile and costly coalitions that had dominated the 1970s were smashed so that opposition to the economic reforms was minimal. Moreover, the Turkish people themselves were relieved, for a time, that the growing political violence and economic disarray of the late 1970s had come to an end.

It became clear that Özal would not devote much effort to reforming the SOE sector. He undertook three initiatives with different objectives. The first was to have the Treasury absorb a good portion of the SOEs' debt. The second was to allow the firms to raise their prices substantially. Large price increases occurred in 1983 and 1988. Through these two measures the SOEs wiped out their deficits and restructured their debt-equity ratios. Price increases were passed on to consumers. Farmers, for instance, saw the price of fertilizers go up fourfold. The third initiative was to begin the gradual conversion of the two hundred thousand or so white-collar administrators of the SOEs to the status of contract personnel. On the one hand, while the conversions could result in higher salaries, at the same time they were based on one-year contracts that could be easily terminated. Moreover contract personnel could not join unions or engage in strikes.

In sum, the quasimonopolistic SOEs are no longer a net drain on the budget, and their management is much less secure in its tenure. Nothing has been done at the firm level to improve performance, although there have been individual successes, such as the turnaround of Sümerbank in the late 1980s.

By 1986 several SOEs had been nominated for privatization, and an order of priority established. In May of that year Law 3291 on Privatization was issued. It provided for the transfer of the shares in targeted SOEs to an off-budget entity known as the Mass Housing and Public Participation Fund (MHPPF). Whatever its long-term objective, this fund became one of Turkey's largest holding companies, and its director served at the behest of the prime minister. It not only held the controlling equity in dozens of SOEs, but it was empowered to change management and restructure the finances and operations of SOEs being prepared for privatization. Most important, it could retain in any privatized SOE a "golden share" that would allow it to veto any decisions taken by the board. Here we have a prime example of the orthodox paradox, with the added dimension of the discretionary use of recentralized power.[47]

It was not until February 1988 that the first privatization was carried out. Ironically it involved a firm, Teletaş, for the manufacture of telephone equipment, that was already legally private. The MHPPF sold 22 percent of the equity that was publicly held through a general share offering.[48]

The authorities may have eschewed further public share offerings given the size of the larger units coming up on the agenda and the shallowness of the Turkish capital market. The next privatization involved five productive units of Çitosan, the public sector cement firm. Ninety percent of the equity in the five units was sold to Société Ciment Français. As part of the deal, the French purchaser committed itself to a $75 million investment program spread over four years. The French company pledged that after three years 39 percent of the equity would be offered to the public. A similar deal was being prepared with SAS for the purchase of USAŞ, a catering service for Turkish Airlines.

These moves were challenged by Özal's principal rivals, the True Path Party and the Social Democrat Party. They went to court to block the Çitosan and USAŞ deals. The Sixth District Court of Ankara, in late 1989, suspended the sales, on the grounds that they were in violation of decrees of the Higher Planning Council and of the MHPPF that stipulated that privatization would take place through share offerings to the workers in SOEs, small savers, expatriate labor, and the people in general.[49]

Since then no privatization has taken place. The government has promised that no block sales to foreign interests will be contemplated. This means turning to Turks in the private sector. It is being proposed that privately-held (i.e., nontraded) Turkish firms swap shares for shares in the SOEs. This would have the double effect of bringing family firms into the capital market, thereby deepening it, and providing an incentive for the

[47] In a similar vein, the Treasury and Foreign Trade Secretariat established a computer network for all SOEs that allowed it to follow the financial and investment status of each firm on a daily basis (*Cumhuriyet*, 24 February 1990).

[48] Karataş Cevat, "Privatization in the U.K. and Turkey," University of Bradford, draft, 1989; Roger Leeds, "Turkey: Rhetoric and Reality," in Raymond Vernon, ed., *The Promise of Privatization* (New York: Council on Foreign Relations, 1989), pp. 149–78; and Yakup Kepenek, *State-Owned Enterprises in Turkey*, in Turkish (Istanbul: Gerçek Yayinevi, 1990).

[49] See Yasushi Hazama, "Politics of Implementation: Privatization in Turkey," Department of Economics (Ankara: Middle East Technical University, 1990); and *Cumhuriyet*, 21 February 1990.

acquisition of the SOEs. Private buyers could form consortia with foreign interests to carry out the swaps. The swaps would be mediated by the MHPPF.[50]

The adjustment and reform efforts of the early 1980s have begun to lose steam. Özal's Motherland Party suffered a heavy defeat in municipal and local elections in March 1989, partially due to continued high rates of inflation. New parliamentary elections in 1992 might lead to the defeat of his party, although he would continue on as President, a post to which the Grand National Assembly elected him in 1989. Özal's attention in recent years has moved away from the reform agenda to the maintenance of the fractious coalition within his own party. The team of young tech-nocrats, with the exception of the governor of the Central Bank and the head of the State Planning Organization, has not been stable, and its im-mediate political bosses have changed rapidly.

The export drive itself has been sustained, although it is slowing due to the phasing out of various subsidies and rebates. The challenge here will be for the private firms involved to keep their market niches and develop new product lines in the absence of the levels of government support to which they have become accustomed.

One cannot say with much confidence that Turkey's course since 1980 is irreversible. Its private firms are highly leveraged and facing very high real rates of interest. Loss of markets abroad due to increased competition or world recession could force widespread bankruptcies. The government and the banks would then be faced with the unpalatable choice of liqui-dating the losers or bailing them out by government takeover. Chile had to do just that in 1983, and there are powerful forces in Turkey that would welcome a reassertion of the state in the economic domain.

The electoral coalition that has kept the Motherland Party in power does not in any direct sense benefit from the economic reforms. Many agricultural producers and small-scale manufacturers have been hurt by trade liberalization, high prices for SOE-supplied inputs, and high interest rates. The large scale private sector generally adopts a stance of political neutrality. The way Özal has placated various interests is by directing some of the growth in the economy into compensatory payments to select constituents within a narrow coalition.[51] With its seven hundred thou-sand workers and employees, the SOE sector has been maintained to

[50] *Cumhuriyet*, 28 November 1989.

[51] I have explored his strategy in some detail in Waterbury, "Export-led Growth." The Turkish electoral law allows a party winning about a third of the national vote to capture over half the seats in the Grand National Assembly. The electoral law adopted in Mexico in 1989 has a provision that *guarantees* that any party winning a third of the national vote will automatically receive 51 percent of the seats in the Chamber of Deputies.

cushion the impact of inflation and unemployment for a strategic segment of the organized workforce.

The very substantial changes wrought in the early 1980s came about as a result of deep crisis and a clean break with a previous set of political and allocational arrangements. But there has been some tendency since 1983 for new entitled claimants to emerge. As in the 1950s, the need to win elections has driven the Motherland Party to use public expenditures and the SOE sector to shore up its narrow coalition. Nonetheless, the export drive has been impressive, and the general commitment to trade liberalization and market-oriented reforms has been repeatedly blessed by Turgut Özal. He assembled a competent change team that, over time however, appears to have lost the attention of the Prime Minister and since 1989 the President. Moreover, the team has found so many complex technical issues facing it that there is a real opportunity cost for its time posed by privatization.

MEXICO

Mexico presents the greatest challenge to conventional understandings of what produces change within seemingly stable political systems. It illustrates the process by which pragmatic, damage control efforts can escalate in the hands of a programmatically-guided change team into policies that, if sustained, would transform the system profoundly. The collapse of petroleum prices and Mexico's inability to service its external debt drove Miguel de la Madrid in the early 1980s to a series of pragmatic reforms that involved reductions in public outlays, layoffs of public personnel, and liquidation or consolidation of several rather minor SOEs. De la Madrid was the product of a system in place since the late 1930s. His object was to reform it so that it could continue to be viable economically and politically.[52]

The SOE sector had grown greatly and incoherently during the 1970s within the *sexenios* of Luís Echeverría and José López Portillo. Failing private sector firms were taken over, a myriad of special funds (*fideicomisos*) founded, and new lumpy assets added to the public domain. In the late 1970s, with the oil boom, the Mexican petroleum company, PEMEX, came to constitute a kind of economic state within the state, controlled in large part by the Petroleum Workers Union (STPRM). The period of wildcat SOE expansion culminated in the nationalization of several large private banks in 1982, ostensibly to stem the capital hem-

[52] This is also how I have interpreted President Sadat's "open-door" policies in Egypt (see Waterbury, *Egypt of Nasser and Sadat*; and "The Soft State and the Open Door: Egypt's Experience with Economic Liberalization, 1974–1984," *Comparative Politics* 18, no. 1 [1985]: 65–84), and I would extend it to Rajiv Gandhi's policies between 1984 and 1989. Özal, by contrast, started out as a system breaker.

orrhage under way at the time. To a degree not evidenced in India, the bank nationalizations undermined the increasingly cordial relations that López Portillo had succeeded in establishing between the private sector and the government.[53]

In 1977 there was an attempt to structure the SOEs into homogeneous sectors with coordinators at the head of each and responsible to the key ministries.[54] With the advent of De la Madrid after 1982, there were further efforts at rationalization, all within the long prevailing philosophy of the *rectoría del estado* espoused by the president at least until the mid-1980s.

In 1986 a new Law for Parastatal Entities was drawn up (although its implementing legislation is apparently still lacking). Its object was to define more explicitly managerial autonomy (in the words of Pardo, "reduce the bureaucratic spider web"),[55] to specify the purview of the three controlling ministries (Finance and Public Credit, Planning and Budgeting, and Auditing), and to redefine the principal sectors. Simultaneously, the government absorbed the heavy debts of several SOEs equivalent to $12 billion.[56] In return the SOEs signed performance contracts (*convenios de rehabilitacíon financiera y cambio estructural*), designed to promote technological upgrading, price reform, and a reduction in idle capacity and in the workforce. These were principal-agent measures similar to those that have constituted the entire reform agenda in Egypt and India.

It was perhaps unrealistic to expect such measures to have much effect when the economy as a whole was registering negative rates of growth and when the SOEs were faced with declining demand and massive debt servicing obligations contracted in the late 1970s and early 1980s. As important, however, was the conclusion in December 1987 of the Pact of Economic Solidarity among the government, labor, and business. It put in place a negotiated system of price and wage controls, accompanied by creeping devaluation of the peso. The pact succeeded in reducing domestic inflation drastically, but it meant that SOEs lost autonomy in adjusting the prices of their goods and services. The pact has been renegotiated periodically since 1987, and its maintenance ironically may vitiate the

---

[53] Maxfield, *Governing Capital*; Carlos Tello, *La Nacionalización de la Banca en México*, 3d ed. (Mexico Distrito Federál: Siglo Veintiuno, 1988).

[54] Secretarías Globalizadoras: Maria del Carmen Pardo, "La Ley Federal de las Entidades Paraestatales: un Nuevo Intento para Regular el Sector Paraestatal," *Foro Internacional* 27, no. 2 (1986): 238; and *Restructuración del Sector Paraestatal* (Mexico D.F.: Cuadernos de Renovación Nacional, 1988).

[55] Pardo, "La Ley Federal," p. 244.

[56] Felix Castrejon and Castrejon Aguilar, "Macro-administrativo-Institutional de la Empresa Publica en México" (National Institute of Public Administration, 1989), p. 11; and Cuadernos de Renovación Nacional, *Restructuración del Sector Paraestate*, pp. 98–108.

effect of a Public Enterprise Reform Loan (PERL) agreed to by the World Bank and Mexico in 1989. It seeks to put teeth in the performance contracts so that good performance is rewarded and mediocre performance penalized particularly through hard budget constraints.[57]

The sequence from public sector reform to divestiture was telescoped in Mexico so that by 1986 both processes were going on simultaneously but with key technocratic skills being devoted to the latter. The qualitative shift came in 1985–86 when Mexico joined the GATT, reduced its tariffs to a degree perhaps unprecedented in the developing world, and also liquidated Fundidora de Monterrey, an integrated steel mill with seven thousand employees. The impatience with gradualism and systemic tinkering grew as a result of inflation running at 180 percent per annum in 1987–88 with no growth in the economy. The government had no funds to invest and the private sector was unwilling to borrow or to bring back flight capital.

There were, then, three major elements that spurred on the privatization drive: deficit reduction, the search for new investment, and, peculiar to Mexico, the overriding concern to establish some modicum of confidence between the private sector and the government. In this vein, the willingness to pursue noncosmetic privatization was signaled by the preparation of the Cananea copper company for sale in 1988–89. Cananea occupied a hallowed place in Mexican nationalist history, and the government's determination to sell it showed that it was prepared to meet strong populist criticism.

By the summer of 1988 some 722 SOEs out of a total of 1,216 were in the process of liquidation or sale. Although estimates differ, the units involved may have produced as much as 25 percent of the SOE sector's gross product, excluding PEMEX.[58] After 1988 and the accession to the presidency of Salinas de Gortari, the process was accelerated. Salinas had headed Planning and Budget under De la Madrid and had designed the sharp cuts in government outlays. He entrusted the Ministry of Finance

[57] On the Mexican public and SOE sector in general, see Maria Casar and Wilson Peres, *El Estado Empresario en México: Agotamiento o Renovación?* (Mexico D.F.: Sieglo Veintiuno, 1988); *Revista de Administración Publica*, "Tamaño de la Administración Publica," no. 73 (1989); René Villareal, *Mitos y Realidades de la Empresa Publica* (Mexico D.F.: Diana, 1988); Cuadernos de Renovación Nacional, *Restructuración del Sector Paraestate*; Benito Rey Romay, *La Ofensiva Empresarial contra la Intervención del Estado* (Mexico D.F.: Siglo Veintiuno, 1987); Raymond Hill, "State Enterprise and Income Distribution in Mexico," in Pedro Aspe and Paul Sigmund, eds., *The Political Economy of Income Distribution in Mexico* (New York: Holmes and Meier, 1984), pp. 357–96.

[58] Ignacio Pichardo Pagaza, *El Proceso de Desincorporación de Entidades Paraestatales: el Caso de México*, Simposio Modernización y Empresa Publica, Colegio Nacional de Economistas, Queretaro, July 1988, p. 26; and Cuadernos de Renovación Nacional, *Restructuración del Sector Paraestate*, p. 91.

and Public Credit, which had primary responsibility for privatization, to Pedro Aspe, a professor of economics. He in turn recruited a team of very young, highly trained economists who espoused, like Aspe, a coherent package of neoclassical reforms for the economy. In another instance of the orthodox paradox, the Office of Privatization, to which shares of companies slated for privatization have been transferred, was itself detached from the Ministry of Energy and Mines and put under the control of Pedro Aspe's ministry.[59]

Facing a time frame of six years, or effectively five, in which to set in motion irreversible policy changes, the team pushed forward at breakneck speed. Salinas appeared to go right along with them, and certainly took some spectacular initiatives of his own. In 1989, he took on the Petroleum Workers Union by jailing its leader on charges of tax fraud. The Armed Forces stood by in case the petroleum workers tried to paralyze the country by closing down the refineries and the delivery of fuels. The signal to other unions was unmistakable, and the fact that there was no groundswell of support for the jailed leader sent an equally clear message. This was a major triumph for Salinas. It complemented less spectacular moves toward Aeromexico and Cananea, both of which were declared bankrupt so that their labor contracts were nullified, allowing major layoffs, and so that new management could be brought in prior to privatization.

It became clear that hardly anything in the SOE sector was off limits to the Aspe team. Telmex, the huge state telephone and telegraph company worth about $7 billion, was put up for sale to a consortium of Mexican and foreign buyers who pledged to bring in several billion dollars in new investment. The state holding company for steel, SIDERMEX, a chronic lossmaker was also targeted, and it appeared likely that over time everything owned by PEMEX in refining and secondary petrochemicals would be sold off, leaving only the extraction facilities. Easily the most important move was the announcement in May 1990 that the government would privatize the nineteen commercial banks it had taken over in 1982. This move required a modification of the constitution achieved by a voting alliance with the Partido de Acción Nacional (PAN), a rightist, pro-business party long anathema to the dominant Partido Revolucionario Institucional (PRI). This move led to the restoration of a considerable measure of government-business confidence.

Real growth returned to the Mexican economy in 1989, and the increased petroleum prices resulting from the 1990–91 Gulf crisis may strengthen the trend. Private investment is picking up, and the drive in nontraditional exports has shown positive results. The Brady Plan com-

[59] *Latin American Monitor*, October 1990, p. 823.

bined with a growing volume of private debt-equity swaps has reduced the external debt substantially ($97 billion at the end of 1990). After nearly a decade of severe depression, inflation, and falling standards of living, the modest upturn may generate enough hope and good will to allow Salinas and his team to push ahead.

In 1994 the result could be an SOE sector built around the oil fields, the railroads, atomic energy, the post office, and the social security administration. The mines, heavy industry, vehicle assembly, shipping, airlines, agricultural marketing, petrochemicals, sugar refineries, and banks will be under private ownership. The place of foreign capital throughout the economy is likely to grow, especially if a free-trade agreement with the United States is worked out. The PRI, for the first time, might retain power having won less than half of the national vote (see note 51), and as its cooperation with the PAN suggests, it will move its center of gravity to the center right, with a greatly diminished SOE sector and an open alliance with private sector interests.

No single factor accounts for this extraordinary shift. Rather it has been a combination of the depth of Mexico's crisis with concomitant discrediting of the defenders of old arrangements, the need for new investment and to restore good relations with the private sector, the assembly of a competent, coherent, and determined change team closely identified with the president, and the time constraints of the *sexenio* itself that have produced the phenomenon of cascading change. Undoubtedly the PRI has been able to control entrenched constituencies during the painful adjustments of the 1980s. That very institutional strength, however, could be turned against Salinas, just as India's Congress Part thwarted Rajiv Gandhi, if his radical reform project savages the interests of labor, the teachers union, and the traditional PRI vote bank among the peasantry.

Conclusion

Efforts to make state enterprise more market- and profit-oriented will probably fail, although there will be isolated examples of success. The goal of reform is incompatible with the *political* logic of the SOE system as it has evolved. Moreover, the partial liberation of SOEs may bestow upon their managers the worst of both worlds; that is, the need to adjust to markets all the while adjusting to continued bureaucratic determination of investment, supply of inputs and of foreign exchange.[60] There are two ways out of this conundrum. The first is to recognize that most SOEs will continue to be saddled with several contradictory objectives that will undermine economic and financial efficiency. These objectives will con-

---

[60] Kornai, "Hungarian Reform Process."

tinue to be politically determined and will have a social welfare component (e.g., subsidized products and services, job creation, or development
of backward regions). Public outlays specific to the SOEs and to the public sector in general will be used to compensate on a selective basis sectors
of society particularly hurt by the adjustment process and to maintain the
support of strategic interests that constitute fairly narrow political coalitions.

The second way out is to seek a kind of mercantilist equilibrium along
the lines of South Korea or Taiwan. The components of the equilibrium
would be the key economic ministries and public banks, the SOEs, and
the large-scale private sector. The goal would be state-supported capitalism (with or without an export orientation) in which public agencies in-
tervene in the economy to support large-scale enterprise both public and
private. This is the model of "embedded autonomy" and "administrative
guidance cartels" examined by Peter Evans in chapter 3 of this volume.[61]
But the model contains a kind of magic ingredient for which there is no
theoretic explanation: the willingness of bureaucrats, managers, and politicians to forego large-scale rent seeking and to refrain from devouring
the units the state seeks to support. It supposes that there will be an equitable use of credit and investment such that SOEs do not crowd out the
private sector. This is the direction in which Turkey was moving in the
early 1980s, but predatory and rent-seeking instincts may have derailed
the process.

Privatization, on the other hand, is equally problematic. It is part of a
broader process whereby fiscally-constrained states unburden themselves
of parts of the social welfare agenda. It is an implicit call upon the private
sector to accept responsibility for meeting the needs of the workforce for
jobs and an acceptable standard of living. It is an implicit admission that
bureaucratic decision-making allocates resources in suboptimal ways and
that partially regulated markets are likely to do a better job.

Privatization, then, places assets somewhat beyond the reach of the
state, thereby reducing the temptation of officials and politicians to use
them for venal ends. It is a step toward making the public authorities
referees in factor markets where the actors are juridically private. If this
is to work, then the private sector itself must, in a way, be privatized; that
is, denied subsidized credit, energy and inputs, licenses and quotas, award
of contracts through noncompetitive bidding, and so forth.

Because so few developing countries have sustained the adjustment
process over long periods of time (authoritarian Chile and South Korea
being notable exceptions), and because a number of experiments have

[61] See also Alice Amsden, "The Diffusion of Development: The Late-Industrializing
Model and Greater East Asia," *American Economic Review* 81, no. 2 (May 1991): 282–86.

aborted (e.g., Argentina and Brazil in the early 1980s), one can only speculate about the dynamics of sustainability. Success may be the enemy of sustained reform and adjustment. Once economies begin to grow and the perception that the crisis is over spreads, the pressures to move from selective compensation to massive transfers may prove irresistible.

The *kind* of change undertaken matters a great deal for successfully sustaining it. We have seen that the new political economy accurately predicts the effective blocking strategies of entitled interests when faced with the reform of the public sector. But it must be stressed that public sector reforms collapse not so much because of successful blocking, but because the reforms themselves are inherently flawed.

This fact may lead "reform mongers" to a more far-reaching assault on entitlements through privatization. The empirical evidence shows surprisingly little resistance when such an assault is launched, although it is at this stage that one would expect concerted blocking efforts to be undertaken. The reason seems to be that seemingly powerful and directly threatened interests dissolve into fragmented grouplets seeking special deals. Because transformational change is so recent, it is too early to tell whether or not affected interests will rally when and if the adjustment process runs into major diffuclties.

Why the response to structural change is so feeble and fragmented can be explained through collective action dynamics. We can conceive of change as a collective good, or, for entitled groups, a collective bad. Rather than these groups acting collectively to thwart change, subunits of them will try to protect their own privileges while foisting the burden of absorbing the costs of change onto others. The result will be that change is facilitated and all those adversely affected will have paid a higher price than had they acted together.

The suboptimal solution for the defenders of the status quo works itself out sequentially. There will be an initial period in which the need for change is denied, although the crisis requiring change may already be full-blown. At this point distributional coalitions put on a brave front, reinterpret evidence, seek other culprits, and act collectively. Until very recently both Egypt and India have been in this stage.

There then comes the stage of avowal. Change can no longer be criticized as betrayal. The issue becomes who will bear the burden of it, and the coalition, as previously suggested, dissolves into *sauve qui peut*. This gives determined leadership the chance to push through transformative programs while the free riders look on, perhaps, until it is too late. For most developing countries we do not yet know when too late is, and even in Mexico, where the assault on entitlements has been the most pronounced, we can only talk of the factors leading to its launching rather than of the likelihood of its success.

PART III

Distributive Politics

CHAPTER FIVE

Poverty, Equity, and the Politics of Adjustment

Joan M. Nelson

BOTH IN international development circles and within countries struggling with economic adjustment, questions about the allocation of the social costs of stabilization and reform have prompted bitter argument. The charge that adjustment bears particularly harshly on the poor has fueled widespread criticism and protest. Conversely, in those few cases where governments have convinced their citizens that they are sensitive to equity issues, adjustment programs have been less politically controversial.

But the nature of the equity issue is much less clear than appears at first glance. Much of the ambiguity turns on differing concepts of the poor. There are also ethical ambiguities: How should small costs imposed on already extremely poor people be weighed against larger costs, both in absolute terms and relative to precrisis living standards, for people somewhat higher (but far from well off) on the income ladder? These ambiguities have heightened acrimony within adjusting nations, between them and external donors, and among international organizations and private agencies concerned with development.

Indeed, as adjustment efforts unfolded in the course of the 1980s, two distinct equity issues emerged. One issue was driven by humanitarian concerns. It was focused on reducing the impact of adjustment on the very poor, most of whom are rural. In most cases pressures from external agencies played a prominent role. In contrast, the second equity issue was defined by domestic political pressures, and focused less on the very poor than on the semipoor and working classes, mainly in the cities.

This chapter opens with a survey of what is known and not known regarding the social costs of adjustment in developing nations and the impact of those costs on different socioeconomic groups. One frustrating but important conclusion is that we have remarkably little detailed empirical data on these questions. However, we can infer a good deal by considering the extent to which different groups are exposed to losses from adjustment, and their means for coping with and minimizing losses.

This chapter has evolved from several separate earlier research efforts, and many people have been helpful with specific portions of it. Particular thanks are due to Carol Graham, Merilee Grindle, Nora Lustig, Helena Ribe, and Elaine Zuckerman on pro-poor policies, and to my colleagues in the *Politics of Adjustment* project on popular class politics.

Based on these inferences and on fragmentary data, the outlines of the two equity issues emerge. Many of the poor have grown somewhat poorer. Urban working and popular classes remain somewhat better off (how much so depends in good part on the level of development of the country). But they have often suffered much larger *relative* losses.

The two equity issues pose quite different political challenges. For most governments, domestic political incentives to assist the very poor are relatively weak, and the risks of certain kinds of pro-poor measures are considerable. By the late 1980s, however, there were considerable and growing international pressures on behalf of the very poor. With largely external financial support, many governments did launch temporary relief programs targeted in good part to the very poor and vulnerable. External agencies also urged governments to retarget subsidies and social services to provide more durable benefits to the poor. Such redistributive measures are much more difficult than distributive relief programs. Usually they have been eroded or defeated by opposition from more politically active middle sectors who stood to lose by the reforms. In some cases, however, influential groups formed alliances with the poor, strengthening the incentive for governments to adopt pro-poor measures imbedded in broader programs.

The often dramatic losses of the urban working and popular classes raise quite different policy dilemmas. In contrast to the very poor, urban middle strata can pressure governments through strikes, protests, and in democracies, the ballot box. Political elites view their opposition as a serious threat to the sustainability of adjustment programs. This can become a self-fulfilling prophecy, since efforts to placate the urban popular sector are likely to undermine the coherence of economic stabilization and adjustment programs.

A closer examination of the three channels of popular sector influence, however, reveals that popular sectors do not always or automatically oppose adjustment efforts. Both political institutions and government tactics are important in mediating the effects of popular sector opposition. More importantly, narrow and short-term calculations of class interests are not the only basis of popular sector reactions. Popular interpretations of the nature of the crisis, the need for government action, and the ability of the government to manage the economy will also condition political reactions.

DISTRIBUTIVE EFFECTS OF ECONOMIC CRISIS AND ADJUSTMENT EFFORTS

Are economic stabilization and structural reforms inherently equitable or inequitable? Do they bear particularly harshly on the poor? Are the rich escaping their share of the costs? The equity issue enters into the domestic politics of adjustment, more or less centrally, in every country confronting serious economic difficulties. In international financial and development circles, however, the issue was initially given scant attention. The view prevailed in the early 1980s that appropriate policy reforms by debtors, though painful, would permit rapid stabilization and recovery. But as the depth of many countries' economic difficulties became clearer and the prospects for rapid recovery receded, an often acrimonious debate emerged regarding the social costs of adjustment.

Journalists, politicians, and popular opinion in debtor nations, joined by many nongovernmental organizations and some international and regional organizations, argued bitterly that devaluations, budget cuts, wage freezes, and subsidy reductions harm the public in general and the poor in particular. Further, they claimed, the medium- and long-run structural changes urged by the international financial institutions would erode governments' abilities to protect and advance the interests of the poor, and would cause widespread misery as local industries withered in the winds of international competition.

Neoorthodox theorists vigorously rejected these views. The critics, they argued, were confounding the effects of economic instability and decline with alleged effects of adjustment efforts to correct the economic problems. Far from being anti-poor, adjustment is crucial to the welfare of the poor. The key to reduced poverty is economic growth. Where growth has been rapid, as in Brazil in the 1970s, poverty has dropped substantially even in the absence of pro-poor measures. Conversely, in the absence of growth even vigorous pro-poor measures have failed to make sustainable inroads on poverty, as in Sri Lanka in the early 1970s. Since stabilization and structural reforms are crucial to resumed and sustainable growth, they work to the advantage of the poor.

Moreover, the argument continued, the structural changes needed in many countries to promote growth also tend to benefit the poor directly. The rich and middle classes, not the poor, have been the primary beneficiaries of direct and indirect subsidies, economic controls and regulations, and import-substituting strategies. For example, apparently pro-poor measures such as minimum wage laws and legally required fringe benefits flow to a minority of workers fortunate enough to find jobs in firms where the laws are enforced. But the broader effect is to discourage labor-intensive patterns of investment, thereby limiting the number of workers who can find industrial jobs. Similarly, crop procurement and price controls designed to ensure low food prices for urban consumers have often been at the expense of poorer cultivators.

These conflicting views regarding the distributive effects of adjustment could not be readily resolved by looking at the facts. Available data documented continuing economic stagnation or decline in much of Latin America and sub-Saharan Africa. Common sense argued and fragmentary data confirmed that where national economies are stagnant or declining, the extent and depth of poverty grows: more people sink below the poverty line (however defined), and those already poor become more so. But virtually no country had sufficiently detailed and timely data to provide empirical answers to the more fine-grained questions: Precisely how were depression and adjustment policies affecting different groups?

By the late 1980s, the still unresolved debates over the distributive impact of adjustment were largely overtaken by a strong international consensus on the need to protect the poor in the course of adjustment. That consensus and some of its implications are discussed in more detail in the second section of this chapter. The remainder of this section briefly surveys the evidence on trends in income, services, and welfare in the 1980s. As a second-best alternative to detailed data on distributive effects within countries, the discussion then considers the channels through which depression and adjustment measures affect welfare and the ways in which these channels bear on different groups.

Trends in Growth and Services in the 1980s

National economic performance powerfully affects the breadth and depth of poverty within nations. Although the 1980s were broadly a decade of crisis, economic performance varied widely both between and within geographic regions.[1]

Economic decline was most acute and widespread in sub-Saharan Africa. Of thirty-two low-income African nations, only five registered positive growth in the 1980s. In thirteen, including a third of the region's population, per capita incomes in 1990 were lower than they were in 1960. On average, real per capita income fell 2.2 percent a year; per capita consumption shrank roughly 1.2 percent a year. In 1985 almost a fifth of the world's extremely poor lived in sub-Saharan Africa.

In Latin America and the Caribbean the picture was less uniformly bleak, and stagnation rather than severe decline was the norm. Region-wide, per capita incomes fell 0.6 percent a year. Private consumption dipped about 0.8 percent a year from 1980 through 1984, then registered slow but positive growth of 1.4 percent for the period 1985–87. Less than 8 percent of the world's extremely poor, as of 1985, were located in Latin America and the Caribbean.

[1] Data for various regions on trends in per capita income during the 1980s are drawn from the World Bank, *World Development Report 1990: Poverty* (Washington, D.C.: World Bank, 1990), table 1.2, p. 11. Data on trends in per capita consumption are drawn from Nanak Kakwani, Elene Makonnen, and Jacques van der Gaag, "Structural Adjustment and Living Conditions in Developing Countries," draft paper, World Bank Population and Human Resources Division, September 1989, p. 32. Data on proportion of the poor in different regions, *World Development Report*, table 2.1, p. 29.

In contrast, real incomes rose in South Asia by 3.2 percent a year, and in East Asia by an impressive 6.7 percent. Consumption in Asian countries (dominated by China's performance) grew more than 5 percent a year in the first half of the decade, then slowed to 1.7 percent in 1985–87. Since close to half of the world's extremely poor live in South Asia, India's considerable though undramatic economic growth during the 1980s is important to note.

Welfare is directly affected by public education, health, and other social services, which often are assumed to have declined dramatically in the 1980s. Available data suggest a less bleak, though far from happy, picture. The rate of growth in outlays on education and health, which had been rapid in many countries in the 1970s, did indeed slow greatly in the 1980s. In many countries, real per capita expenditures shrank in the sharpest periods of austerity. But many others managed to sustain or even increase social service outlays, or were able to restore growth after initial cuts. Among thirty-four countries in Asia, Africa, and Latin America, real per capita expenditures by central government for education, health, and other social services between 1980 and 1986 increased in twenty and declined in fourteen cases.[2] Another study of twenty-seven sub-Saharan African countries found real outlays on education and health dropping steeply in the early 1980s but then tending to rise; by 1986–87 about ten still were spending less than in 1980, but some others were spending far more.[3] In ten countries in Latin America, Africa, and Asia that launched adjustment programs early in the 1980s and continued to pursue adjustment vigorously, average real per capita expenditures on education stayed roughly stable; outlays on health shrank 1.8 percent yearly in 1981–84 but then recovered somewhat, increasing 3.4 percent annually during 1985–87. But these averages mask tremendous variation among the ten countries, as table A5.1 reveals.[4]

Trends in infant mortality, the incidence of malnutrition and illness, and school enrollments measure welfare more directly than do trends in incomes or services.[5] Infant mortality might be expected to respond rap-

[2] Kakwani et al., "Structural Adjustment," p. 32. The figures hide considerable variation in expenditures on particular categories, but outlays on education, health, and other services taken separately also increased in nineteen or twenty of the countries over the seven-year period.

[3] David E. Sahn, "Fiscal and Exchange Rate Reforms in Africa: Considering the Impact on the Poor" (Cornell University Food and Nutrition Policy Program, report prepared for the African Bureau of the Agency for International Development, Washington, D.C., March 1990), fig. 10, p. 49 and table 10, p. 51.

[4] World Bank Country Economics Department, *Adjustment Lending Policies for Sustainable Growth* (Washington, D.C.: World Bank Policy and Research Series No. 14, 1990), table 3.5, p. 34.

[5] Life expectancy data might be considered as another direct measure of welfare, but they

idly to widespread shortages of food and medicines and deteriorating public health service. Therefore it is particularly interesting that in the 1980s, infant mortality rates continued their long-term decline throughout most of the developing world, including sub-Saharan Africa. However, African rates remained very high, and fell more slowly in the 1980s than the 1970s.[6]

Undernourishment was already much more prevalent in sub-Saharan Africa than elsewhere in the world in 1980. In the next six years the situation worsened in a third of twenty-nine countries. However, many of the countries with the most severe malnutrition were victims of protracted drought (especially in the Sahel) or pervasive civil violence (as in Mozambique), rather than adverse international economic pressures or government economic policies. With a few exceptions such as Bangladesh and Haiti, undernutrition is generally much less severe in other regions, and showed either positive or no clear trends during the 1980s.[7]

Perhaps surprisingly, school enrollment seems to be a more prompt and sensitive reflector of economic distress: net primary school enrollment ratios dropped between 1980 and 1985 in thirty-two of eighty-five developing countries.[8] The reasons almost surely have more to do with family decisions to keep children at home (to save expenses or to help earn money) than with dwindling space in schools.

Costs of Adjustment for Different Groups: Differential Exposure and Coping Mechanisms

Those few nations for which income distribution data are available for two or more points during the 1980s confirm the commonsense assumption that trends in poverty mirror trends in overall economic performance. Poverty declined in parts of Asia, including India, Indonesia, Malaysia, and Pakistan.[9] In contrast, in Argentina, Brazil, Guatemala, and Mexico the incidence of poverty clearly increased.[10] However, attempts to probe beneath these national statistics to trace what has happened to different income groups within countries usually stall for lack of data.

Since the data are so fragmentary, it is more useful to approach the

---

reflect many factors and are unlikely to change rapidly. Moreover, life expectancy figures are usually based on census data and are simply extrapolated for intercensus years.

[6] Kakwani et al., Structural Adjustment, p. 46. See also World Bank Country Economics Department, Adjustment Lending Policies, pp. 31–32.

[7] Kakwani et al., Structural Adjustment, pp. 67–68 and annex 2, table 7.

[8] Kakwani et al., Structural Adjustment, p. 82, table 25.

[9] World Bank, World Development Report 1990, p. 10.

[10] Nora Lustig, "Poverty and Income Distribution in Latin America in the 1980s," Brookings Institution, Washington, D.C., 1990; M. Louise Fox and Samuel A. Morley, "Who Paid the Bill? Adjustment and Poverty in Brazil 1980–1995" (World Bank, 22 January 1990), p. 8.

question by considering how different groups are exposed to economic policies and trends. Economic trends and government policies affect individuals and households through three channels: changes in employment status and labor incomes (and, for the wealthy, returns on assets); changes in the prices of goods and services consumed; and changes in the provision of public services (including transfers). Individuals and households vary widely in the degree to which they are exposed, through their patterns of earning and consumption, to changes in these three channels. They also have varying resources and options for coping with hard times.

Broadly, those groups and households that are least integrated into domestic and foreign markets are least exposed to changes in those markets. In sub-Saharan Africa and Asia, four-fifths or more of the poor are rural.[11] Purely subsistence cultivators have virtually vanished, even in Africa. But semisubsistence cultivators in remote regions have only limited links with domestic markets and little access to public services. Therefore many changes in price levels (including devaluation) or cutbacks in public services may have relatively little impact.

Even in many African countries, however, an increasing percentage of rural households earn much of their income from wage labor: data from Malawi, Mali, Senegal, Somalia, and Rwanda indicate that between two-fifths and two-thirds of rural households are net buyers of cereals.[12] Throughout the developing world, agricultural laborers on commercial farms are still more integrated into markets and therefore more exposed. They buy much or all of their food and other consumer goods and are vulnerable to price changes. They are more likely to use public schools and clinics, and therefore to suffer from reduced services. Prolonged recession may also slow migration to the cities and swell the agricultural labor force, tending to lower wages. However, where governments increase producer prices for agricultural goods as part of broader structural reforms, demand for labor and wages may improve, benefiting farm workers as well as small and larger landowners. Devaluation may have similar effects for cultivators and farm workers producing export or import-substituting crops.

City dwellers in general, including the poor and semipoor, are highly exposed to changes in consumer prices (including devaluation) and the availability, quality, and costs of public services. Urbanites consume more imported goods (or import substitutes, the prices of which are affected by devaluation) and they also use more public services, including schools, clinics and hospitals, buses, water, electricity, and garbage collection. Working classes are likely to be particularly strongly affected by deteriorating quality and increased fees, since they use a wider range of services

[11] World Bank, *World Development Report 1990*, table 2.2, p. 31.
[12] Sahn, *Fiscal and Exchange Rate Reforms*, p. 73.

and facilities than the poor, but lack the upper-middle-class and elite options of shifting to (or continuing to rely on) private schools, doctors, and other services. Reduced subsidies or removal of price controls for a wide range of consumer goods also hits hardest at the urban middle sectors, again because they are more likely than the very poor to include such goods in their budgets, but less able than the upper middle classes to afford steep price increases.

The impact of depression and adjustment policies on urban employment and wages bears differently on informal and formal sector workers, and, within the formal sector, on public versus private employees. Formal sector workers are more fully and directly exposed to losses. In many developing nations, between a quarter and a half of all wage earners are public sector employees; in several African countries in 1980, 60 to 80 percent of nonagricultural workers were in the public sector. Shrinking revenues and rising interest payments have sharply squeezed public sector wages, even though most governments have tried to avoid layoffs and wage cuts by slashing expenditures on equipment, materials, and public investment.[13] Stabilization programs generally tighten the pressure.[14] Private sector wages are less directly in governments' control, but many stabilization and adjustment programs include wage restraints to temporarily compress overall demand. Legal or institutional measures to permit more flexible wage arrangements are often part of the medium-term structural reform agenda, and generally entail direct or indirect erosion of union power and the privileges of those already employed.

These pressures are reflected in real wages. Despite measurement problems,[15] it is clear that formal sector real wages dropped considerably in most of the nations adopting strong adjustment programs in the 1980s, though manufacturing sector wages registered a comeback in the later 1980s in some. In Mexico, for example, average real wages fell a quarter between 1980 and 1984, and continued to erode thereafter. In Turkey real wages dropped 30 percent between 1980 and 1987. In both countries wage trends were part of deliberate adjustment strategy, in contrast to some other countries such as Peru, where even more dramatic drops resulted from economic collapse. In most of sub-Saharan Africa, real wages

[13] Peter S. Heller and Alan A. Tait, *Government Employment and Pay: Some International Comparisons*, Occasional Paper No. 24 (Washington, D.C.: International Monetary Fund, March 1984), table 22, p. 42 provides data on the size of the public sector circa 1980, for more than thirty-five developing countries in Latin America, Africa, and Asia.

[14] In some cases the IMF has urged governments to increase decimated salaries to restore public sector morale and work incentives, but this advice is generally coupled with encouragement to lay off redundant workers.

[15] Trends in real wages are difficult to measure for many reasons, including the substantial and shifting importance of nonwage compensation in total compensation packages.

in the public sector (comprising the bulk of the formal sector) dwindled dramatically in the 1980s. In Costa Rica and Uruguay, average real wages shrank sharply in the most acute stabilization periods but were then restored roughly to precrisis levels. Still other countries, such as Brazil and Argentina, did not seek or were not able to contain nominal wage increases, contributing to inflation and the collapse of adjustment efforts.[16]

It seems likely that organized labor often or usually bears a greater share of the costs of adjustment than other factors of production. Manuel Pastor, analyzing the effects of IMF programs in Latin American nations between 1965 and 1981, found a reduction in labor shares of income to be the most statistically significant among nine categories of outcomes tested.[17] In Mexico, the wage share of national income dwindled from 35.9 percent in 1982 to 26.6 percent in 1987. In Turkey, wages and salaries as a share of nonagricultural factor income are estimated to have declined still more dramatically, from 52 percent in 1977 to 22 percent in 1986.[18] As discussed later in this chapter, unions' political power is limited in most developing nations, while business and financial interests have better access to policymakers. Moreover, the ever-present threat of capital flight dissuades governments from trying to shift a larger share of the costs to capital.

Both public and private formal sector workers cope with shrinking real wages in various ways, including seeking second or third jobs in the informal sector. Often other members of their households also look for part- or full-time informal sector work to supplement household income. Therefore one effect of dwindling real wages in the formal sector is to further blur the already murky distinction between formal and informal sectors. In some African countries, many public sector workers may earn as little as a tenth of their incomes from their "regular" government jobs.

Depression and market-oriented reforms affect employment and in-

---

[16] Annual real average wage data are available for most Latin American countries in the annual reports on *Economic and Social Progress in Latin America* published by the Inter-American Development Bank. Data for African countries are much more difficult to find, but David Lindauer, Oey Astra Meesook, and Parita Suebsaeng, "Government Wage Policy in Africa," *World Bank Research Observer* 3, no. 1 (January 1988): 7, 15, 18–19 provide evidence of drastic drops in real public sector wages in Africa during the 1980s. Data for Turkey are from the World Bank, *Turkey: Country Economic Memorandum: Towards Sustainable Growth* (Washington, D.C.: World Bank, 12 October, 1988), pp. 70–75.

[17] Manuel Pastor, Jr., "The Effects of IMF Programs in the Third World: Debate and Evidence from Latin America," *World Development* 15, no. 2 (February 1987): 254, 258.

[18] Kevin J. Middlebrook, "The Sounds of Silence: Organized Labour's Response to Economic Crisis in Mexico," *Journal of Latin American Studies* 21, no. 2 (1989): 199. World Bank, *Turkey: Country Economic Memorandum*, citing Ozmucur, "National Income Estimates by Quarters, in Dollar Terms and by Income Types" (Istanbul Chamber of Commerce, 1987).

comes in the informal sector less directly. Informal sector workers are not directly exposed to government wage and employment policies. But pressure on wages and employment in the formal sector pushes both primary and secondary earners into the informal sector, increasing competition and reducing earnings. The urban informal sector in Brazil is estimated to have grown 70 percent between 1980 and 1987; in Mexico the corresponding figure was 82 percent; in Colombia (where recession and adjustment were much less drastic) 48 percent. These sharp increases broke the pattern of the three previous decades, during which the informal urban sector held a roughly constant share of the non-agricultural economically active population.[19]

In addition to the competition of increased numbers, informal sector workers may also suffer indirectly from stagnation or decline in the formal sector. Many small enterprises work on consignment for formal sector firms. Although hard times may cause some shift from formal to lower-cost informal suppliers, consignment orders and consumer demand for market vendors' goods and informal sector services (not only personal, but also construction and transport services) rise and fall with formal sector employment and wages.

Nevertheless, recent analyses from many Latin American and African countries suggest that the urban informal sector is the most flexible, innovative, and rapidly responsive to new incentives flowing from adjustment measures, including less distorted prices and some degree of import liberalization. As a result, informal sector incomes may decline less, and later improve more rapidly than government and other formal sector wages.

The discussion thus far has focussed on the varying *exposure* of different groups to effects of adjustment on employment and wages, consumer prices, and services. *Ability to cope* with hard times varies independently from exposure. Multiple sources of income can help households and individuals preserve living standards even when a major earnings source dries up. Studies at the village or urban neighborhood level suggest that many households in developing countries hold diverse portfolios of activities and reallocate their resources and time among these activities as circumstances change. A rural household may own small parcels of land, rent other parcels, get seasonal jobs as agricultural or construction workers, and send household members to the cities or abroad, seasonally or for longer periods, to find wage jobs and remit earnings. Its members may engage in part-time artisan activities, offer personal or repair services to

[19] Economic Commission for Latin America and the Caribbean, "The Dynamics of Social Deterioration in Latin America and the Caribbean in the 1980s," paper prepared for the Regional Preparatory Meeting for the Eighth United Nations Congress on the Prevention of Crime and the Treatment of Offenders, May 1989, p. 10.

neighbors, and engage in trade. Similarly, in hard times urban households increase the number of members (including children) trying to earn money full- or part-time. They may also rent a room, grow food or keep small livestock, and maintain ties with rural kin and relatives abroad who send food and remittances.[20]

The broader the portfolio, the less the vulnerability. Broader portfolios are often associated with higher income; the poorest rural and urban households may have very few options. Even migrating costs money; therefore, the poorest seldom migrate. Thus while those with few market ties and little access to services are less exposed to depression, options for coping are likely to increase with income level.

The rich, of course, can defend themselves with options not open to others, including reducing risk through capital flight and escaping deteriorating services by going abroad for schooling and medical attention. Some of the wealthy also gain directly from stabilization measures, for instance through increased interest rates on debt owed to them, or speculation on exchange rate changes. The impression is widespread that the wealthy have suffered little harm, and many of them have benefited from the disruptions of the 1980s. While hard to prove empirically, the impression itself has important political repercussions.

Taking into account both exposure to national economic trends and adjustment policies, and ability to cope during hard times, we can sketch some plausible hypotheses regarding distributive impact. Semisubsistence cultivators in remote areas are little exposed, although they also have few coping mechanisms. In most countries this category is a small percent of the population. The impact on small cultivators and rural wage earners varies, reflecting trends in consumer prices for staples and in producer prices for cash crops. In cities all groups (save perhaps the wealthiest) are highly exposed to losses. The very poor have the most limited options for coping with deepened hardship. The most exposed, however, and those who have suffered the largest drops in income relative to precrisis levels, may well be formal sector workers.

Two Equity Dilemmas

Two separate equity issues flow from the way in which the costs of depression and adjustment have typically affected different groups. The first issue focuses on the very poor, and on the highly vulnerable, particularly

---

[20] See, for example, Jennifer Widner, "Interest Group Structure and Organization in Kenya's Informal Sector," *Comparative Political Studies* (Spring 1991); and, on Mexico, Merilee Grindle, "The Response to Austerity: Political and Economic Strategies of Mexico's Rural Poor," in William L. Canak, *Lost Promises: Debt, Austerity, and Development in Latin America* (Boulder, Colo.: Westview Press, 1989), pp. 190–215.

young children and pregnant and nursing mothers whose health may be permanently impaired by even a few months' severe deprivation. The very poor are overwhelmingly rural, even in those Latin American countries that are now heavily urbanized. Many, perhaps most, of the poorest were poor before the crisis of the 1980s. But that crisis has deepened their poverty and pushed many others, including many in the cities, into poverty. Their plight poses an immediate and acute humanitarian challenge. International concern about the social costs of adjustment focuses largely on these groups. But political incentives for governments to help the very poor are usually weak. Indeed, measures that shift resources away from middle deciles or wealthier groups to help the poor provoke political opposition.

Domestic political pressures within debtor nations almost always stress a different equity issue: the grievances of urban working classes and middle strata. These groups remain better off than the poor (though the gap has narrowed), and are less at immediate risk of hunger and disease. But compared to their precrisis standards of living, they have suffered still larger relative drops. Their sense of inequity is intensified where the wealthy appear to have escaped unscathed, or even to have wrung gains from instability and scarcities. And in contrast to the very poor, urban working classes and middle strata can exercise considerable political pressure on governments, through strikes, protests, and voting.

The tension between the two versions of the equity issue is heightened by economic and technical considerations. In most countries, at least some of the very poor can be helped without jeopardizing the economic requirements and constraints of adjustment. This is true for three reasons. The very poor have usually benefited little if at all from the various forms of state control of prices, wages, and trade, and from biases in the allocation of services and subsidies. Adjustment measures that seek to reduce those controls and reorient services and subsidies therefore do not threaten them, and may indeed help them. Second, the very poor can often benefit from modest, low-cost aid, such as inoculations, vitamins, or oral rehydration packets for children. Finally, in middle-income countries, the very poor are relatively few.

In contrast, it is much more difficult to significantly buffer urban formal sector workers and middle strata from the social costs of adjustment, without undercutting the adjustment effort itself. Especially in middle-income countries, these groups may represent a larger share of the population. More important, unlike the very poor, formal sector workers and much of the urban popular sectors do benefit to some degree (though less than elites and middle classes) from existing controls, preferences, pricing patterns, and subsidies. Structural reforms are likely to impose transitional costs on them, even if they ultimately gain as the reforms play out in the economy. Put slightly differently, the very poor are either isolated from or victims of "the system"; much of the urban working and popular classes are hooked into it, and must suffer some losses if the system is to be changed. Finally, concessions to the urban working and popular classes are likely to be more costly than assistance to the very poor, since very modest assistance provides a smaller relative boost to their welfare.

In short, the impact of depression and adjustment on some among the very poor, and on urban popular classes, has created two distinct equity issues. The remainder of this chapter considers the politics of each in turn.

THE POLITICS OF PROTECTING THE POOR

Incentives for Pro-Poor Measures

Most politicians and governments profess concern for the poor. For some, the concern is sincere, even strong. But even strong commitment must be balanced against competing goals, including the imperative of political survival. When resources dwindle and pressures mount, governments are likely to give highest priority to demands from groups whose support is crucial to continued control. In general, for well-known reasons, the poor are much less influential than better-off groups, including not just wealthy elites but also urban and rural middle deciles.

The political dynamics of attempting to help the very poor can be better understood by distinguishing between pro-poor measures that are distributive and those that are redistributive in nature. We start with the presumption that most governments have little incentive to protect or promote the interests of the very poor. The problem is not simply the weakness of the poor and the indifference of elites. Working and popular classes, themselves fairly poor, often demand more government attention to their needs, and predictably resist government attempts to retarget subsidies and social programs such as education and health to better serve the truly needy. The key question then becomes the conditions under which governments are nonetheless likely to adopt pro-poor measures.

Both external and domestic pressures can somewhat alter the incentives in favor of the poor. International pressures on behalf of the poor intensified in the late 1980s and early 1990s. External donors can offer support available solely for pro-poor programs, thus transforming them from redistributive into distributive measures that may benefit the incumbent government. In addition, external donors can make pro-poor measures partial conditions of broader assistance, although this raises the many questions of conditionality discussed by Kahler in chapter 2 of this volume.

Domestic political circumstances and institutions can also have the effect of widening the coalition of beneficiaries, by including the poor, or some among them, in alliances with more influential groups. The poor can derive benefits from such alliances, even though they remain subordinate partners. But such alliances confront governments with a different dilemma: programs that benefit broader groups are more politically sustainable but may be inconsistent with the economic constraints of adjustment.

International Pressures for Pro-Poor Measures

As the debt crisis continued unresolved throughout the 1980s, international concern over its social costs mounted and supplanted earlier debates over whether adjustment harmed or helped the poor in the long run. By the late 1980s, even the strongest proponents of the need for stabilization and structural reforms conceded that adjustment can have adverse short-run effects on the poor. Austerity measures reduce consumption of both poor and non-poor; the cuts are far more threatening to those already very poor. And lags between policy adoption and market responses may increase unemployment and raise prices.[21] Many critics of adjustment, meanwhile, had modified their stance as a result of growing understanding of the need for reforms. When the United Nations' Childrens' Fund (UNICEF) published its eloquent study *Adjustment with a Human Face* in 1987, it did not advocate a halt to adjustment efforts. Rather, it urged far more attention to protecting the poor and vulnerable in the course of adjustment and called for designing both macroeconomic and sectoral or middle-level economic policies so as to promote the longer-run interests of the poor. Both parts of this prescription commanded broad agreement within international circles.

By 1990 measures to buffer the poor and to improve their access to social services were increasingly common elements of adjustment programs. Before 1985, fewer than one in six World Bank adjustment loans included either conditions or understandings with the government regarding social policies. By the late 1980s the proportion rose to a quarter, and in 1989 a third of loans gave some attention to social policy reforms.[22] Bilateral donors also launched their own projects in some nations, and contributed funds to World Bank-coordinated efforts in others.

As relief and compensatory programs were launched, questions and disagreements surfaced over which groups of poor should be given pri-

---

[21] World Bank, *World Development Report 1990: Poverty* (Washington, D.C., 1990), p. 103.

[22] The World Bank, *Adjustment Lending Policies for Sustainable Growth*, World Bank Policy and Research Series No. 14 (Washington, D.C.: World Bank, 1990), p. 35.

ority. Many humanitarian and religious organizations were concerned with "the poorest of the poor."[23] UNICEF, in accord with its mandate, focused on the vulnerable poor—young children and pregnant women in particular—for whom even fairly short periods of deprivation threaten permanent physical and mental damage. In hard times and in very poor countries, the vulnerable might be found even in families near the middle of the income distribution. The World Bank, and many bilateral aid agencies, defined the poor more broadly: using cross-nationally comparable criteria, the bottom 30 percent of sub-Saharan African and South Asian populations (a third of India) are extremely poor, half are poor. In Latin America and the Caribbean, 12 percent of the people are extremely poor and 19 percent are poor. World Bank analyses often also distinguished between the "new poor," resulting from depression and adjustment, and the "structural poor," reflecting levels of development. The relief and compensatory programs launched in the late 1980s often included components aimed at the new poor—for instance, laid-off government workers—who were fairly clearly not among the poorest or most vulnerable.

By 1990, international development institutions were also focusing on the second half of UNICEF's prescription—that in addition to emergency relief efforts, much greater attention should be given to designing macroeconomic, sectoral, and subsectoral policies and programs so as to improve the longer-run opportunities for the poor. In substantial degree, this could be interpreted as a return to the predebt-crisis priorities of the 1970s, which had stressed meeting basic human needs. However, the renewed initiatives tended to place greater emphasis on designing broad development policies and strategies so as to expand productive employment opportunities, in addition to reorienting and strengthening social sector programs and rural development.[24]

Domestic Political Pressures from or for the Poor

External efforts to encourage pro-poor policies, like any outsiders' attempts to influence reforms, will meet with varying receptions by different governments. A few, already committed to such efforts, will welcome

[23] Michael Lipton provides a working definition of the ultrapoor as those who spend virtually all of their incomes on food yet cannot afford adequate caloric intake. Fragmentary data suggest that they constitute perhaps 10 to 20 percent of the population in the low-income African and South Asian nations, and a smaller proportion in somewhat better off countries. See Michael Lipton, *The Poor and the Poorest: Some Interim Findings*, World Bank Discussion Paper No. 25 (Washington, D.C.: World Bank, 1988).

[24] The World Bank's *World Development Report* for 1990 spotlighted poverty issues and urged that the Bank take systematic steps to consider the effects on income distribution and poverty in all aspects of its analysis and advice to borrowers. The report also proposed linking the allocation of funding in part to the vigor of governments' antipoverty efforts.

additional advice and financial support. In most cases, some agencies and officials will be receptive, while others will resist. Governments' responses to external pro-poor pressures will be shaped largely by the governments' own priorities and commitments, in turn reflecting domestic pressures.

The degree to which the poor lack political influence depends in part on which poor one has in mind. The ultra-poor are simply politically in-active. They may, however, have non-poor advocates with considerable influence, at least in regard to particular programs and policies. In a few countries, well-established social welfare bureaucracies are effective advocates for the very poor: Costa Rica and Chile offer examples. And as noted, domestic and international private voluntary organizations (PVOs) and churches also press for benefits for the very poor. The vulner-able poor—especially children—also are not politially active on their own behalf, but programs targeted to them can attract considerable political support.

Even if the poor are defined more broadly as the poorest half (in much of sub-Saharan Africa and South Asia), or the poorest fifth (in Latin America) of the population, a range of well-known factors tends to limit their political participation and autonomy. Most of the poor are rural, and tend to be geographically dispersed, isolated, and uneducated. They are frequently controlled by landlords, large farmers, or local notables. Even in towns and cities, the poorest groups are usually politically inac-tive, or sometimes controlled by local bosses or patrons.

However, both rural and urban poor may gain salience to the extent that they are allied with better-off groups in a position to exercise some leverage. Many of the poor have ethnic, clan, patronage, or other ties to more vocal and organized groups. Those groups in turn may exercise con-siderable influence on local politics, including pressing for some attention to the needs of poorer members.[25] The political influence of the poor also is heightened when governments fear they will be attracted by dissident or radical groups (usually organized by the non-poor). Regional or radi-cal guerrilla movements appealing to the rural poor have prompted rural antipoverty campaigns in a number of countries, including Negros Orien-tale in the Philippines or in Peru during the first years of Alan Garcia's government. In Indonesia, memories of the powerful rural communist movement of the early 1960s spurred vigorous agricultural and rural de-velopment policies in the 1970s and 1980s. Similarly, fear of urban pro-tests may heighten the political salience of the urban poor.

Political institutions also shape the influence of the poor and the incen-

[25] For a detailed analysis of the effects of such ties on political mobilization, see Joan M. Nelson, *Access to Power: Politics and the Urban Poor in Developing Nations* (Princeton, N.J.: Princeton University Press, 1979), chaps. 5 and 6 on "Traditional Leaders, Patrons, and Urban Political Machines" and "Ethnic Politics and the Urban Poor," pp. 168–248.

tive for governments to adopt pro-poor policies. Competitive democratic elections are no guarantee of influence for the poor. A great deal of historical evidence supports the generalization that at early stages of development, the extension of electoral and other channels for popular participation empowers urban and rural middle strata and skews government policies in their favor.[26] As participation spreads among the poor at later stages, the balance may be partly redressed, but middle class and upper-level working class groups usually retain advantages in organization, information, contacts, and financial resources. However, more specific institutional features can enhance the influence of poorer groups in democratic contexts. Electoral arrangements that overrepresent rural areas, large turnouts, and close contests all tend to have that effect: Costa Rica, Sri Lanka, Chile in the 1960s and early 1970s, and some of the states of India offer illustrations. Some revolutionary or nationalist regimes seeking to consolidate or broaden their power bases are also pro-poor: China, Cuba, and Zimbabwe are among the obvious examples.

Below the level of the political system as a whole, the structure as well as the strategy of political parties affects the influence of the poor. For instance, in West Bengal in India, the Communist Party of India, Marxist (CPM) has built its strategy on a concerted attack on rural poverty. The CPM successfully based its power on the rural poor in part through organizational features that retained strong central direction combined with decentralized penetration of local village councils.[27]

Decentralized governmental authority and increased use of grassroots organizations are often advocated as additional institutional channels to increased influence for the poor. Again the effect depends on more specific details, including organizational arrangements and the relative strength of local interest groups. Local elites are not necessarily more progressive than national ones. And many nongovernmental organizations in which the poor and near-poor participate are dominated by slightly better-off members, whose priorities are not neccesarily the same as those of their poorer associates. But there are also many examples of effective local organization by quite poor cultivators, normally focused on specific needs or problems. Occasionally such organizations lead to improved access for the poor to local decision-making more broadly.

Whether the poor exert pressure as part of a larger threat to government security, as voters in highly competitive elections, or as members of

[26] For evidence on this point, see Samuel P. Huntington and Joan M. Nelson, *No Easy Choice: Political Participation in Developing Countries* (Cambridge, Mass.: Harvard University Press, 1976), pp. 75–78.

[27] For a detailed discussion of CPM organization and programs, see Atul Kohli, *The State and Poverty in India* (Cambridge, England: Cambridge University Press, 1987), chap. 3, "West Bengal: Parliamentary Communism and Reform from Above," pp. 95–144.

community organizations, a similar theme emerges: when governments respond to "popular" pressures, the poor are subordinate partners. They are likely to benefit to the degree that their needs overlap those of their allies. On issues where their interests diverge, the poor are unlikely to prevail.[28] The principle applies not only in developing but also in industrialized nations. Domestic U.S. efforts to help the poor have proved durable where they have been imbedded in larger programs carrying benefits for the working and middle classes; programs targeted narrowly to the very poor have usually been eroded or discontinued.[29]

Distributive versus Redistributive Pro-Poor Efforts

In addition to the national and international pressures that shape the priority governments assign to pro-poor measures, political responses, and thus program viability, are also likely to be affected by the design of the programs themselves. As previously noted, a key distinction in this regard is between distributive and redistributive measures. Pro-poor policies are much more difficult to the extent that they transfer, or are seen to transfer, resources directly or indirectly from more to less privileged groups. However, the following elements of program design can provide political leaders with some leeway in shaping political responses to pro-poor measures.

First, the difficulty of implementing such programs increases to the extent that resource transfers are *obvious, long-term,* and *large* (relative to the incomes or assets of the losers). As an extension of that principle, transfers of assets (like land) are usually more difficult than transfers of income.

The *target group* also matters. The simplest theory is that broadly distributed benefits are more attractive politically than narrowly targeted programs. But the relationship between scope of targeting and political acceptability may be more U-shaped. Transfers narrowly targeted to the deserving or appealing poor (especially poor or ill children) are difficult to oppose. Broadly targeted programs have a large clientele. Programs falling between these categories may be much less attractive and are likely to rely on "upward leakage"—that is, permitting benefits to flow to people technically not poor enough to qualify—in order to survive politically.

Measures that require considerable *institutional change,* or that re-

---

[28] William Ascher, analyzing the history of pro-poor reforms in Latin America, reaches the same conclusion: such reforms require the support of some middle class or elite groups, and alliances are often formed around measures that serve the interests of middle sectors as well as the poor. William Ascher, *Scheming for the Poor: The Politics of Redistribution in Latin America* (Cambridge, Mass.: Harvard University Press, 1984), p. 316.

[29] Theda Skocpol, "Universal Appeal: Politically Viable Policies to Combat Poverty," *The Brookings Review* (Summer 1991): 29–33.

move *control over patronage* from the government, are more difficult than those that do not have those qualities.

Experience with different kinds of pro-poor measures reflects these principles. In particular, relief programs (which are essentially distributive) pose far fewer political problems than reorienting social services and subsidies (which are substantially redistributive).

Relief Programs

Relief programs are the most widespread and least politically controversial category of pro-poor measures in the context of stabilization. The countries that put such programs into effect most rapidly and effectively during the 1980s were those with well-established social welfare programs and bureaucracies, such as Chile and Costa Rica. Those bureaucracies are the product of long histories of highly competitive political systems including strong equity-oriented parties. In Chile, for example, the bureacracies had survived the repression of parties and competitive politics in the early 1970s. Costa Rica launched a temporary emergency food packets program (with substantial foreign assistance) and expanded other employment and social programs. Chile broadened work relief to cover almost an eighth of the labor force in the most severe depression year of 1983. At the same time, nutrition and health programs for children and mothers (available to and used by much of the population, not only the poor) were expanded and strengthened. The programs were well-accepted politically.

As international concern with the social costs of adjustment increased in the second half of the 1980s, external agencies encouraged multifaceted relief programs in many other countries. Two of the most ambitious and well-publicized were the Bolivian Emergency Social Fund (ESF) and Ghana's Program of Action to Mitigate the Costs of Adjustment (PAMSCAD). Both of these programs financed small local public works and a variety of education, health, and other social projects to simultaneously generate jobs and improve conditions. By 1991 somewhat similar programs were under way in Guinea-Bissau and Guinea and under discussion in Guatemala, Guyana, and Haiti in Latin America.[30]

These programs share several features that increase their political acceptability. They are overwhelmingly externally financed, and therefore do not entail domestic resource transfers. Moreover, much of the funding is (or is believed to be) available only for these activities, that is, the opportunity costs are zero. Perhaps equally important, most of the actual and proposed programs are fairly broadly targeted to rural and urban

[30] Elaine Zuckerman, "Compensatory Programs: Redressing the Social Costs of Adjustment," draft paper (Washington, D.C.: World Bank, February 1989); World Bank Country Economics Department, *Adjustment Lending Policies*, p. 36.

popular classes. Fifty-six percent of the workers employed on ESF projects were drawn from the lower four deciles of the income distribution, and 41 percent from the fifth through eighth deciles.[31] Moreover, the small public works and social welfare projects financed by ESF served a broad spectrum of social groups and were widely distributed geographically. Both ESF and PAMSCAD include compensatory programs for workers laid off from the public sector: tin miners in Bolivia, and Cocoa Board and other employees in Ghana. Indeed, in Ghana much of the early benefits of PAMSCAD seem to have flowed to some of the more than forty thousand public sector workers who lost their jobs in 1987–89. In Bolivia relatively few miners took jobs on ESF projects, in part because the wages were too low to attract them.[32]

The programs were explicitly temporary when they were launched, which facilitated funding from both external donors and governments. In Bolivia the temporary and urgent character of the program was used to justify establishing a special unit outside of normal government agencies to administer the program.[33] The efficiency and honesty of that unit, and its reliance on local governments and NGOs to propose and administer projects, contributed to the wide popularity of the program. PAMSCAD encountered far more obstacles in getting under way. Some of those obstacles reflected conflicts between the donors' priorities and those of the Ghanaian agencies. For instance, procurement and shipment of medical supplies was delayed because external donors and government agencies could not agree on safeguards to channel the supplies to clinics accessible to the poor rather than to urban hospitals serving mainly middle strata. Such conflicts in objectives and priorities were still more obvious and central with respect to a different category of pro-poor measures: the retargeting of social programs.

[31] World Bank, *Adjustment Lending Policies*, box 3.3, p. 38. Surveys showed that almost all those employed on ESF projects were prime-aged male household heads, most were toward the lower end of the education and skills scales for construction workers, and roughly 30 percent were former construction workers. It should be noted that ESF administrators did not administer projects or hire workers directly; they approved projects proposed by local governments and private voluntary agencies, which assumed responsibility for administering the projects and hired workers on the local labor market. (John Newman, Steen Jorgensen, and Menno Pradhan, "How Did Workers Benefit from Bolivia's Emergency Social Fund?" [World Bank staff study, Washington, D.C., November 1989.])

[32] Richard Jolly and Rolph von der Hoeven, "Protecting the Poor and Vulnerable During Adjustment: The Case of Ghana" (UNICEF preliminary staff paper, New York, June 1989), p. 6. Newman, Jorgensen, and Pradhan found that about 10 percent of 3,051 workers on ESF-funded projects at the time surveys were taken had been miners. This represents a tiny fraction of the twenty-three thousand miners who lost their jobs when the state-owned mining company was closed (p. 10). See also Carol Graham, "The Politics of Bolivia's Emergency Social Fund" (Brookings Institution, Washington D.C., 1990), p. 8 and note 21.

[33] As of 1991, the temporary and autonomous ESF administration had been converted into a longer-term arrangement within more orthodox bureaucratic channels.

Retargeting Social Programs: Food Subsidies

Many developing countries directly or indirectly subsidize the prices consumers pay for basic (and sometimes not so basic) foods. In some cases, the subsidies substantially benefit many of the poor; in others subsidies may fail to reach the rural poor at all and the choice of items subsidized or the channels of distribution may exclude even the urban poor. Even where the poor do benefit, the bulk of nontargeted subsidies often go to the non-poor, because they buy more of the foods. General or broadly targeted subsidies also add to budget deficits. Therefore the World Bank, the International Monetary Fund, and other external organizations have long urged substituting targeted for general subsidies, to better serve the poor while easing fiscal pressures.

Acute fiscal pressures in the 1980s did indeed cause many governments to lower or eliminate broad consumer subsidies. But few simultaneously launched or enlarged targeted programs for the poor. It is not easy to set up and operate targeted programs, although a number of approaches are available. Means tests pose administrative problems and can be exploited politically. Food stamps or "inferior goods" approaches to targeting are often thought to demean the beneficiaries.[34] But probably the main reason why targeted programs are rarely installed as part of a broader subsidy reduction effort is that the political incentives are weak. In several of the cases where the approach was attempted, the targeting turned out to be quite broad—in essence, screening out the well-to-do, rather than targeting only the most needy.

Sri Lanka provides the most instructive case, because political and economic conditions for shifting from global to targeted subsidies were unusually favorable yet only a moderate degree of targeting turned out to be politically sustainable. Rice subsidies (at times a free ration) for the entire population had been introduced in World War II. The subsidy soon became a serious fiscal burden, but several attempts to reduce it were political disasters. In 1977, after almost a decade of deepening economic stagnation and political turmoil, a new government took office elected by an overwhelming majority and committed to economic liberalization. Opposition parties were in disarray, and the public was receptive to reforms. The new government also benefited in its early years from massive external economic aid, good weather, and strong international prices for the island's export crops. Regarding subsidies specifically, rice farmers, a politically important group, viewed the rice ration as a price depressant and favored its reform.

[34] An "inferior good" is one that is purchased primarily by the poor or constitutes a large part of the diets of the poor but not of better-off people, who prefer better tasting, more convenient, or higher status foods. Subsidizing the price of an inferior good is likely to benefit the poor without much leakage to the better off.

In this uniquely favorable economic and political setting, the government moved to convert the rice subsidy into a food stamp program targeted to the poor. It proceeded in two steps. In 1978 the subsidy was removed from the better-off half of the population. In 1979, the government converted the remaining subsidy for the poorer half to a food stamps system. Simultaneously, it tried to check the rolls and tighten the targeting to focus on the poorest third in order to permit somewhat increased benefits. But many households reported less than their real income, especially in rural areas where their claims were hard to verify. Members of Parliament pressured government officials not to challenge declared incomes. Later studies found that about 30 percent of households in the top half of the income distribution were receiving food stamps; worse, about an equal proportion of eligible poor households were *not* receiving them.[35]

In 1985 the government tried again to tighten the targeting. Inflation had reduced the real value of the stamps by half, and studies indicated a disturbing incidence of nutritional deficiencies among the poor. Again, however, strong pressure from the legislature defeated the technicians' proposals, although special feeding programs for the poor were adopted. A later study concludes:

> The government's concern in targeting the scheme to households who were genuinely in need was only halfhearted. A scheme which benefited half the population evidently made it politically more acceptable and rendered the problem of selection less demanding.[36]

In short, even (or perhaps especially) in a strongly democratic and equity-oriented society like Sri Lanka's, cutting the benefits of the middle sectors to help the poor was not politically acceptable.

Somewhat similar tales can be told regarding Morocco and Mexico, even though the details of the broad subsidy arrangements, the economic and political settings, and the precise ways in which the governments sought to cut back the subsidies while protecting poorer consumers were quite different. Morocco had long subsidized both high-grade and coarser wheat flour. Reforms introduced in 1988 removed the subsidy for high-quality flour and altered arrangements for subsidizing coarser flour, but

[35] M.D.D. Pieris, "Decade of Food Policy Reforms: Sri Lanka 1977–1987" (Paper prepared for the Seminar on Economic Policy Change and Governmental Process, sponsored by the Korean Development Institute and the Economic Development Institute of the World Bank, Seoul, Korea, 9–12 November 1987). See also Neville Edirisinghe, "Food Subsidy Changes in Sri Lanka: The Short-Run Effect on the Poor," in Per Pinstrup Anderson, ed., *Food Subsidies in Developing Countries* (Baltimore, Md.: Johns Hopkins University Press, 1988).

[36] Godfrey Gunatilleke, "Government Policies and Nutrition in Sri Lanka: Changes During the Last Ten Years and Lessons Learned" (Ithaca, N.Y.: PEW/Cornell Lecture Series on Food and Nutrition Policy, 26 September 1989).

the general effect was to remove the subsidy from the wealthy rather than to target it to the truly poor. In Mexico in the mid-1980s a variety of subsidies were cut but subsidies were increased for tortillas—a product purchased solely in the cities.

Reorienting Social Programs: Education and Health Services

At least since the 1970s (and earlier in many instances) development agencies urged governments to spend less on universities and hospitals, and more on primary schools and clinics. But the politics of restructuring social expenditures on education or health are similar to substituting targeted for general food subsidies: resources must be shifted from relatively privileged middle classes and less privileged popular classes to the most neglected groups. Where governments introduced such measures (save in exceptional political circumstances, as in Zimbabwe in the period immediately following independence) they have encountered stiff political resistance.

In Morocco, for example, university enrollments increased by 6 to 10 percent annually in the early 1980s. As part of a program supported by the World Bank, Morocco undertook to hold expansion of university enrollment to 2 percent a year and to phase down subsidies for university students' living expenses and books, in order to expand and improve primary education especially in rural areas. The agreement held for one year. In the second year, political intervention from the highest levels breached the ceiling: enrollment jumped by 25 percent.[37] A package of education reforms with similar broad goals (but with no cap on university admissions) was launched in Ghana at about the same time. Reduced university bursaries prompted protests and closed campuses in both 1987 and 1988. Neither government has abandoned the reforms, and both may gradually implement them. But the political struggle is on-going and intense.

Reorienting consumer subsidies and education and health services provoke political resistance because, unlike relief programs (especially those largely financed from abroad) these reforms quite obviously shift resources from more politically active and vocal groups to less potent ones. Experience with both relief and social sector programs supports the proposition stated early in this chapter: while it is often technically feasible to buffer some among the poor, political incentives for such action are usu-

---

[37] Among the government's reasons for deciding to undertake the reforms was concern that the rapidly swelling number of university graduates would not be able to find the kinds of employment that they expected and that had been virtually guaranteed to earlier graduates. The reform, in other words, was partly intended to help reduce a potentially severe future political problem of frustrated highly educated youth. Easing immediate political pressures, however, soon took priority over reducing a future problem, even when the short-run solution led predictably to the longer-run difficulty.

ally weak. Thus short-run compensatory programs are likely to flow as much to middle strata as to the very poor, and attempts to target expenditures on consumer subsidies and social services to the poor at the expense of middle strata face stiff opposition.

URBAN POPULAR CLASSES AND THE POLITICS OF ADJUSTMENT

In broad outline, the second equity issue raises political questions that are virtually the reverse of the politics of pro-poor measures. The domestic political incentives for governments to buffer the poor in the course of adjustment are usually weak. The domestic incentives to slow the downward slide of urban working classes and popular sectors are often all too strong.

International pressures, however, are also reversed and lean against domestic forces. While the World Bank, the IMF, and other external donors encourage governments to protect the poor, they often urge them to stand firm against the demands of labor unions and urban popular classes.

That characterization, of course, both oversimplifies and exaggerates the dichotomy between the two equity issues. Especially in the least developed countries, the absolute gap in living standards between very poor and much of the urban population is not great. The latter are still very poor (more so in 1990 than in 1980), and many of their needs are similar to those of the very poor. The gap between the very poor and the working and popular classes widens in the cities of the more industrialized countries.

Even in the poorer countries, however, urban popular classes are likely to be more active politically than both the rural poor and the poorest fringes of urban society. Coupled with this political potential is the high exposure of urban workers and popular classes to the costs of adjustment, discussed earlier in this chapter. Popular classes are more active politically, in part because they tend to be somewhat better educated and more self-confident than the very poor. In part, their political potential grows from higher levels of affiliation with organized groups of all kinds, including neighborhood and occupational associations, migrants' home place associations, churches, sports and parents' clubs, and labor unions. Political participation is stimulated by and often mediated through such organizations. And while political parties usually ignore the very poor, they often compete for support from urban popular sectors, in part through sponsoring or seeking to co-opt their associations.

It is obvious why governments worry about political reactions from these sectors. Yet several factors mitigate their political responses to adjustment measures. The urban popular classes are not a uniform social or economic category, nor are they normally a cohesive political group. Their widely diverse ways of earning livings and their varied lifestyles

mean considerable divergence in specific political concerns. They are often also divided by religion and ethnicity. In cities comprised heavily of
migrants they may be further split by loyalties to the regions from which
they came. Political parties often build on and intensify these splits.

With respect to many specific structural reforms, too, urban political
classes are often divided among themselves. Some segments may ally with
business or other elite interests. This is probably clearest with respect to
import liberalization and trade policies more generally, where workers in
export-oriented industries may have quite different reactions than their
counterparts in inefficient import-substituting firms.

Macroeconomic stabilization measures, in contrast, affect much of the
urban popular classes similarly, simultaneously, and transparently; hence
the much-publicized, and real, risk of large-scale protest. Formal sector
workers are more directly targeted by stabilization and by many structural reforms than other formal sector groups: their weapon, facilitated
by preestablished organization, is of course the strike. And although the
urban popular classes seldom constitute an organized and cohesive voting
bloc, their numbers and the probability of high participation rates makes
their electoral support or opposition an important element in politicians'
electoral calculations.

While strikes and protests often gain wide publicity, the most noteworthy fact about them is that they happen at all; large-scale protests and
large sustained strikes are exceptional political responses to adjustment
efforts. Labor unions and the urban popular classes are more often qui-
escent in the face of adjustment programs and may even temporarily support aspects of the programs. The following discussion probes why adjustment sometimes prompts broad and strong opposition and in other
cases leads to at least temporary acquiescence. The discussion focuses on
the three major channels of popular political action—strikes, protests,
and electoral behavior.

Unionized Labor and Strikes

Among the urban popular classes, unionized labor is usually best-orga-
nized to defend its interests, and strikes are widely assumed to be the most
likely cause of the erosion or abandonment of adjustment programs.
Most stabilization and adjustment programs have been accompanied by
some strike action. Yet there are very few instances where union pressure
alone derailed adjustment efforts, although labor combined with other
elements of the urban popular sectors has done so in some instances.

At first glance, strikes as a response to adjustment seem to accord with
simple interest group explanations: the intensity of protest reflects the
strength of the interests concerned. Capacity to mount large and sus-

tained strikes clearly relates to union size and autonomy.[38] John Walton and Charles Ragin found a strong correlation between the proportion of the labor force in unions (as of 1975) and the severity of protests against austerity between 1976 and 1987 in twenty-six countries in Latin America, Asia, and Africa.[39] Brazilian and especially Argentine unions have a long history of undermining or killing adjustment programs. Workers in strategic sectors may exercise tremendous economic and political leverage, even where they are only a small fraction of organized labor. Copper workers in Zambia and Chile, tin miners in Bolivia, bauxite/alumina workers in Jamaica, oil workers in Nigeria, Venezuela, Mexico, and other countries have been able to throttle national export earnings and government revenues and have used their leverage to maintain wages markedly out of line with the rest of the economy.

In general, however, unions in developing countries are not strong. The most heavily unionized nations, including Venezuela, Nicaragua, Guyana, Sri Lanka and Mauritius, count roughly a third of the work force as union members (with agricultural estate workers an important component in the last two named). Argentine unions claim about 28 percent of the labor force; roughly a quarter of Jamaican workers are unionized; perhaps a fifth in Tunisia and Mexico; and far fewer elsewhere.[40] More

[38] In advanced industrial democracies, links between union strength and strike activity are more complex. One set of studies has found strike activity negatively correlated to strong labor movements and highly centralized wage bargaining, reflecting cooperative or "corporatist" relationships among unions, business associations, and governments. See, for example, David R. Cameron, "Social Democracy, Corporatism, Labour Quiescence and the Representation of Economic Interest in Advanced Capitalist Society," in John H. Goldthorpe, ed., *Order and Conflict in Contemporary Capitalism* (Oxford: Oxford University Press, 1984). A second set of studies suggests a nonlinear relationship, with strikes and union militance most pronounced where unions are neither weak and fragmented nor powerful and highly centralized. See, for example, Lars Calmfors and John Driffill, "Bargaining Structure, Corporatism, and Macroeconomic Performance," *Economic Policy* 6 (April 1988): 13–62. But no developing countries have union movements comparable to those at the top end of the scale in industrialized nations. See Joan M. Nelson, "Organized Labor, Politics, and Labor Market Flexibility in Developing Countries," *The World Bank Research Observer* 6 (January 1991): 38–46 for a fuller discussion of links between union structure and union militance in developing nations.

[39] John Walton and Charles Ragin, "Austerity and Dissent: Social Bases of Popular Struggle in Latin America," in William L. Canak, ed., *Lost Promises: Debt, Austerity, and Development in Latin America* (Boulder, Colo.: Westview Press, 1988), table 10.3, p. 224.

[40] The most extensive sets of data on union members as a proportion of the labor force are found in Charles Lewis Taylor and David Jodice, *World Handbook of Political and Social Indicators*, 3d ed. (New Haven, Conn.: Yale University Press,1983), and in the U.S. Central Intelligence Agency, *World Factbook 1989*. But the former is now dated (referring to the mid-1970s) and some of the data from the latter are startlingly out of line with other sources. For example, the World Factbook gives Mexican union membership as 35 percent of the workforce, compared to Middlebrook's figure for 1979 of 16.3 percent (Middlebrook, "The Sounds of Silence," p. 212), and George Grayson's estimate for the late 1980s of 20 percent given at a conference on Mexican trade unions at the Overseas Development

important, in most developing countries unions tend to be fragmented and often poorly led. A wave of wildcat strikes is normally not a menace either to political stability or to the continuity of adjustment efforts. The opening section of this chapter noted that organized labor has usually not been powerful enough to prevent falling wages and growing unemployment, nor to forestall a shrinking factor share of national income.

The simple strength or weakness of unions only partially determines their behavior and their influence. Economic circumstances are a second important factor. Even strong unions do not automatically respond to hard times with strikes. Union militance and strike action in established industrial democracies tend to decline in hard times, since slack labor markets and rising unemployment reduce strike effectiveness. Strike data for seven Latin America countries with strong unions for the period 1976–84 indicate that rising unemployment clearly discouraged strikes, although falling real wages did not relate systematically to strikes.[41] The underlying logic of decreased militance in hard times may also be affected by the longer-term outlook. Peter Lange suggests that where prospects are truly bleak, workers may conclude that there is little to be gained by restraint: "Things will not get better anyway without major disruptions to their economic lives, and . . . it is therefore best to try to get as much as possible while it can still be had." In such situations, a key variable shaping union militance or restraint, Lange says, is workers' perceptions that "the fruits of their restraint will redound to their future economic advantage." This perception, in turn, rests on two factors: the credibility of the government's broader recovery program, and explicit or implicit assurances that their interests will be protected during industrial restructuring.[42] In short, when the long-term economic outlook is grim, political factors and institutions become much more important in determining labor responses.

Regime type would seem to be the most obvious institutional factor

Council in 1989. Recent data for many countries are also available in the periodic U.S. embassy reports for individual countries (*Foreign Labor Trends*, released through the U.S. Department of Labor, Bureau of International Labor Affairs). This source is the main basis for the estimates in the text for Argentina, Venezuela, and Jamaica.

[41] Edward C. Epstein, "Austerity and Trade Unions in Latin America," in William L. Canak, editor, *Lost Promises: Debt, Austerity, and Development in Latin America* (Boulder, Colo.: Westview Press, 1989), pp. 176–77. Annual data on the number and severity of strikes are available for many other developing nations in the yearbooks of the International Labour Organization. But the links between strike activity and economic prosperity or hard times is harder to trace in developing countries as a group than in industrialized democracies because frequent changes of regime in the developing nations abruptly and erratically alter legal and political constraint on strikes.

[42] Peter Lange, "Unions, Workers, and Wage Regulation: The Rational Bases of Consent," in John H. Goldthorpe, ed., *Order and Conflict in Contemporary Capitalism* (Oxford, England: Oxford University Press, 1984), p. 115.

shaping governments' behavior towards strikes, and therefore affecting the options available to unions. Broadly, one would expect democratic governments to rely more on persuasion and compensation tactics, while authoritarian regimes are less reluctant to use repression. But regime type turns out to be too crude a variable to reliably predict government tactics toward labor. Some democracies have laws hedging in union activity quite tightly, and many have been willing to ignore or put down labor protests. Both the Jayawardene government in Sri Lanka in 1980 and the Paz Estenssoro government in Bolivia in 1985 put down major strikes promptly and decisively. In 1985 in Jamaica, Seaga simply ignored a general strike entailing unprecedented cooperation between the two major rival labor federations. Conversely, some long-established one- or dominant-party governments grant unions considerable influence, despite frequent tension and occasional repression. Among the many examples are the dominant Tunisian Neodestour Party's long history of relations with the major labor federation, and Kenneth Kaunda's relations with Zambian copper miners.

More fine-grained features of the relations between unions, governments, and parties, including the channels and degrees of access to decision-making circles, are key in determining available options and therefore behavior of both unions and governments. The range of institutional arrangements can be arrayed from those where unions exercise most influence to those where they are weakest. Extremely rarely, unions are strong forces within a party holding power, as during periods of Peronist control in Argentina. In several durable dominant-party systems, including Mexico, Tunisia, and Singapore, union federations are incorporated into the party as subordinate partners with varying (though not great) influence. In Colombia, Venezuela, Costa Rica, and Jamaica unions have links with both of two centrist parties that alternate power: in these cases labor has access to but does not dominate the government regardless of the party in power. In Peru and Argentina, labor has been linked to one strong party within a deeply polarized system, leading to drastic swings in influence in Argentina and to exclusion in Peru. In Uruguay and (less clearly) the Dominican Republic, unions are mainly linked with weak radical parties, resulting in semiexclusion. And in Korea until recently, Chile under Pinochet, and many African countries organized labor has been effectively excluded from restricted political arenas.

Broadly, it appears that either incorporation into an established dominant party or links with parties that alternate in power encourages negotiation and compromise and dampens confrontation (see Stephan Haggard and Robert R. Kaufman, chapter 6 of this volume). But incentives for the party in power to make concessions to labor differ sharply under the two party systems. Where a dominant party incorporates major unions, it may assume that labor has no plausible alternative to cooperation. In more competitive two-party systems, access to both major parties assures labor leaders that their interests will get a hearing—the kind of assurance Lange suggests is likely to moderate the militance of desperation in very hard times. In contrast to both of these two possibilities, polarized party systems are likely to stimulate union militance, whether or not the party with which labor is affiliated stands a good chance of taking office. Exclusion and repression stifle large-scale strikes; scattered wildcat strikes may still erupt but are not likely to be effective.

In sum, unions—the most organized segment of the urban popular classes—are seldom strong enough to threaten entire adjustment programs, although they can certainly raise the costs to the government of specific measures. More interesting because less obvious, even strong unions do not necessarily or automatically oppose adjustment measures. Their responses are shaped by calculations of both short- and longer-run costs and benefits, reflecting both their appraisal of economic prospects and their ties with and confidence in the political institutions that affect their likely shares in future benefits.

Urban Protest

Urban protests and demonstrations span a wide range of actions. They vary on at least four key dimensions: number of people involved (from a few dozen to many thousands); degree of organization (ranging from entirely spontaneous to carefully planned and orchestrated); orderly versus violent character; and duration (from minutes to days or even weeks). Generalizing about such a heterogeneous range of action is hazardous, but some patterns do emerge. Much protest activity is spontaneous, triggered by some specific government action, directed solely to reversing or redressing that action, and short-lived. The commonest triggers are increased prices (reduced or removed subsidies) for foods, utilities, gasoline, or bus fares. Unions or opposition parties are often involved in larger protests, and sometimes play a key role in initiating them, but they usually do not control or represent most of the participants.[43]

Some urban protests take on a much more organized and sustained character, and draw in not only popular classes but business and professional elites. Such cases usually involve not only specific economic grievances, but broader political issues. For instance, in Jamaica in the course of 1985, unions, business associations, church groups and the opposition party were all involved in cumulative protests against both austerity measures and repeated postponement of municipal elections, viewed as an abridgement of democracy. In Chile a similarly broad front of urban in-

[43] Henry S. Bienen and Mark Gersovitz, "Consumer Subsidy Cuts, Violence, and Political Stability," *Comparative Politics* 19, no. 1 (October 1986): 25–44.

terests, spearheaded by labor unions, took part in a coordinated series of demonstrations against both economic policy and authoritarian rule in 1983–84. Urban protests can of course merge into popular revolutions, changing not only governments but regime types, as in the Philippines in 1985 and Eastern Europe in 1989.

Large protests, especially where they turn violent or actually bring down governments, capture world headlines. But when one considers the number of devaluations, subsidy cuts, and other adjustment measures adopted throughout Latin America and Africa and in much of Asia during the 1980s, it is clear that large protests are a comparatively rare response, while popular revolutions are still rarer. Small and scattered protests pose little or no threat, even to weak governments.

What causes no or only scattered protests in reaction to adjustment measures in some cases, and mass explosions in others? Research has focused on actual protests, and there has been almost no systematic analysis of the factors determining occurrence versus nonoccurrence of protests.[44] As a poor substitute, we can speculate that at least five sets of factors are at work. Fragmentary evidence supports the speculation.

The actual short-term economic impact of adjustment measures presumably is an important determinant of popular responses. Assessing that impact, even for comparatively direct measures like cuts in food subsidies, is more complicated than appears at first glance. For example, sharp hikes in prices for subsidized food staples may in fact have little impact on popular classes or the poor if supplies of the goods have been so scarce that most people could not buy them at the official subsidized price. This seems to have been part of the explanation for the absence of protests when Tanzania announced steep increases in the previously subsidized price of maize meal in mid-1984. Simultaneous compensatory measures also can soften the effect of price increases. In Tanzania, government salaries were increased on a sliding scale simultaneously with the rise in maize meal prices in amounts calculated to largely cover increased costs. In short, pocketbook impact is determined by a variety of factors operating simultaneously.

Protest or lack of protest is also influenced by two dimensions of broad public opinion. The first of these is the degree to which much of the public is convinced that the economy is in dire straits and strong policies are required to restore stability and growth. When the government of Tunisia announced increases of 115 percent in previously heavily subsidized prices for wheat products in January 1984, there was little popular per-

---

[44] A modest attempt to assess occurrence versus nonoccurrence of protest in reaction to adjustment measures is available in Joan M. Nelson, "Short-run Public Reactions to Food Subsidy Cuts in Selected Sub-Saharan and North African Countries" (Research report submitted to the U.S. Department of State and the Agency for International Development, contract 1722–420142, Washington, D.C., February 1985).

ception of economic crisis, ironically because the government was trying to deal in timely fashion with real difficulties to prevent their becoming a crisis. Similarly, when the Venezuelan government hiked gasoline prices 90 percent and bus fares 30 percent in February 1989, public opinion did not perceive an economic crisis justifying the move. In both countries, the urban popular sectors had become accustomed to steady economic improvement, and subsidy cuts prompted large-scale riots in each. In contrast, protests did not erupt in Ghana in 1983 and in Tanzania in 1984 despite price hikes; in both countries much of the public was convinced that prolonged and severe economic decline could only be reversed by drastic measures—although that attitude did not necessarily mean approval of the specific decisions taken.

The second dimension of public opinion that shapes popular reactions is confidence in the government's plan or competence to manage the economy. The newly elected Monge government in Costa Rica promptly introduced strong measures to bring the economy out of the worst tailspin in its history, prompting little popular protest despite a number of strikes. The vigorous and coherent Sri Lanka adjustment program in the late 1970s and the adjustment efforts in Turkey in the early 1980s similarly prompted little general protest. In contrast, the perception that the government is vacillating or confused and that events have spun beyond its control are likely to provoke protest. A popular explosion in Santo Domingo in April 1984 was triggered by attempted subsidy cuts, but capped months of growing popular-sector protest in reaction to vacillating and confused government policies. Similarly, urban riots in Zambia in December 1986 were touched off by subsidy cuts but reflected a longer history of inept administration and confusing signals, in turn the product of a deeply divided government.

More obvious political circumstances, such as the legitimacy and popularity of the government or, conversely, linkage with other grievances, also shape the probability of large-scale urban protest against adjustment. Acceptance of subsidy cuts in Zimbabwe in the early 1980s was facilitated by the strong popularity of the government that had recently won independence after a long struggle. In contrast, raising wheat prices in Tunisia in 1983 provided a catalyst for long-simmering political grievances against an old and tired dominant-party system, and distaste for the increasingly blatant maneuvering between rival factions for Bourguiba's mantle. The dramatic events of the mid- and late 1980s in the Philippines, Chile, and Eastern Europe reflected still deeper and more pervasive political dissatisfactions coupled with economic grievances.

Finally, government tactics can also make a considerable difference in the likelihood that protests will occur, or will spread, in response to government measures. Within months after the riots of April 1984, the government of the Dominican Republic was convinced that it could no longer avoid devaluation and associated price increases being urged by the international agencies. Certain steps were taken in August 1984 and a larger package was announced in January 1985. In both instances, in sharp contrast to its performance in early 1984, the government made considerable efforts to persuade or offer partial compensations to key groups, and to take preemptive measures to round up potential opposition leaders and place troops on the streets. There were no protests.

In the 1990s, increasing organization and political sophistication within the urban popular sectors may lead to new patterns of urban protest. In the past, the rich array of small-scale popular sector organizations based on neighborhood, place of origin, ethnic group or clan, or type of work (for instance, venders' syndicates) sometimes pressed local or national officials for services or benefits or to retract some harmful regulation or decision. But they seldom tried to alter government policies or overall budget allocations. Federations (most commonly of neighborhood associations) were more powerful in principle, but were often hampered by distrust and rivalries among member groups, controlled by parties or co-opted or repressed by governments.[45]

Recently, however, converging trends have strengthened ties among such organizations and drawn them increasingly into the political arena. Rising education levels and access to mass media contributes to increasing sophistication and confidence. The economic pressures of the 1980s and governments' demonstrated failure to cope with urban problems spurred discontent. In many countries, increasing disillusion with established parties or the disintegration (or destruction by authoritarian governments) of party systems has led urban popular groups to rely increasingly on their own resources and initiatives. The outcome has been the increased political participation of private voluntary organizations and associations of all kinds.

Often loosely coordinated, though with no single leader or ideology or plan for political action, these groups are entering public debate and pressuring political authorities with respect to a wide range of policy decisions. Access to the media through special newspaper columns and radio or television talk shows may greatly increase the power of such groups. Sometimes their participation takes on highly creative forms: in Mexico City in the late 1980s a mysterious figure calling himself "Superbarrio" led protests of tens of thousands, insisting that representatives of the bureaucracy negotiate with him on the street in the full glare of newspaper and television coverage.[46]

[45] These points are developed in detail in Nelson, *Access to Power*, chap. 7, "Special-Interest Associations Among the Urban Poor," pp. 249–317.

[46] Sheldon Annis, "What is Not the Same About the Urban Poor: The Case of Mexico City," in John P. Lewis, ed., *Strengthening the Poor: What Have We Learned?*, Policy Per-

The upshot is new forms of urban popular sector protest and lobbying. These popular pressures are more planned, sustained, and often coordinated than spontaneous outbursts. They pose new challenges for governments but also permit new forms of dialogue and potentially constructive popular sector participation in some elements of policy-making.

Elections

Elections are the third major channel through which urban popular sectors can express their reactions to economic trends and adjustment efforts. In contrast to strikes and protests, the timing of elections is predictable or within the control of the government. Governments, of course, anticipate adverse popular reactions, and the effects of electoral cycles on macro-economic policies are much analyzed (see, for instance, the discussion of electoral effects as part of Haggard and Kaufman's analysis of causes of inflationary cycles in chapter 6 of this volume). Fiscal stringency in particular tends to loosen before elections. And it is conventional wisdom that unpopular reforms are best announced shortly after an electoral victory.

Elections can express support as well as opposition. The question at its simplest is: Given an opportunity at the polls, do voters reject leaders who seek reelection (or their designated successors) because they imposed austerity programs and related reforms? Or for imposing adjustment programs that *fail*? Evidence on political responses to adjustment drawn from election outcomes offers a useful complement to evidence drawn from strikes and protests. While the latter usually represents immediate reactions to unpopular government measures, elections often come several years after adjustment programs have been introduced, so that the economic effects have had a chance to play out. Moreover, while participation in strikes or protests requires extraordinary action, in most countries voting is a more routine step for ordinary citizens.

To start from the obvious: Where an economy is in severe difficulty, voters punish politicians or their parties demonstrably unable to adopt or pursue consistent policies to regain balance. Among the many elections demonstrating powerful public reactions against perceived economic mismanagement are those in Jamaica in 1980, Costa Rica in 1982, Bolivia in 1985, Peru in 1985 and 1990, and Brazil in 1989.

But how do voters respond when governments do adopt vigorous and sustained adjustment efforts? In 1990 the World Bank listed twenty-five countries as having conducted intensive and sustained structural adjust-

---

spectives Series No. 10 (Washington, D.C., Overseas Development Council, 1988), pp. 140–42.

ment programs starting in or before 1985.[47] Almost all of these countries undertook simultaneous stabilization programs with IMF support. To this list can be added Sri Lanka, which had adopted a vigorous set of structural reforms in the late 1970s predating the introduction of adjustment loans as World Bank instruments. Some of these countries have not held presidential elections since the adjustment program was launched, or constrain opposition so tightly that election results can not be interpreted as evidence of popular views. But in fifteen countries, competitive or semicompetitive presidential elections were held between the launching of adjustment programs and 1990; two such elections occured in Turkey. (Appendix table A5.2 lists all the countries in the initial pool and the reasons for excluding certain elections from analysis.)

Table 5.1 arrays these elections and their outcomes. A plurality of the popular vote for the incumbent or his designated successor is labeled as a victory (V); defeats are labeled (D). For the purposes of this analysis, the table also records three quasidefeats ("D"), where opposition votes in dominant party systems reached unprecedented levels (Mexico, Senegal, Madagascar) although the ruling parties were not displaced. Table 5.1 also includes two quasivictories ("V"). In Bolivia in 1989, Paz Estenssoro's designated heir won a narrow plurality of the popular vote, but an unlikely legislative coalition denied him the office. In Turkey in 1983, winner Turgut Özal definitely was not the designated heir of the military government in power from 1980 to 1983; indeed, that government opposed him vigorously. But Özal had been the key technical architect of the military government's adjustment program, and was elected in large part on his reputation as a skilled economic manager. His election was a "victory" for the adjustment effort, although not for the outgoing military government. Appendix table A5.3 gives more detailed data on election outcomes.

The elections in table 5.1 are grouped according to a rough ranking of overall economic performance and trends in conditions for the urban popular sectors in the year of the election and the two preceeding years.[48] Overall economic performance is assessed on a scale from + + (strong growth) to − (deterioration) based on rates of growth of GNP, exports, and investment. Trends in conditions for the urban popular sectors are classified as improving (+), stagnant (0), or deteriorating (−), based on level and trends in the consumer price index, real average wages, private per capita consumption, and unemployment. Not all indicators are avail-

[47] These countries received at least two Structural Adjustment Loans (SALs), or three or more Sector Adjustment Loans (SECALs), or a combination of three or more SALs and SECALs, with the first adjustment operation funded in or before 1985.

[48] Where the election occurred early in the calendar year, the economic data are shown for the three years prior to the election.

TABLE 5.1
Electoral Responses to Intensively Adjusting Governments

	Date of Election	Election Outcome for Incumbent or Heir	In Election Year and Two Previous Years		Important Non-adjustment Issues (Harmed Incumbent Except as Noted)
			Overall Economic Performance	Urban Popular Impact	
Korea	12/87	V	+ +	+ +	Political reform, relations with North Korea
Mauritius	8/87	V	+ +	+ +	
Chile	12/89	D	+ +	+	Restore democracy
Sri Lanka	10/82	V	+	+	Ethnic relations
Thailand	7/88	V	+ +	+	Political reform
Costa Rica	2/86	V	0 +	+ +	
Colombia	5/86	D	+	+	Political violence
Pakistan	11/88	D	+	0?	Restore democracy
Turkey	11/83	"V"	+	−	Restore democracy (helped Özal)
Turkey	11/87	V	+	−	
Jamaica	2/89	D	0 +	0 +	No third term
Senegal	2/88	"D"	0	0	Political reform
Bolivia	5/89	"V"	0	0	
Mexico	7/89	"D"	0	0	Political reform
Madagascar	3/89	"D"	−	−	
Philippines	2/86	D	−	−	Restore democracy

Key: V = victory
      D = defeat
      "V" = quasi-victory
      "D" = quasi-defeat

able for each country. The order of listing within broad categories is not intended as a ranking. The data on overall performance and on conditions for the urban popular sectors are shown in appendix table A5.4.

Table 5.1 clearly does no more than provide extremely rough impressions regarding links—or lack of links—between adjustment performance and voter responses. Four problems blur the analysis. First, issues other than economic management were central in several of these elections, sometimes reinforcing and sometimes countervailing voter reactions to good or bad economic performance. The last column of table 5 briefly indicates such issues. Second, not all elections featured either an incumbent or a clearly designated "successor". In some cases the presidential candidate from the out-going president's party was not his heir and could even be interpreted as his rival. Third, the usual data problems apply particularly to economic indicators most relevant to the urban popular sectors. Unemployment data are notoriously unreliable. Real wage data apply only to formal sector workers or still narrower categories. Even for such workers, the varying importance of nonwage compensation erodes the significance of real wage trends, especially for cross-national comparisons. Therefore the level and trend of inflation, as measured by the Consumer Price Index (CPI), is emphasized somewhat more heavily in the rough scores. Fourth, national electoral returns obviously may diverge substantially from the urban popular class vote, or even from the broader urban vote.

Despite these strong caveats, table 5.1 confirms the common sense assumption that, given a reasonably free election, voters will usually reward effective economic management and punish failure. The deviant cases are those where noneconomic issues weighed heavily against incumbents. The first seven elections listed in table 5.1 were held in situations of overall economic improvement that was almost surely benefiting many among the popular sectors: Korea in December 1987, Mauritius in August 1987, Chile in December 1989, Sri Lanka in October 1982, Thailand in July 1988, and Costa Rica in February 1986. In five of these seven elections, the incumbents or their designated successors won, although not always with wide margins. In Chile, desire for democratization gave Patricio Aylwin a 26-point margin over the candidate sponsored by Pinochet. Barco's victory in Colombia similarly turned on noneconomic issues (and neither Colombia's economic difficulties nor her adjustment program had been severe).

In contrast to these economic success stories, the last five elections listed in Table 5.1 were held when overall economic performance was weak and conditions for the urban popular sectors were stagnant or deteriorating, despite (or perhaps in some respects because of) adjustment efforts: Senegal in February 1988, Bolivia in May 1989, Mexico in July 1989, Madagascar in March 1989, and the Philippines in February 1986. In all these cases, it should be noted, some or considerable progress had been made in stabilizing the economy and undertaking important longer-term reforms, but they had not yet translated into economic growth. In Senegal and Madagascar, previously weak opposition parties captured roughly a quarter of the popular votes, and far higher proportions in the capital cities. In Mexico, according to official but contested figures the PRI won a hair's breadth majority of 50.36 percent, while challenger Cuatémoc Cárdenas garnered over 31 percent, with particularly strong support in major urban areas.

In Bolivia, the interpretation is more complicated. Gonzalo Sanchez de Lozada, Paz Estenssorro's designated heir, had been his minister of economics and chief architect of the New Economic Policy that had stopped hyperinflation in its tracks and introduced major reforms. Although the economy remained stagnant and hardship was widespread, all three major candidates contesting the election pledged to continue the basic policies of the Paz Estenssoro government. Sanchez de Lozada won a plurality in the closely fought election, but was defeated by an unlikely left-right coalition when the election was decided by congressional vote. For the purposes of this discussion, it is clear that the election represented broad popular support for the stabilization program.

More interesting because less obvious are the intermediate cases in Table 5.1, where strong adjustment efforts had produced more stable economic conditions and some or considerable growth, but conditions for urban popular sectors had improved little or continued to deteriorate. Turkey fits this description fairly clearly; arguably it also applies to Jamaica, although the island's economic recovery was set back in 1988 by hurricane damage before the elections. Pakistan fits less comfortably in this middle category in part because it confronted a much less serious economic crisis, and in part because noneconomic issues strongly affected the election outcome.

Turkey had suffered severe economic and political problems in the late 1970s. A major adjustment program was launched in early 1980 and was continued and strengthened by the military government that took power later in the year. Early effects on growth and exports were dramatic, but the social impact of adjustment was mixed. Average real wages fell steeply throughout the decade until 1988, although the legal minimum wage increased 85 percent in real terms between 1980 and 1987 and jumped particularly sharply in each of the two election years.[49]

Turgut Özal's string of electoral victories, in national elections in 1983, municipal elections in 1984, and national elections in 1987 all hinged substantially on his abilities as an economic manager. The 1983 win also reflected the voters' desire to end military dominance of politics. Although Özal had been the architect of the highly effective adjustment efforts under military rule from 1980 to 1982, in 1983 he was the major challenger of the military-endorsed candidate. The 1984 local elections (not included in table 5.1) saw "an important shift to the center-right in the big cities [which Özal's party carried by over 80 percent], despite their large working class constituencies and traditional support for social democratic candidates."[50] By the general elections of 1987, however, resurgent economic problems were cooling enthusiasm for Özal. Economic issues dominated the election, and with more than 91 percent of the electorate participating, Özal's party won by a razor-thin majority of 50.17 percent. And by March 1989, Özal's party took only 22 percent of

[49] World Bank, *Turkey: Country Economic Memorandum* (Washington, D.C.: World Bank, 1988), table 3.7, p. 73.

[50] *Keesing's Record of World Events*, vol. 8 (1983–84), p. 724.

the municipal election vote and placed third, losing the three biggest cities. Analysts explained the outcome largely in terms of inflation that peaked at 87 percent in late 1988 and dropped to 72 percent on an annualized basis before the elections.[51]

In Bolivia in 1989 and Turkey in 1983 and 1984, a great many voters evidently were prepared to vote for economic management that inspired their confidence, even though their own gains were limited. In Jamaica in the late 1980s, overall economic indicators were more encouraging than they had been in many years: some growth, little inflation, investment increasing and some return of flight capital. Urban unemployment was at its lowest level in years. However, Jamaicans were tired of austerity and poorer Jamaicans expected Manley to be much more sensitive to their needs: the issue of equity was central to the campaign. Moreover, a victory for Edward Seaga, the architect of the adjustment effort since 1980, would have meant an unprecedented third term. Nonetheless, Seaga's defeat was not clearly a popular mandate against adjustment measures. Indeed, Manley and his party made clear that they accepted many of the main principles of Seaga's reforms.

Election outcomes broadly concur with fragmentary evidence from the occurrence or nonoccurrence of protests and with analysis of strike behavior to suggest the broad principle that confidence—more precisely, the belief that the government in power has the will and capacity to cope with current economic difficulties and to lay the basis for resumed growth—may sustain political acquiescence even where conditions for the popular classes remain bad. In economists' analyses of successful and unsuccessful adjustment efforts, the role of investor confidence (or government credibility) is widely acknowledged to be crucial, since it determines the degree to which firms respond to government measures with resumed activity and increased investment (including repatriation of flight capital). Confidence plays a directly analagous role in shaping popular political responses to adjustment programs. Political acquiescence means accepting diminished consumption now in hopes that this sacrifice will prove to be an investment in a more prosperous future. Like businessmen's decisions to resume investment, urban popular classes' acceptance of adjustment measures reflects two judgments: the government's capacity to manage the economy appropriately, and the likelihood that the particular groups concerned will gain a fair share of future benefits from current behavior.

CONCLUSIONS: OPTIONS FOR GOVERNMENTS

Both governments and external development agencies have tended to focus concern for political sustainability on tactics, rather than longer-run

[51] *Keesing's*, vol. 34 (1988), p. 35909 and vol. 35 (1989), p. 36528.

strategies. In politics as in war, tactics reflect immediate circumstances, and generalizations are difficult. Governments seek to prevent strikes and protests by varying combinations of persuasion, partial compensation, occasional obfuscation, and tacit or explicit threats or other deterrent actions. When strikes or protests do occur, governments again have a range of tactical options, including outright repression, stonewalling or ignoring the pressure, or making limited or broader concessions. While some combinations have clearly been much more effective than others, what worked in one set of circumstances may well not work elsewhere.

As it has become clear that adjustment in most African and Latin American countries is no quick fix, but a long, drawn-out process, longer-run strategies for dealing with urban popular sector pressures become imperative. Even where there has been broad public acceptance of temporary stabilization measures—as not infrequently happens—such acquiescence predictably erodes. Pressure for more relaxed macroeconomic policies will mount. So will resentment of those longer-term reforms that impose obvious near-term costs but produce only deferred and often diffuse benefits. Where economic reforms and supply response are slow or international conditions remain difficult—as was the case for so many countries during the 1980s and may well continue during the 1990s—urban popular sectors are likely to become increasingly restive. If it is no longer economically feasible simply to yield to such pressures, what are the options available to governments?

Korea and Taiwan since the 1960s and Chile since 1973 appear to offer one approach. However morally repugnant, sustained repression of urban popular sectors in these countries clearly facilitated effective economic restructuring. Several factors contributed to the feasibility of repression in these cases: widespread agreement that the nation faced an extreme internal or external threat justifying authoritarian rule; strong military and police forces loyal to the executive; and (after initial stages) considerable economic growth benefiting much of the population. Most developing countries lack one or more of these conditions. Where large-scale popular sector protests (often in alliance with business elements) have been sustained over weeks or months, even so strong an authoritarian government as Pinochet's has had to respond with some concessions. Moreover, the changing international political climate is likely to be less tolerant of repression in the 1990s, and potential dissenters within many countries will become more aggressive as a result of political openings in other countries.

Constructive alternatives to repressive approaches to containing urban popular pressures essentially require either building strong support coalitions based mainly on other groups or finding ways to gain support from at least some urban popular elements. Proponents of market-oriented economic reforms often assume that the beneficiaries of the reforms, including much of the previously neglected or exploited agricultural sector, will provide political support for continuing adjustment. At best, such support will be slow to materialize. In a few countries such as Costa Rica, nontraditional agricultural exports have boomed, and have generated some new political support for aspects of reform. But in Ghana, although cocoa farmers and other rural groups have benefited from reforms launched in 1983, the government has yet to figure out how to mobilize their potential political support without also enfranchising disaffected urban groups. In many cases, beneficiaries are not organized politically, or putative beneficiaries are not yet convinced that the new opportunities are real or sustainable. In some cases, particularly in sub-Saharan Africa and in Central and Eastern Europe, the most obvious beneficiaries of structural reforms are foreign or alien resident business groups, who are hardly in a position to enter the national political arena.

In short, many, perhaps most, governments will not be able to build adequate political counterweights to urban popular sectors. They will have to address, rather than finesse discontent from those sectors. The global trend toward more open political systems further strengthens the assumption. Since loosening macroeconomic discipline to satisfy popular pressures is self-defeating, the remaining alternative is considerably more energetic and creative attention to sectoral, subsectoral, and micromeasures designed to address some of the more pressing problems of the urban popular classes.

Ordinary people must be able to see some positive returns from adjustment, if they are to convert what is at best initial skepticism into more durable grumbling acquiescence. Several approaches are consistent with tight fiscal constraints. The list is not new, but deserves (and in many countries is now receiving) much higher priority. One approach is increasing the efficiency of existing programs and services and reorienting existing programs, probably mainly in social services, to better serve broad popular sectors. User fees will probably have to be introduced for many services, with exceptions for the poorest; the political acceptability of such fees may hinge on simultaneous improvements in quality. Public funds and foreign aid can be stretched by channeling them through or combining them with the resources of private voluntary organizations. In many countries, perhaps especially in Latin America, enforcement of tax laws already on the books should be tightened, not only for the additional revenue but also to reduce the anger that is widespread among popular classes that the wealthy are evading their share of adjustment costs.

None of these measures is easy, politically or administratively. But they are more feasible politically where the results are targeted fairly broadly, rather than emphasizing tight targeting to the poorest groups.

In addition to programmatic reforms and more extensive dialogue, governments should consider institutional innovations to encourage urban popular acquiescence. Analysis of strike, protest, and electoral patterns suggested a common underlying theme: urban working and popular class responses to adjustment reflect the degree to which current loss is softened by hopes for the future. Two perceptions are key: confidence in the government's ability to manage the economy, and the belief that they will share in future benefits. As Haggard and Kaufman discuss in their introduction to this volume, effective economic management usually requires that central economic authorities be shielded from popular political pressures. Nevertheless, in the context of global trends toward more open political systems, there is scope for creating or broadening channels through which urban working and popular classes can influence some of the allocational choices that bear on them directly. Tripartite wage and price commissions, or reforms in the process of setting priorities for municipal budgets offer examples. The growing sophistication and coordination among popular sector organizations mentioned earlier may strengthen both the need for and the feasibility of such institutional and procedural reforms. In short, institutional arrangements shape political responses, but institutions themselves can change. In the 1990s they are likely to draw more attention as policy variables than they received in the previous decade.

TABLE A5.1

Intensive Adjustment Countries: Annual Percentage Change in Real Government Expenditure Per Capita

	Education			Health		
	1970–80	1981–84	1985–87	1970–80	1981–84	1985–87
Chile	3.1	−3.4	−3.4	2.2	−4.8	−2.9
Costa Rica	8.6	−9.7	7.3	117.6	−7.0	1.7
Korea, Republic of	10.8	8.7	6.9	13.2	10.6	29.9
Mauritius	15.2	−2.5	0.0	5.6	3.6	4.1
Mexico	11.4	−1.8	−13.8	1.4	−4.8	−9.0
Morocco	8.1	−2.1	−1.9	1.8	−6.7	0.5
Pakistan	24.8	14.9	6.1	10.5	2.3	0.1
Thailand	6.4	5.3	−0.3	8.2	12.0	6.1
Togo	9.8	−1.1	3.0	−0.2	2.9	−8.0
Turkey	10.0	2.6	3.8	5.7	−25.7	12.0
Average	10.8	1.1	0.8	16.6	−1.8	3.4

Source: World Bank Country Economics Department, Adjustment Lending Policies for Sustainable Growth (1990), table 3.5.

TABLE A5.2
Selection of National Elections for Analysis

In 1990 the World Bank listed twenty-five "early intensive adjusting" countries, e.g., those having received two World Bank Structural Adjustment Loans (SALs), or three or more "adjustment operations" (SALs and sector adjustment loans) with the initial loan in 1985 or earlier. From these twenty-five countries, those were selected where national elections for the chief executive had been held after the adjustment program was launched, with opposition parties permitted to compete and winning at least fifteen percent of the popular vote. The full list of intensive adjusters is shown below, with those holding no or non-competitive elections identified in the second section.

Intensive Adjusters with Elections Meeting the Criteria

Bolivia 1989	Mauritius 1987
Chile 1989	Mexico 1989
Colombia 1986	Pakistan 1988
Costa Rica 1986	Philippines 1986
Jamaica 1989	Senegal 1988
Korea 1987	Thailand 1988
Madagascar 1989	Turkey: 1983, 1987

Intensive Adjusters Where no Elections Were Held or Elections Did Not Meet Criteria for Competitiveness

Brazil: The December 1989 election was held almost two years after the adjustment effort of the mid-1980s had collapsed.

Cote D'Ivoire: One-party elections October 1990.

Ghana: No national elections since adjustment program started in 1983. (District assembly elections were held.)

Jamaica: December 1983 elections were boycotted by the opposition party.

Kenya: One-party elections March 1988.

Malawi: No elections; President Banda holds life term.

Mauritania: No national elections since program launched. (Municipal elections were held 1986.)

Morocco: No national elections second half of the 1980s.

Nigeria: No national elections second half of the 1980s.

Tanzania: One-party elections October 1985.

Togo: One-party elections December 1986.

Zambia: One-party elections October 1988.

TABLE A5.3
Electoral Outcomes in Countries Undertaking Intensive Adjustment

Date of Election	Outcome	Popular Vote (%)	Noneconomic Issues and Other Comments
Korea December 1987	V	Dem. Justice (Roh)[a] 35.9 Reunification (Kim Y.) 27.5 Peace & Dem. (Kim D.) 26.5	Better relations with North Korea; reduced military role in politics.
Mauritius August 1987	V	Alliance (Jugnauth)[b] 49.3 Union 47.5	Alliance won 39 of 62 legislative seats.
Chile December 1989	D	DDC (Aylwin) 55.2 RN (Buchi)[a] 29.4 DP (Errazuriz) 15.4	Democratization issue dominant. Buchi ran on economic management issue.
Sri Lanka October 1982	V	UNP (Jayawardene)[b] 52.9 SLFP (Kobbekaduwa) 39.1	Ethnic violence a major issue. UNP stressed economic record and ability to maintain record.
Costa Rica February 1986	V	PLN (Arias)[a] 52.3 PUSC (Calderon) 45.8	Public support for good PLN economic management overcame tradition of alternating parties.
Thailand July 1988	V	Chart Thai[a] 24.1[c] Social Action 15.1 Dem. Party 13.4	King appoints Prime Minister. Economic reform minor issue.
Colombia May 1986	D	Liberals (Barco) 58.3 Conservatives (Gomez)[a] 35.9	Political violence a major issue.

TABLE A5.3 (*cont.*)

Date of Election	Outcome	Popular Vote (%)		Noneconomic Issues and Other Comments
Pakistan November 1988	D	PPP (Bhutto) IJI (Sharif)[a]	39.0 32.0	Democratization a major issue.
Turkey November 1983	"V"	ANAP (Özal) SDPP NDP	45.1 30.4 23.2	Özal had designed outgoing government's adjustment program but was not designated heir, which probably helped him win.
Turkey November 1987	V	ANAP (Özal)[b] SDPP TPP	36.3 24.7 19.1	Corruption issue harmed Özal.
Senegal February 1988		PS (Diouf)[b] PDS (Wade)	73.2 25.8	Democratization a major issue. PDS support strong in Dakar. Official results disputed.
Jamaica February 1989	D	PNP (Manley) JLP (Seaga)[b]	55.8 44.1	Lack of perceived concern for equity, and third term issues harmed Seaga.
Bolivia May 1989	"V"	MNR (Lozada)[a] ADN (Banzer) Mir (Paz Zamora)	23.0 22.7 19.6	All candidates endorsed adj. program. Lozada defeated in legislative run off.

Mexico July 1989	"D"	PRI (Salinas)[a] PPS (Cárdenas) PAN (Clouthier)	48.8 30.2 16.5	Unprecedentedly large non-PRI vote. Official results disputed. Political reform a major issue, adjustment also key. PPS support strong in Mexico City.
Madagascar March 1989	"D"	AREMA (Ratsiraka)[b] MFM/MFT Vonjy/VITM	62.6 22.0 14.0	Unprecedentedly large non-AREMA vote. Official results disputed. Political reform a major issue. All major candidates endorsed economic adjustment but social costs an issue.
Philippines February 1986	D	Aquino (Marcos)[b]	55 45	Democratization key issue.

Sources: Keesing's Record of World Events, World Elections, New York Times. Data on Pakistan from Pakistan Elections: Foundation for Democracy (Washington, D.C.: National Democratic Institute for International Affairs, 1989); data on Mauritius from Colin Legum and Marion E. Doro, eds., Africa Contemporary Record: 1987–88, vol. 20. (New York and London: Africana Publishing Co., 1989), p. B354.

[a] = incumbent's designated successor, or candidate of incumbent's party.

[b] = incumbent (running for re-election)

[c] Percent of legislative seats.

Key:　V　=　victory
　　　D　=　defeat
　　　"V"　=　quasi-victory
　　　"D"　=　quasi-defeat

TABLE A5.4
Economic Performance Indicators and Urban Popular Impact Indicators

| | Economic Performance Indicators | | | | Urban Popular Impact Indicators | | | | |
| | Overall Performance Summary | % annual growth in | | Gross Domestic Investment as % of GDP | Urban Impact Summary | CPI | % annual change in | | Urban Unemployment Level |
		GDP	Exports of GNFS				Real Average Wage	Private Consumption	
Korea 12/87	++				++				low
1985		6.9	4.5	29.3		2.5	4.7	4.6	
1986		12.3	26.1	28.8		2.8	2.9	6.0	
1987		11.6	21.6	29.2		3.0	13.0	6.9	
Mauritius 8/87	++				++				
1985		7.3	11.9	23.5		6.7	0	3.8	14.0
1986		10.3	27.0	21.9		1.9	6.9	2.6	NA
1987		10.6	16.9	26.0		0.5	21.3	13.7	5.0
Chile 12/89	++				+				
1987		5.7	9.8	16.9		21.5	−0.3	4.1	11.9
1988		7.4	8.8	17.0		12.7	6.7	8.3	10.2
1989		8.5	NA	NA		21.1	1.0	NA	7.5
Sri Lanka 10/82	+				+				
1980		5.5	3.6	33.8		26.2	−16.9	7.1	>13.6
1981		5.6	10.0	27.8		17.9	−10.0	3.1	>11.7
1982		3.8	4.5	30.7		10.8	17.9	12.7	
Thailand 7/88	++				+				fairly low
1985		3.4	10.5	24.0		2.4	4.2	−0.7	
1986		4.6	14.6	22.0		1.8	1.7	3.8	
1987		8.6	20.6	25.8		2.5	NA	6.3	
1988		11.1	19.6	27.5		3.9	NA	17.9	

Costa Rica 2/86	0+				++				
1983		2.8	−1.3	24.2		32.6	10.9	−1.9	8.5
1984		7.9	11.3	22.7		12.0	7.8	5.0	6.6
1985		0.8	−4.0	25.4		15.1	9.1	1.0	6.7
Colombia 5/86	+				+				
1983		1.6	−0.9	19.9		19.8	5.2	−0.8	11.7
1984		3.6	10.3	19.0		16.1	7.2	2.1	13.4
1985		3.3	14.4	19.0		24.0	−2.9	1.3	14.1
1986		6.1	20.7	18.0		18.9	4.8	−2.0	13.8
Pakistan 11/88	+				0?				
1986		5.6	32.8	18.3		3.5	NA	−3.8	low
1987		6.3	12.3	18.3		4.7	NA	0.5	
1988		7.5	−1.6	18.8		8.8	NA	7.4	
Turkey 11/83	+				−				
1981		4.4	85.1	22.0		30.6	−30.1	−3.4	11.2
1982		4.9	40.1	20.6		30.8	−13.1	−2.0	11.8
1983		3.9	13.7	19.6		32.9	0.6	4.0	12.4
Turkey 11/87	+				−				
1985		5.1	12.3	21.0		45.0	−5.8	0.8	12.6
1986		8.3	−1.5	24.4		34.6	−13.5	7.9	12.3
1987		7.5	27.3	25.4		38.8	−17.2	4.6	12.0
Jamaica 2/89	0+				0+				
1986		2.3	−6.7	18.5		10.5	NA	−2.0	10.9
1987		5.5	12.0	22.6		8.4	NA	2.0	8.6
1988		0.8	2.0	27.1		8.8	NA	NA	8.7
Senegal 2/88	0				0				
1985		3.9	−12.7	13.7		13.0	falling	7.4	fairly high
1986		4.8	5.0	14.6		6.2		−1.9	
1987		4.0	1.5	15.3		−4.1		−0.4	

Table A5.4 (cont.)
Economic Performance Indicators and Urban Popular Impact Indicators

	Economic Performance Indicators					Urban Popular Impact Indicators			
	Overall Performance Summary	% annual growth in		Gross Domestic Investment as % of GDP	Urban Impact Summary	% annual change in			Urban Unemployment Level
		GDP	Exports of GNFS			CPI	Real Average Wage	Private Consumption	
Bolivia 5/89	0				0				
1986		−2.9	12.1	5.6		66.0	−39.2	−4.7	7.0
1987		2.1	1.5	6.4		10.7	35.0	1.4	7.2
1988		2.8	11.6	10.5		21.5	21.2	−5.7	11.5
1989		2.5	NA	NA		15.7	NA	NA	10.2
Mexico 7/89	0				0				
1986		−4.0	−3.2	18.4		105.7	−5.6	−3.8	4.3
1987		1.6	9.8	18.6		139.2	2.1	−2.1	3.9
1988		1.5	3.0	20.8		51.7	−1.0	3.1	3.5
1989		3.0	—	—		18.2	—	NA	3.0
Madagascar 3/89	—				—				
1986		1.9	−1.9	8.9		14.5	falling	−2.3	Perhaps
1987		1.1	29.2	10.0		15.0		−9.5	lower in
1988		3.8	−5.0	13.0		NA		0.9	1988?
Philippines 2/86	—				—				
1983		1.2	9.0	26.7		10.0	23.1	3.3	
1984		−6.5	8.3	17.0		50.3	−13.7	−1.9	
1985		−4.6	−7.4	13.9		23.1	−3.0	−7.7	

Key: Overall Performance Summary   Urban Impact Summary
      + + = Strong Growth   + + = Considerable improvement
      +   = Growth   +   = Improvement
      0   = Stagnation   0   = Stagnation
      –   = Deterioration   –   = Deterioration

Sources: Annual growth of GDP, annual growth of exports of goods and nonfactor services, gross domestic investment as a percent of GDP, and annual change in private consumption per capita: World Bank, country data sheets for the 1990 "Adjustment Lending Policy Paper—Macroeconomic Indicators." Data available through 1988. 1989 growth in Bolivia, Mexico, and Chile are from ECLAC, *Preliminary Overview of the Economy of Latin America and the Caribbean* (1989), table 2, p. 18.

Consumer price index: For most countries: IMF, *International Financial Statistics Yearbook 1989.* For Chile, Mexico, and Bolivia: ECLAC, *Preliminary Overview,* table 5, p. 20 (used instead of IFS because elections occurred in 1989 or 1990 and ECLAC data covered 1988.)

Average real wages: Brazil, Colombia, Costa Rica, Chile, Mexico: ECLAC, *Preliminary Overview,* table 6, p. 20. Data cover workers in manufacturing, except Costa Rica (persons covered by social security system) and Chile (wage-earners not in agriculture). Brazil data are for São Paulo. Data from Rio de Janeiro are: 1984, 6.7%; 1985, 7.2%; 1986, 8.1%. Bolivia: ECLA, *Economic and Social Progress in Latin America 1989,* p. 276. Mauritius: World Bank, *Mauritius* (1989), table X.2, p. 145, covering real average monthly earnings in large establishments. Turkey: World Bank, *Turkey: Country Economic Memorandum,* table 16, p. 115. Data shown in table 1 are for workers in private sector establishments covered by SIS. A different index for private sector workers, in the same source, showed more positive wage trends. Sri Lanka: David Sahn. Data shown are for "all nonexecutive officers" in public service. Real minimum wages for Wage Boards Trade (private formal sector) workers in industry and commerce fell steadily: 1980, 4.9%; 1981, 12.5%; 1982, 1.9%. Senegal, Madagascar: descriptive estimates from World Bank staff. "Changes in the Living Standards of the Poor in Sri Lanka during a Period of Macroeconomic Restructuring," *World Development* 15, no. 16 (June 1987): 822 (table 8).

Urban unemployment: Latin American cases: ECLAC, *Preliminary Overview,* table 3, p. 19. Mauritius: World Bank, *Mauritius* (1989), table 5.1, p. 58. (Data given for every second year.) Sri Lanka: Surjit S. Bhalla and Paul Glewwe, "Growth and Equity in Developing Countries: A Reinterpretation of the Sri Lankan Experience," *World Bank Economic Review* (1987?), table 6, Data for the two consecutive years are based on two different indicators. Turkey: World Bank, *Turkey: Country Economic Memorandum,* table 3.1, p. 60. Madagascar: Descriptive estimate from World Bank staff.

CHAPTER SIX

The Political Economy of Inflation and Stabilization in Middle-Income Countries

Stephan Haggard and Robert R. Kaufman

IN A NUMBER of middle-income developing countries, the collapse of authoritarian governments and the widening of the arena of distributive politics coincided with severe inflationary crises. This confluence of political change and macroeconomic instability raises questions that have recurred throughout the post–World War II period. To what extent do distributive conflicts among contending social groups create macroeconomic imbalances? How are such political pressures affected by systems of representation? Are authoritarian regimes necessary for bringing high inflations under control? This chapter explores these questions through a comparative analysis of the politics of inflation and stabilization in seventeen Latin American and Asian countries. We focus in particular on the role of institutions, including the nature of the regime and party system, in structuring the incentives to both political elites and organized social groups.

We are interested in explaining two sets of macroeconomic outcomes, the first being differences in the *level* and *variability* of inflation over the long run. Why do some developing countries have high inflation while others maintain relative price stability? And why do countries with high mean inflation rates exhibit cycles of stop-go macroeconomic policy, cycles that may be more damaging for economic activity and political stability than high levels of inflation per se?[1] Our second concern is how political factors affect the timing of the initiation of stabilization packages and the ability to consolidate them in the face of political resistance.

The first section provides a theoretical overview. We outline the ways

We would like to thank Alberto Alesina, Bela Balassa, Richard Cooper, Vittorio Corbo, Max Corden, Merilee Grindle, Steven Webb, John Williamson, and the participants at workshops hosted by the World Bank, the Overseas Development Council, and the Center for International Affairs, Harvard University. We also thank the other members of this project—Miles Kahler, Barbara Stallings, Joan Nelson, Tom Callaghy, and John Waterbury—for comments on numerous earlier drafts.

[1] See Dani Rodrik, "Liberalization, Sustainability and the Design of Structural Adjustment Programs," Kennedy School of Government, Discussion Paper Series No. 177D Harvard University, March 1989.

in which macroeconomic policy and performance are influenced by the organizational strength of contending economic groups and by the political and institutional milieu in which they operate. The second section examines the way these factors have shaped the long-run inflation histories of three groups of middle-income countries: those that have maintained relatively stable macroeconomic policies and price levels over the long-run; those that have periodically experienced severe macroeconomic imbalances, but managed to adjust; and those that have experienced recurrent cycles of very high inflation over extended periods. The final section draws more extensively on case studies of particular inflation episodes to explore the conditions under which inflation has been brought down.

The political patterns that emerge from this analysis are extremely complex, and their influence must be weighed against the effect of a variety of economic factors that operate independently of politics.[2] Nonetheless, the country experiences we review provide evidence for three interrelated sets of propositions. The first and most general finding is that macroeconomic stability is profoundly affected by the political security of governmental elites and the extent of their independence from the pull of short-term distributive political pressures. Security of tenure is conditioned in part by electoral cycles, but viewed comparatively a more important factor is the overall degree of institutional stability. Political systems characterized by threats of coups and frequent changes of regime tend to have higher and more variable long-term inflation paths than more institutionalized systems, whether democratic or authoritarian.

A second broad theme concerns the role played by the organization of the party system in the maintenance of macroeconomic stability. In systems characterized by party fragmentation or by the recurrent exclusion of important political contenders from the electoral game, macroeconomic policy is more likely to be driven by "bidding wars" among contending political elites vying for support. These bidding wars reinforce cleavages among social groups and undermine efforts to maintain macroeconomic discipline. Conversely, long-term rates of inflation have been low in political systems in which strong authoritarian governments have managed either to establish dominant-party systems or to proscribe electoral politics entirely over extended periods of time. We find, however, that competitive constitutional regimes in the developing world are capable of sustaining macroeconomic stability where broad catchall parties mute the conflicts among contending social forces, facilitate relatively sta-

---

[2] Our effort to do this through pooled time-series regression analysis is contained in Stephan Haggard, Robert Kaufman, Karim Shariff, and Steven B. Webb, "Politics, Inflation, and Stabilization in Middle-Income Countries" (World Bank, 1990).

ble ruling majorities, and thus discourage abrupt swings in policy from one administration to the next.

Our third conclusion directly addresses the question of the ability of democratic and authoritarian regimes to restore price stability once inflation has accelerated.[3] We argue that the relative capacity of different types of regimes to stabilize is a function of the political dynamics that underlie inflationary pressures in the first place. Where rates of inflation have historically been low or moderate, constitutional and authoritarian regimes seem equally able to implement stabilization policies in the face of temporary shocks. On the other hand, in economies characterized by very high and persistent inflation, price stability has generally been restored under the auspices of labor-repressive authoritarian regimes. This pattern appears most prevalent precisely where fragmented party systems contribute to increased social conflict and the entrenchment of inflationary expectations.

Before beginning our analysis, two objections might be raised to the particular emphasis we place on the domestic political sources of inflation. It could be argued that domestic political conflict is less important for understanding inflation and stabilization than exogenous shocks, including particularly external ones. International shocks do figure prominently in our story, but we find that countries' vulnerability to these shocks and their ability to adjust are closely related to domestic policy and politics.

It could also be argued that a preoccupation with inflation and stabilization too readily accepts "orthodox" and monetarist prescriptions of the problems facing developing countries. First, orthodox stabilization measures may be inappropriate for managing very high inflations or where strong inertial forces are at work. Second, it is wrong to portray stabilization as an end in itself. Macroeconomic management is ultimately a tool for achieving growth objectives, and some inflation may be tolerable if the costs of stabilization in terms of lost output are high. Resistance to stabilization may thus stem not only from the play of political interests, but from substantive disagreements over development strategy, tradeoffs among different economic objectives, and the efficacy of orthodox policy prescriptions.[4]

Though these caveats are important, we find an increasing consensus that high inflation has proved extremely costly and that coherent demand management policies are a necessary prerequisite for sustainable eco-

[3] For a review of this debate, see Stephan Haggard and Robert Kaufman, "The Politics of Stabilization and Structural Adjustment," in Jeffrey D. Sachs, ed., *Developing Country Debt and Economic Performance* (Chicago: University of Chicago Press, 1989), pp. 232–39.

[4] See for example, Lance Taylor, *Structuralist Macroeconomics: Applicable Models for the Third World* (New York: Basic Books, 1983), chap. 11.

nomic growth.[5] Even advocates of "heterodox" stabilization policies that involve wage and price controls or the use of the exchange rate as a nominal anchor recognize that such measures have never worked in the absence of complementary orthodox measures of fiscal and monetary control. There is also increasing agreement that longer-term measures of structural adjustment will not be effective unless inflation is brought under control.

THE POLITICAL ECONOMY OF INFLATION

Albert Hirschman has pointed out that "the explanation of inflation in terms of social conflict between groups, each aspiring to a greater share of the social product, has become the sociologist's monotonous equivalent of the economist's untiring stress on the undue expansion of the money supply."[6] To make such an approach plausible, we must provide an account of the economic mechanisms through which group conflicts translate into inflation and show how political paramaters might affect these conflicts.

There are several mechanisms through which distributive conflicts might translate into higher prices by creating political pressures for an accommodative monetary policy. One is cost-push; where unions and popular sector groups are strong, whether because of government support or a high degree of organization, wage settlements are likely to be more generous than in those countries where such groups are organizationally weak.[7] Similarly, inflationary pressures may arise or be exacerbated by the monopoly or oligopoly pricing practices of concentrated industrial and agricultural groups. Whether cost-push pressures emanate from labor or capital, they take on particular significance in countries where wages and prices are indexed to past rates of inflation. In such systems, price shocks emanating from one sector will be transmitted rapidly throughout the rest of the economy.

[5] See for example John Williamson, ed., *Latin American Adjustment: How Much Has Happened?* (Washington, D.C.: Institute of International Economics, 1990).

[6] Albert Hirschman, "Reflections on the Latin American Experience," in Leon Lindberg and Charles S. Maier, *The Politics of Inflation and Stagnation* (Washington, D.C.: The Brookings Institution, 1985), pp. 57–58.

[7] This mechanism has been a central concern of much of the literature on the political economy of inflation in the advanced industrial states. See for example R. Michael Alvarez, Geoffrey Garrett and Peter Lange, "The Political Economy of Macroeconomic Performance: the Advanced Industrial Democracies, 1967–1984" (Paper prepared for the annual meetings of the American Political Science Association, Atlanta GA, 30 August–3 September 1989). Labor strength can also result in inflationary pressures indirectly through indexation. Indexation reduces opposition to inflation, and increases the vulnerability of the economy to exogenous price shocks; we return to this problem below.

A second source of inflationary pressure lies with fiscal policy, which in turn can be traced to competing claims on fiscal resources either in the form of increased spending or resistance to taxation. The inflationary impact of a given fiscal stance will depend on the share of budget deficits that are financed by money creation, the size of the monetary base, and the demand for money. Nonetheless, a growing literature has documented that budget deficits financed by seignorage have played a crucial role in developing country inflation.[8]

Under what conditions are inflationary pressures contained? Our case studies suggest that part of the answer lies in aspects of state organization discussed by Peter Evans and John Waterbury in chapters 3 and 4 of this volume. In particular, we note the importance of the degree of political insulation of technocratic elites within finance ministries, central banks, and budgeting offices. Yet any analysis of the influence of technocratic groups must be placed in the context of the broader social and political influences that structure their relationship with political elites and organized social interests.

Sociological Approaches to Inflation

We therefore begin with approaches that focus directly on social structure and the presence and strength of what Mancur Olson has called "distributive coalitions."[9] In our cross-regional sample, a variety of social cleavages appear that might influence macroeconomic policy, including sectoral, ethnic, regional, and religious ones. But industrial and public sector unions are likely to be particularly important, since they have been at the core of urban-based "populist" movements that have pressed not only for higher wages, but for an expansion of transfers, social services, and patronage.

Demographic data presented in table 6.1 provide some indirect evidence that popular sector groups arising out of the processes of urbanization and industrialization may have some effect on inflation. Mean annual inflation rates in our sample for the period from 1960 through 1980 correlate fairly strongly with urbanization in 1960 (0.61) and with indus-

[8] The monetization of fiscal deficits can contribute to inflation through an indirect route as well. Where exchange rates are fixed, sometimes in the effort to post a nominal anchor to the economy, overvaluation can result. When the exchange rate is subsequently devalued, it can exacerbate inflation. For a comparison of the fiscal and exchange rate approaches to inflation, see Peter Montiel, "Empirical Analysis of High-Inflation Episodes in Argentina, Brazil, and Israel," *IMF Staff Papers* 36, no. 3 (September 1989): 527–49. It should also be noted that *anticipated* cost-push pressures, fiscal deficits, and exchange rate movements can also have an influence on current inflation under the assumption of rational expectations; we return to these expectational factors in our discussion of particular cases.

[9] Mancur Olson, *The Rise and Decline of Nations* (New Haven: Yale University Press, 1982).

try's share of GDP in 1960 (0.56). On the other hand, more direct indicators of distributive conflict, such as the extent of labor organization and the degree of income inequality, suggest a far weaker relationship. Though the data must be viewed with caution, the simple correlation between unionization and inflation from 1960–80 for this sample of countries is low (0.17). The relationship between inequality and inflation is actually negative (−0.23).[10] High-inflation countries such as Chile, Argentina, and Uruguay have comparatively low levels of inequality, while Malaysia, Venezuela, and Colombia have long records of price stability and high levels of income concentration.

These results may spring from the fact that the proxies for measuring the strength of distributional coalitions and the intensity of the conflicts among them are not good. A large industrial work force can be weakly organized, as those in Korea and Taiwan have been until quite recently, while a relatively small urban population can play a political role disproportionate to its actual numbers. Nevertheless, even with better measures, an exclusive focus on the strength of contending groups and the relationship among them is likely to obscure the actual political processes that contribute to inflation. Keeping these underlying sociological factors in mind, we turn, therefore, to a more extended discussion of several alternative political explanations that will recur in the empirical sections that follow, including: electoral constraints and changes of government, the constitutent base and ideological orientations of governments, and the organization of party systems and the nature of the regime.

Electoral Cycles and Changes of Government

Strategic models of elections focus on the time horizons of politicians, and assume some ability to exploit a trade-off between inflation and output.[11]

---

[10] For two accounts that stress the importance of income distribution for macroeconomic performance, see Jeffrey D. Sachs, "External Debt and Macroeconomic Performance in Latin America and East Asia," *Brookings Papers on Economic Activity* 2 (1985): 523–73 and "Social Conflict and Populist Policies in Latin America," National Bureau of Economic Research Working Paper No. 2897 (March 1989).

[11] The original statement of this perspective is William Nordhaus, "The Political Business Cycle," *Review of Economic Studies* 42: 169–90. For an empirical treatment with reference to the developing countries, see Barry Ames, *Political Survival: Politicians and Public Policy in Latin America* (Berkeley: University of California Press, 1987). The rational expectations literature has made the assumption of myopic voters and a Phillips curve tradeoff controversial. For a critique along these lines, see Brian Barry, "Does Democracy Cause Inflation? Political Ideas of Some Economists," in Leon N. Lindberg and Charles S. Maier, *The Politics of Inflation and Economic Stagnation* (Washington, D.C.: The Brookings Institution, 1985). For attempts to defend the expectations-augmented Phillips curve, see Robert E. Lucas, Jr., "An Equilibrium Model of Business Cycles," *Journal of Political Economy* 83, no. 6 (December 1975): 1113–44; Stanley Fischer, "Long-term Contracts, Rational Expectations, and the Optimal Money Supply Rule," *Journal of Political Economy* 85, no. 1 (Feb-

TABLE 6.1
Social and Economic Structure and Inflation in East Asia and Latin America

	Urban Population/ Total (1960)	Industry/ GDP (1960)	Share of Labor Force in Unions (c. 1975)	Income: Highest Fifth/ Lowest Fifth	Average Annual Inflation	
					1965–80	1980–86
Argentina	71%	38%	25%	11.4	78.3%	326.2%
Brazil	45	35	na	33.3	31.3	157.1
Chile	69	38	25	11.4	129.9	20.2
Colombia	47	26	13	21.1	17.4	22.6
Costa Rica	34	19	12	16.6	11.3	32.3
Jamaica	30	38	25	na	12.8	19.8
Mexico	50	29	20	15.1	13.1	63.7
Peru	47	29	37	32.1	20.5	100.1
Uruguay	73	28	25	10.8	57.8	50.4
Venezuela	68	22	45	18.0	8.7	8.7
Mean, Latin America	53.4	30.2	25.2	18.9	38.1	80.1
Indonesia	15	17	10	na	34.3	8.9
Korea	28	19	10	7.5	18.8	5.4
Malaysia	26	18	15	16.0	4.9	1.4
Philippines	30	28	na	13.6	11.7	18.2
Taiwan	35	29	11	4.2	8.3	5.8
Thailand	13	19	na	8.9	6.8	3.0
Turkey	30	21	8	na	20.7	37.3
Mean, Asia	25.3	21.6	10.8	10.0	15.1	11.4

Sources: World Bank, World Development Report 1978 (Washington, D.C.: World Bank, 1978); World Bank, World Bank Development Report 1988 (New York: Oxford University Press, 1988); Republic of China, Council on Economic Planning and Development, Taiwan Statistical Data Book 1988 (Taipei: CEPD, 1988); Charles Lewis Taylor and David Jodice, World Handbook of Political and Social Indicators (New Haven: Yale University Press, 1983); Jeffrey Sachs, "Social Conflict and Populist Policies in Latin America," National Bureau of Economic Research Working Paper No. 2897 (March 1989).

Note: Means are unweighted averages. Data on income distribution is from household surveys in the late 1960s or early 1970s. Industry share of GDP is probably biased upwards for the Latin American countries because of higher levels of protection.

In the preelection period, incumbent governments will be sensitive to unemployment, particularly if popular sector groups are politically mobilized. This sensitivity may be equally acute in new democratic regimes seeking to consolidate their power or in military regimes engineering a transition to democracy. Inflationary macroeconomic policy may thus also be a product of regime changes, as well as institutionalized electoral cycles.[12]

Though this strategic view of macroeconomic policy has been used to explain cyclical movements of output and prices within individual countries, it can be expanded to explain cross-national differences in inflation. Political instability shortens the time horizons of politicians, and can provide recurrent incentives to inflate, overvalue the currency, and borrow. This results in an inflation path that is higher than would occur under a more stable political setting.[13] In our cross-sectional analysis, we expect that political systems in which there are frequent elections and changes of government, recurrent challenges to the security of officeholders, or frequent changes of regime will have both higher and more variable inflation.

Political Orientation of the Government in Power

A related set of arguments focuses on differences in the political strategies and constituent bases of governments. In this line of analysis, the preferences of politicians for accommodative or restrictive macroeconomic policies are related not to elections or broader political changes, but to the interests of different constituent bases.[14] One problem with such argu-

ruary 1977): 191–206. For a discussion of several models of the political business cycle that attempt to incorporate rational expectations, see Alberto Alesina, "Politics and Business Cycles in Industrial Democracies," *Economic Policy* 9 (April 1989): 63–64 and William Nordhaus, "Alternative Approaches to the Political Business Cycle," *Brookings Papers on Economic Activity* 2 (1989): 1–68.

[12] For a further analysis of the constraints on new democratic governments, see Stephan Haggard and Robert Kaufman, "Economic Adjustment in New Democracies," in Joan Nelson, ed., *Fragile Coalitions: The Politics of Economic Adjustment* (New Brunswick, N.J.: Transaction Books, 1989).

[13] For theoretical attempts to model why changes of government are likely to result in macroeconomic instability, see Alberto Alesina, "Macroeconomic Policy in a Two-Party System as a Repeated Game," *Quarterly Journal of Economics* 102 (August 1987): 651–78; Alberto Alesina and Allan Drazen, "Why Are Stabilizations Delayed? A Political-Economic Model" (Unpublished ms., 1990); and Alex Cukierman, Sebastian Edwards and Guido Tabellini, "Seignorage and Political Instability" (Paper presented at the National Bureau of Economic Research (NBER) conference on Political Economy, May 1989).

[14] This line of work was pioneered by Douglas Hibbs, "Political Parties and Macroeconomic Policy," *American Political Science Review* 71 (December 1977): 146–87. For reviews, see James E. Alt and K. Alec Chrystal, *Political Economics* (Berkeley: University of California Press, 1980), pp. 103–25; Douglas A. Hibbs, Jr., *The American Political Econ-*

ments is that they say little about the circumstances in which the different types of government are likely to come to power. The presence of a "left" or "right" government in power may be endogenous to other social and political variables, including the strength of different social groups and the logic of political competition under alternative party structures. Nonetheless, it is still necessary to assess the connection between different coalitional appeals and macroeconomic strategies.

The range of political orientations in the developing world is wider than in the advanced industrial states, with greater representation at the extremes. Rather than the simple right-left distinction employed in the advanced industrial democracies, we divide governments into four categories based principally on our judgement of the extent to which they seek to defend or change existing distributions of income and assets. At one extreme are rightist governments that are explicitly antagonistic toward labor and seek to defend the position of business elites, large landowners, and upper middle-class groups. These governments might be expected to pursue the most conservative macroeconomic policy, although their constituents might well seek subsidies that could have macroeconomic consequences, particularly given their likely resistance to taxation. At the other extreme are governments committed to a radical redistribution of income and assets toward organized labor and other low-income groups. We will call these governments populist, although the category includes socialist experiments, such as the Allende period in Chile and the Manley governments of the 1970s in Jamaica as well. Because their political commitments to redistribution are likely to involve extensive fiscal commitments, difficulties in raising taxes, and favorable wage settlements for public and private sector workers, we expect these governments to have the most expansionist macroeconomic policies and the highest inflation. In between these extremes are center-right governments, which correspond roughly to this category among the advanced industrial states, and moderately reformist governments of the center-left, typified by the reformist Latin American governments of the 1960s that were favored by the Alliance for Progress.

Party Systems

The final theoretical approach stresses the independent effect of institutional arrangements on macroeconomic policy. As we have suggested, there are a number of institutional variables that may be of significance, including the independence of the central bank and the role of techno-

---

omy (Cambridge, Mass.: Harvard University Press, 1987), pp. 213–32; Alesina, "Politics and Business Cycles in Industrial Democracies"; Nordhaus, "Alternative Approaches to the Political Business Cycle."

cratic agencies in the budgetary process.[15] We focus here, however, on the effects of political parties, distinguishing between so-called fragmented, aggregative, and monist party systems.

Fragmented party systems are ones in which social cleavages, ideological divisions, and/or electoral rules (particularly proportional representation) result in a proliferation of parties. There are several reasons why such systems may intensify distributive conflicts and macroeconomic instability. Fragmentation encourages bidding wars among rival political elites seeking to strength their base of support with relatively narrow, ideologically-oriented constituencies. Such systems are more likely than others to polarize into blocs that define their interests in zero-sum terms. Fragmented party systems are also more likely to generate coalition governments held together by extensive, and costly, sidepayments.[16] Particularly where centrist forces are weak and coalition governments unstable, alternations of government in these systems may be expected to result in wider swings of basic policy orientation and a greater likelihood of sharp oscillations in macroeconomic policy.[17]

Aggregative party systems are those in which governments can consistently mobilize electoral support through one or two broadly-based centrist parties. This would include party systems such as Malaysia's and Mexico's that permit opposition, but incorporate contending ethnic or class groups within the framework of a semi-official party organization, as well as dominant party systems such as India's. We would also include in this category institutionalized two-party systems such as Venezuela, Colombia, Costa Rica, and the Philippines in the 1950s and 1960s in which multiclass parties compete for similar constituencies, and either share power or alternate in office.

Aggregative party systems are by no means immune to inflationary pressures. In most of these systems, patronage has at times placed major strains on fiscal resources. In at least one instance, Jamaica, strong left forces *within* one of the major parties contributed to a broader polarization of the political system. Nonetheless, the features of such systems place important limits on tendencies toward macroeconomic instability. Precisely because catchall parties cut broadly across major social cleavages, they restrict opportunities for linking electoral appeals to class or

[15] See Robert Lacey, "The Management of Public Expenditures: An Evolving Bank Approach," World Bank Policy, Planning and Research Working Paper No. 46, January 1989; John T. Woolley, *Monetary Politics: The Federal Reserve and the Politics of Monetary Policy* (Cambridge: Cambridge University Press, 1984).

[16] Jeffrey D. Sachs and Nouriel Roubini, "Political and Economic Determinants of Budget Deficits in the Industrial Democracies," NBER Working Paper No. 2682, 1988.

[17] This effect is emphasized in Alberto Alesina, "Macroeconomic Policy in a Two-Party System," and Alesina and Drazen, "Why are Stabilizations Delayed?"

narrow sectoral interests, encourage policy continuity across successive administrations, and diminish the freedom of maneuver of opposition forces outside of the broad center.

Finally, distributive conflicts are likely to be weakest in monist systems where state elites have suppressed electoral competition, or where an official party has effectively claimed a monopoly of power. Our expectations about distributive conflict in such systems are empirical as much as theoretical, and may simply reflect the absence of revolutionary governments in our sample. Some revolutionary governments, such as Cuba, Nicaragua, and Vietnam, have used an offical party apparatus to spearhead class struggles and to enforce substantial redistribution of income and assets. Where political competition has been restricted in middle-income countries, however, it is usually to *limit* the play of distributive politics and to block antielite challenges from gaining momentum.

Our reasoning is also theoretical, however. No-party authoritarian regimes or those based on exclusive dominant parties will provide less political space for interest groups to organize or gain effective representation, and greater autonomy for technocratic elites.

Monist systems are by definition authoritarian, but it is important to underline that not all authoritarian regimes are willing or able to suppress electoral politics. Electoral mobilization is possible in authoritarian systems during periods of transition to democratic rule, when opposition forces have coalesced against the government's wishes, or where an opposition is allowed to operate under some constraints. In such circumstances, nominally authoritarian polities may exhibit characteristics of fragmented or aggregative party systems.

POLITICAL SOURCES OF INFLATION OVER THE LONG RUN

In this section, we focus on the political correlates of inflation over the long run. Table 6.2 provides two ways of assessing the inflation histories of the countries in our sample. The first is the mean annual rate of inflation covering the periods from 1960–80 and from 1981–86. To obtain a picture of the variability of inflation over time, and to isolate the way political factors affect specific stabilization efforts, we have also identified various "inflation episodes"; years during which inflations peak over a specific threshold. Peaks between 15 and 29 percent are considered episodes of "moderate" inflation, those between 30 and 89 percent are considered "high," and those over 90 percent, "very high."[18]

[18] Identifying an "episode" is difficult, since inflation may creep upward for a number of years before finally crossing an arbitrary dividing line, or may cross the threshold and remain at a constant, but higher level. Our method here is to group together those years when the *rate* of inflation increased without interruption into a single episode, based on the highest

Both the mean annual inflation rates since 1960 and the incidence of inflation episodes suggest three broad national inflation histories. One group of countries has been characterized by a consistent record of price stability for most of the last three decades. We include in this group Malaysia, Thailand, Taiwan, and Venezuela. For reasons we will explain, we place Colombia in this category despite its somewhat higher level of inflation. At the other extreme are a group of very high inflation countries that experienced recurrent and severe cycles of inflation over extended periods: Argentina, Brazil, Uruguay, and Chile before the mid-1970s.

The remainder of the countries have mixed records, but fall into one of several categories. Jamaica, Turkey, Indonesia, and Costa Rica have had relatively severe inflations that were confined to short periods of time, and Korea and the Philippines have had recurrent cycles of moderate inflation. We also include in this category Mexico and Peru, two countries that had long histories of low inflation, but experienced serious and sustained inflationary pressures in the 1980s.

Low Inflation Countries

Countries with extended records of price stability provide a useful comparative backdrop for understanding those cases in which more serious inflationary pressures emerge. Malaysia, Thailand, Taiwan, and Venezuela all maintained annual average inflation rates of less than 10 percent from 1960 through 1986. These countries have not been immune from periods of accelerating inflation: Malaysia in 1974; Thailand in 1973–74 and 1980; Venezuela in 1979–80 and 1987; and Taiwan in 1960, 1973, and 1980. With the exception of the episode in 1960 in Taiwan which was the result of increased government spending in connection with the Taiwan Straits crisis, and Venezuela's difficulties in the 1980s these inflations were largely the result of external shocks.

The range of countries that fall into this category suggests that it is possible to sustain price stability within the context of different economic structures and development strategies. It could be argued that export in-

---

annual inflation rate reached. Similarly, we group together all years of stable, but higher inflation as a single episode (see appendix table A6.1)

A second problem is that crossing an artificial threshold may not be viewed by authorities as constituting a policy problem, while changes within categories may be. Moreover, in selecting and analyzing cases, it is essential to be attentive to the rates of change of inflation as well as inflation itself. An increase in the rate of inflation from 5 to 10 percent may be as explosive for a society accustomed to stable prices as a change from 50 percent to 100 percent in a country that has lived with rapid price increases for long periods of time. We believe that we have captured all of the relevant inflation/stabilization episodes through our strategy, but in gauging the political and policy significance of price increases, there is no substitute for the analysis of particular cases.

TABLE 6.2
Cross-national Patterns of Inflation

	Mean Annual Inflation		Inflation Episodes (Year of Peak Inflation; Inflation Rate)
	1960–80	1980–86	
Low Inflation Countries			
Malaysia	4.9	1.4	1974 (16.1)
Taiwan	8.3	5.8	1960 (18.4); 1974 (47.5); 1980 (19.0)
Thailand	6.8	3.0	1974 (24.3); 1980 (19.7)
Venezuela	8.7	8.7	1980 (21.5)
Colombia	17.4	22.6	1963 (32.0); 1966 (19.1); 1977 (33.1)
Countries with Mixed Records			
Costa Rica	11.3	32.3	1974 (30.1); 1982 (90.1)
Jamaica	12.8	19.8	1974 (27.2); 1978 (34.9); 1984 (27.8)
Mexico	13.1	63.7	1977 (29.0); 1987 (131.8)
Peru	20.5	100.1	1968 (19.0); 1975 (23.6); 1981 (75.4) 1985 (163.4)
Indonesia	34.3	8.9	1966 (1044.8); 1973 (40.6); 1978 (18.2)
Korea	18.8	5.4	1964 (29.5); 1970 (16.1); 1975 (25.3); 1980 (28.7)
Philippines	11.7	18.2	1971 (21.4); 1974 (34.2); 1980 (18.2); 1984 (50.3)
Turkey	20.7	37.3	1975 (19.2); 1980 (110.2)
High Inflation Countries			
Argentina	78.3	326.2	1952 (38.1); 1959 (113.9); 1966 (31.7); 1971 (61.2); 1976 (443.2); 1985 (672.1); 1987 (229.7)
Brazil	31.3	157.1	1956 (21.8); 1959 (51.9); 1964 (91.4); 1979 (52.7); 1987 (227.1)
Chile	129.9	20.2	1955 (84.0); 1959 (33.3); 1963 (45.3); 1970 (34.9); 1974 (504.7)
Uruguay	57.8	50.4	1959 (39.5); 1968 (125.3); 1973 (97.0); 1986 (76.4)

Sources: International Monetary Fund, International Financial Statistics (various issues); Republic of China, Council on Economic Planning and Development, Taiwan Statistical Data Book 1988 (Taipei: CEPD, 1988).

Note: Inflation is year-on-year change in the consumer price index. Inflation episodes are years when the inflation rate crosses one of three thresholds: moderate inflations exceed 15 percent for a calendar year, high inflations exceed 30 percent, and very high inflations, 90 percent. An episode includes all those years when the rate of inflation increased without interruption, based on the highest annual inflation rate reached; peak inflation rate is in parentheses.

terests are particularly sensitive to relative price changes, and that the Asian economies have lower inflation than their Latin American counterparts because they are more open to trade. The contrast between Taiwan and Korea suggests interesting differences among the export-oriented East Asian newly industrialized countries (NICs), however, with inflation substantially higher in Korea. Moreover, macroeconomic stability was a prerequisite to export-oriented policies. Taiwan and Korea both became more open to trade only *after* stabilizing their economies.[19]

It could also be argued that Venezuela's status as an oil exporter makes it a special case. But Venezuela resembles the other Latin American countries in terms of its industrial strategy, with a large state-owned enterprise sector devoted to secondary import substitution in intermediate and capital goods and high levels of protection. Moreover, Mexico is also an oil exporter and had much higher inflation in the 1980s.

The political systems of the low-inflation countries appear to be quite diverse. Venezuela is a two-party democracy. Malaysia has been democratic since independence, with the exception of a brief interlude of emergency rule. It has been governed continuously by a ruling coalition that integrates conservative parties from the three ethnic communities, but in which the dominant Malay party is primus inter pares. Until the mid-1970s, Thailand had a long history of military rule. A brief liberalization in 1973–74 was reversed by a military coup, but since 1978, the country has undergone a process of democratization. The Kuomintang party (KMT) has ruled Taiwan continuously since 1945, but began a far-reaching political liberalization in the mid-1980s.

Notwithstanding the apparent differences, these political systems exhibit certain commonalities. First, politicians were insulated from distributive claims "from below," either because popular sector groups were weak, or because party structures or other institutional arrangements limited their organizational and coalitional possibilities, or some combination of the two. Second, these institutions generally exhibited continuity over a substantial period of time, providing the policy system with a high degree of stability. Finally, in part because of these political characteristics, politicians appeared more willing to delegate authority to technocratic decision makers who in turn enjoyed both organizational autonomy and a high degree of credibility.

Taiwan and Thailand achieved stable macroeconomic policy under authoritarian auspices. Taiwan experienced a hyperinflation in the late 1940s as a result of the expansive monetary policy used to finance the

[19] Jeffrey D. Sachs, "Trade and Exchange Rate Policies in Growth-Oriented Adjustment Programs," in Vittorio Corbo, Morris Goldstein, and Mohsin Khan, eds., *Growth-Oriented Adjustment Programs* (Washington, D.C.: International Monetary Fund and World Bank, 1987).

KMT's military efforts on the mainland. Under strong pressure from the United States and rapidly declining reserves, the government instituted an innovative currency and financial reform that raised real interest rates for savers. Drawing a close connection between the hyperinflation and the political disaster on the mainland, the political leadership vested the monetary authorities with substantial authority and committed themselves to gold standard rules of adjustment under a fixed exchange rate regime. The head of the Central Bank has usually been a person of high political stature, and both fiscal and monetary policy have been tightly controlled by technocrats. The scope for any independent organization by interest-groups or parties has been severely limited until recently; needless to say, their influence on macroeconomic policy has been nil.

Thailand provides a sharp contrast to Taiwan. Since a military coup in 1932 introduced a constitutional monarchy, the country's politics have been dominated by the military, but with a number of coups, coup attempts, and ongoing intramilitary conflicts. Urban political mobilization also increased during the political liberalization of 1973–74 and in the 1980s. During these controlled democratic openings, the party system has been extremely fragmented.

The apparent instability associated with government changes and the fragmented nature of the party system runs counter to several of the hypotheses concerning low-inflation countries previously elaborated. To an important extent, however, macroeconomic stability has been sustained because of other social and institutional factors that limit the impact of distributive conflicts. The urban population and industrial work force is small compared to other countries in our sample, limiting the political importance of the union movement until recently. In spite of democratic openings, moreover, the political system has been dominated more or less continuously by an alliance between the military, the monarchy, and the civil bureaucracy. In one of the few reversals in the recent global wave of democratization, the military launched a coup in February 1991, revealing once again their veto power over nominally democratic politics. Although the party system is severely fragmented, it is not divided sharply in ideological terms, the legislature has not been a significant locus of economic policy initiatives, even during democratic interludes, and all of the parties maintain links to key military factions. A relatively insulated Budget Office and Central Bank, built up during the extended and continuous period of military rule under Generals Sarit and Thanom from 1959 through 1973, continued to exercise tight control over macroeconomic decision-making throughout the 1970s and 1980s.

Venezuela and Malaysia are important cases, since they demonstrate that similar outcomes are possible under democratic as well as authoritarian auspices. In Venezuela, oil income has no doubt played an important role in mitigating social conflict. Nonetheless, economic decision-making has also been insulated from popular sector pressures by the electoral dominance of two nationally-organized, vertically-integrated, multiclass parties, the Acción Democrática (AD) and the Comité de Organización Política Electoral Independiente (COPEI). De facto, the parties have established a collaborative relationship and limited the space for independent popular sector or leftist forces to operate. Labor's relationship with the parties, particularly AD, has been institutionalized, but it has not translated directly into influence since each party also has substantial support from business groups and competes for roughly the same cross-class constituency.

These structures have not wholly immunized Venezuela against either inflation or other macroeconomic imbalances, and as the partisan theory of inflation would predict, the alternation of parties in office has produced important policy shifts. The administration of Carlos Andrés Pérez (1973–78) initially adopted a populist stance. This was shortly toned down, but the government did initiate a major expansion of public employment and investment in the state-owned enterprise sector, exploiting Venezuela's status as an oil exporter to borrow heavily on the Euromarkets. An overvalued exchange rate dampened pressure on prices over the 1970s. By 1979, however, an increase in inflation and perceptions of economic mismanagement contributed to a COPEI victory at the polls, followed quickly by a stabilization plan.

Precisely because of fears of inflation, the COPEI government persisted in supporting the overvalued bolivar, which encouraged capital flight and further pressure on the currency. Venezuela's debt crisis broke in February 1983. The core of the adjustment program was a large devaluation coupled with the initiation of a multiple exchange rate system designed to insulate the real sector from the effects of speculative capital movements. The government also took strong fiscal measures, which probably contributed to COPEI's electoral defeat later that year.

By now, however, the rival AD leaders also accepted the importance of reversing inflationary expectations and both the Lusinchi (1984–88) and the Pérez (1989–) governments undertook stabilization plans that included controversial elements, such as subsidy cuts and curbs on public investment. The AD was also able to restrain wage increases through its direct links with, and control over, the Venezuelan Workers' Confederation, which accounts for approximately 80 percent of the country's organized workforce. Stabilization efforts were complicated under Lusinchi by the collapse of oil prices and under Pérez by widespread riots against adjustment measures in 1989, and it remains far from clear Venezuela has finally returned to its low-inflation equilibrium. Nonetheless, it is clear that the two-party system has facilitated the imposition of stabilization programs in a democratic context.

Malaysia also demonstrates the importance of institutional arrangements for managing group conflicts, though the salient cleavages are different. Prior to the general election of 1969, serious violence erupted between the Chinese and Malay communities. Following a brief suspension of democratic rule, a new government moved to construct a "grand coalition" that would integrate conservative leaders of the Chinese and Indian communities, while maintaining and further institutionalizing Malay dominance of the political system.

Policies designed to assist the Malays (*bumiputra*), including an expansion of the state-owned enterprise sector, contributed to large fiscal deficits in the early 1970s, but high domestic savings rates and lucrative trade taxes have made it possible to finance them in a noninflationary way; indeed, there is only a weak relationship between fiscal deficits and inflation in Malaysia.[20] These economic features of the Malaysian economy have clearly contributed to the low-inflation outcome. Yet it can be argued that the political insulation and conservative orientation of the Malaysian monetary authorities, a legacy of the British currency board, also contributed to the outcome. Monetary policy has been used actively in the face of economic downturns, but has also responded quickly to sterilize increases in net foreign assets as well. Moreover, such other favorable factors as the country's high savings rates are attributable to government policy, which, among other measures, forces savings through high social security contributions. In general, the Alliance party has shielded macroeconomic policy from political contention.

Colombia constitutes somewhat of a special case. Higher rates of inflation set it apart from other low-inflation countries, but like them Colombia has been relatively successful in avoiding sharp fluctuations in the price level. Colombia experienced an increase in inflation rates in the 1970s, but managed to maintain a relatively constant level of inflation of about 20 percent thereafter; the standard deviation of Colombia's mean inflation from 1960 through 1987 is virtually the same as Thailand's.

Colombia's two-party system resembles Venezuela's in its cross-class electoral appeal. As Barbara Stallings has argued, the "quasidemocratic" alliance between the two major parties, the Liberals and Conservatives, "placed boundaries on the types of policies that could be followed, preventing the violent economic swings that typified Chile and Peru."[21] In

[20] Mohamed Ariff, "Inflation in Malaysia—An Empirical Survey," in Chung-Hua Institution for Economic Research, *Conference on Inflation in East Asian Countries* (Taipei: Chung-Hua Institution, Conference Series No. 2, 1983).

[21] Barbara Stallings, "Politics and Economic Crisis: A Comparative Study of Chile, Peru,

1968, constitutional reforms backed by the leaders of the two dominant parties virtually eliminated congressional control over fiscal and monetary policy, further enhancing executive autonomy.

Colombia has faced political constraints on its macroeconomic policymaking. In the presidential elections of 1970 the joint candidate of the traditional parties was almost defeated by the ex-dictator, Gustavo Rojas-Panilla, who campaigned on a strongly redistributionist platform. Organized labor, which in contrast to Venezuela generally operated outside the framework of the party system, became more militant in the 1970s. Fiscal policy loosened in 1972–73, resulting in a jump in inflation even prior to the oil shock. By the mid-1970s, the first oil shock and a strong boom in coffee exports added to the problem of maintaining price stability. Moreover, the general political climate has undergone a steady deterioration due to the explosion of drug-related violence.

Financial authorities nonetheless managed to maintain a generally cautious macroeconomic stance, in part through policies that maintained the support of key groups. Union demands had long been muted by an implicit system of wage and salary indexation and the limited room for political maneuvering the system allowed. Exporters gained from a crawling peg exchange rate, even if adjustments were not always adequately fast. More generally a close intertwining of political, economic and financial elites and the two-party system itself left few institutionalized channels for leftist or populist forces. This political structure helps explain the periodic eruption of antisystemic leftist political action, both rural and urban. But it also helps explain why Colombian officials were successful in partially sterilizing the effects of the coffee boom, avoiding political pressures to increase public expenditures, and limiting foreign borrowing.

Public investment did surge in the early 1980s, partly as a result of the ascent of a mildly populist president, Belisario Betancur, in 1982. With the coffee boom over, this increased investment lead to higher fiscal deficits, but in 1984, pressures within Betancur's own party resulted in a turn toward a more conservative stance. This relatively orthodox adjustment strategy, including substantial fiscal adjustments, was sustained by his successor.

Mixed Records: The Moderate Inflation Countries

Countries with mixed records are those which have experienced severe episodes of inflation for short periods or recurrent problems of moderate inflation over a longer time period. One striking difference between this

---

and Colombia," in Joan M. Nelson, ed., *Economic Crisis and Policy Choice* (Princeton, N.J.: Princeton University Press, 1989), p. 160.

group and the low inflation countries is the shift in the relative importance of external and domestic sources of inflation. Many of the inflation episodes in these countries overlapped with the two oil shocks, and Peru, Mexico, Turkey, and the Philippines faced severe budgetary problems as a result of the withdrawal of external financing. Yet domestic policy stance appears to have seriously aggravated the effects of external shocks.

The political characteristics of these countries also differ predictably from the low inflation cases. Governments are more vulnerable to electoral constraints, more inclined toward redistributive orientations, and more likely to have fragmented party systems. There are, however, important political differences among these cases that are reflected in different inflation histories. Three subpatterns can be distinguished. In Indonesia, Turkey, and Peru, well-organized political groups were temporarily mobilized in settings of party fragmentation or polarization and governments with strong redistributive orientations, resulting in periods of severe macroeconomic imbalance. In Korea and the Philippines, by contrast, opposition forces have generally remained weakly organized or vulnerable to repression. The legitimacy of incumbent governments has periodically been challenged, however, giving rise to political business cycles.

Mexico, Costa Rica, and Jamaica constitute partial anomalies, since the general security of officeholders and the nature of the party system seem otherwise conducive to stable macroeconomic policy. We argue that the ability of these countries to adjust, despite serious inflation problems, provides some vindication for the institutional argument we have advanced.

INDONESIA, TURKEY, AND PERU

The Indonesian inflation is a clear case of political fragmentation giving rise to conflicting demands on the government. The initiation of the so-called Guided Democracy in 1959 established an uneasy balance of power between the radical nationalist Sukarno, the army, and the Communist Party (PKI). The reduced influence of technocrats and efforts by Sukarno to placate the demands of increasingly polarized political groups resulted in massive fiscal deficits, financed largely by money creation. A grandiose eight-year plan announced in 1961 contained a variety of expensive projects. The Planning Council degenerated into a purely political entity, and the increasing entry of the army into the government resulted in ongoing interference in policy-making. Technocrats attempted a stabilization program in 1963, but the bureaucracy, army, Communists and Sukarno's policy of military *confrontasi* with Malaysia derailed the program. In 1965, the country slipped into hyperinflation.

Stabilization came only after a military coup resulted in Suharto's assumption of power. The massacre of the PKI leadership and cadre by the army and its mobilized Muslim and anti-Chinese supporters in Java freed Suharto from one important source of political pressure. Unions and business groups were weak, and in any case supported stabilization, as did the civil service, and export interests ravaged by Sukarno's inflationary policies. In 1966, Suharto's ear was captured by a group of Western-trained economists who assisted in the design of a stabilization plan that included a constitutional provision that the budget be balanced; expenditures could not exceed revenues plus counterpart funds generated by the aid program. This provision limited the crucial mechanism that had produced the hyperinflation: unlimited central bank emissions.

By 1970, Indonesia resembled the authoritarian low-inflation countries: a stable, single-party government with a low level of independent group mobilization, no electoral constraints, and a relatively insulated economic bureaucracy. Although the large state-owned enterprise sector periodically put pressure on the budget, Indonesia's subsequent bouts with inflation stemmed largely from the inflow of foreign exchange associated with oil, and every effort was made to manage them quickly.

Inflationary pressures in Turkey and Peru have also been linked to intense partisan conflicts in which governments with strong redistributive orientations played a role. Initially, independent popular-sector groups in these two countries were relatively weak, and the primary impetus for expansionist policies came from political elites. Over the course of the 1970s, however, growing political mobilization and the redistributive conflicts spawned by inflation itself made it increasingly difficult for these countries to stabilize. Fragmented party systems clearly contributed to this outcome.

Turkey demonstrates the way institutional structures can produce perverse incentives that undermine macroeconomic stability. In the mid-1970s, an ambitious program of investment in state-owned enterprises was sustained with foreign borrowing despite the first oil shock. Although the electorate continued to show overwhelming loyalty to the two major parties, extremist political forces on both the left and the right placed increasing strains on the center. In a classic case of the political fragmentation that can occur under proportional representation, governing coalitions proved difficult to form, were hostage to the demands of small antisystem parties, and were pulled toward policy positions more radical than those of the electorate as a whole. In this setting, it proved extremely difficult to cut government expenditure or adjust to the withdrawal of foreign lending. A stabilization program was announced under democratic auspices in January 1980, but the government was quickly deadlocked over political issues and was ousted by the military in September of that year.

In Peru, the military's democratic successors had to contend not only with the inflationary legacy of the ambitious redistributive and developmentalist policies of the populist phase of military rule, but also the increasingly independent social and political movements that period had spawned. These forces played themselves out in an extremely fragmented party system that also became increasingly polarized over the 1980s. Labor and business protests against austerity and municipal elections combined to scuttle a stabilization program under Belaúnde in 1983–84. The electoral victory of the APRA party in 1985 against political forces on both the left and right held forth the promise of a centrist reformism anchored in a strong, multiclass party. In fact, the Alianza Popular Revolucionoria Americana (APRA) was severely fractionalized and the political tactics of President Alan García had the effect of further polarizing the political system. By 1987, any semblance of coherent policy had disappeared and the economy spiraled into hyperinflation.

KOREA AND THE PHILIPPINES

In these two countries, governments were more conservative than in Turkey and Peru, and popular sector groups were less well organized and subject to outright repression. In both countries, authoritarian leaders also lacked strong party organizations, however, and faced recurrent problems of representation and legitimation. Governments in both countries used macroeconomic policy to cope with electoral and nonelectoral challenges. While those are considered relatively low-inflation countries, the strategic use of macroeconomic policy and politically-motivated delays in stabilization help explain a pattern of recurrent, if moderate, inflation.

Korea shows evidence of a political business cycle. Large expansions of the money supply coincide with the election of 1963 and the 1969 referendum on a constitutional amendment that allowed Park Chung Hee to run for a third term. In 1973, in response to protest over the initiation of the authoritarian Yushin constitution, Park pursued a number of policies such as preferential tax breaks for the working class that were designed to reduce the likelihood that opposition leaders would exploit the grievances of labor and the urban poor. During the second half of the decade, the government's commitment to industrial deepening led to rapid growth of domestic credit and external debt and strong pressure on labor markets. The inflationary episode of 1979 is partially attributable to these policies. Unlike most developing countries, a commitment to stabilization emerged prior to the second oil shock, but it was not fully implemented due to the political instability both before and after the assassination of Park in October 1979. Not until the consolidation of power under General Chun Doo Hwan were consistent stabilization measures adopted.

These, in turn, came under strong pressure with the transition to democratic rule.

Notwithstanding the numerous differences between Korea and the Philippines, there are also some interesting similarities. The upsurge of inflation in 1971 was directly linked to expansionary policies undertaken in support of Marcos' unprecedented bid for a second term as president. Inflation in the 1970s was mainly the result of the oil shocks, but Marcos also borrowed heavily to finance an ambitious expansion of the public sector. With many projects tied to cronies of the Marcoses, the government proved slow in adjusting to the adverse trends in its terms of trade in the early 1980s. The acceleration of inflation in 1984 followed the loss of confidence on the part of external creditors after the assassination of Benigno Aquino in 1983 and the upsurge of protest that followed. One reason for the rapid expansion of the money supply in early 1984 was to deflect attention from the opposition in anticipation of a critical election in May 1984. Stabilization was achieved under Marcos, and since 1986 the new democratic government, dominated by Aquino's center-right coalition in a traditional two-party system, has maintained low inflation.

MEXICO, COSTA RICA, AND JAMAICA

Until at least the early 1970s, all three of these countries experienced sustained records of macroeconomic stability, records that may be attributed at least in part to the tendency of multiclass party systems to limit the range of distributive conflicts. Notwithstanding these institutional arrangements, however, each experienced serious episodes of inflation during the next two decades.

The economic impulses behind these episodes stemmed primarily from the commodity and borrowing booms of the 1970s, which financed the growth of large state-owned enterprise sectors with links to import-substituting business interests. Expanding fiscal commitments left these economies particularly vulnerable to sharp declines in commodity prices and to the freeze on commercial bank lending of the early 1980s. The brief, but severe, inflation in Costa Rica can be traced largely to this conjuncture. The conservative but deeply divided Carazo administration delayed in responding to the collapse of coffee prices and the first oil price shock. Under a new government, stabilization and structural adjustment measures were rapidly put in place, and Costa Rica resumed its previous low-inflation trajectory.

In Mexico and Jamaica, such pressures were exacerbated considerably by escalating conflicts within the political system. Through the 1960s, Jamaica was the archetype of a stable, two-party democracy built around relatively nonideological parties. Manley's presidential campaign in 1972 was populist in orientation, but his election did not initially appear to represent a radicalization of the system. The strengthening of the left wing of Manley's People's National Party, his turn toward socialism after 1974, and the hostility of the private sector, however, transformed the party system into an ideologically polarized one. Elections in 1976 and 1980 were accompanied by violent clashes among partisans who were largely outside the control of political elites. Increasing political polarization overlapped with the economic shocks of the 1970s, contributing to a loss of control over macroeconomic policy and intense conflicts with the IMF over the terms of adjustment.

In Mexico, growing elite concerns about social unrest led the governments of the 1970s to launch both ambitious industrial initiatives and to increase the emphasis on social welfare. These efforts were accompanied by severe strains on fiscal policy and recurrent problems of inflation. Luis Echeverría's mildly populist administration (1970–76) pushed through ambitious developmentalist plans in spite of business opposition to tax reform, culminating in a stabilization crisis in 1976. The López Portillo administration (1977–82) engaged in heavy borrowing against oil revenues and delayed adjustments during the years immediately preceding the electoral campaign of 1982. By the time the more orthodox de la Madrid administration came to office, ballooning service costs on government debt made fiscal deficits difficult to control and tended to undermine the harsh wage and credit policies undertaken by the government in response to the crisis of 1982.

These episodes of inflaton, occurring as they did within institutionalized political regimes with cross-class party structures, present a challenge to the institutional explanation of inflation we have offered. It should be noted, however, that even after the emergence of macroeconomic instability in the 1970s and 1980s, there were several ways in which both the electoral and party systems pushed in predictable directions.

First, electoral cycles played an important role in all three stories; upcoming presidential elections increased the reluctance of governments in both Mexico and Costa Rica to undertake fiscal adjustments and deepened political polarization in Jamaica during the 1970s. Second, aggregative features of the party systems in the three countries played a role in efforts to bring inflation under control. Following the change of administration in Costa Rica in 1982, the new Monge government moved rapidly to put stabilization and adjustment measures into place, and Costa Rica quickly resumed its low inflation trajectory. In Jamaica, similarly, some of the centripetal tendencies of a two-party system reemerged in the 1980s. In 1980, voters rejected Manley and turned to the openly orthodox Seaga. By the end of the decade Manley himself had returned to power on a platform espousing a far more cautious economic policy agenda.

Mexico's inflation during the 1980s was higher and more persistent than Costa Rica's or Jamaica's, but it eventually proved more manageable than in the polarized political systems of the Southern Cone. The de la Madrid administration deployed the control mechanisms of the dominant party to implement a substantial change in the overall direction of macroeconomic policy after 1982. Although there is debate over the consistency with which the government maintained fiscal discipline, noninterest expenditures were slashed and credit remained very tight. Using its extensive leverage over the official labor organizations, the government maintained strict control over nominal wage increases throughout the administration. Overall austerity was relaxed at two points during the de la Madrid administration in anticipation of elections, but when inflation began to accelerate, the government responded with new austerity packages that combined tough fiscal retrenchment with wage and price controls. Despite Mexico's high inflation, its efforts at stabilization since 1983 and its willingness to pursue an orthodox policy line toward creditors reflect a continuing ability to absorb costs that would have been extremely difficult under different political-institutional arrangements.

The High Inflation Countries: Argentina, Brazil, Chile, and Uruguay

Table 6.2 shows that Argentina, Brazil, Uruguay, and Chile prior to Pinochet have had inflation histories that differ quite substantially from the other countries in the sample. These countries experienced both high average inflation rates over the long run and a high degree of volatility in prices. Among them, these four countries account for twelve of the twenty-one episodes of high inflation and nine of the fourteen very high inflation episodes.

External shocks are clearly one component of the story. The oil shocks contributed to the acceleration of Brazilian and Argentine inflation in the mid-1970s and early 1980s. After 1981, a number of adverse external developments coincided, though the interruption of external lending constituted a particularly profound shock. Reduced access to international capital markets cut off a major source of government financing, and forced governments to assume responsibility for private sector liabilities. The sheer size and speed of the required adjustment led governments to rely heavily on central bank financing.[22] The need to generate substantial current account surpluses to adjust to the lack of finance and to service existing obligations also resulted in large devaluations; these contributed

[22] See William R. Easterly, *Fiscal Adjustment and Deficit Financing During the Debt Crisis*, World Bank Policy, Planning and Research Working Paper No. 138, January 1989.

to inflation as well.[23] The influence of these debt-related shocks was significant in four episodes in the 1980s: Brazil, 1981–87; Argentina, 1982–85 and 1987; and Uruguay, 1983–86.

For reasons that we have already spelled out in our introduction to this volume, it is likely that the South American inflations have domestic roots as well. Some simple statistical tests suggest that the relationship between external shocks and inflation cannot simply be assumed. For a sample of seventy-one developing countries for which there was adequate data, there was no statistically significant relationship (0.05 level) between the size of interest rate and terms of trade shocks in 1981–84 and either growth or inflation in 1981–84 or 1985–88. Nor did any such relationship hold for a subsample of heavily-indebted countries.[24] More complex

[23] This problem was particularly severe where the government attempted to use the exchange rate as a nominal anchor through the policy of a fixed exchange rate or preannounced devaluations. These policies were adopted under military governments in Chile, Argentina and Uruguay as components of ultraconservative political projects designed to permanently reduce the influence of leftist and labor groups, in part through the discipline of the external market. In all three cases, however, the exchange rate overvaluation became substantial, speculation against the monetary authorities grew intense, and the experiments collapsed with capital flight, major external accounts crisis and in Argentina, near hyperinflation. See Max Corden, "Exchange Rate Policy in Developing Countries," World Bank, February 1990; Nicolas Ardito Barletta, Mario I. Blejer and Luis Landau, eds., *Economic Liberalization and Stabilization Policies in Argentina, Chile, and Uruguay* (Washington, D.C.: The World Bank, 1984); John Williamson, *Inflation and Indexation: Argentina, Brazil and Israel* (Washington, D.C.: Institute of International Economics, 1987); Peter Montiel, "Empirical Analysis of High-Inflation Episodes."

[24] The exercise was repeated for countries in four regions: sub-Saharan Africa, Latin America, East and South Asia, and the Middle East. Again, we found no significant relationship. We separated out the middle income countries, which include all of the larger debtors. There was a statistically significant relationship (0.05 level) between the size of the external shock in 1981–84 and growth in the 1985–88 period, but not surprisingly, the adjusted R-squared for this regression was low, 0.08. Moreover, there was *no* relationship between the shocks of the early 1980s and subsequent inflation. Finally, we ran the regression for the countries which the World Bank has designated "severely indebted middle-income countries," countries in which three of four key ratios are above critical levels: debt to GNP (above 50 percent); debt to exports of goods and services (above 275 percent); accrued debt service to exports (above 30 percent) and accrued interest to exports (above 20 percent). None of the relationships was statistically significant. These tests are, to be sure, extremely primitive but they suggest that the importance of international shocks cannot be presumed.

The independent variable in the regression was a measure of the combined interest rate and terms of trade shocks as a share of GDP for the period 1981–84 relative to the average size of these shocks in 1970–80. The interest rate shock was calculated using the change in real interest rate between the base period and subsequent period times the stock of external debt as a share of GDP. The terms of trade shock was calculated for both export and import prices. The dependent variables were inflation, measured as the annual change in the consumer price index measured for two separate periods, 1981–84 and 1985–88, and GDP growth for the same periods. For a full description of the construction of the indices, see

models might well reveal a larger role for international shocks, but the existing evidence is not compelling enough to dismiss domestic explanations altogether. More importantly, however, the history of price instability in Brazil and the Southern Cone dates back for many decades, indicating that longer-term domestic factors have interacted with and compounded the effects of the external shocks of the 1970s and 1980s.

Details of the political struggles within the high-inflation countries differ from case to case. Each of the countries, however, has been characterized by party fragmentation and tenure insecurity for extended periods of time, and several have experienced the emergence of governments with strongly redistributive orientations. It is difficult to sort out the independent effects of different political variables in these cases, since several that we have emphasized operate simultaneously. An additional methodological problem arises in that these political factors are not altogether exogenous to high inflation itself.

Nonetheless, it is plausible that institutional features of the party and electoral systems have contributed both to inflation and to other political characteristics of these polities, such as tenure insecurity and the emergence of populist political forces. Historically, centrifugal forces have been most evident within the party systems of Chile, Brazil, and Argentina. Until the military coup of 1973, the Chilean system was divided into bitterly competing left, center, and rightist currents, each with its own internal party cleavages. In the contemporary Brazilian party system, initially formed at the end of the Estado Novo in 1945, stable governing electoral majorities (and recurrent attempts at stabilization) have been consistently undermined by the divisive effects of geographic localism, struggles over state patronage, and redistributive appeals from the populist left. Fragmentation became particularly evident from the late 1950s to 1964, and again after the return of civilian government in 1985.

In Argentina, finally, the party system that evolved between the overthrow of Perón in 1955 and the military dictatorship of the late 1970s was composed of two, then three, competing Radical party organizations, and the deeply divided Peronists. The latter, though generally proscribed from participation in electoral politics, maintained its presence on the political scene through its influence within the union movement; Peronist-led strike activities became an important impediment to both military and civilian attempts to stabilize the economy.

Uruguay is a partial exception to this pattern of party fragmentation, since the Colorado and Blanco parties traditionally engaged in cross-class appeals. However, the complex "double simultaneous" electoral system

World Bank, Macroeconomics and Growth Division, *Report on Adjustment Lending II: Policies for the Recovery of Growth* (Washington, D.C.: The World Bank, 1990), p. 14.

allowed conflicting factions within each party to compete directly for control of the presidency and congress.[25] During the inflationary crises of the 1960s and early 1970s both parties had become internally polarized along left-right lines and a third political coalition, the left-of-center Frente Amplio (Broad Front) had gained a strong base of support in Montevideo and in the labor movement.[26]

Within the party contexts just described, tenure insecurities also contributed to macroeconomic instability. In ten of the fourteen very high inflation episodes, sharply contested elections or broader challenges to the security of tenure constituted major constraints on economic decision-making. Prior to the military coups of 1973, electoral cycles were especially important in the comparatively institutionalized constitutional systems of Chile and Uruguay. In four of the Chilean episodes (1953–55, 1958–59, 1962–64, and 1968–70), surges of inflation at the end of a presidential term could be traced to expansionary programs instituted as each new president took office. Successive incumbent presidents found themselves politically unable to resist the inflationary wage and credit demands of the business and labor interests linked to contending party forces. In Uruguay, the inflation episodes of 1968 and 1973 were also preceded by large increases in public sector wages and fiscal deficits implemented by incumbent governments during the electoral campaigns of 1967 and 1971.

In less institutionalized systems, of course, there were even broader challenges to the legitimacy of incumbent governments. Elected civilian presidents in Argentina and Brazil faced ongoing military pressures. But military governments also had to face serious political challenges, particularly as internal divisions and opposition pressures opened the way to a relaxation of coercion and the reemergence of long-standing political forces. In the face of mounting protest, authoritarian regimes pursued expansionist policies or delayed stabilization in Brazil in the late 1970s, Uruguay in the early 1980s, and in Argentina in both 1971–73 and in

[25] The double simultaneous system is, in effect, a combined primary and general election. The winning *candidate* of the winning *party* becomes president.

[26] It should be noted that traditional left-right splits were compounded in both Argentina and Uruguay by structural features of the economy that created intense *sectoral* conflicts as well. In both countries, the principal exports are wage goods. Conflicts between popular-sector groups and their opponents were frequently triggered by devaluations. These would first shift the internal terms of trade toward agroexport groups in the tradables sector, then generate strong popular sector pressures for compensating wage and price increases. Somewhat similar sectoral pressures on the budget were visible in Brazil during the inflationary surges of 1956, 1959, and 1964. Governments that had sought to implement fiscal adjustments to counter declines in coffee prices were caught between the demands of the growers, the demands of industrialists for price supports and credit, and growing wage demands from an increasingly radicalized labor movement.

1981–83. Only in Chile did the long period of authoritarian rule result in "successful" stabilization and a fundamental break in the previous pattern of partisan politics. New democratic governments in Argentina, Brazil, and Uruguay, by contrast, inherited very high inflations from their authoritarian predecessors.

Finally, the dynamics of party conflict intermittently led to the emergence of strongly redistributive governments that have used macroeconomic instruments to engineer increases in the real incomes of urban popular sector groups. Notwithstanding important differences in their long-term goals, the major examples would include the Peronist governments in Argentina, Goulart and Sarney in Brazil, and Ibáñez and Allende in Chile. The García government, elected in an increasingly polarized context in Peru, represents an additional example. While inflationary episodes have occurred in these countries under all types of governments, including nominally conservative ones, these radical-redistributive governments have tended to push inflation peaks to new heights within their respective countries.

As Sachs and Dornbusch and Edwards have argued, there is a remarkable similarity in the economic programs initiated by these "populist" governments.[27] The objective of increasing the real income to urban groups is usually coupled with a "developmentalist" program of structural reform designed to relieve productive bottlenecks. In its radical-transformative variant, populism aims at a more basic redistribution of assets through land reform or nationalization.

New populist governments uniformly reject the claim that deficit financing is inflationary, arguing that the mobilization of unused spare capacity, declining costs, and price controls can be used both to stimulate growth and lower inflation. They typically combine support for real wage increases with rapid monetary and fiscal expansion which, under a fixed exchange rate, also raises urban wages and industrial profits at the expense of the tradable goods sector. During the initial phases, policy makers enjoy a honeymoon, as their prescriptions appear to be vindicated. Reserves inherited from the previous government provided a crucial cushion for meeting import demand. Output, real wages and employment all improve, while direct controls are deployed to manage inflationary pressures.

Within two or three years, however, domestic demand generates a foreign exchange constraint, and the deterioration of existing reserves places increasing pressure on the exchange rate. Devaluation is initially rejected,

[27] Rudiger Dornbusch and Sebastian Edwards, "The Macroeconomics of Populism in Latin America," World Bank Policy, Planning and Research Working Paper No. 316, December 1989; Jeffrey D. Sachs, "Social Conflict and Populist Policies in Latin America," National Bureau of Economic Research Working Paper No. 2897, March 1989.

both because of its inflationary and distributional consequences. Controls on trade and capital movements proliferate, the budget deficit widens, and reserves shrink. In the third phase, the disparity between official and black market exchange rates and general lack of confidence leads to capital flight and large devaluations. Inflation soars, and stabilization finally becomes a political priority.

Popular sector groups generally have emerged as losers in such struggles, as temporary gains in real income are quickly eroded by inflation. Nonetheless, in a polarized political setting where contending forces represent sharply contending preferences, labor may face few good choices. For groups that are economically weak and vulnerable to repression, stabilization also implies disproportionately heavy costs, with few assurances of future benefits. Thus, in the types of cycles described above, the most prudent course for labor is to press for a defense of real wages when political conditions permit, even if it is likely that inflation will increase and that real gains will be eroded by the counterclaims of other, more powerful groups.

HOW INFLATIONS END: THE POLITICAL ECONOMY OF STABILIZATION

In the previous section, we focused on some long-run political correlates of inflation; here we turn to the circumstances under which inflations have been brought under control. We are concerned with three outcomes: the timing of stabilization efforts and whether adjustment was delayed; the nature of the stabilization package, particularly the mix between orthodox and heterodox adjustment measures; and the success in sustaining stabilization efforts.

We are particularly interested in understanding the relative capacity of authoritarian and democratic governments in managing inflation. Is a suppression of distributive conflicts a necessary component of successful stabilization? As previously stated, our hypothesis is that this will depend on the level of inflation, the political dynamics that underlie it, and the nature of the institutional setting. Higher inflations require more severe fiscal and monetary policies, in part because government reputation is likely to have been eroded and inflationary expectations deeply engrained. We expect that democratic governments will have greater difficulty stabilizing higher inflations, but that this will be particularly true in fragmented party systems where political conflicts have contributed to price instability over a number of recurring stop-go cycles.

To explore these issues, we look more closely at the outcomes of the inflation episodes. Tables 6.3 through 6.5 array these episodes in terms of the level of inflation, the political circumstances at the time of the episode, the type of political regime that attempted stabilization, and the outcome.

The criterion for success is whether inflation is brought below the inflation threshold for three years. Thus, moderate inflations are successfully stabilized if the government brings inflation below 15 percent for three years following its peak level, high inflations if the government achieves inflation rates below 30 percent for three years, and very high inflations if the government reduces inflation below 90 percent for three years. Such a definition of success is extremely generous, since it sets loose standards for higher inflations, deals only with the medium term and does not incorporate information about growth rates and employment.

Though the small number of cases demands caution in drawing firm conclusions, three important points emerge from Tables 6.3, 6.4, and 6.5. First, even by these loose standards of success, inflations were increasingly difficult to control as they moved toward higher levels. About two-thirds of the moderate inflations were reduced below the 15 percent threshold, but only half of the high and very high inflations were brought down for three years.

The second point is that regime type has made more of a difference at higher levels of inflation. At moderate levels, a majority of authoritarian and democratic regimes manage successful reductions in inflation. At high levels of inflation, however, only three of the eleven democratic governments were able to reduce inflation and these were at the low end of the high inflation range, between 30 and 40 percent. In the very high inflation category, three of seven democratic regimes managed to stabilize, but these were at the low end of the very high inflation range. Moreover, in two of these three cases, there were significant limitations placed on civil liberties. In contrast, six of nine authoritarian governments stabilized high inflation episodes, and five of seven were able to reduce very high inflations.

Finally, Table 6.6 contrasts the performance of those party systems that are fragmented with aggregative democratic and authoritarian regimes and monist systems. Only about one-third of the inflations in fragmented systems were brought down for three years, as compared to almost 70 percent of inflations in political systems where conflict was mediated by catchall parties or suppressed. In the nonfragmented settings, democracies did about as well as authoritarian regimes, each having a failure rate of roughly 30 percent. In fragmented party systems, however, democratic regimes had great difficulty stabilizing. In the three that did, two nominally democratic governments, in Uruguay and Argentina, operated under significant limits posed by the military, while in the third, Thailand, stabilization appears to have been the result of external price developments more than domestic policy. Two of the three authoritarian regimes with fragmented party systems also failed to stabilize.

TABLE 6.3
Political Correlates of Stabilization: Moderate Inflation Cases

Inflation Reduced Below 15 Percent for at Least 3 Years

	Election	Orientation	Fragmentation
Democratic			
Colombia 1966	1	2	2
Venezuela 1979–81	0	2	2
Malaysia 1974	1	3	2
Thailand 1980	0	2	3
Authoritarian			
Indonesia 1978–79	0	1	1
Korea 1963–64	1	1	1
1970	1	1	1
1974–75	0	1	1
1979–80	1	1	3
Taiwan 1960	0	1	1
1980	0	1	1
Thailand 1973–74	1	2	3
Peru 1965–68	0	3	3

Inflation Persists

	Election	Orientation	Fragmentation
Democratic			
Brazil 1952–56	1	4	3
Jamaica 1973–75	0	4	2
Turkey 1971–76	1	3	3
Authoritarian			
Philippines 1970–71	0	2	2
1980	0	1	1
Peru 1973–75	0	3	1
Mexico 1974–77	1	3	2

Notes: Elections: 1, national election for chief executive during the episode or within the following year; 0, no election.

Government orientation during majority of the episode: 1, conservative, antilabor, antileft government; 2, center-right government or coalition including both center-right and center-left parties; 3, center-left government; 4, Socialist or populist government.

Fragmentation: 1, monist: no-party or exclusive one-party systems; 2, aggregative: inclusive or corporatist one-party dominant systems or two-party systems dominated by broad, catch-all parties; 3, fragmented: multiparty systems.

TABLE 6.4
Political Correlates of Stabilization: High Inflation Cases

	Inflation Reduced Below 30 Percent for at Least 3 Years				Inflation Persists		
	Election	Orientation	Fragmentation		Election	Orientation	Fragmentation
Democratic							
Colombia 1963	0	2	2	Brazil 1959	1	3	3
Costa Rica 1973–75	0	3	2	Chile 1953–55	0	4	3
Jamaica 1978–80	0	4	2	1958–59	1	4	3
				1962–64	1	2	3
				1968–70	1	3	3
				Colombia 1973–77	0	3	2
				Peru 1976–81	1	2	3
				Uruguay 1959–60	0	1	2
Authoritarian							
Argentina 1949–52	0	1	1	Argentina 1971–73	1	2	3
1962–67	1	2	3	Brazil 1974–79	0	2	1
Indonesia 1972–73	0	1	1	Uruguay 1983–86	1	1	1
Philippines 1973–74	0	1	1				
1984	0	1	3				
Taiwan 1973–74	0	1	1				

Notes: See table 6.3.

TABLE 6.5
Political Correlates of Stabilization: Very High Inflation Cases

Inflation Reduced Below 90 Percent for at Least 3 Years

	Election	Orientation	Fragmentation
Democratic			
Costa Rica 1981–83	1	3	2
Argentina 1958–59	1	2	3
Uruguay 1964–68	1	1	3
Authoritarian			
Brazil 1962–64	0	4	3
Chile 1972–74	1	4	3
Mexico 1983–87	1	1	2
Indonesia 1962–66	0	4	3
Turkey 1977–80	1	2	3

Inflation Persists

	Election	Orientation	Fragmentation
Democratic			
Argentina 1982–85,	1	1	2
1987	1	3	2
Brazil 1981–87	1	3	3
Peru 1983–85	1	4	3
Authoritarian			
Argentina 1975–77	0	3	3
Uruguay 1972–75	1	1	3

Notes: See table 6.3.

TABLE 6.6
Party Fragmentation, Political Regimes, and Stabilization

	Democratic		Authoritarian	
	Successful Stabilization	*Inflation Persists*	*Successful Stabilization*	*Inflation Persists*
Monist or Aggregative				
	Colombia 1966	Colombia 1963	Argentina 1952	Argentina 1977
	Colombia 1977	Uruguay 1959	Argentina 1966	Brazil 1979
	Costa Rica 1974	Jamaica 1973	Brazil 1964	Mexico 1977
	Costa Rica 1982	Argentina 1985	Chile 1974	Peru 1975
	Jamaica 1978		Peru 1968	Uruguay 1973
	Jamaica 1984		Indonesia 1966	Uruguay 1983
	Venezuela 1980		Indonesia 1973	Philippines 1971
	Korea 1964		Indonesia 1978	
	Malaysia 1974		Korea 1970	
			Korea 1974	
			Korea 1980	
			Philippines 1974	
			Taiwan 1960	
			Taiwan 1974	
			Taiwan 1980	
			Turkey 1980	
Fragmented				
	Argentina 1959	Brazil 1956	Philippines 1984	Argentina 1973
	Uruguay 1968	Chile 1955		Philippines 1980
	Thailand 1973	Chile 1959		
	Thailand 1980	Chile 1962		
		Chile 1968		
		Peru 1981		
		Turkey 1971		

Note: See text for definitions of successful stabilization and persistent inflation. Episodes identified by peak inflation year. Inflations peaking after 1985 are not included.

Stabilizing Moderate Inflations

A closer examination of each category of inflation episodes provides some basis for understanding the political dynamics of inflation, as well as the timing and content of stabilization packages. We begin with an analysis of the moderate inflation episodes. Arguably, the same political factors that limited inflationary pressures in the first place also allowed for a quick return to price stability. Most of these cases were in the low-inflation countries where broader political pressures were muted in some form and where conservative economic decision makers enjoyed substantial autonomy. Most of the successful stabilizations in this category came in countries that had long-term records of low or controlled inflation, and in which governments enjoyed a high degree of credibility.

Favorable changes in the external environment—especially the leveling off of oil prices—contributed significantly to the decline of inflation in several episodes. This was true in Korea 1973–74, Malaysia 1974, Taiwan 1980 and Thailand in 1973–74 and 1980; these constitute nearly half of the successful cases. In most instances, however, both democratic and authoritarian governments also moved relatively quickly to counter external disturbances with some types of stabilization measures. Although there was often considerable debate over such measures, most successful responses included at least some significant steps to reduce demand.

The episodes in Korea and Venezuela provide useful illustrations of the range of policies adopted and their apparent consequences. Park Chung Hee, facing increasing potential threats from an urban political opposition, responded to the first oil shock with a relatively heterodox adjustment strategy. The government did, it should be noted, pursue a generally conservative fiscal policy. On the other hand, it borrowed heavily to maintain investment in export industries and a high level of growth, and relied heavily on price controls. This gamble paid off when growth resumed in Korea's major export markets and inflationary pressures subsided with the subsequent stabilization of world oil prices.

The Venezuelan government, by contrast, adopted a quite orthodox approach, which implied a very different set of tradeoffs. The strong, multiclass parties worked to discourage challenges to the stabilization program imposed in the late 1970s, and tight monetary and fiscal policy contributed to bringing inflation down in the early 1980s. This came at the cost of a severe recession, however, as well as sharp cuts in capital expenditure and investment. As in many other Latin American countries, the government also maintained an overvalued currency, which left it extremely vulnerable to the debt shock and forced adjustments of 1983.

Although lower levels of inflation were generally easier to control than higher ones, stabilization of moderate inflations did frequently pose political difficulties for governments. Although most of the governments in this group were able to return quickly to price stability, seven governments were not able to do so: Brazil 1952–56; Turkey, 1971–76; the Philippines 1970–71 and 1980; Jamaica, 1973–74; Peru 1973–75; and Mexico 1974–77. Democratic governments in Turkey and Brazil operated in fragmented party systems, and Jamaica and the Philippines (1971), though two-party systems, were increasingly polarized. The military government in Peru also faced increased distributional conflicts over its policies. Mexico experienced no basic change in its political structure, but it did begin a political liberalization that made the ruling party more sensitive to electoral constraints.

As in Korea, governments in these societies responded to balance-of-payments problems by seeking increased external financing and stepping up investment programs to counter recession. In at least one case—Brazil in the mid-1950s—this strategy paid off in high growth rates. Unlike Korea, however, these governments could not count on foreign exchange earnings from a diversified export sector and did not have the political capacity to control fiscal deficits. Both problems left them highly vulnerable to external shocks in subsequent years.

Stabilizing High Inflations

As table 6.4 shows, the success in taming high inflations was more limited than efforts to stabilize moderate ones. Eleven of the twenty episodes (55 percent) were followed by a rapid recurrence of the inflationary cycle. Four of these occurred in Chile, but as we have shown, long-term inflationary problems also plagued Argentina, Uruguay, and Brazil. Fragmented party systems were present in six of the eight democratic failures, and one of the three authoritarian ones.

Successful efforts to reduce inflation tended to occur at the lower end of the 30 to 90 percent range, and in several instances was attributable as much to changes in the external environment as adjustments in domestic policy. This was the case in the Philippines (1973–74) and Costa Rica (1973–75), which increased their borrowing in response to the first oil shock, and arguably in Jamaica in the early 1980s. To contain a pressing balance-of-payments crisis, the conservative Seaga government initially avoided conventional stabilization, relying instead on generous foreign assistance and an overvalued exchange rate. By 1984, however, inflationary pressures had reemerged, and Seaga turned more directly to fiscal austerity.

Effective, medium-term stabilizations were achieved in only two of the eight episodes in which price increases peaked at over 40 percent, Indonesia and the Philippines. In Indonesia, where the main cause of the inflation had been the monetization of oil surpluses, stabilization came under unusual conditions. Inflation was brought down in part through the adoption of more effective techniques of monetary management, but the financial difficulties of the overextended state-owned oil enterprise, Pertamina, also forced the government to repay a portion of its external debt, effectively sterilizing the growth of foreign assets.

External constraints, particularly the unavailability of credit in the wake of the assassination of Benigno Aquino and strong pressures from the IMF and banks, were important in forcing stabilization on the Philippines in mid-1984. Once the decision to stabilize was made—and it was delayed in anticipation of elections in May—the absence of a strong labor movement or of indexation contributed to the speed with which prices could be brought down. The program hit extremely hard at urban living standards, however, and the Marcos government was overthrown less than two years after launching the program.

With a few exceptions, such as Korea's supply-side adjustment strategy in the mid-1970s, stabilization in the moderate inflation cases generally centered on traditional instruments of demand management: fiscal, monetary, and wage policy. Because stabilizing higher levels of inflation entails higher political and economic risks, several governments turned to comparatively heterodox means of stabilizing prices in the high inflation episodes.

The stabilization program launched by the Onganía government in Argentina (1966–70) is noteworthy in this regard, since it departed substantially from the conventional IMF recipes of the time. Devaluation, a reduction of fiscal deficits, and strict wage controls were instituted, but the government also took additional measures aimed at avoiding the recessionary effects that had accompanied earlier IMF programs. A large tax on traditional exports allowed the Treasury, rather than agricultural exporters, to capture the gains from the devaluation. With fiscal problems eased by increased revenues, the government was in a position to maintain a moderate flow of credit to the private sector and to engage in a mildly expansionist program of public construction and subsidies to manufactured exports, supplementing these measures with controls on some key prices. Within six months, inflation had been reduced to single digits and growth had resumed, all without a major drop in real wages. In 1969 and 1970, however, the program was abandoned in the face of increasing pressure from landowners opposed to export taxes, small import-substituting firms, and Peronist-dominated unions that had been excluded from political power under the military.

A second heterodox alternative is to sidestep the political costs of stabilization in the short run by indexing prices and wages.[28] This was the route chosen by both Colombia and Brazil during the late 1960s. Minidevaluations were pioneered by the Colombian government to counter the tendency toward real appreciation that had contributed to payments disequilibria in earlier years. The minidevaluations, however, contributed to mounting pressure from the organized labor movement. In response

[28] For a review, see John Williamson, ed., *Inflation and Indexation: Argentina, Brazil, and Israel* (Washington, D.C.: Institute for International Economics, 1985).

the Colombian government established an implicit system of wage and salary indexation. An extensive system of indexing allowed the Brazilian military regime to accomplish roughly similar objectives between 1968 and the mid-1970s.

For both the Brazilian and Colombian governments, indexing appeared to reduce the distributional conflicts that accompanied high inflation and was thus a tool for depoliticizing devaluations and industrial relations more generally. In both cases, the ultimate success of the strategy rested on fiscal conservatism, which in turn was related to the underlying political context. Brazil's move to indexation was preceded by a very harsh orthodox stabilization program imposed by the military from 1964–67 that involved a particularly severe compression of real wages. As the Brazilian military regime began to relax political controls during the second half of the 1970s, long-standing distributional pressures resurfaced. Government concessions and its own developmentalist objectives were reflected in growing fiscal and current account deficits and increasing inflation. Indexing also resulted in the price effects of adverse supply shocks being transmitted quickly throughout the economy. Inflation doubled to about 50 percent in the wake of the first oil shock, and to 100 percent after the second, remaining at that level between 1980 and 1983 in spite of an exceptionally tight monetary policy imposed by the regime.

Stabilizing Very High Inflations

Stabilizing very high inflations poses a number of technical problems that are different from the stabilization of inflation at lower levels. These can only be outlined briefly here, but some exposition of these problems is necessary to understand the particular political problems at issue.[29] First, inertial forces are likely to operate quite independently of government intentions. When financial instruments are indexed in a high-inflation setting, government debt and interest payments can grow explosively even if fiscal authorities sharply reduce discretionary spending. Inflation, lags in tax collection and in the adjustment of tax brackets can all result in a decline in the real value of tax revenue, contributing to rapid increases in government deficits.

Expectations play a critical role in this inertial process. In setting prices and wages, firms and workers will take past inflation as a baseline prediction of future inflation. This reduces the scope of adjustment that can be achieved by traditional demand restraint measures alone. If prices are increasing at 200 percent annually, for example, and firms were able to

[29] This is particularly true for hyperinflations, and a large technical literature has emerged on them, although we do not address it here. The following draws on Rudiger Dornbusch, "Mexico: Stabilization, Debt and Growth," in *Economic Policy* 7 (October 1988): 251–62.

hold nominal wage increases to 180 percent, this would represent a draconian cut in real wages, but would only have a slow and marginal effect on inflation. More importantly, however, deindexing poses classic collective action dilemmas. While all might be better off, the player who is deindexed first risks substantial real income losses and is likely to resist strongly.

These particular problems of high inflation explain why some sort of heterodox strategy of inflation management involving wage and price freezes is likely to be not only politically attractive, but economically necessary. Yet as the failed heterodox experiments in Peru, Argentina, and Brazil have made clear, heterodox experiments cannot work unless there are also adjustments in the monetary and fiscal fundamentals. This is true not only because of the economic effects of continued fiscal and monetary expansion, but because of the crucial role government policy will have on expectations. Incredible adjustment programs will quickly be undermined by forward-looking economic agents, particularly as wage and price controls are eased, as they inevitably must be to allow relative prices to adjust.

It needs little elaboration to see that these "technical" difficulties of coordination are related to political challenges of the first order. For this reason very high inflations have raised most clearly the question of the relationship between regime type and stabilization.[30] The past record is not very comforting. Two of the democratic failures, in Peru and Brazil, have come in relatively new democracies with fragmented party systems. In Argentina, expectations rooted in earlier periods of political fragmentation remained strong, although by the mid-1980s, there were encouraging signs that the party system was evolving into two relatively cohesive blocs of Peronists and Radicals.

For these governments, all of which inherited high inflation from their military predecessors, heterodoxy appeared to have political as well as economic advantages. All three experimented with stabilization packages involving wage-price controls and currency reforms, but all proved un-

[30] See Thomas E. Skidmore, "The Politics of Economic Stabilization in Postwar Latin America," in James Malloy, ed., *Authoritarianism and Corporatism in Latin America* (Pittsburgh, Pa.: University of Pittsburgh Press, 1977); John Sheahan, "Market-oriented Policies and Political Repression in Latin America," *Economic Development and Cultural Change* 28, no. 2 (1980): 267–91; Karen Remmer, "The Politics of Economic Stabilization: IMF Standby Programs in Latin America, 1954–1984," *Comparative Politics* 19 (October 1986): 1–25; Stephan Haggard, "The Politics of Adjustment: Lessons from the IMF's Extended Fund Facility," in Miles Kahler, ed., *The Politics of International Debt* (Ithaca, N.Y.: Cornell University Press, 1986); and the review of the literature in Haggard and Kaufman, "The Politics of Stabilization and Structural Adjustment," in Jeff D. Sachs, ed., *Developing Country Debt and Economic Performance* (Chicago: Chicago University Press, 1989), pp. 232–39.

able to sustain the fiscal and monetary control required to make the heterodox component of the stabilization viable.

Under Sarney in Brazil, but particularly under Alan García in Peru, wage and price controls were components of populist programs and deployed as substitutes for, rather than complements to, more orthodox measures. Real wages were allowed to rise substantially, and there was virtually no effort to limit subsidies or control spending. When pressure on prices ultimately forced the relaxation of controls, a new spiral of inflation began. Brazil experienced three such cycles between 1985 and 1989 associated with three successive plans: the Cruzado plan of 1986, the Bresser plan of 1987, and the so-called summer plan of 1988.

The Argentine attempt at heterodoxy, instituted in 1985 under much tighter foreign exchange conditions and a different political party context, placed greater emphasis on maintaining wage restraint and bringing fiscal deficits under control. The efforts of the Alfonsín administration weakened, however, and then collapsed in the face of strong electoral challenges from the Peronist opposition, strong resistance to tax reform, and the continuing drain of debt servicing on fiscal resources. Since 1989, the Peronist government that succeeded the Radicals in office has pursued a considerably more orthodox stabilization approach, combining this with significant steps toward privatization and trade liberalization. As implied, the evolution toward a two-party system may have contributed to this surprising policy turnaround; nevertheless, the strong momentum of earlier decades of instability remains a major impediment to success.

Only in three instances did very high inflation come down under civilian governments, and in two of these three cases, Uruguay in the 1960s and Argentina in 1959, these civilian regimes significantly curtailed civil liberties. Significant limitations on civil liberties was also evident in another success story not included in this sample, the stabilization of the Bolivian hyperinflation in 1985, when several hundred union leaders were arrested and the union movement virtually destroyed. This leaves the case of Costa Rica as the only fully democratic regime in our sample which managed to stabilize a very high inflation, and this came at the low end of the very high-inflation range.[31]

There are, however, important variations among the successful high inflation stabilizations in the degree of political continuity, the extent of political repression and the severity with which costs are imposed on the organized working class. These are related in predictable ways to the nature of the political institutions and the degree of polarization and social conflict which accompanied the inflation episodes.

[31] Israel constitutes another case in which a hyperinflation was brought down under democratic auspices.

At one extreme are stabilizations that remain broadly within the constitutional framework. In Uruguay in 1968, the death of moderate president Oscar Gestido lead to the succession of conservative vice president Jorge Areco, who used new constitutional powers to declare a state of seige and impose an austerity program. The program was characterized by a wage freeze, price controls, a fixed exchange rate, and very tight fiscal and monetary policies. Censorship was instituted and attempts made to repress unions. Prices came down, but confrontations with increasingly militant labor and left groups continued, and the stabilization package unravelled during the sharply contested election campaign of 1971. The Argentine stabilization of 1959 was more orthodox, relying on a large devaluation followed by strict wage controls and very tight monetary policy. The program was implemented after the military had forced Frondizi to install a finance minister of their choosing, and had insisted on the continued proscription of the Peronist party.

Mexico also exhibits continuity in its basic political structure, and has had substantial success in reducing inflation in a context which, while authoritarian, has not been harshly repressive. In December 1987, the de la Madrid government brokered a "Solidarity Pact" after five years of reliance on traditional demand-management approaches. The pact, negotiated with business elites and "official" unions, provided for wage and price controls that were crucial ingredients in lowering inflation over the next two years. This was possible because official unions were integrated into the party structure. Mexico is the one very high inflation case in which the government was able to gain voluntary compliance from at least some portions of organized labor. Nevertheless, the pact was accompanied by the continuation of very tight wage and credit policies that probably could not have been sustained under more open and competitive political conditions.

The combination of high levels of social polarization and conflict and high levels of inflation has been an important factor in authoritarian installations in a number of the cases in our sample. In these cases, the tasks of restructuring politics and the economy have been closely linked in the programmatic statements of incoming military governments. The military has generally sought not only to control inflation and restore private sector confidence, but to curtail partisan conflict and the activities of labor and the left, which are held accountable for the economic deterioration.

Important distinctions can be drawn among these new authoritarian regimes. Far-reaching changes in both the economy and polity followed the coup in Indonesia (1965–66). Unlike the Latin American cases, however, inflation in Indonesia was less directly the result of the competing demands of organized social groups as it was of the political leadership itself, and thus the link between repression and economic strategy was less clear. Reform could be effective by changing procedures within the government itself. Following the advice of a cadre of foreign advisors known as "the Berkeley mafia," and painfully aware of the extreme costs associated with Sukarno's inflationary course, Suharto institutionalized a budget process that provided checks on the ability of the central government to pursue expansionist fiscal policies. Though these constraints were somewhat relaxed by the oil boom of the 1970s, the government has nonetheless maintained a relatively tight fiscal control.

Turkey and Brazil typify more repressive military interventions, although with a difference in the degree of institutionalization of military rule. The Turkish military stated clearly its intention to return the country to democratic rule when it intervened in 1980; moreover, the promise was generally credible, given that the military had intervened briefly in Turkish politics before. The military's main objective was to put an end to the escalating social violence which had claimed over five thousand lives in the late 1970s. This program included an effective ban on union activity and the arrest of thousands of activists from both right-wing and left-wing groups, with well-documented instances of torture and other human rights abuses. Although the motive for these actions was as much political as economic, it fit with the government's strong commitment to stabilization and structural adjustment. The military provided the political space for a team of technocrats to continue the reforms that had been initiated under the weak and divided coalition government of Suleiman Demirel.

While Turkey's adjustment program was launched under civilian auspices, the Goulart government in Brazil appeared unable to formulate any coherent economic policy. Brazil's military intervention also proved more institutionalized. Otherwise, the pattern in the two countries is remarkably similar: a harsh stabilization introduced immediately following the military's intervention, followed by some relaxation as the military sought to exit politics. It is interesting to note that in both of these cases, inflationary pressures resurfaced as the military liberalized politics; in Turkey in 1983, and in Brazil, in a more extended process after 1975.

The most radical economic experiments came in Chile under Pinochet and Argentina in the late 1970s, also the two cases in which partisan conflict, popular sector mobilization, and subsequent repression of labor were the most intense. In these cases, militaries allied with neo-liberal technocrats not only to stabilize, but to introduce market-oriented reforms that went beyond those launched in Brazil and Turkey.

The Argentine experiment collapsed under the combined weight of an unsustainable exchange rate policy and the military's adventurism. This leaves Chile as the only country with a long history of high inflation that was capable of achieving relative price stability in the 1980s, and this in spite of significant fiscal burdens associated with servicing the external debt. The question is whether the conservative demand-management policies pursued under the Pinochet government will be maintained under the new democratic government or whether, as in Brazil and Turkey, the opening of the political arena will place new distributive pressures on the government.

The possibilities for macroeconomic stability are enhanced by several changes, both political and economic, that took place under military rule. First, the substantial liberalization of trade, deindustrialization, and the weakening of the union movement have seriously reduced the organizational base of the left. Second, perhaps because of the economic and political shock of the Allende government and its aftermath, there is a strong consensus among the leaders of the major parties that inflation should be kept in check. Finally, there have been important institutional changes in the management of economic policy, including greater independence for the central bank, which should contribute to greater stability. Nonetheless, the capacity of the party system to prevent the polarization of distributive politics has not been tested.

These patterns naturally raise serious questions about the ability of new democracies in Argentina, Brazil, and Peru to cope effectively with the hyperinflations of the late 1980s and early 1990s. Does Costa Rica provide the basis for optimism concerning democratic stabilization of very high inflations? In 1982, the Social Democrats were returned to power with a strong majority in both the popular vote and in the Assembly. President Monge instituted strict foreign exchange controls, but coupled them with very tight budget policies and an appreciation of the exchange rate that cut inflation. The program was supported by the IMF from late 1982 on and by concessional American assistance on a very large scale. Inflation came down more rapidly than IMF targets. The case seems to suggest that democratic stabilization of high inflations is possible where incoming governments exploit electoral honeymoons, broad public disenchantment with the policies of the previous regime, and substantial external support to launch comprehensive programs.

Yet even a cursory look at this case reveals that the circumstances surrounding its success are very different than in the other high inflation democracies. Costa Rica was the only case of very high inflation in a democracy where the party system was not fragmented and seriously polarized. Inflation had not been a long-term phenomenon, so there were fewer problems with indexation or the credibility of government policy. Finally, the country received external assistance that was much larger relative to GNP than Argentina, Brazil, or Peru could expect to enjoy.

We close with two possible sources of hope for the democracies experiencing very high inflation. The first is that as inflation accelerates, public opinion may be more receptive to very strong measures, regardless of their distributive implications. This is suggested not only by the strong support for the Monge program, but also by apparent support within the Chilean public for Pinochet's antiinflationary achievements and by the successful stabilization of the Israeli hyperinflation under democratic auspices in the mid-1980s.

Finally, there is hope that as electoral competition becomes institutionalized in countries like Argentina, Brazil, and Peru, it will extend the time horizons of both political elites and competing distributive groups. In the newer democracies, the second and third round of elections have brought governments to power that favored relatively conservative economic programs; this is not simply a function of economic circumstance, but of political learning. As experiences in Costa Rica, Colombia, and Venezuela suggest, democratic compromises on stabilization issues might well be more enduring than the "solutions" imposed—and reimposed—by successive authoritarian governments, only to be undermined by their successors.

Yet as we have argued, this result is likely to hinge on the institutional arrangements for managing political conflict. In fragmented party systems such as those in Peru and Brazil that block the formation of a national consensus for reform, continued economic stagnation is likely to further polarize politics. In this case the prospects are poor not only for adjustment, but for democracy as well.

TABLE A6.1
Inflation Episodes

	Years of Episode	Inflation in Prior Year (percent)	Peak Inflation (percent)/(year)
Moderate Inflations			
Korea	1970	12.5	16.1 (1970)
Malaysia	1974	10.5	17.4 (1974)
Philippines	1979–80	7.3	18.2 (1980)
Indonesia	1978–79	6.7	18.2 (1978)
Taiwan	1960	n.a	18.4 (1960)
Peru	1965–68	9.1	19.0 (1968)
Colombia	1966	3.5	19.1 (1966)
Turkey	1971–76	6.1	19.2 (1975)
Thailand	1980	9.9	19.7 (1980)
Philippines	1970–71	1.3	21.4 (1971)
Venezuela	1979–81	7.1	21.5 (1980)
Brazil	1952–56	10.8	21.8 (1956)
Peru	1973–75	7.2	23.6 (1975)
Thailand	1973–74	4.9	24.3 (1974)
Korea	1974–75	3.2	25.3 (1975)
Jamaica	1973–75	5.0	27.2 (1974)
Jamaica	1984–85	11.6	27.8 (1984)
Korea	1979–80	14.5	28.7 (1980)
Mexico	1974–77	12.0	29.0 (1977)
Korea	1963–64	6.7	29.5 (1964)
High Inflations			
Costa Rica	1973–75	4.6	30.1 (1974)
Argentina	1962–67	14.0	31.7 (1966)
Colombia	1963	2.7	32.0 (1963)
Colombia	1973–77	13.1	33.1 (1977)
Chile	1958–59	17.3	33.3 (1959)
Chile	1968–70	17.0	34.9 (1970)
Philippines	1973–74	8.2	34.2 (1974)
Jamaica	1978–80	11.2	34.9 (1978)
Argentina	1949–52	13.0	38.1 (1952)
Uruguay	1959–60	6.0	39.5 (1959)
Indonesia	1972–73	4.4	40.6 (1973)
Chile	1962–64	9.6	45.3 (1963)
Taiwan	1973–74	8.2	47.5 (1974)
Philippines	1984	8.3	50.3 (1984)
Brazil	1959	17.3	51.9 (1959)
Brazil	1974–79	12.7	52.7 (1979)
Argentina	1971–73	13.6	61.2 (1973)
Peru	1976–81	23.6	75.4 (1981)
Uruguay	1983–86	19.0	76.4 (1986)
Chile	1953–55	12.0	84.0 (1955)

TABLE A6.1 *(cont.)*

	Years of Episode	Inflation in Prior Year (percent)	Peak Inflation (percent)/(year)
Very High Inflations			
Costa Rica	1981–83	18.1	90.1 (1982)
Brazil	1962–64	32.3	91.4 (1964)
Uruguay	1972–75	24.0	97.0 (1973)
Turkey	1977–80	17.4	110.2 (1980)
Argentina	1958–59	13.1	113.9 (1959)
Uruguay	1964–68	21.3	125.3 (1968)
Mexico	1983–87	27.9	131.8 (1987)
Peru	1983–85	64.4	163.4 (1985)
Brazil	1981–87	19.1	227.7 (1987)
Argentina	1986–87	145.2	229.7 (1987)
Argentina	1975–76	23.5	443.2 (1976)
Chile	1972–74	19.2	504.7 (1974)
Argentina	1982–85	104.5	672.1 (1985)
Indonesia	1962–66	30.7	1044.8 (1966)

Notes: The inflation episodes are derived on the basis of the following criteria:

Years when inflation (CPI) for the whole year crossed the threshhold and all following years that it stayed roughly constant with no evidence of stabilization;

For the "high" and "very high" inflation cases, all years prior to the highest annual level of inflation that are marked by an increase in inflation above the respective threshold in the rate of inflation;

Within the very high inflation category, episodes are differentiated if inflation is reduced significantly, but remains above the 90 percent threshold, and then increases again.

Moderate inflations: threshold, 15 percent; N = 21; range, 15.7–29.5 percent.

High inflations: threshold, 30 percent; N = 20; range, 30.1–84.0 percent.

Very high inflations: threshold, 90 percent; N = 14; range, 90.1–1044.8 percent.

PART IV

Conclusion

CHAPTER SEVEN

Economic Adjustment and the Prospects for Democracy

Stephan Haggard and Robert R. Kaufman

STUDENTS OF political economy are concerned both with the way political factors condition economic behavior and how market forces and economic policies influence politics. This volume has focused on the first of these concerns—the effects of politics on economic policy choice and performance—but has not considered the impact of the adjustment process on political development. In this essay, we take up this challenge, less as a conclusion drawn from assembled evidence than as a speculative look at several new issues that will dominate the research agenda of comparative political economy over the next decade.

Our principal concern is with the effect of the economic changes of the 1980s on efforts to establish and consolidate democratic governance. We define democracy in institutional terms, as a political regime that guarantees fundamental civil liberties and is based on public contestation and competitive elections. In a fuller sense, democratization might also be conceived as an extension of popular control and the expansion of rights beyond the sphere of the political to other social institutions.[1] But the establishment of a pluralistic electoral system is an important aspect of democratization however defined, and probably necessary for the realization of any broader conception of the term.

Despite the fact that economic crisis overlapped a new wave of democratization in the developing world, recent literature on the transition to democracy has largely eschewed economic variables.[2] Emphasizing the

We would like to thank Jorge Domínguez, Lisa Martin, Eric Nordlinger, Minxin Pei, and participants in seminars at Georgetown, Brown, and Princeton Universities and the University of California, San Diego for helpful comments on earlier drafts. Particular thanks are due to Matthew Shugart for his careful reading.

[1] Robert Dahl, *Democracy and Its Critics* (New Haven: Yale University Press, 1989), pp. 218–24.

[2] See for example Guillermo O'Donnnel and Philippe Schmitter, "Tentative Conclusions about Uncertain Democracies," in O'Donnell, Schmitter and Lawrence Whitehead, *Transitions from Authoritarian Rule: Prospects for Democracy*, part 4 (Baltimore, Md.: Johns Hopkins University Press, 1986), pp. 3–78; Larry Diamond, Juan J. Linz, and Seymour Martin Lipset, *Politics in Developing Countries: Comparing Experiences with Democracy* (Boulder, Colo.: Lynne Rienner Publishers, 1990); and the influential Juan J. Linz and Al-

autonomy of the political realm, this analysis has focused rather on factors such as pact-making among political elites, institutional relations between civilian and military authorities, and the way electoral and constitutional rules structured opportunities for the democratic opposition under authoritarian rule.

We do not contest the importance of these factors, and in fact seek to integrate them into our analysis, but it is misleading to ignore the ways in which the political realm has been affected by recent economic crises and adjustments. Throughout the 1980s, economic problems constituted the most salient issue on the political agenda of most developing countries. Adjustment efforts implied important shifts in the balance of political power among contending interests; for example, between the export and import-competing sectors and between capital and labor.[3] As Peter Evans argues in chap. 3 of this volume, the sharp squeeze on government resources also sparked fundamental debates about the role of the state in the development process. In some instances, economic crisis has even jeopardized the ability of central governments to maintain control over population and territory.

In this essay we focus on a sample of twenty-three cases, including most of the countries in East and Southeast Asia and Latin America, as well as several important African cases. We began with the thirteen countries that formed the core of the first phase of this research project, and are analyzed in *Economic Crisis and Policy Choice* (1990). As nine of these were Latin American countries, we expanded the sample to include seven additional countries from Africa and Asia, as well as three Latin American countries not included in our original case studies. This yields a sample that, while not scientific, includes a wide array of middle-income countries outside of the Middle East.

The relationship between economic forces and democratization is discussed in three steps. In the first section, we examine the extent to which the international shocks of the 1980s led to regime change. We argue that the effects of external shocks were mediated by preexisting institutional arrangements for managing political conflict and by the ability of governments to maintain the support of key private sector interests. In a substantial number of countries, both democratic and authoritarian, political conditions allowed incumbent regimes to survive the crisis. In an important subset of cases, however, institutional structures and bases of support were weak, and economic crisis contributed to fundamental political transformation.

---

fred Stepan, eds., *The Breakdown of Democratic Regimes* (Baltimore, Md.: The Johns Hopkins University Press, 1978).

[3] On the coalitional consequences of shifts in relative prices, see Ronald Rogowski, *Commerce and Coalitions: How Trade Affects Domestic Political Alignments* (Princeton, N.J.: Princeton University Press, 1989).

In the second section, we turn to the effect of adjustment policies on the pattern of political conflict in newly democratizing countries. A host of factors will influence the nature of political cleavages in new democracies, including characteristics of the transition, the constitution, voting rules, and the party structure. Nonetheless, we explore how the implementation and timing of economic adjustment initiatives—whether they were undertaken before, during, or after the transition to democratic rule—affect post-transition political alignments.

Over the long run, the consolidation of economic reform will hinge critically on the governability of new democracies, and vice versa. In the final section of the essay we consider how alternative party systems might reconcile democratic politics and a market-oriented economy. We close on a cautionary note. The current wave of democratization is frequently considered irreversible, but new democratic experiments may prove quite fragile in the face of continued poor economic performance.

ECONOMIC CRISIS AND REGIME CHANGE

To explore the linkages between economic crisis and political outcomes, we begin with a simple, if not simplistic, model that links international shocks, domestic performance, and the likelihood of government and regime change. Economic crises are generally unfavorable to officeholders. Where institutionalized mechanisms are available for removing leaders, crises will increase the likelihood that governments will change. Over some (unknown) threshold, we might expect external shocks to generate challenges not only to the government, but to the basic economic and political project on which incumbent rule is based, and to the regime itself.

Two hypotheses follow. First, we should expect an increase in the incidence of regime change during global depressions; second, we should expect regime change to be more likely the greater the intensity of the external shock a country faces.

A systematic test of the first hypothesis would demand a comparison of political developments during periods of rapid and slow growth, an exercise that is beyond the scope of this study. Nonetheless, the hypothesis appears to find support from the Great Depression. With the exception of Czechoslovakia, every one of the fragile democracies established in Eastern Europe after World War I had collapsed by 1939; economic distress played an important role in each case.[4] Paul Drake has indicated that in Latin America during the 1930s, regime changes occurred in ten

[4] See Joseph Rothschild, *East Central Europe between the Two World Wars* (Seattle: University of Washington Press, 1974).

of the twenty countries he examined.[5] These changes usually involved a shift from elected civilian governments to military-backed, dictatorial ones, but this was largely the result of the fact that civilian administrations were in power at the time. In some instances, such as the collapse of the Ibáñez regime in Chile, authoritarian governments gave way to elected successors.

The coincidence of economic crisis and an upsurge in the number of regime changes in the 1980s, particularly toward democracy, would also seem to provide some prima facie evidence for the first hypothesis. On closer inspection, however, the relationship between economic shocks and regime change appears somewhat more tenuous. Table 7.1 presents data on twenty-three countries. The general point of reference is the global recession of 1982–83, which affected most of the countries in our group, albeit not uniformly. In a few cases, the recession hit somewhat earlier or later, and the relevant dates are indicated in parentheses. The last column indicates whether the economic crisis contributed to a change of political regime, either from authoritarian to democratic (AD) or from democratic to authoritarian (DA). These are distinguished from those countries in which regimes persisted, and also from those which experienced regime changes that were not linked directly to economic shocks.

As in the 1930s, crisis did lead to important political changes. In four Latin American countries—Argentina, Brazil, Bolivia, and Uruguay—sharp economic downturns intensified democratic oppositions to incumbent military governments and lead reasonably quickly to their withdrawal from power. Similar processes also occurred in the transition from Marcos to Aquino in the Philippines. In Nigeria, Ghana, and Turkey, regime changes were also associated with economic shocks, but in these cases, elected governments gave way to military rule. In Korea, a brief political opening in 1980 was aborted by a military coup d'etat that left the authoritarian structure of the previous regime largely intact.

As with the effort to draw a direct causal link between external shocks and economic policy choice analyzed in the introduction, the relationship between declining economic performance and regime change must be substantially qualified. First, the majority of countries did *not* experience regime changes as a result of the shocks of the 1980s. A number of established democratic regimes survived the crisis, as did a number of authoritarian ones. By the end of the 1980s, virtually all authoritarian governments in the sample were coming under substantial pressure to liberalize,

[5] Paul Drake, "Debt and Democracy in Latin America, 1920s–1980s," in Barbara Stallings and Robert R. Kaufman, eds., *Debt and Democracy in Latin America* (Boulder, Colo.: Westview Press, 1989), p. 40.

TABLE 7.1
Economic Shocks and Regime Change in the 1980s

	Average GDP Growth			Regime Change Tied to Economic Shock
	1978–81	1982–83[a]	1984–87	
Latin America				
Argentina	−0.3	−1.3	0.9	AD (1983)
Brazil	4.5	−1.6	6.3	AD (1985)
Bolivia	0.7	−5.6	−0.8	AD (1980–82)[c]
Chile	7.5	−7.5	4.9	No[d]
Colombia	5.0	1.3	4.0	No
Costa Rica	2.4	−2.7	4.1	No
Jamaica	−1.3	1.5	0.4	No
Mexico	8.5	−3.0	0.9	No
Peru	3.8	−6.0	5.9	No[e]
Uruguay	4.8	−7.8	2.7	AD (1985)
Venezuela	0.3	1.5	2.0	No
Africa				
Ghana[b]	1.5	−4.5	4.8	DA (1981)
Kenya	5.4	1.3	4.4	No
Nigeria	0.0	−4.1	−0.5	DA (1983)
Zaire	0.1	−0.9	2.0	No
Zambia	1.7	−2.4	0.4	No
Asia				
Indonesia	7.3	1.5	3.9	No
Korea[b]	10.4	−3.0 (1980)	9.3	AA (1980)[f]
Philippines[b]	4.2	−5.4 (1984–85)	3.4	AD (1986)
Thailand	7.0	5.0	4.4	No
Turkey[b]	7.0	−0.8	4.7	DA (1980)[g]

Source: For GDP growth data, The World Bank.

Key and Notes: AD = transition from authoritarian to democratic government; DA, transition from democratic to authoritarian government; AA = an irregular change of authoritarian government.

[a] Different years for the economic downturn are indicated in parentheses.

[b] First and third columns show averages for five years preceding and following the crisis respectively.

[c] Bolivian politics in this period are characterized by a rapid succession of military and civilian governments. The Siles government (1982–85) came to power through negotiations with the military, but Siles had received a plurality vote in the 1980 elections. Even though the first directly elected government came to power in 1985, we therefore date the transition to the early 1980s.

[d] Chile underwent a regime change in the late 1980s, after the severe crisis of the early 1980s.

[e] Peru experienced a democratic transition in 1980, but this was prior to the debt crisis of the 1980s.

[f] Korea underwent a transition to democracy in 1987–88, but under conditions of rapid growth.

[g] Turkey returned to democratic rule in 1983, but under improving economic circumstances.

but their endurance in the face of continuing economic and political pressures must be explained.

Even if the hypothesis about the global incidence of regime change during periods of international economic distress were sustained, there does not appear to be any clear correlation between the magnitude of country-specific economic shocks and changes in regime. Authoritarian Chile experienced a drop in GDP during 1982–83 that was the second largest in the group. Although the Pinochet dictatorship confronted massive protest, it survived for most of the rest of the decade, and when it did undergo a regime change, the economy was in a strong recovery. Taiwan and Korea launched or completed political transitions by the end of the 1980s, yet these changes also occurred against the background of strong growth and could in no way be attributed to the shocks of the early 1980s. Among the other authoritarian governments that survived the decade, Mexico, Zambia, and Zaire all had extremely poor economic performance.

These variations raise a number of questions. Under what conditions do sudden economic downturns galvanize political opposition to the regime in power? What determines whether incumbent authorities survive or succumb to these pressures? And what determines whether the ensuing political change involves a new government, or a more fundamental reorganization of the polity itself? We can gain some purchase on these questions by considering more closely the differences between those regimes that changed as a result of the crisis of the early 1980s and those that survived the initial shocks. Each of these two types can be divided into those governments that were democratic at the beginning of the decade, and those that were authoritarian. These distinctions are displayed in table 7.2.

Although it is beyond the scope of this chapter to specify fully the conditions for regime persistence and change, two factors appear particularly important. First, regime survival appeared to depend on the existence of mechanisms of interest representation that channeled, and therefore controlled, group conflict; in short, what Samuel Huntington called "institutionalization."[6] The second recurrent factor is the extent to which international shocks resulted in the defection of key political, military, and business supporters of the regime. This, in turn, rested on a variety of conjunctural conditions, including the effects of the economic shock on major business interests and the extent to which the opposition was viewed as moderate or radical.

Among the democracies, survival appeared to depend heavily on mechanisms for limiting the degree of conflict among competing electoral

[6] See Samuel Huntington, *Political Order in Changing Societies* (New Haven: Yale University Press, 1968).

TABLE 7.2
Regime Persistence and Change in the 1980s

	Initial Regime Type (1980)	
	Democratic	Authoritarian
	(1)	(2)
Regime change attributable in part to economic crisis	Turkey (1980)[a] Ghana Nigeria (1983)[b]	Argentina Bolivia Brazil Philippines Nigeria (1985)[b] Nigeria (1987)[b] Korea (1980)[c]
	(3)	(4)
Regime endures or undergoes change not attributable to economic crisis	Costa Rica Colombia Jamaica Peru Venezuela Thailand Dominican Republic	Chile Mexico Korea (1987)[c] Taiwan Zaire Zambia Kenya Indonesia Turkey (1983)[a]

[a] Turkey had a military coup in 1980 that can be traced in part to deteriorating economic conditions. The military handed power back to a civilian government in 1983, but not due to worsening economic circumstance.

[b] Nigeria had a military coup in 1983 attributable in part to the poor performance and corruption of the civilian government. A second coup in 1985 can be attributed in part to the effects of declining oil prices. The initiation of a democratic opening in 1987 might also be traced to continuing dissatisfaction with the economy.

[c] Korea experienced a brief political opening in 1980 following the assassination of Park Chung Hee in 1979, but the military quickly returned to power in a coup in the same year. This coup might be interpreted in part as the result of poor economic conditions, exacerbated by the first oil shock. The transition to democracy, however, came during a period of strong growth later in the decade.

elites. Costa Rica, Colombia, Jamaica, and Venezuela were all relatively established, two-party democracies at the beginning of the 1980s and managed to stay that way despite wrenching economic changes. Although the Dominican Republic's experience with democracy is of more recent vintage, the party of Joaquin Balaguer, which dominated Dominican politics following the American intervention in 1965, did cede power to the opposition in 1978. In these systems, oppositions had reasons to expect that they could exercise influence through the electoral mechanism.[7] De-

[7] On the small Latin American two-party democracies, see Joan M. Nelson, "The Politics

spite violent clashes among competing partisan groups in Jamaica and the eruption of rioting in Venezuela in 1989, the severity of protest and anti-government activity was muted in these countries by the shared interests of competing party leaders in the survival of the constitutional system.[8]

Peru and Thailand are new democracies, and present somewhat different cases. Peru underwent a democratic transition in 1980, and the discrediting of military governments helped to prevent bitter partisan rivalries from spilling over into antidemocratic civil-military alliances. Moreover, as in the more established democracies, the opposition to the Belaúnde government that grew in the wake of the economic downturn of 1982–83 could look forward to upcoming elections.[9] In Thailand, a sort of semi- or quasidemocracy at best, the troika of the military, the bureaucracy, and the monarchy has provided strong institutional continuity to the system of political rule despite changes in formal regime char-

---

of Adjustment in Small Democracies: Costa Rica, the Dominican Republic and Jamaica," and Barbara Stallings, "Politics and Economic Crisis: A Comparative Study of Chile, Peru, and Colombia," in Nelson, ed., *Economic Crisis and Policy Choice: the Politics of Adjustment in the Third World* (Princeton, N.J.: Princeton University Press, 1990), pp. 169–214 and 113–68; John A. Booth, "Costa Rica: The Roots of Democratic Stability," Jonathan Hartlyn, "Colombia: The Politics of Violence and Accommodation," Howard Wiarda, "The Dominican Republic: Mirror Legacies of Democracy and Authoritarianism," all in Larry Diamond, Juan Linz, and Seymour Martin Lipset, *Democracy in Developing Countries: Latin America* (Boulder, Colo.: Lynn Rienner, 1989), pp. 387–423, 291–335, 423–59; Mitchell Seligson, "Costa Rica and Jamaica," in Myron Weiner and Ergun Ozbudan, eds., *Competitive Elections in Developing Countries* (Durham, N.C.: Duke University Press, 1987), pp. 147–200; Evelyne Huber Stephens and John D. Stephens, *Democratic Socialism in Jamaica* (Princeton, N.J.: Princeton University Press, 1986) and Omar Davies, "An Analysis of the Management of the Jamaican Economy, 1972–1985," *Social and Economic Studies* 35, no. 1 (March 1986): 73–109. On party, state, and labor relations, see Ruth Berins Collier and David Collier, *Shaping the Political Arena: Critical Junctures, Trade Unions, and the State in Latin America* (Princeton, N.J.: Princeton University Press, 1990), which contains treatments of Colombia and Venezuela, among other cases.

[8] On Venezuela, see Daniel Levine, "Venezuela: The Nature, Sources and Future Prospects of Democracy," in Diamond, Linz, and Lipset, *Democracy in Developing Countries: Latin America*, pp. 247–91; Terry Lynn Karl, "Petroleum and Political Pacts: The Transition to Democracy in Latin America," in O'Donnell, Schmitter, and Whitehead, *Transitions from Authoritarian Rule: Prospects for Democracy* (Baltimore, Md.: Johns Hopkins University Press, 1986), pp. 196–221; Michael Coppedge, "Strong Parties and Lame Ducks: A Study of the Quality and Stability of Venezuelan Democracy" (Ph.D. diss., Yale University, 1988).

[9] See Carol Wise, "Democratization, Crisis and the APRA's Modernization Project in Peru," in Stallings and Kaufman, *Debt and Democracy*, pp. 169–72; Cynthia McClintock, "Peru: Precarious Regimes, Authoritarian and Democratic," in Diamond, Linz, and Lipset, *Democracy in Developing Countries: Latin America*, pp. 335–87; Luis Abugattas, "Populism and After: The Peruvian Experience," in James M. Malloy and Mitchell A. Seligson, *Authoritarians and Democrats: Regime Transition in Latin America* (Pittsburgh, Pa.: University of Pittsburgh Press, 1987), pp. 121–44.

acteristics. These three pillars of the Thai polity accepted a liberalization of the political system since the late 1970s, in part because it did not fundamentally challenge their prerogatives.[10] Yet, interestingly, both Peru and Thailand have proved more fragile than their more institutionalized two-party counterparts. Peru's democracy is probably the most vulnerable in the region, and in February 1991, the Thai military interrupted the country's political development by reentering politics, one of the few outright reversals of the current democratic wave.

The authoritarian regimes that persisted over the decade or underwent changes not linked to the crisis also show several interesting commonalities. First, we found in this category all of the one-party authoritarian regimes in our sample. In contrast to those military governments that collapsed, political elites in Taiwan, Mexico, Zambia, and arguably Indonesia and Kenya could rely not only on coercion, but on institutionalized party mechanisms for co-opting and controlling opposition tendencies.

Mexico presents a clear case of how developed party structures provide incumbent elites with substantial advantages. The government has been pressed from the right since the mid-1970s by well-organized business groups and the conservative Partido de Acción Nacional. In the 1988 presidential election, it faced an unprecedented electoral challenge from left opposition groups led by Cuauhtémoc Cárdenas. Despite these pressures, however, the PRI remained a formidable instrument of elite political control, with substantial organizational resources, continuing ties to key unions, and an impressive electoral and patronage machine.[11]

A second, related feature of those authoritarian polities that survived was the continuing loyalty to the political status quo on the part of key support groups, even in the face of severe economic distress. Regime continuity was more likely where crucial bases of support in the private sector, the middle class, and within the military itself held firm. The reasons for this continuing loyalty varied, but included fears of aligning with an intemperate or radical opposition and the absence of organizational alternatives, often precisely because of the institutional arrangements just outlined.

The Pinochet regime in Chile shows the importance of social support or acquiescence, particularly given that the government was not willing

[10] See Chai-Anan Samudavanija, "Thailand: A Stable Semi-Democracy," in Larry Diamond, Juan J. Linz, and Seymour Martin Lipset, *Democracy in Developing Countries: Asia* (Boulder, Colo.: Lynne Rienner, 1989), pp. 305–46.

[11] See Robert Kaufman, *The Politics of Debt in Argentina, Brazil and Mexico: Economic Stabilization in the 1980s* (Berkeley: Institute of International Studies, University of California, 1988); Collier and Collier, *Shaping the Political Arena*, pp. 104–206; Daniel Levy, "Mexico: Sustained Civilian Rule without Democracy," in Diamond, Linz, and Lipset, *Democracy in Developing Countries: Latin America*, pp. 459–98.

or able to construct an official party organization to provide it with electoral legitimation. In fact, the absence of an official party did contribute significantly to Pinochet's defeat in the 1989 plebiscite, which in turn led to the opposition's victory in the 1990 presidential elections. The capacity of the regime to weather the exceptionally severe economic crisis of the early 1980s, however, highlights the importance of elite support in determining the survival or demise of other authoritarian regimes. Key private sector groups continued to accept the regime in spite of their opposition to specific economic policies. In large part, this behavior was a function of the way such groups perceived their political alternatives. During the early 1980s, fear of a resurgent political left deterred defections to the democratic opposition; by the end of the decade, these fears had receded as the opposition itself moved toward more moderate positions.[12]

The Pinochet regime also benefited from a highly institutionalized tradition of corporate cohesion and hierarchical discipline within the military establishment, a tradition that predated the 1973 coup. Unlike his counterparts in countries such as Argentina and Brazil, Pinochet was able to control internal rivalries within the officer corps, and could rely on the support of the armed forces at least until his loss in the plebiscite undercut his claims to legal authority.[13]

When we turn to those governments that underwent regime change, we see a lower level of institutionalization and elite cohesion, regardless of whether the regime is democratic or authoritarian. This in turn contributed to policy stalemates that exacerbated economic difficulties and led to the political defection of key support groups.

Those governments that saw the collapse of democratic rule include two African states, Nigeria and Ghana, with long histories of oscillation between democratic and military rule and well-documented institutional weaknesses.[14] Both had only recently exited from military governance in

[12] Barbara Stallings, "The Political Economy of Democratic Transition: Chile in the 1980s," in Stallings and Kaufman, eds., *Debt and Democracy in Latin America*, pp. 193–97.

[13] Manuel Antonio Garreton, "The Political Evolution of the Chilean Military Regime and Problems in the Transition to Democracy," in O'Donnell, Schmitter, and Whitehead, *Transitions from Authoritarian Rule*, pp. 100–111.

[14] See Thomas Callaghy, "Lost Between State and Market: The Politics of Economic Adjustment in Ghana, Zambia, and Nigeria," in Nelson, *Economic Crisis and Policy Choice*, pp. 257–321; Thomas Biersteker, "The Relationship between Economic and Political Reforms: Structural Adjustment and the Political Transition in Nigeria" (University of Southern California, August 1990); Larry Diamond, "Nigeria: Pluralism, Statism and the Struggle for Democracy," and Naomi Chazan, "Ghana: Problems of Governance and the Emergence of Civil Society," in Larry Diamond, Juan Linz, and Seymour Martin Lipset, *Democracy in Developing Countries: Africa* (Boulder, Colo.: Lynne Rienner, 1989), pp. 33–92, 93–140.

1979, but new democratic governments immediately faced a variety of challenges to the legitimacy of their rule. In Nigeria, these included serious public doubt about the probity of elections in 1979 and 1983 and growing public outrage at corruption. Survey evidence from 1983 suggests widespread public support for a military coup.[15] The coup cycle was repeated again in 1985 before bringing to power a military government once again committed to attempting a transition to democracy. Economic problems and the political inability to manage them were even more obviously responsible for the failure of the Limann government in Ghana (1979–81), which faced opposition from its inception from the bureaucracy, the military, newly-mobilized populist forces, and major ethnic groups.

Turkey had a longer tradition of democratic governance, but also a history of brief, "corrective" military interventions followed by a swift return to democratic rule.[16] When Turkey's debt crisis broke, the political landscape was becoming increasingly polarized through the activities of antisystem parties and radical groups willing to use violence. Though the newly elected Demirel government initiated a bold economic adjustment plan in early 1980, the institutions of government, including both the legislature and the bureaucracy, became increasingly paralyzed over the course of the year. The government proved unable to manage growing civil violence. As in Nigeria and Ghana, military intervention was actually welcomed by substantial segments of the population.

The authoritarian governments that ceded power to democratic successors (type 2 in table 7.2) also exhibited characteristics that distinguished them sharply from those that survived (Type 4). Military regimes in Argentina, Brazil, and Uruguay and the authoritarian government of Ferdinand Marcos in the Philippines failed to develop durable institutional mechanisms linking state and society during the 1970s and early 1980s. In contrast to Chile, moreover, the problem of a lack of durable representative structures was compounded by increasing factionalization of the military. Finally, these governments all faced moderate oppositions that were acceptable to the business and middle-class groups that had initially backed, or at least tolerated, military rule.[17]

[15] Diamond, "Nigeria," p. 53.

[16] Ergun Ozbudan, "Turkey: Crises, Interruptions, and Reequilibrations," in Diamond, Linz, and Lipset, *Democracy in Developing Countries: Asia*, pp. 187–230; Ilkay Sunar and Sabri Sayari, "Democracy in Turkey: Problems and Prospects," in O'Donnell, Schmitter, and Whitehead, *Transitions from Authoritarian Rule*, part 1, pp. 165–86.

[17] Guillermo O'Donnell, "Tensions in the Bureaucratic-Authoritarian State and the Question of Democracy," in David Collier, ed., *The New Authoritarianism in Latin America* (Princeton, N.J.: Princeton University Press, 1979), pp. 285–319; Stephan Haggard, "The Political Economy of the Philippine Debt Crisis," in Nelson, *Economic Crisis and Policy Choice*, pp. 215–56.

The economic crisis exacerbated internal conflicts in these governments and provided a new focal point for opposition energies. As the crisis deepened, important economic interest groups came to view political opening as a means of increasing their policy influence and enhancing their chances for economic relief. In Argentina and Brazil, this was particularly true of those industrial groups with substantial fixed investments in import-substituting activities and ties to the state sector. In the early 1980s, their swing toward the opposition severely weakened the position of the military incumbents.[18] In the Philippines, the defection of business groups and the middle class provided an important impetus to the democratic opposition and added substantially to the pressure on the Marcos government.[19]

The puzzle of why regime changes tended to move in the direction of more, rather than less, democracy remains. Even in two of the three cases in which economic factors initially contributed to authoritarian installations, the military either handed power back to a civilian government (Turkey) or came under strong pressure to do so (Nigeria). In the 1930s, the global tendency was for economic shocks to encourage authoritarian solutions; the reasons for the different outcomes in the 1980s are by no means as obvious as they might first appear. Before turning to the question of democratic consolidation, therefore, we need to look more closely at the factors influencing the direction of regime change.

One reason for the general tendency toward democratic transitions may simply be that the majority of Third World governments were authoritarian at the time that the crisis hit. Authoritarian regimes tended to rely more heavily than democratic ones on purely instrumental appeals and were thus particularly vulnerable to "legitimation crises" when economic conditions turned sour. Moreover, the demand for democratic constitutionalism provided a useful common denominator for an otherwise heterogeneous array of opposition forces. For example, the demand for the direct election of the president played a galvanizing role for the opposition in both Brazil and Korea and has been a recurrent theme of the opposition in Taiwan.

It is not entirely plausible, however, to explain democratizing tendencies simply as reactions to authoritarian rulers. There is no a priori reason why incumbent authoritarian regimes might not have been replaced by

[18] The economic objectives of such groups generally involved an increase in state assistance rather than more orthodox structural adjustment, a position that complicated the efforts of incoming governments to deal with the economic crisis. See Jeffry Frieden, "Winners and Losers in the Latin American Debt Crisis: The Political Implications," and Sylvia Maxfield, "National Business, Debt-led Growth, and Political Transition in Latin America," both in Stallings and Kaufman, *Debt and Democracy in Latin America*, pp. 23–39, 75–91.

[19] Haggard, "The Political Economy of the Philippine Debt Crisis," pp. 245–48.

authoritarian successors. Military coups did in fact occur in Korea and Nigeria. In interwar Europe, economic crisis contributed to the growth of right-wing political movements advocating authoritarian solutions.

The most persuasive explanation for the general political trend toward democracy in the 1980s appears to lie in the international realm, including ideological influences, international and regional demonstration effects, and the more direct influence wielded by the major powers in support of democratic governments. In the Depression era, both Soviet communism and Italian fascism provided alternative models of governance and economic development that had wide appeal in parts of the developing world. During the 1980s, even before the collapse of the Soviet empire in Eastern Europe, the international political climate favored movement toward more liberal political systems, in form, though not always in substance. This was especially true in those areas that lay within the American sphere of influence, including the Philippines, the Caribbean, and Central America. The disintegration of the Soviet bloc contributed a powerful impetus to this ideological climate, since it undercut both the strategic rationale in the West and the ideological rationale in the East for continuing to support authoritarian client states. Regional and international demonstration effects worked through a variety of channels. Democratic developments in Spain and Portugal influenced Latin American political thinking, the Philippines had some influence on subsequent developments in Korea, Taiwan, and less successfully, Indonesia, and Gorbachev's political opening profoundly influenced events in Eastern Europe.

In important respects, these observations about the importance of global influences on political change correspond closely with Kahler's and Stallings' arguments about the international political and ideological pressures toward economic liberalization. Whether political and economic changes were set in motion by external shocks or not, they were frequently reinforced by ideological shifts in the international milieu. By the end of the decade, political elites in the developed world increasingly came to view political democratization and economic liberalization as mutually interdependent processes. Aid donors increasingly argued that improved "governance" was a prerequisite for economic reform, and that attention to political liberalization and even "political conditionality" should be added to economic policy conditionality.[20]

---

[20] A surprising admission of the centrality of "governance" in explaining economic outcomes is contained in *Sub-Saharan Africa: From Crisis to Sustainable Growth* (Washington, D.C.: The World Bank, 1989), pp. 60–61. See also Ernst and Young, *Development of an ANE Democratic Pluralism Initiative: Rationale, Operating Principles, and Potential Projects* (Draft report prepared by SRI International for Bureau for Asia and Near East/Office

The key question became the compatibility of the twin processes of economic and political liberalization. Could countries undergoing a transition from authoritarian rule also manage the complex political conflicts associated with market-oriented reforms? It is to this question that we now turn.

DEMOCRATIZATION AND ECONOMIC REFORM: THE POLITICS OF THE TRANSITION PROCESS

Governments undertaking market-oriented policies confront a tradeoff between the need to insulate decision makers and the pressure to respond to constituent interests. These tradeoffs can be difficult even in authoritarian settings; in polities undergoing a transition to democratic governance, they become more complex and severe since the rules of the political game are not set. In this section, we explore some of the political dilemmas of combining democratic reform and economic adjustment, particularly those adjustments that are likely to have short-run costs, such as stabilization and liberalizing prices and trade. The political conflicts that emerge in such situations will be influenced by the strength of competing economic interests and by the political and institutional factors discussed in the preceding section. Here, however, we focus primarily on the reform *processes* themselves.

We argue that the political effects of these reforms are likely to be contingent on the *sequencing* of economic and political liberalization. Figure 7.1 outlines three stylized reform sequences: economic adjustments may be implemented before, during, or after the political transition. As will be seen, these do not always constitute clear choices; governments may be pushed toward a given sequence by circumstances beyond their control. We suggest, however, that each sequence has predictable consequences both for the nature of the democratic transition and for political alignments and conflicts in the posttransition period.

Sequence I: Economic Reform First

One way of "resolving" the tensions between political and economic liberalization is to attempt to suppress opposition to economic reform—often for an extended period—prior to reopening the political sphere. This was the strategy pursued by the "bureaucratic-authoritarian" regimes in Argentina, Brazil, Chile, and Uruguay in the 1960s and 1970s,

---

of Technical Resources, U.S. Agency for International Development, October 1989), pp. 8–13.

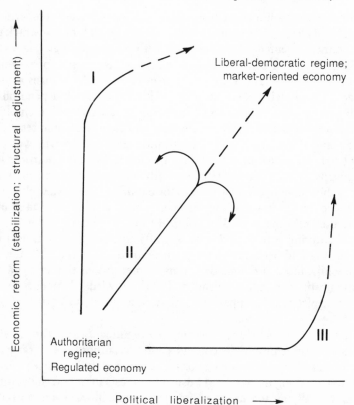

Figure 7.1. Sequences of Economic and Political Liberalization
   Note: Dashed lines indicate that the sustainability of the path is problematic.
   Sequence I: Chile, Korea, Taiwan, Turkey
   Sequence II: Mexico, Nigeria, the USSR (?)
   Sequence III: Argentina, Bolivia, Brazil, Peru, the Philippines, Uruguay,
            Eastern Europe (?)

to which Turkey in the early 1980s also bears some resemblance.[21] It also conforms to the pronouncements of authoritarian leaderships in the East Asian newly industrialized countries (NICs). In the early 1960s, Lee Kuan Yew in Singapore and Park Chung Hee in Korea argued explicitly that economic development should be given precedence over democratic rule.[22] Most recently, this authoritarian model of development found fa-

[21] See Guillermo O'Donnell, *Bureaucratic-Authoritarianism: Argentina 1966–1973 in Comparative Perspective* (Berkeley: University of California Press, 1988).
[22] See Stephan Haggard, *Pathways from the Periphery: The Politics of Growth in the*

vor among the politically conservative but economically modernizing elite around Deng Zhao-ping in China, which argued for a two-track policy of market-oriented reforms coupled with continued single-party rule.

The implications of this sequence for the consolidation of economic policy reform hinge critically on the extent to which the reforms actually change the underlying social structure. This, in turn, will depend on the length and consistency with which new policies are pursued, their ability to effectively reorient economic activity, and their economic results. In Taiwan and Korea, the import-substitution phase of growth was relatively brief and export-oriented policies were sustained uninterrupted for over twenty years. By the 1980s, virtually all segments of business and labor in these countries had a stake in the export sector. Results elsewhere were more mixed. In Chile and Turkey, military governments used market-oriented reforms to weaken political forces on the left and in the import-substituting private sector as well. By the 1980s, new export-oriented groups had become an important political force in both countries, and in Chile, most of the major left and center groups that once backed import substitution industrialization (ISI) acknowledged the new "social facts" and pledged to support a continuation of outward-oriented policies.

As we will discuss below, however, in Argentina, Brazil, and the Philippines, governments initially committed to this authoritarian strategy ultimately lacked either the interest or the capacity to fully realize their initial designs. Strong military and business interests in import-substituting sectors were significant impediments to economic liberalism in both Brazil and Argentina. In the Philippines, Marcos turned to the creation of state-sanctioned monopolies as a way of consolidating his patronage network. Where reform efforts were not consistently pursued, the post-transition political landscape is more likely to resemble its pre-authoritarian past.

Yet even where these authoritarian reform projects succeeded on their own terms—as in Korea, Chile, Turkey, and Taiwan—they left distinctive political problems for their democratic successors to resolve. These have to do with the nature of the political transition and the management of posttransition distributive and political conflicts that had been suppressed under authoritarian rule.

Partly because of the new social facts associated with sustained market-oriented policies, and partly because of the capacity of relatively strong authoritarian governments to control the nature of the democratic transition, the new democratic governments in these countries have tended to

---

Newly Industrializing Countries (Ithaca, N.Y.: Cornell University Press, 1990), pp. 62, 106–7.

be led by political elites of the center and center-right, though in Chile, the moderate left backed the incoming president as well. Business groups with ties to the old regime retained political influence, as did the military itself, either through explicit agreements or constitutional provisions, as in Chile and Turkey, or through the continuity in personnel, as was the case in Korea. In contrast to cases where military regimes collapsed in the context of generalized economic failure, right-wing forces may be more disposed to reassert their control or, at a minimum, to act as a veto group if they perceive that new democratic governments falter in their management of the economy or of resurgent political conflict.

The continuing strength of groups linked to the old regime also constrains efforts by incoming civilian governments to integrate previously excluded groups, particularly the labor movement, into the social and political system. In Turkey, which has experienced the longest period of democratic rule in the 1980s, the Özal government has attempted to deal with this problem through a rather precarious balancing act that has combined strong emphasis on exports through an active exchange-rate policy with expansive fiscal policy and extensive state patronage directed at urban workers, small businesses, and disadvantaged regions. Under the Özal strategy, however, real wages and labor's share of income fell dramatically over the 1980s. By the end of the decade, the organized labor movement, which had significant restrictions placed on its activities under the transitional constitution, was once again becoming more militant.[23]

New governments in Korea and Chile face similar difficulties revolving around the role of organized labor and the political left. In Korea, the expansion and consolidation of democracy will depend heavily on how officials and employers institutionalize relations with a militant labor movement that emerged following decades of repression.[24] The position of the government has vacillated between an arm's length stance toward labor disputes and support for the repressive solutions to strikes favored by more conservative employers. The formation of a "grand coalition" of center and right parties in 1989 has been interpreted as an effort to build support for more decisive policies vis-à-vis the left.

In Chile, the left's decision to participate in the coalition backing Patricio Aylwin contributed significantly to the reopening of the political system, but the left has yet fully to define its role with respect to the "social deficit" accumulated under Pinochet. Whether or not the Aylwin government proves successful in managing the economy, the incentives of electoral competition are likely to pull its leftist allies away from their role as

[23] John Waterbury, "Coalition-Building, Export-led Growth and the Public Sector in Turkey" (Paper presented at the Annual Conference of the Middle East Studies Association, Los Angeles, November 1988).
[24] See Haggard, *Pathways from the Periphery*, pp. 135–38.

coalition partners, raising again the possibility of left-right polarization and the problem of organizing a stable base of electoral support for the government in power.[25]

Sequence II: Simultaneous Economic and Political Liberalization

Efforts to engage in concurrent political and economic reform constitute a second possible course of change. This pattern is most likely to occur under authoritarian regimes that face mounting economic problems and growing threats to their authority, but are still relatively secure in power and capable of controlling the pace of political change. Governments in this context are likely to view political reform partly, if not largely, in instrumental terms. Political liberalization is seen to provide opportunities for new groups favored by the economic reform to counterbalance losers; it could also be used as a form of symbolic compensation. Nonetheless, this pattern raises most clearly the dilemmas of democratic reformism, and is likely to be unstable.

Among the countries examined in this study, the best examples are provided by Nigeria under Ibrahim Babangida and Mexico under both Miguel de la Madrid and Carlos Salinas, although reform efforts in Poland under Jaruzelski prior to 1990 and in the Soviet Union may also fit into this model. In Nigeria, the structural adjustment program launched in 1987 was accompanied by the announcement of plans calling for the establishment of an electoral commission, the convening of a Constituent Assembly, and a gradual lifting of the ban on party politics. National elections were scheduled for 1992, implying a long transitional period.[26] In Mexico, the dominant party government experimented with piecemeal electoral reform in the administration of López Portillo (1977–82).[27] After the severe crisis of 1985–86, however, the dominant faction within the PRI came to view a broader reform of the party system as an important means of breaking the power of old-style "corporatist" unions and business groups that opposed economic liberalization.[28] In the Soviet

[25] On the background to party alignments during the transition, see J. Samuel Valenzuela, "Party Oppositions under the Chilean Authoritarian Regime," in J. Samuel Valenzuela and Arturo Valenzuela, *Military Rule in Chile: Dictatorship and Oppositions* (Baltimore, Md.: Johns Hopkins University Press, 1986), pp. 184–229.

[26] Thomas Biersteker, "The Relationship between Political and Economic Reforms," p. 28.

[27] Kevin Middlebrook, "Political Liberalization in an Authoritarian Regime: The Case of Mexico," in O'Donnell, Schmitter, and Whitehead, *Transitions from Authoritarian Rule*, part 2, pp. 123–48.

[28] Wayne A. Cornelius, Judith Gentleman, and Peter H. Smith, eds., *Mexico's Alternative Political Futures* (San Diego: Center for U.S.-Mexican Studies, University of California,

Union and Poland, a gradual liberalization, though initially not democratization, of the political system was undertaken simultaneously with efforts to initiate economic reforms.

Although the results of these decisions are still unfolding, there have been few clear winners from the adjustment process and signs of overall recovery have been slow to materialize. Thus, it has been predictably difficult for these governments to maintain the intended balance between political and economic reforms. In Nigeria, inflation did fall and agricultural production increased slightly in 1987 and 1988. But as the program began to affect the interests of key urban groups, particularly organized labor and the import-substituting manufacturing sector, protest against the structural adjustment program (SAP) began to mount. The government faced crippling strikes in 1988, and in 1989 widespread "SAP riots" exploded through the southern part of the country when the government lifted its ban on political activity. Rather than providing a form of compensation for the costs of economic reform or strengthening the political voice of potential winners, political liberalization provided the opposition with new opportunities to pillory the government. Caught in these cross-pressures, the government's initial response was to vacillate. On the economic front, the government first appeared to relax its commitment to structural adjustment, then reaffirmed its course by mid-1988. It did so, however, at the cost of considerable damage to its political reform program: increasing use of censorship; repression of strikes; arrests of political opponents to maintain control of its economic program; and the delay of the political transition itself.[29]

As we have already suggested, Mexico's dominant party system allowed ruling elites to deal with such predicaments with greater flexibility than their counterparts in military governments. As in Nigeria, however, political reforms tended to weaken the government's capacity to implement its economic reform program, and forced the government to retreat from its commitment to a more open politics. Notwithstanding their calls for greater political pluralism, both de la Madrid and Salinas, for example, relied heavily on their control of the corporatist portions of the labor movement to impose and sustain the wage controls in the antiinflationary Solidarity Pact with business groups. In line with the strategy of courting support from the beneficiaries of reform, the government permitted considerable latitude for the right-wing opposition, allowing the PAN to win an unprecedented victory in a gubernatorial election in 1990. However, the PAN showed a close programmatic affinity to the Salinas gov-

---

1989); Ruth Berins Collier, "The Contradictory Alliance: State-Labor Relations and Regime Change in Mexico" (University of California, Berkeley, May 1990).

[29] Biersteker, "The Relationship between Economic and Political Reforms," p. 53.

ernment, and was openly allied with the government on a number of economic reform issues. By contrast, after the surprisingly strong showing of the Cárdenas movement in the 1988 presidential election, the government has relied on previous tactics of harassment and intimidation in its dealings with the political left, which was openly opposed to Salinas' liberalizing project.

The hope expressed by the government at the onset of Salinas' term was that improvements resulting from economic adjustment, coupled with internal reforms of the PRI, would allow that party to compete more effectively in the 1991 midterm elections and the 1994 presidential race. Such an outcome, however, is by no means assured and it is unclear how the government will mix concession and repression if its plans for building electoral support do not materialize.[30]

In both countries, the prolonged nature of the political and economic reform processes created predictable tensions. For the opposition, costly economic reforms provided a useful point of political attack in their effort to build a base of support against the government. As opposition to liberalization mounted, governments dealt with the threats to their own authority by slowing down or reversing their projects of political liberalization. Such decisions were shaped in part by the fact that both governments were still relatively secure, and by the fact that political reforms were seen largely in instrumental terms, as a means of achieving economic objectives. When events proved that perception to be mistaken, political reforms were allowed to lag behind economic ones. Other governments under more political pressure might conceivably have taken the opposite decision: to abandon the program of economic reforms in order to maintain support during the process of political transition, even at the potential cost of more severe political problems at a later stage. In either case, however, the Nigerian and Mexican cases suggest that the strategy of pursuing political and economic reforms simultaneously results in a highly unstable equilibrium, and that governments are likely to be pushed toward one of the other two stylized sequences.

Sequence III: Democracy First

The final sequence is one in which authoritarian regimes cede power to democratic governments without having implemented structural adjustment measures, or even achieving a sustainable macroeconomic position. This scenario was most likely to occur where the military was substantially weakened through internal divisions and opposition protest. On the defensive, these governments proved unable either to make credible eco-

---

[30] Cornelius et al., *Mexico's Alternative Political Futures.*

nomic policy commitments that would stabilize expectations or to control the pace of political change. During the 1980s, this was a rather common scenario in Latin America, as with Argentina, Bolivia, Brazil, and Peru. The Philippines is a hybrid case. While the Marcos government stabilized the economy, it left the Aquino government a myriad of structural adjustment problems.[31] If the first stirrings of political liberalization now visible in a number of African countries prove durable, these new regimes may face similar problems, as did the short-lived democratic experiments in Ghana and Nigeria in the early 1980s.

In one respect, the new governments emerging through this reform sequence gain an important advantage from the ineptitude of the preceding regime. More than in Korea, Chile or Turkey, the divisions that prevented the old regime from instituting effective economic adjustment also reduced the short-term dangers of a military coup, providing incoming governments with increased space for political maneuver. On the other hand, incoming governments have also had to deal with far more severe macroeconomic problems, including not only structural adjustment measures but macroeconomic stabilization. Although some regimes have begun projects of economic reform, few, if any, have yet seen sustained economic results from these efforts.

The difficulties in managing these issues was compounded by the nature of the political transition itself. In several of these cases, notably Argentina and Bolivia, regime change occurred through what O'Donnell and Schmitter have termed a rupture.[32] Authoritarian rule collapsed swiftly in the absence of negotiated pacts or clear mutual guarantees among contending political forces. Even where democratization occurred somewhat less dramatically, elites in such situations faced greater challenges in managing the mobilization of previously repressed groups than did their counterparts where transitions were guided "from above" or achieved through explicit pact.

Given these features of the transition, it can be expected that there will be considerable uncertainty with respect to new decision-making structures and the stance of key interest groups and political parties.[33] Under these circumstances, it is not surprising that economic crises deepened during the initial stages of these new regimes, and although all survived the decade of the 1980s, difficulties in achieving sustainable adjustment and growth posed a major risk to their long-term prospects for political stability.

[31] Haggard, "The Political Economy of the Philippine Debt Crisis," pp. 245–55.

[32] O'Donnell and Schmitter, "Tentative Conclusions," p. 45.

[33] See Haggard and Kaufman, "Economic Adjustment in New Democracies," in Joan Nelson, ed., *Fragile Coalitions: The Politics of Economic Adjustment* (New Brunswick, N.J.: Transaction Books for the Overseas Development Council, 1989), pp. 57–77.

In these new democratic regimes, the key political as well as economic challenge is the routinization of politics and the reduction of the high level of uncertainty associated with the transition.[34] In the first instance, this demands the stabilization of expectations regarding the basic rules of the political game, including the opportunities of the major power contenders to participate regularly in honest elections and the expectation that incumbent governments will in fact serve out their constitutional terms. Once this context is established, the consolidation of democratic rule will also demand a downward adjustment of expectations concerning the ability of the state to respond to distributive claims carried into the political arena, whether by the left or the right. Timely and substantial external assistance might help smooth the transition to such lowered expectations, but it cannot substitute for them and might, in some cases, result in delayed adjustment.

Such changes in expectations are in part a function of time: the routinization of access to decision-making, the successful alternation of governments, and the increasing "responsibility" of oppositions. In several countries that have experienced democratic transitions prior to economic reform, the second or third electoral cycle has produced governments willing to run the risks of difficult stabilization and adjustment programs, and have even gained political credit for doing so. The shock program of the Menem government is one example, but Nelson's contribution to this volume suggests that democratic support for difficult adjustment measures may be a more widespread occurrence than is often thought.[35]

Constitutional design can also play an important role in this learning process, although the effects of specific arrangements are still widely disputed. In recent years, considerable debate has focused on the relative merits of parliamentary and presidential systems. Parliamentary systems are more vulnerable to cabinet instability, but they may provide stronger incentives for the formation of centrist coalitions than do winner-take-all presidential systems. Presumably, parliamentary systems would also be less prone to prolonged, politically dangerous stalemates between the executive and legislature. As we will suggest in more detail in the following section, however, the economic governability of either presidential or parliamentary systems can also depend heavily on the electoral system and on arrangements that protect areas of the decision-making bureaucracy from the immediate impact of electoral politics.

[34] Lawrence Whitehead, "Democratization and Disinflation: A Comparative Approach," in Nelson, *Fragile Coalitions*, pp. 79–83.

[35] The evolution from economic radicalism to macroeconomic caution during the Portuguese democratic transition of the 1970s indicates that such shifts can also occur at times when international pressures toward orthodoxy were less compelling than they have been during the 1980s.

Regardless of the sequence followed, political consolidation in new democracies will hinge on at least two additional developments. The first is the evolution of party systems that can effectively channel distributional struggles, including those unleashed in the transition process itself. The second is the extent to which adjustment policies actually result in economic recovery. In the next section, we turn to a discussion of these broad challenges and the way they are likely to influence the long-term relationship between market economies and democratic politics.

THE POLITICAL CONSEQUENCES OF ADJUSTMENT OUTCOMES

The experiences of the developed and developing countries have yielded up somewhat different answers to the question of the compatibility of capitalism and democracy. The dominant view derived from the Western experience is that a market economy is wholly compatible with democracy and even its prerequisite. Historically, those classes tied to the emergence of market relations opposed the status hierarchies and interventions associated with traditional forms of rule, sought to check the growth of arbitrary state power through law, and supported competition in the political, as well as economic realm. To the extent that liberal economies encourage the emergence of groups that do not depend on the state, and to the extent that they have the broadly equalizing effect of spawning middle classes, they contribute to the creation of an autonomous civil society that is the social foundation of a liberal democratic polity.[36]

On the other hand, it has been argued that economic liberalism and political democracy may be in conflict for countries at certain stages of growth. This is due, first, to the social dislocations and increasing inequality characteristic of the early stages of development. These inevitable strains are only exacerbated by market-oriented reforms. This argument was advanced to account for the installation of economically liberalizing, but politically authoritarian governments in the 1960s and 1970s in Latin America and East Asia. Though many of these governments have given way to democratic successors, it is clear that the "Western" pattern of development has also included nondemocratic interludes in many countries and that authoritarianism can coexist with capitalist relations of production over some fairly long run.[37]

[36] See Robert Dahl, *Polyarchy: Participation and Opposition* (New Haven: Yale University Press, 1971), pp. 48–81; Barrington Moore, *Social Origins of Dictatorship and Democracy: Lord and Peasant in the Making of the Modern World* (Boston: Beacon Press, 1966), pp. 413–33.

[37] This is a conclusion shared by Samuel Huntington, *Political Order in Changing Societies*, pp. 32–78 and Guillermo O'Donnell, *Modernization and Bureaucratic Authoritarian-*

A second, and more fundamental, source of tension between capitalism and democracy in the Third World resides in the nature of the social structure. Highly unequal distributions of assets and income, and particularly severe rural inequalities, pose threats to political stability. Thus while all democratic capitalist systems face the tension between stratified societies and open polities, these tensions are likely to be particularly acute in the developing world, increasing the likelihood of either revolutionary or reactionary political outcomes.[38]

Given the contradictory nature of these accounts about the relationship between regime type and a market-oriented economy, it is likely that democratic outcomes are compatible with a fairly wide range of social and economic conditions, including high levels of inequality and weak growth performance. However, the effect of these conditions will be mediated by the nature of political institutions, and particularly the nature of the party system. Party systems shape distributional conflicts over economic adjustment questions and are thus likely to play an important role not only in the "governability" of new democracies, but also in determining their stability in the face of continuing economic challenges. It is worthwhile to explore in more detail why this is likely to be the case.

Distribution, Legitimation, and the Organization of Party Systems

In his classic study, *The Great Transformation*, Karl Polanyi chronicled the revolt against the liberal utopianism of early Victorian "radicalism."[39] This revolt consisted of successive political efforts to protect the individual from the dislocations associated with the market. Some of these efforts, namely Leninism and fascism, were explicitly anti-democratic. In the advanced industrial democracies that were spared these extreme solutions, a key feature of political stability was the gradual incorporation of the working class into the political and economic system. This incorporation occurred not only through the expansion of the franchise, but through the creation of institutions for managing industrial relations, networks of social security, and policies for alleviating absolute poverty. As John Ruggie has argued, they also rested on a liberalizing, but by no means laissez-faire posture toward integration with the world economy, a mix he labeled "embedded liberalism."[40]

---

ism: Studies in South American Politics (Berkeley, Calif.: Institute of International Studies, 1973), pp. 55–79.

[38] Fernando Henrique Cardoso and Enzo Faletto, *Dependency and Development in Latin America* (Berkeley: University of California Press, 1979), pp. 163–71.

[39] Karl Polanyi, *The Great Transformation: The Political and Economic Origins of Our Time* (Boston: Beacon Press, 1957).

[40] John Gerard Ruggie, "International Regimes, Transactions, and Change: Embedded

There are, however, various ways in which the bargain of "embedded liberalism" might be struck. The idea that the stability of democratic capitalist polities is contingent on forms of social compensation, not only to the poor but to the middle and working classes, has already been raised by Joan Nelson in chapter 5 of this volume. The configuration of the party system will be a crucial component of these bargains. As Samuel Huntington argued over twenty years ago, societies with weak parties are prone to periods of praetorian instability and/or a disproportionate degree of state control over interest group organization.[41] Clientelism is also likely to be a pervasive feature of such systems. As we have suggested in our chapter on inflation, fragmented party systems can result in perverse incentives that are detrimental not only to macroeconomic stability but to democratic governance as well.

Whether transitional democracies can avoid such problems depends in part on historically determined social and political cleavages. These factors should not be overemphasized however. Political institutions will also depend on the balance of political forces *at the time* of the transition and the agreements and subsequent processes of interaction among political elites that result. It is possible to conceive of a variety of party system arrangements that would avoid the problems of political polarization and fragmentation and provide stable support for the functioning of capitalist democracy. We identify four: catchall two-party systems, consociationalism, and multiparty systems dominated by either the center-left or center-right. We consider the conditions under which these alternative party structures are likely to arise and the characteristic political dilemmas that accompany them, particularly with reference to the pursuit of economic reform.

A two-party system based on broad, catchall parties is likely to emerge where there is a relatively high degree of elite consensus on the appropriate economic model and a weakly mobilized or controlled left. This model is encouraged by an electoral system based on plurality voting for the president, and would be reinforced by concurrently elected legislatures based on single-member districts.[42] It would provide some role for labor and left forces, but as distinctly "junior partners" to elite-dominated centrist parties that compete for overlapping cross-class constituencies. This party system is characteristic of Venezuela as well as the more patronage-based and clientelistic parties of Colombia and Costa Rica. Among tran-

---

Liberalism in the Postwar Economic Order," in Stephen D. Krasner, ed., *International Regimes* (Ithaca, N.Y.: Cornell University Press, 1983), pp. 195–232.

[41] Huntington, *Political Order in Changing Societies*, pp. 192–264.

[42] See Matthew Soberg Shugart and John Carey, "Assemblies and Executives: Institutional Dynamics of Presidential Democracy" (University of California, San Diego, February 1991).

sitional democracies, this is a pattern that has already been approximated in Uruguay, where the traditional Colorado and Blanco parties resurfaced after the withdrawal of the military. It is theoretically possible that these kinds of party arrangements would evolve in other countries where popular-sector forces have been severely weakened by the economic crisis of the 1980s, or where ethnic or class conflicts were not highly politicized in the past. Interestingly, however, most new democracies have not opted for institutional designs that would support such a party system.

As we argued in our discussion of inflation, stable two-party systems have generally had a good record in maintaining stable macroeconomic policies, a record relevant to the maintenance of electoral democracy as well. On the other hand, these systems do have characteristic problems. First, parties in such systems may become little more than elite-dominated patronage machines, with the risk both of undermining coherent economic policy and taking on exclusionary features that can undermine the legitimacy of the political system as a whole. The exclusionary side of such parties account in part for the widespread alienation evident in the Venezuelan riots of 1990, and even more fundamentally, for the ongoing guerrilla welfare that characterized the Philippines in the immediate postwar period and Colombia today.

The challenge in such systems is to find ways to broaden participation and extend social compensation without recourse to the large and inflationary state sectors that were characteristic of developmentalism in the 1960s and 1970s. Party competition might provide the basis for a kind of mild reformism and social compensation, perhaps similar to that envisioned in the Alliance for Progress, but projects of this sort demand an extremely delicate balancing act. Michael Manley's experience in Jamaica provides a good illustration. The goal of the first Manley government was precisely to broaden the political and economic base of an elite-dominated two-party system, but the expansion of the role of the state coincided with the collapse of the bauxite market and the first oil crisis. The resulting deterioration in economic performance contributed to a dramatic increase in political polarization. During the 1980s, as might be expected, both electoral pressures and economic constraints pushed Manley back toward the center. Efforts to reestablish elite consensus, however, have once again substantially reduced the scope for participation available to the Jamaican left.

Multiparty systems, encouraged by electoral systems of proportional representation, are more likely to emerge in ethnically divided societies or where political movements on the left succeed in winning the loyalties of substantial portions of the working class. In ethnically plural societies, an important path toward democratic consolidation might rest on consociationalism and/or federalism. Power-sharing agreements could be negotiated among the major contending ethnic or regional groups, or power might devolve to the regional level in the name of autonomy.

Arend Lijphart has attempted to make the case that consociational agreements can provide an effective base for governance in advanced industrial societies characterized by ethnic pluralism.[43] Although this has been advanced as an option for a number of developing countries, particularly in Africa, the stability of such arrangements is problematic. In such settings, distributional issues are not formulated along left-right lines, but along lines given by the ethnic and regional structure. Where one group is dominant, it will be tempted to exploit its position to monopolize the political gains of office. Where ethnic or regional divisions are more evenly balanced, political bargains are likely to deepen the fundamental challenges of fiscal stability and economic growth faced by developing countries. Unlike the growth-oriented class compromises that are theoretically possible in systems divided along left-right lines, the basis of political mobilization is more likely to focus on purely distributive claims and take on a zero-sum character.

Partly for these reasons, there has been a growing interest in the design of electoral rules that would force ethnically-based parties to form cross-ethnic constituencies, for example, by demanding that parties achieve thresholds of support in all regions.[44] While such rules might help to stabilize democratic politics, it would do so precisely by pushing the principle of party organization and competition toward one of the other alternatives discussed in this section.

Finally, democratic consolidation might be achieved around long-term governing coalitions centered either on the social-democratic left or the center-right. This last pair of multiparty alternatives are most likely to emerge in societies such as Chile, Korea, or perhaps Brazil where ideological divisions have been sharpened by historic partisan loyalties, working-class political subcultures, or the recent mobilization of working-class movements. In such circumstances, the shape of the party system is likely to turn heavily on the political allegiances of the middle classes and agriculture. Alliances of these groups with working-class movements would make it possible to form relatively stable, European-style "social democratic" coalitions. Rural and/or middle-class alignment with the right would create a basis for more conservative coalitions, such as that in Japan. Depending on specific national conditions, either model could conceivably form a viable basis for the electoral legitimation of democratic

---

[43] Arend Lijphart, *Democracy in Plural Societies* (New Haven, Conn.: Yale University Press, 1977).

[44] See for example, Donald L. Horowitz, *A Democratic South Africa: Constitutional Engineering in a Divided Society* (Berkeley: University of California Press, 1991), chap. 7.

capitalist systems; yet as with the other alternatives, both face characteristic problems.

The "Japanese model" rests on more or less permanent rule by a dominant center-right party or coalition, and on an economic model that emphasizes the prerogatives of business, investment over consumption and
transfers, and an instrumental legitimating formula based on the promise
of rapid growth.[45] Organized labor and the left would be relegated to a
position of long-term opposition, perhaps even with legal and political
guarantees that provide various checks on their freedom of maneuver.
Examples might include voting rules that limit the entry of small leftist
parties or systems of industrial relations that restrict the political activities of unions.

Whatever the purported advantages of this model in terms of providing
support for growth-oriented policies, its exclusionary features pose
greater problems of legitimation than the two-party option discussed
above. These systems would require governments to produce high rates
of economic growth, substantial opportunities for upward mobility, and
at least a modicum of welfare concessions to the opposition. All of these
might be undermined by economic forces beyond the government's control.

A second dilemma of the center-right model is more explicitly political.
The conditions likely for this outcome to emerge in the first place include
a labor movement weakened by some combination of market conditions
and transitional "guarantees"; an ideologically coherent and politically
strong right-wing, both inside and outside the state apparatus; and middle-class groups that are disinclined to ally with the left. If these conditions are coupled with a political alienation among radicals on the left,
they could lead to political polarization and the acceptance of quasiau-
thoritarian "solutions." These risks are clearly present in Korea and Thailand.

The social-democratic model is in many respects the mirror image of
the "Japanese" alternative.[46] The principal elements in this model would
be strong, if not dominant, center-left parties based on an alliance between industrial workers and middle-class groups, or, as in the classic
"red-green" alliance, between the urban working class and agriculture. In

[45] For two different expositions of the "Japanese model," see Gerald Curtis, *The Japanese
Way of Politics* (New York: Columbia University Press, 1988), particularly pp. 45–79; and
Kent E. Calder, *Crisis and Compensation: Public Policy and Political Stability in Japan:
1949–1986* (Princeton, N.J.: Princeton University Press, 1988).

[46] For an exposition centered on the small, open European economies that might have
relevance for some developing countries, see Peter J. Katzenstein, *Small States in World
Markets: Industrial Policy in Europe* (Ithaca, N.Y.: Cornell University Press, 1985), particularly pp. 80–135.

a corporatist variant, this might include direct representation of peak labor and business associations into the policy-making process. Whatever its precise institutional form, the core bargain is that capitalists trade predictability and consensual decision-making for the dominance of center-left governments, welfare state policies, strong labor involvement in politics and even in the investment decision-making process. As Peter Katzenstein has argued most clearly for the small European states, this alternative is not necessarily antithetical to the maintenance of open markets; to the contrary, such political systems are likely to invest in labor mobility and training that facilitates openness.[47]

Compared to center-right systems and possibly even to the two-party model, inclusionary features of the social-democratic outcome would provide it with a relatively broad base of legitimacy. Precisely because of their identification with the left, moreover, social democratic governments might be in a better position to moderate wage and welfare demands emanating from their core constituency; this point has been made widely in the literature on Western European social democracies.[48]

While this model is normatively appealing, it is far from clear that the social conditions for its emergence are widespread in the middle-income developing countries. These conditions include muted differences between left and right, a strong but disciplined labor movement, and a private sector that is both relatively weak yet sufficiently cohesive to negotiate class compromises. Where labor is relatively well-organized and militant, it may have little interest in the proposed bargain. With the possible exception of Chile, there is no evidence that militant labor movements emerging from long periods of repression are willing to provide private sector groups the guarantees that form the core of the social democratic bargain. Even where the left has become an important political actor, the organization of the working class has suffered substantially over the last two decades, first as a result of authoritarian rule, then due to the recession of the 1980s. As a result, in most countries it does not yet possess the coherent structure to make it a unified and forceful political player or to provide the basis for strong left parties. In less developed countries, the problem is structural: labor is simply not large enough to play a key political role.

A third and even more daunting problem with the social-democratic model is that it implies a reconciliation between the left and military and

[47] Peter Katzenstein, *Small States in World Markets* (Ithaca, N.Y.: Cornell University Press, 1988).

[48] The theoretical foundation for this argument is spelled out in Peter Lange, "Unions, Workers, and Wage Regulation: The Rational Bases of Consent," in John H. Goldthorpe, ed., *Order and Conflict in Contemporary Capitalism* (Oxford: Oxford University Press, 1984), pp. 98–123.

business elites, which in many countries remain relatively strong and hostile to the compromises on which such a system must rest. The sources of right strength might include the continuing presence of external threats, a memory of disorder associated with political openings to the left, or middle classes disinclined to play the role of a swing force because of the factors just cited. In countries such as Brazil and the Philippines in which the "rural problem" remains unresolved, landed interests are likely to constitute a further barrier to this solution.

Growth and the Consolidation of Democratic Rule

In all of the party systems discussed, the tradeoffs associated with the organization of political support and the provision of compensation would be ameliorated by sustained economic recovery. Economic growth can reduce frustrations derived from distributional inequalities by increasing mobility, and provide the material base for social compromises. A long record of successful economic performance can strengthen general beliefs in the effectiveness and legitimacy of the system as a whole.

A return to the high rates of growth of the 1960s and 1970s seems highly unlikely, however. During the 1980s, most developing countries had lower growth than in the 1970s, and a number of heavily-indebted countries experienced prolonged recession. Investment remained low, even in countries that implemented major structural adjustment programs, including Bolivia and Mexico, and many faced highly unfavorable international conditions beyond their immediate control.[49]

Assessments of the political implications of such difficulties have undergone a change over the course of the last ten years. It was once widely argued that if economic performance in developing countries remained poor, it would imperil the prospects for democracy; this argument was advanced as a rationale for debt relief and increased financial assistance. As of the early 1990s, however, with virtually all of the new democracies still functioning, it has become clear that the effects of recession and modest growth rates were less straightforward than anticipated. Why?

Sharp economic shocks are likely to lead to widespread demands for public assistance and possibly changes of regime. Long periods of slow growth, by contrast, do not necessarily produce destabilizing political responses. Citizens and firms lower expectations and make individual, nonpolitical adjustments, such as sending more family members into the work force, entering into informal sector activities, and reducing consumption.

---

[49] On the continuing problem of low investment, even among countries launching adjustment programs, see the World Bank, Country Economics Department, *Adjustment Lending Policies for Sustainable Growth*, Policy and Research Series No. 14 (Washington, D.C.: World Bank, 1990), pp. 81–91.

Even if demands for relief are politicized, they are just as likely to be directed at the government in power as they are at the system as a whole. This may be particularly true in new democracies, in which the democratic system enjoys a reservoir of political toleration on which it can draw.

Even if poor economic performance does not result in a collapse of elected governments, however, the nature and content of political life and can be profoundly affected by stagnant growth in real incomes. Emphasis on the durability of liberal constitutional institutions in the face of such hardships may be a useful corrective for earlier pessimism, but it also tends to mispecify the nature of the threat to the consolidation of democratic rule. The principal danger to democratic consolidation in the 1990s is less likely to be a reversion to military rule than a decay of state institutions and in the capacity of groups within civil society to engage in sustained and constructive collective action. In some new democracies, including Peru, the Philippines, and Bolivia, severe economic difficulties have already contributed to a profound disarticulation of social relations and a contraction of the state's capacity to sustain order. A number of other democratic regimes in Latin America face similar problems, as will liberalizing Africa.

Drawing on the experience of many countries over the last decade, it is possible to sketch a stylized process of political decay that while stopping short of formal regime change would nonetheless drain constitutional institutions of their democratic content. Such a cycle would begin with developments already evident in a number of developing countries: an increase in political cynicism and apathy, a decline in effective political participation, and an inability for the political system to generate representative ruling coalitions. In a next stage, crime, civil violence, and organized revolutionary or antirevolutionary ("death squad") activity could contribute to a gradual erosion of the substance of democratic rule through intermittent repression of opposition groups, "emergency" measures, and a decline in the integrity of legal guarantees, such as habeas corpus.

At a final stage—still short of a formal transition to authoritarian rule or constitutional change—electoral institutions could be rendered a facade. Elected officials could be subject to the veto power of military elites, could come under pressure from military elites, as happened in 1990 in Pakistan, or could become little more than fronts for them. This was the case with the highly repressive Uruguayan model from 1973 to 1985 in which civilians formally held the presidency for extended periods, and is increasingly true in Guatemala and Honduras.

Finally, we can by no means rule out the possibility of open reversals of democratic rule. This could occur in several ways. It is at least possible that authoritarian reversals would result from the military triumph of revolutionary movements spawned by the crisis, though this seems highly unlikely at present. A more likely scenario is that a general erosion of faith in the capacity of democratic government to manage the economy increases the appeal, not only to elites, but to larger publics, of authoritarian solutions to the crisis. The erosion of support for democratic institutions would lead to the election of leaders or parties with plebiscitarian or openly authoritarian ambitions, or reduce the perceived costs to the military of intervening.

Economic crisis might reverse democratization in a more indirect route. Sustained poor performance or sudden economic deterioration could lead to an increase in crime, strikes, riots, and civil violence. Rapid social changes and downward mobility for members of the middle and working classes could increase the appeal of political movements on the extreme left and right, including revolutionary ones. The deterioration of social order and increasing social polarization are classic justifications for military intervention.

Index